ASP.NET 4 Social Networking

A truly hands-on book for Microsoft ASP.NET 4 Developers

Atul Gupta

Sudhanshu Hate

Andrew Siemer

BIRMINGHAM - MUMBAI

ASP.NET 4 Social Networking

First published: March 2011

Production Reference: 1180311

Published by Packt Publishing Ltd.
32 Lincoln Road
Olton
Birmingham, B27 6PA, UK.

ISBN 978-1-849690-82-9

www.packtpub.com

Cover Image by Vinayak Chittar (vinayak.chittar@gmail.com)

Credits

Authors
Atul Gupta
Sudhanshu Hate
Andrew Siemer

Reviewers
Robert S Robbins
Sergey Suchok
Steven M Swafford

Acquisition Editor
David Barnes

Development Editors
Dhiraj Chandiramani
Sushmita Panda

Technical Editor
Pallavi Kachare

Indexer
Rekha Nair

Editorial Team Leader
Aanchal Kumar

Project Team Leader
Priya Mukherji

Project Coordinator
Shubhanjan Chatterjee

Proofreader
Mario Cecere
Lesley Harrison

Graphics
Geetanjali Sawant

Production Coordinator
Arvindkumar Gupta

Cover Work
Arvindkumar Gupta

About the Authors

Atul Gupta is a Principal Technology Architect at Infosys Technologies Limited. He has more than 15 years of experience working on Microsoft Technologies. The technology experience is spread across VC++, MFC, COM/DCOM, SQL, .NET, Microsoft ASP.NET, Microsoft ASP.NET AJAX, Microsoft ASP.NET MVC, C#, ADO.NET, VS (various versions), BizTalk Server, Commerce Server and he has worked across all SDLC life cycle phases like architecture definition, design, development, and testing.

His current focus is User Experience Technologies from Microsoft like Windows Presentation Foundation and Silverlight. He is also exploring Microsoft Surface, Windows Touch, Windows Phone 7, Pivot, and Augmented Reality. He blogs on latest technologies at: `http://blogs.infosys.com/microsoft`. Some of his other publications can be accessed at Infosys' Technology Showcase (`http://www.infosys.com/microsoft/resource-center/Pages/technology-showcase.aspx`). Working on latest technologies is his passion and this had helped him bag the Microsoft's Most Valuable Professional (MVP) award for six consecutive years. He has also spoken on events like Microsoft Virtual Tech Days.

Atul holds a Bachelor's degree in Chemical Engineering and Master's in Software Systems from Premier Universities in India.

He recently helped review the book titled *Refactoring with Microsoft Visual Studio 2010* from Packt Publishing.

Acknowledgement

I have had experience in writing short notes, blogs and even hand books, and always thought about writing a book. The credit to finally get me into this space clearly goes to Neha Patwari, the Development Editor at Packt who convinced me that I could write and introduced me to other fellow editors who reached out to me for this particular book.

Next I would like to acknowledge Sudhanshu Hate, my co-author in this book, who kindly agreed to work on this book with me, inspite of his very busy schedule. We have had many an interesting debates when writing this book over a cup of hot tea in the afternoons.

My co-workers and managers, with special mention of Naveen Kumar and Prasad Joshi, at Infosys were kind enough to support my time and effort in writing this book and always provided necessary guidance as and when required.

I cannot thank my immediate team members enough for their support as well. They continued to drive their work even when I would disappear for days when working on various chapters in this book. Shashikant, Vidyadhar, Nimisha, Deepika, Ravi, Nachiket, and Vikas, I appreciate your support.

Andrew Siemer, the author of the previous edition of this book, also needs a special mention. He has indeed done a wonderful work in writing the .NET 3.5 Social Networking book. We got lot of help from his work and the code snippets. I also would like to acknowledge the support and guidance from the editorial team at Packt and also the various technical reviewers. Their comments have helped bring out the finer shades in this book that will make it interesting to read.

Finally, significant credit also goes to my wife, Shilpi and daughter, Anukriti, who waited patiently for me on numerous weekends to finish my work and spend time with them. Their understanding and patience helped me concentrate on the book and get it out quickly.

Sudhanshu Hate is a Senior Technology Architect at Infosys Technologies Limited. He has 13 years of industry experience working across various stages of SDLC.

Sudhanshu has diverse technology experience starting from Oracle, Delphi, Java to Microsoft .NET (.NET Framework, WCF, WF, Entity Framework) and Microsoft SQL Server BI platform.

For last eight years, he has been responsible for technology research, envisioning, building, and consulting on Microsoft technology based solutions. He has also been instrumental in taking solutions to Fortune 500 customers in EMEA and US.

Sudhanshu is passionate about understanding technology levers and aligning it for business benefits. These days he is working on Cloud Computing with focus around Microsoft Azure as a platform.

Sudhanshu has authored papers that are available at Infosys' Technology Showcase (`http://www.infosys.com/microsoft/resource-center/Pages/technology-showcase.aspx`), presented in external forums such as Microsoft Virtual TechDays, 3rd India Software Engineering Conference (ISEC 2010) and blogs at `http://blogs.infosys.com/Microsoft`.

Sudhanshu was ranked third in Univ. for Bachelor's degree in Industrial Engineering.

Acknowledgement

Effort of this kind needs help wishes and blessings from many, colleagues, co-workers, mentors, and personal friends. Though the book has been a result of work of last one year but over this period of life I have been blessed to have support from many in many forms without which I would not have reached thus far.

I would like to profusely acknowledge my co-author Atul Gupta, who provided me an opportunity to work with him on this book. With each other's help and encouragement, we kept sailing through the difficult times in this book.

I would also like to also profusely thank my managers and mentors Naveen Kumar, and Prasad Joshi for their executive support and directions in shaping this book. They not only displayed faith in my abilities on every turn at Infosys which has kept me going but were kind enough to support my time and effort in writing this book.

Andrew Siemer's excellent work provided us nice foundation to take off. Reviewers did a stupendous job of keeping us sharp. This book wouldn't have been possible without the help from some key people from publishing house Susmita Panda, Shubhanjan Chatterjee, and Pallavi Kachare who patiently answered our several queries in the journey of completing this book.

Last but not least, significant credit goes to my beloved parents, younger brother Gaurav, wife Amruta, and two year old son, Aalhaad. I draw my daily source of energy and motivation to come to work with smile from Aalhaad, and love from Amruta; sustain it with extraordinary support from my extremely loving parents and brother.

Andrew Siemer is the co-founder of the .NET user group `VirtualDNUG.com`, and is currently an architect/engineer at OTX Research. He has worked as a software engineer, architect, trainer, and author since 1998 when he left the Army. Andrew has provided consultancy to many companies on the topics of ecommerce, social networking, and business systems. He has worked with eUniverse (`AllYouCanInk.com`), PointVantage (`MyInks.com`), Callaway Golf (`CallawayConnect.com`), Guidance Software (`GuidanceSoftware.com`), Intermix Media (`FlowGo.com`, `Grab.com`), and FOX Interactive (`AmericanIdol.com`, `FoxSports.com`) to name a few. In addition to his daily duties, he also conducts classes in .NET, C#, and other web technologies, blogs on numerous topics (`blog.andrewsiemer.com`, `socialnetworkingin.net` to name a couple), and works on fun new communities such as `Fisharoo.com` and `GymEd.com`.

I would like to first thank my wife Jessica Siemer. Without her love and understanding this project and all the others before it would not have been able to get off the ground, let alone get anywhere near completion! For this book project in particular though Jess gave me everything I needed to make it through to the end. My day to day successes in life would be nothing without you.

I would also like to thank Brian Loesgen from Neudesic for getting me started down the book writing path. He has been there for me time and time again keeping me headed in the right direction. And to the friends I made while at Intermix Media, Adam Wolkov and David Higbee. This book was inspired by our many early morning coffee and juice brainstorming sessions. Thank you for igniting the initial spark to get this project started.

About the Reviewers

Robert S. Robbins is a freelance web developer with 11 years of experience in software development. He has an Associate's Degree in Computer Science.

Currently, he is a programmer for a community action agency which still maintains programs written in the old IBM mainframe language RPG II. But in his spare time he continues web application development in Microsoft ASP.NET and PHP. Robert's involvement in social networking began with the YouTube community which eventually led to customizing the Ning platform for a group of vloggers. He now creates plugins for the Elgg open source social networking web application.

He blogs at `http://www.williamsportwebdeveloper.com/cgi/wp/index.php` and could be reached at `robert@williamsportwebdeveloper.com`. You can also follow him on twitter `http://twitter.com/#!/Robert_Robbins`.

Sergey Suchok graduated in 2004 with honors from the Faculty of Cybernetics, Taras Shevchenko National University of Kyiv (Ukraine) and has since then been keen on information technology. He is currently working in the banking area. Sergey is the co-author of more than 45 articles and participated in more than 20 scientific and practical conferences devoted to the economic and mathematical modeling. He is a member of the 'New Atlantis' Youth Public Organization (`newatlantida.org.ua`) and devotes his leisure time to environmental protection issues, historical and patriotic development, and popularization of a grateful attitude toward the Earth. He is also developing a social network for Kombucha's owners called Latusho, and he also writes poetry and short stories and makes macramé.

I would like to express gratitude to the author for this opportunity to improve my knowledge of social networking, as well as Packt Publishing for providing such an interesting experience in the reviewing process.

Steven M. Swafford works as a web-based Application Developer and Team Lead in a wide variety of web-based business applications built upon the Microsoft .NET platform. He is particularly interested in making a positive impact upon technology as it relates to the mission of the enterprise. This includes addressing aspects of software engineering that are often overlooked. For example, accessibility, usability, code libraries, application security, and standardizing the toolsets. Steven is goal-oriented and desires to serve more as a technology generalist rather than a specialist in any given field.

I wish to thank my wife Su Ok and my daughter Sarah. For without them I would be lost.

www.PacktPub.com

Support files, eBooks, discount offers, and more

You might want to visit www.PacktPub.com for support files and downloads related to your book.

Did you know that Packt offers eBook versions of every book published, with PDF and ePub files available? You can upgrade to the eBook version at www.PacktPub.com and as a print book customer, you are entitled to a discount on the eBook copy. Get in touch with us at service@packtpub.com for more details.

At www.PacktPub.com, you can also read a collection of free technical articles, sign up for a range of free newsletters, and receive exclusive discounts and offers on Packt books and eBooks.

http://PacktLib.PacktPub.com

Do you need instant solutions to your IT questions? PacktLib is Packt's online digital book library. Here, you can access, read, and search across Packt's entire library of books.

Why Subscribe?

- Fully searchable across every book published by Packt
- Copy and paste, print, and bookmark content
- On demand and accessible via web browser

Free Access for Packt account holders

If you have an account with Packt at www.PacktPub.com, you can use this to access PacktLib today and view nine entirely free books. Simply use your login credentials for immediate access.

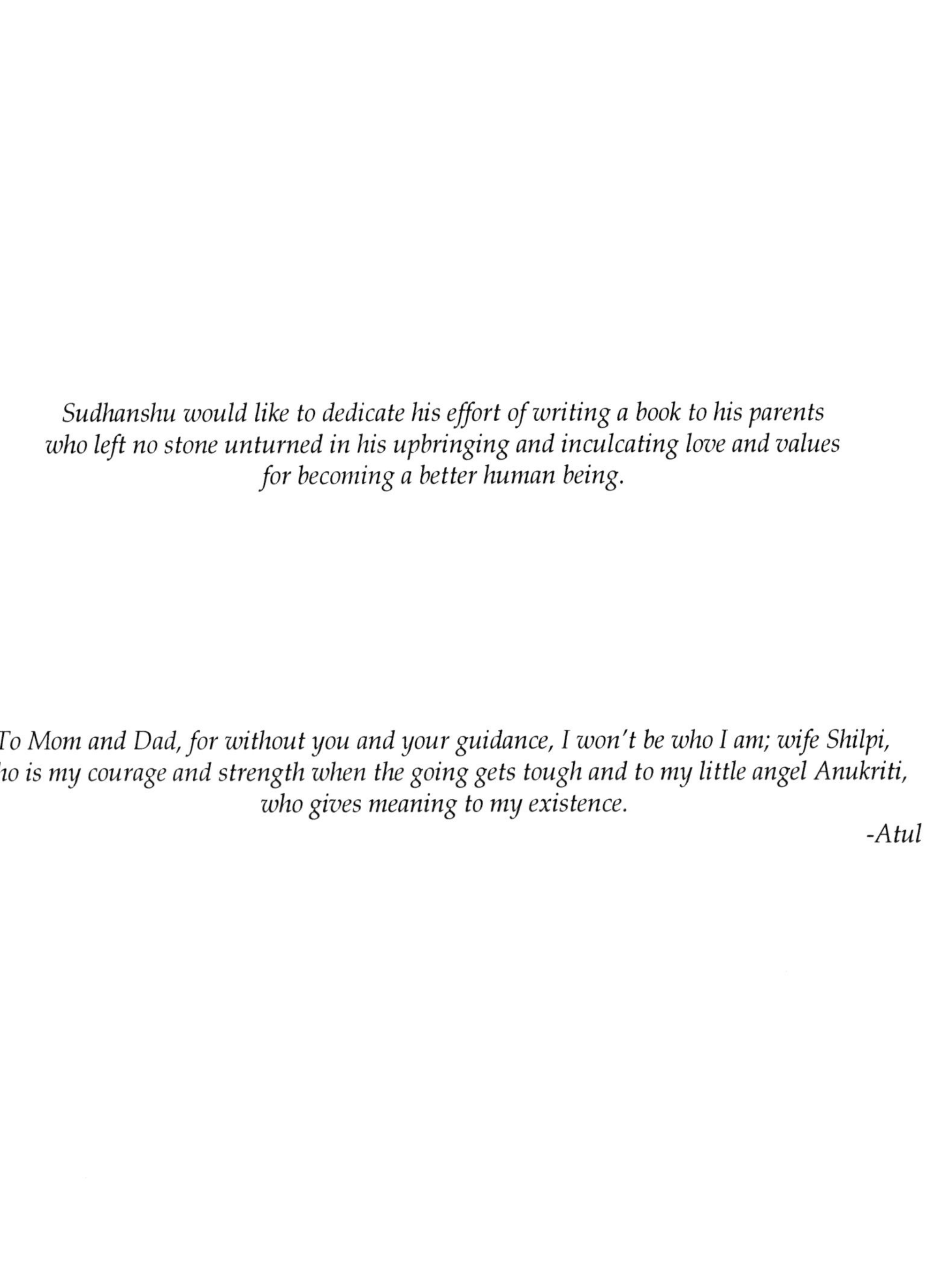

Sudhanshu would like to dedicate his effort of writing a book to his parents who left no stone unturned in his upbringing and inculcating love and values for becoming a better human being.

To Mom and Dad, for without you and your guidance, I won't be who I am; wife Shilpi, who is my courage and strength when the going gets tough and to my little angel Anukriti, who gives meaning to my existence.

-Atul

Table of Contents

Preface

Social networking has become a driving force on the Internet. Many people are part of at least one social network, while more often people are members of many different communities. For this reason many business people are trying to capitalize on this movement and are in a rush to put up their own social network. As the growth of social networks continues, we have started to see more and more niche communities popping up all over in favor of the larger, all-encompassing networks in an attempt to capture a sliver of the market.

In this book, we will discuss the many aspects and features of what makes up the majority of today's social networks or online communities. Not only will we discuss the features, their purpose, and how to go about building them, but we will also take a look at the construction of these features from a large scale enterprise perspective. The goal is to discuss the creation of a community in a scalable fashion.

What this book covers

Chapter 1, Social Networking gives you an overall structure of this book, that is, what a reader can expect from this book.

Chapter 2, An Enterprise Approach to our Community Framework helps you create an enterprise framework to handle the needs of most web applications. It discusses design patterns, best practices, and certain tools to make things easier. It also covers error handling and logging.

Chapter 3, User Accounts covers registration and account creation process by means of an email verification system and a permission system to ensure security. It also touches upon password encryption/decryption techniques.

Chapter 4, User Profiles covers the creation of a user's profile and an avatar in a manner that is flexible enough for all systems to use. In this chapter, we also implement some form of privacy to allow users to hide parts of their profile that they don't want to share with others.

Chapter 5, Friends shows you how to implement friends, how to search for them, find them in the site's listings, and import your contacts into the site to find your friends.

Chapter 6, Messaging helps you create a messaging system that will resemble a web-based email application similar to Hotmail or Gmail. We will also learn how to implement the Xinha WYSIWYG editor in a way that can be re-used easily across the site for complex inputs.

Chapter 7, Media Galleries covers details on how to build a generic media management system that will allow you to host video, photos, resumes, or any number of physical files with minimal tweaking. It also addresses the issue of multi-file uploads via RIA technologies like Flash and Silverlight.

Chapter 8, Blogs is all about Blogging. With search engines, users, and security in mind, we invest a part of this chapter to address an issue that plagues many dynamic websites—query string data being used to determine page output.

Chapter 9, Forums discusses the creation of the core features of a discussion forum—categories, forums, threads, and posts. Along with these features, the chapter also extends the friendly URLs concept to make our content more suitable for search engine optimization.

Chapter 10, Groups covers the concept of Groups. It focuses on how groups can be used to bring many different systems together in a way to start creation of sub-communities.

Chapter 11, User Interactivity helps us build controls to allow our users to express their opinions about various content areas of our site—tagging, rating, commenting, voting and mark as answer. It also discusses how these in turn allow users to earn medals and hence reputation on the site.

Chapter 12, Moderation focuses on Moderation, that is, the means to manage community provided content using a very simple flagging tool. It also covers methods such as Gagging to deal with habitual rule breakers. It also takes a look at how to filter specific words from content on the site.

Chapter 13, Scaling discusses some concepts to help you support a large number of users on your social network. It starts by looking at some key concepts of tiered architecture and web farming. It also discusses ways to create and search indexed data, methods to optimize data retrieval and content creation, and some mail queuing concepts.

Appendix covers a discussion on the Microsoft ASP.NET MVP and MVC patterns and explains why we continued to use the MVP pattern for this book.

What you need for this book

This book describes how to build a Social Network using Microsoft ASP.NET 4, Microsoft C# 4, and Microsoft SQL Server 2008. To use this book effectively, you will need access to Microsoft Visual Studio 2010 and Microsoft SQL Server 2008. Most of this book can be used with the various Express editions of Microsoft Visual Studio 2010 and SQL Express, but you will find that having the Professional edition of Microsoft Visual Studio 2010 will make your work flow more efficient. As we are not just discussing Microsoft ASP.NET, but are instead more interested in what is needed for the features of social networking, there may be times when we turn to an open source solution. All the examples in this book will clearly point out where to get the needed software, and how to configure that software as we work through our examples.

Who is this book for

This book is written for Microsoft ASP.NET and C# developers who want to build an enterprise-grade Social Network, either for their own business purposes or as a contract job for another company. The book assumes you have prior experience of developing web applications using Microsoft ASP.NET 4, Microsoft C# 4, Microsoft SQL Server 2008, and Microsoft Visual Studio 2010; it focuses on topics that will be of interest to existing developers—not on providing step-by-step examples for each detail.

Conventions

In this book, you will find a number of styles of text that distinguish between different kinds of information. Here are some examples of these styles, and an explanation of their meaning.

Code words in text are shown as follows: "Create a new class in the `Fisharoo/BusinessLogic` directory called `ProfileService`."

A block of code will be set as follows:

```
if (profile != null && profile.ProfileID > 0)
    {
        attributes = _profileAttributeService.
                     GetProfileAttributesByProfileID
                     (profile.ProfileID);
        levelOfExperienceType =
                             _levelOfExperienceTypeRepository.
                              GetLevelOfExperienceTypeByID
                              (profile.LevelOfExperienceTypeID);

        profile.Attributes = attributes;
        profile.LevelOfExperienceType = levelOfExperienceType;
    }
```

When we wish to draw your attention to a particular part of a code block, the relevant lines or items will be made bold:

```
Account account = _accountService.GetAccountByID(AccountID);
Profile profile = _profileService.LoadProfileByAccountID(AccountID);
if(profile != null)
{
    account.Profile = profile;
}
```

New terms and **important words** are introduced in a bold-type font. Words that you see on the screen, in menus or dialog boxes for example, appear in our text like this: "Click the **Test Connection** button to see if your settings are acceptable."

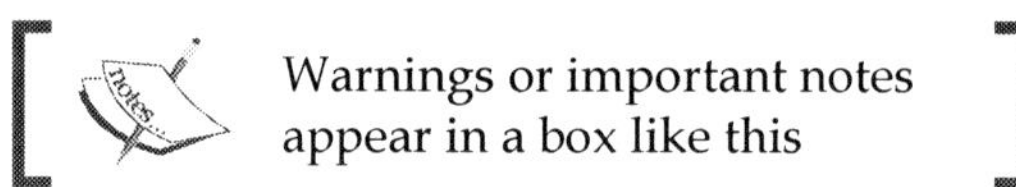

Warnings or important notes appear in a box like this

Reader feedback

Feedback from our readers is always welcome. Let us know what you think about this book, what you liked or may have disliked. Reader feedback is important for us to develop titles that you really get the most out of.

To send us general feedback, simply drop an email to `feedback@packtpub.com`, making sure to mention the book title in the subject of your message.

If there is a book that you need and would like to see us publish, please send us a note in the **SUGGEST A TITLE** form on `www.packtpub.com` or email `suggest@packtpub.com`.

If there is a topic that you have expertise in and you are interested in either writing or contributing to a book, see our author guide on `www.packtpub.com/authors`.

Customer support

Now that you are the proud owner of a Packt book, we have a number of things to help you to get the most from your purchase.

Downloading the example code for the book

You can download the example code files for all Packt books you have purchased from your account at `http://www.PacktPub.com`. If you have purchased this book elsewhere, you can visit `http://www.PacktPub.com/support` and register to have the files e-mailed directly to you.

The downloadable files contain instructions on how to use them.

Errata

Although we have taken every care to ensure the accuracy of our contents, mistakes do happen. If you find a mistake in one of our books—maybe a mistake in text or code—we would be grateful if you would report this to us. By doing this you can save other readers from frustration, and help to improve subsequent versions of this book. If you find any errata, report them by visiting `http://www.packtpub.com/support`, selecting your book, clicking on the **errata submission form** link, and entering the details of your errata. Once your errata are verified, your submission will be accepted and the errata are added to the list of existing errata. The existing errata can be viewed by selecting your title from `http://www.packtpub.com/support`.

Piracy

Piracy of copyright material on the Internet is an ongoing problem across all media. At Packt, we take the protection of our copyright and licenses very seriously. If you come across any illegal copies of our works in any form on the Internet, please provide the location address or website name immediately so we can pursue a remedy.

Please contact us at `copyright@packtpub.com` with a link to the suspected pirated material.

We appreciate your help in protecting our authors, and our ability to bring you valuable content.

Questions

You can contact us at `questions@packtpub.com` if you are having a problem with some aspect of the book, and we will do our best to address it.

1
Social Networking

Given the boom in the Internet and mobile devices industry, people across the world are more connected than ever before. Social networking is the in thing. This book is all about how to build a social networking site or a community site. In this book, we will take a look at a few well-known social networks and some not-so-well-known networks to get an idea of what features are popular. Then we will discuss the community that we will be building in this book. Once we have an idea of what others are doing and what our community will look like, we will dive right in to start building our own demo community.

What makes this topic so important

Social networking is all about developing connections or ties between friends and associates. While people have always networked with one another, the Internet has allowed us to do this in a global manner. Some great examples of popular social networks are Digg, LinkedIn, Facebook, and Twitter. Most people have heard of these services and many use them on a daily basis. These communities are able to generate income from advertising and additional paid services.

Communities Galore

`Digg.com` is an aggregator of information from other sites. They allow people to post links to interesting videos, blogs, news feeds, and other forms of media and content. This posting is then pushed to the top of their site based on how many others on the site also enjoy that post. Eventually, the posting will fall below the fold and fade into oblivion. The key with their site is that you are not actually viewing the body of the content on their site. This service is essentially a dynamic link *farm times ten*.

`LinkedIn.com` has taken the concept of a social network and polished it with a professional touch. With this service you can build a professional profile, connect with recruiters, connect with other professionals in your area, and most importantly, connect with everyone with whom they are connected. LinkedIn has really latched onto the power of the extended network concept.

`Facebook.com` originally started at Harvard University. This site was essentially a digital version of the book that the school gave to its incoming students so that everyone could get to know one another. This site is very much about building profiles and linking those profiles through an eavesdropping feature that Facebook calls "the wall". This feature essentially catches all the activity that your friends are performing on the site. The wall is another form of aggregation. Facebook is also well-known for its extensibility features that allow developers to create and host applications directly in the Facebook environment.

`Twitter.com` is what most would call a microblog. This site allows you to post very small blurbs to your blog that are then fed out to your subscribers (friends). This service is largely used for letting people know what you are up to. A great use of this feature is posting: "I am at such and such coffee shop. If anyone is nearby feel free to stop by and have a cup with me".

Each of these are really large community sites and can easily boast of having millions of subscribers/members. It is however also interesting to note that of the usually large user population, only a small percentage is typically active and most others are passive users. People may join the sites more for social status, but may not really be active users.

There are also many examples of successful community sites that operate on a much smaller scale. Some of these include `Rockero.com`, `AnimeDates.com`, and `Ning.com`. While not as large or as well-known as LinkedIn, Facebook, and so on, these are very active communities that are able to generate a living by means of advertisements on their community. Some communities like Ning even have a membership fee.

Once I have my own social network, then what?

In spite of there being so many social networking sites out there, more still keep cropping up. Everyone wants to build one of their own and think they have a better idea and can do a better job than the next guy. Listed below are some of the key considerations for any social network site that often get missed out.

Customer service

In order to keep your site successful you must pay attention to your community. You need to keep your users happy by addressing their needs and by continuously making your site better. A social network is no different from any other business from your customers' perspective. They expect service of some kind or another. The better the service, the more your users will turn to you instead of the next one.

If you have 5,000 users, you will have a fairly steady flow of communication between them. A user might report a broken feature on your site. They may want to shoot the breeze with you. They may need to report another user. They may want to suggest a feature. You need to stay responsive to your users.

It is said that a happy customer will tell a few of his/her friends about the good experience he/she had with your company. An unhappy customer, on the other hand, will tell everyone they know about the bad experience they had with your company. Keep this in mind! The more users, the more this becomes important.

Content moderation

If you have a lot of users, you (or someone else) will have to manage their activities. They will be adding content to your site on a regular basis. You will need to protect your users from inappropriate content. This means keeping an eye on all of the content in your site. Also as your users will be able to interact with one another through your site, you will need to ensure that there are features that at the very least allow users to protect themselves from other users. If you don't have this sort of feature then you will need a way for your users to report other users to you so that you can deal with it.

If you don't do this, you could end up with at least two problems. You might have a user uploading inappropriate content. This content might offend some of your users. These users could easily take you to court and create havoc for you (even if your terms clearly say that you are not responsible...blah blah blah). The other possible problem is that if a user is offended, he/she may not come back to your site. This may not sound bad, but a social network is all about its users after all!

Growing infrastructure requirements

With any successful site—and not just social networks—it is very important that you keep your infrastructure two steps ahead of your users' needs. If your site is all about video feeds, then you will be required to keep a watchful eye on your bandwidth capabilities and disk space. If either of these starts to fail, the user experience of your site will start to diminish or cease altogether.

If your site has a large number of users regardless of your topic, you will need to watch your web server's usage. You may be required to have your site hosted on many servers. Or you may need to upgrade the overall robustness of your servers to support the heavier demand.

If you are not capable of infrastructure management, it is certainly well worth your while to find someone who can take care of this for you like the cloud computing solutions from the likes of Microsoft, Amazon and Google, etc.

POST and SLATES

In October 2007 independent research firm Forrester Research, Inc. introduced a method called POST in its report Objectives: The Key To Creating A Social Strategy (`http://www.forrester.com/rb/Research/objectives_key_to_creating_social_strategy/q/id/43656/t/2`)—People, Objective, Strategy, and Technology which highlighted the important aspects one should keep in mind when creating a social strategy. These are:

- **People**: This is about knowing your target audience's social behaviors and attitudes.
- **Objective**: This is about what you want to accomplish. Is it to address some concern of people, is it to talk to them, is it for collaboration etc.
- **Strategy**: This is essentially about how you will accomplish your objectives and how this will change your relationship with customers.
- **Technology**: This is about selecting and deploying the appropriate technologies. Is it mainly a wiki type site or a blog site or for picture sharing etc.?

These ideas were later published as the book called Groundswell (`http://www.amazon.com/Groundswell-Winning-Transformed-Social-Technologies/dp/1422125009`). Forrester also has a consulting offering around this methodology (`http://www.forrester.com/Consulting/POST`).

Another related concept is SLATES. It is a term coined by Professor Andrew McAfee and stands for:

- **Search**: Ability to search for information on the site. Note that search is different to query, in that search can be ambiguous and not always fit in the typical WHERE clause of SQL statements.
- **Links**: Ability to interconnect pieces of content by linking them together. Allow quick navigation from a content to another.
- **Authorship**: Ability for users to author content.
- **Tags**: Ability to tag content and organize in a manner that allows an easy way to figure out which content occurs the most and allows navigation to it quickly.
- **Extensions**: Ability to provide additional value added information like Amazon does by showing 'People who purchased this book also purchased these additional books'.
- **Signaling**: Ability to notice change of state like user being online or offline or some change in profile information and ability to navigate to this changed item directly.

These are important aspects when planning to write a social networking site. We will highlight which of these principles is being used as we discuss the features for the site we will be building.

Our social network—Fisharoo

In this book, we will discuss many of the common features that are required for a social network or a community to succeed. We will discuss these features as they pertain to a community about salt water aquariums, their care, and about the people who are so involved in this hobby.

In this book, we will not just discuss core concepts with demos in the form of snippets, but we will build an entire working site from the ground up. And we will build our site in such a way that if by chance you become the founder of the next MySpace, you have a site that will form a great foundation for your community. With that in mind, this book will follow a common problem, design, and solution approach to building the site.

This social network will focus on helping new and old owners of salt water aquariums set up and take care of their salt water tanks. It will also help them to choose the right fish combinations. And, as it is a community, it will give them a place to go to give advice as well as receive it.

This book's approach

In each chapter we will follow a pattern to build a feature or set of features. We will start with the problem that the chapter addresses. We will then attempt to figure out a design that addresses the feature that we need to build. Finally, we will discuss what is needed to meet the design requirements.

Problem

In the problem section we will outline exactly what we need to do to achieve success for the chapter's topic. We will show you some screenshots of the finished product. And we will cover any major gotchas for building out the features.

Design

This section of each chapter is about defining what exactly we want from a feature or features. Here we will decide on and write down the physical requirements so that in the next section we can start to build out the feature set. Here we will start to look at what the database might look like, whether or not we need to make a page or two, or if a user control might work better, and if an open source tool might help us address our needs.

Solution

In the solution section of our chapters we will discuss how to implement all the requirements for each feature. This section will go deep into the actual code for implementing the feature from the database, out to the user interface. We will be using ASP.NET 4 for the implementation with Visual Studio 2010 as the IDE for this. Along with ASP.NET we will also be leveraging certain features from .NET Framework 4, third party tools, and SDKs in our implementation. We will provide the relevant code inline in the book. The entire code can be downloaded from the Packt website. At the end of this section, you should have something that you can play with.

Features of our social network

Following are the desirable features that our social networking site will possess:

Accounts

User accounts are pretty much given on any data-driven site where you have users who are contributing to the site. If you need to know who your users are, then you need some way of tracking their accounts. Instead of showing you accounts from the pure ASP.NET way, this section will show you how to build your own **Account** system from scratch.

This will include looking at the registration process where our users create their initial accounts. To make sure that we block bots and other programs from creating accounts in an automated manner, we will implement a reCAPTCHA system and discuss some other options that are out there for this. We will implement an email verification system to make sure that our users actually are what they claim to be. With all this in place we will also discuss setting up a permissions system that we can build onto over time. And no chapter on account creation is complete until we discuss password encryptions (an often missed topic).

Profiles

A user's profile is really just an extension of his/her account. The difference being that the account holds the login information and the profile holds all the personal identifiers. It holds the description of the user, the user's attributes, and their photo (avatar). We will discuss creating a user's profile in a way that is flexible enough for all systems to use. We will also discuss how to handle creating an avatar in such a way that a user can upload a picture and then crop it suitably. As the profile contains a great deal of information about the user, we will also implement some forms of privacy to allow them to hide some bits and show others. Finally, we will discuss the creation of a personal page for our user that will allow them to have a vanity URL, implemented using the URL routing feature of ASP.NET, (`www.site.com/profiles/AtulGupta`) to send to their friends.

Friends

The concept of having friends in a community is the glue that keeps people coming back to your site. A friend is a user whom you have stated, whom you trust and allow to see information about you, and about whom you are generally interested in knowing. Think of a friend as a connection, a colleague, and so on. Different terms describe the same concept for different community topics.

In this section, we will not only show you how to implement the **Friends** feature, but will also discuss how to search for them, find them in the site's listings, and import your contacts into the site to find your friends. We will also implement a microblog allowing your users to provide a status about where they are and what they are currently doing.

This status will then show up on your microblog and your friend's microblog as an alert.

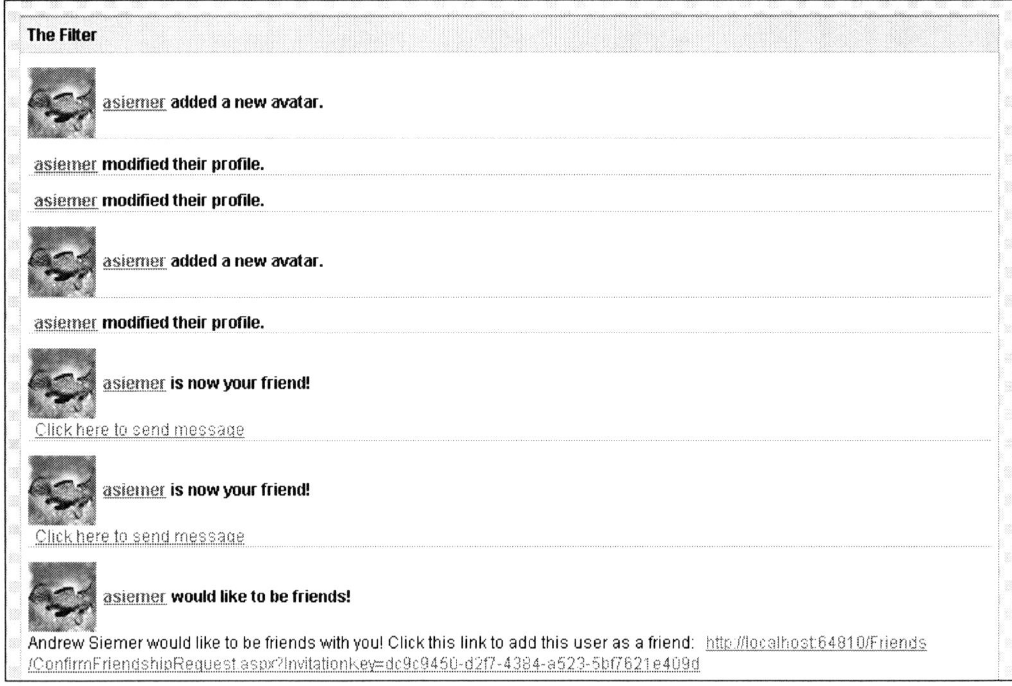

Messaging

Messaging is essential to any community site as it allows users to communicate with one another directly. This can come in many forms. You can send a message to a user, that is sent directly to the user via email. Or you can allow your user to send a message via the site, that is then stored in the recipient's inbox. A notification is then sent out to the recipient. This last form will be easier for you to manage as a site administrator.

In this section we will create a full blown messaging system that will resemble a web-based email application similar to Hotmail or Gmail. As part of our interface we will show a list of existing friends to send messages to. And we will learn how to implement the Xinha WYSIWYG editor in a way that can be re-used easily across the site for complex input. We will cover Xinha editor in more detail in later chapters.

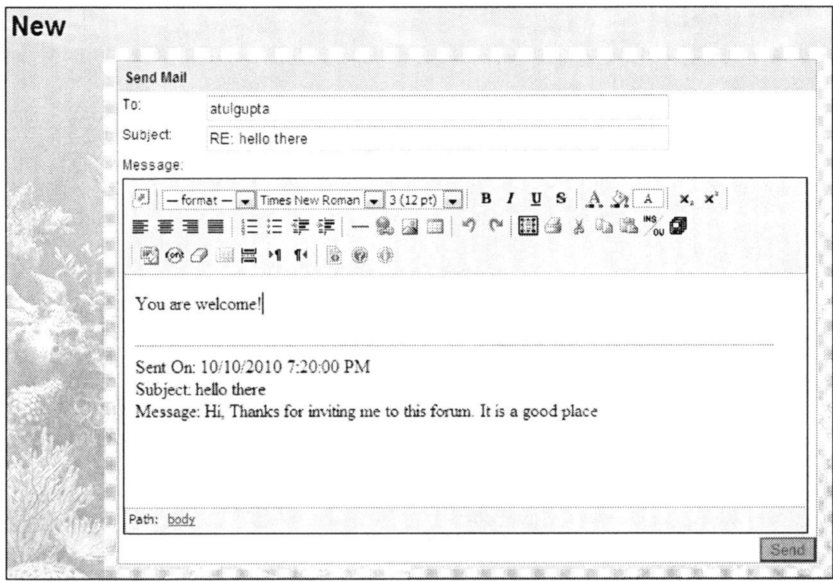

Media galleries

There are many communities that are very dependent upon media galleries. An example of this is YouTube or something similar. This is frequently the feature that can draw the largest percentage of your community back to your site. For that reason, it is very important to understand how to build a media system rather than an image gallery, video gallery, and so on. We will build a generic media management system that will allow you to host videos, photos, resumes, or any number of physical files with limited additional tweaking.

In addition to the media management system, we will take a look at addressing one of the biggest limitations of many web programming environments—multi-file upload. ASP.NET is great at handling one file at a time, but when managing a photo gallery, for instance, you will find that you frequently have a handful or hundreds of photos to upload. Rather than creating a Java-based or Active-X-based control, which may require some additional installations to your users' systems, we will look at a Silverlight and also a Flash-based implementation.

With this we will be able to browse to a directory and upload as many files as we want as shown in the following screenshot:

Blogging

Blogging is often a major feature in any community site as it gives those who enjoy speaking to the world a tool to do just that. On the other hand though, the output of your blog generates free content for those who are more on the voyeuristic side to read up and follow along with your blogs. One of the biggest benefits for a community with active bloggers is that you are acquiring a large amount of free content to feed the various search engine spiders with. This in turn will help you get your search ranking up, that will drive more traffic to your site, and will in turn grow your community.

With search engines, users, and security in mind, we will invest some time to address an issue that plagues many dynamic websites—query string data being used to determine page output. Let's face it, from a user's point of view, seeing a bunch of variable names in the query string with random auto-generated record IDs and 32 character GUIDs is just not that user-friendly and at times downright confusing. Add to this that search engines these days seem to be able to navigate some of this query string mumbo jumbo, but we are losing a key opportunity to optimize our site for keywords by spoofing URLs as though our keywords were directories. We will continue from our profile's example and extend our vanity URL support so that we can have something along the lines of `www.sitename.com/blogs/AtulGupta/my-article-name.aspx`.

Forums

Everyone is well aware of what a forum is. For a social network, it is a disconnected form of communication where people can post something to discuss and others can happen across the posted item over time to add their two cents. Frequently in the developer world, you will have a community that is 100 percent focused around this sort of feature in the form of a technical help forum. For our site that centers on helping others figure out how to run an aquarium, we will find this feature useful.

The above screenshot shows how the message board will look.

Groups

Groups to me are a form of container for like-minded individuals. It allows a community to pool its resources. A group could comprise of people who are interested in the same topic, people for or against a certain presidential candidate, or people representing a company. The common focus for a group is that when someone who is part of the group posts content to the site, all the members of that group are notified. If a user sends a message to a group, then all the members become recipients of that message.

In our site, we will support common concepts such as public and private groups. For private groups you will have to request a membership and should be granted access prior to getting into the group. We will also extend the group concept and provide all our groups with a private forum.

Comments

Commenting is just another way of allowing your users to interact with the content and other members of your social network. There isn't a lot that is special about the commenting concept. We will build out a custom user control to handle commenting any physical object in our system that has a supporting table behind it. This means that we can have comments on anything such as photos, videos, profiles, forum postings, blogs, and so on. To sum up, anything can have a comment!

Tags

Tags are very important to the navigation of your community. A **tag** is usually one or two keywords attached to some content or item in your site. This keyword may be attached to one or many items in the site by one or many users of the site. The more frequently the tag is applied, the larger its subscription base becomes. We can then show the tag in a cloud of other tags. This cloud would be sorted with the most frequently used keywords. Again, the more the keywords are used, the more they get displayed in the cloud.

We can then place a tag cloud in various places of our site such as the homepage, on a user's profile, or on a group's homepage. This will then act as a jumping off point for all of their most frequently tagged content. Usually, this promotes clicking around on the site. The more people move around on the site, the more likely they are to add tags of their own or some other form of content. This will give some activity to your community. We will build our tagging and tag cloud feature as another user control that can be attached to any object with a handful of different display types.

Ratings

Ratings are often a very important part of any community-supplied content site. This allows the whole community to be in charge of what content takes precedence on the site. While the ASP.NET AJAX Toolkit provides us with a rating tool, we will look at creating a custom rating tool. Our rating tool will not only use the AJAX rating tool but will also extend, so that rather than applying a rating directly to an item, we can rate individual attributes of an item. All those ratings will then be rolled up, and that score will be the rating that is displayed for the actual item.

This feature will have the ability to be attached to any item in the site as well. Once built, this feature will really help us get the right content for our community. It also provides our users with the sense of belonging, as they are now able to provide their opinion on just about anything. The screenshot below shows how tagging or commenting can be done.

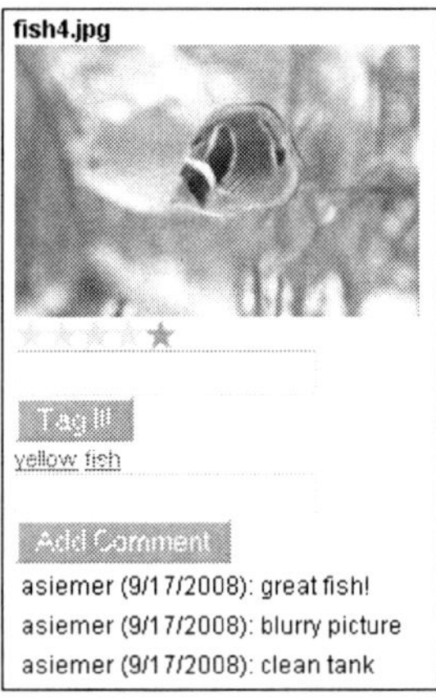

Mark as Answer

For any forum to be successful, it is important to have the basic infrastructure to post a question and reply. Once this is available, the next important thing is to ensure resolution/responses to posted queries because ultimately that is what will drive the number of users to the forums. To ensure forums are successful, the forums should provide ability to mark a reply as answer. A correctly marked answer will result in specific points being awarded to the user and this helps build his/her reputation on the site.

Voting

Voting is a way to moderate the content on a community site and also recognize people who are contributing by providing valuable comments in forums. Users need to have the right to vote positively and negatively on a question or a reply posted on the forum. This helps other users to not read the entire question and associated replies, but focus on those that are voted higher. Similar to *Mark as Answer*, Voting also helps build an individual's reputation.

Medals

Once users start to accrue points based on their replies that are either marked as answers or voted in favor of, they start to earn medals. This is a visual indication of their reputation (see the following screenshot) on the site and the higher the number of medals, the higher the confidence that community will have in what this person has to say.

Framework

Anyone can build a mom and pop community site with the features that we discussed. However, if you want to build a site that can grow with your community, we will want to start building it in a certain way from the beginning. For that reason we will follow a few design patterns and concepts upfront. We will use an n-layered approach to build our site using Domain-driven design, Model View Presenter, Factory Pattern, and Repository Pattern. We will also make use of **Managed Extensibility Framework (MEF)**, the ADO.NET Entity framework and related tools and Windows Server AppFabric that Microsoft has provided with .NET 4 as well as a few great open source tool sets such as Lucene.NET, and MemCached.

Scaling up

Once we have our core community built out, we will begin discussing some concepts to help you support a large number of users on your social network. We will discuss how application can be tiered, transformed into Service Oriented Architecture (SOA), deployment on IIS and look at some key concepts around web farming. We will discuss how to create and search indexed data with Lucene.NET. We will also cover how to optimize your data retrieval and content creation by implementing a caching farm inside your web farm using the new Windows Server AppFabric or MemCached Win32 server. We can also look at optimizing our email communications by implementing some form of mail queuing concepts.

Summary

We have taken a look at some of the features that constitute a social networking site and looked at some examples of successful community sites. Next, we discussed key features that a community site must provide and also briefly looked at POST and SLATES. Finally, we discussed what features we will build through the course of this book.

2

An Enterprise Approach to our Community Framework

We have all worked on application development. It typically starts small with limited feature requirements and doesn't seem to have a need in the future. However, then you found yourself constantly adding features to this application. It continued to grow and grow uncontrollably. Had you known that this application was going to be so important and was going to be used so extensively, you would probably have built it differently? It is most likely that you would have designed your application with extensibility in mind rather than just hurrying to get the project finished and out of the door!

Application design

The application design is as follows:

Key principles

While designing Fisharoo solution, we will try to adhere to certain architecture principles, some of the important ones are:

- **Modular and Loosely Coupled**: We will try to build Fisharoo by dividing the related functionality into various modules having no or relatively low inter-dependencies.
- **Separation of Concerns (SoC)**: It is the process of breaking down your application into specific units of functionality in such a way that each unit only addresses the needs of one concern with as little overlap as possible with other units in terms of functionality. More information regarding this topic is at: `http://en.wikipedia.org/wiki/Separation_of_concerns`.

- **Extensibility**: We will try to build the greater part of the application in extensible manner so that if needed to we can replace parts of the functionality without having to recompile the entire application or even redesign.
- **Build versus Buy**: Wherever possible we will try and utilize out-of-box functionality in the .NET stack or look for third party/open source components that can help fill the gap.

Each of the above principles is discussed in the following section. As we go along, we will also see how they can be realized with the help of technology and architectural patterns.

Layered architecture

Knowing that our application is going to be a large undertaking that should last for some time, we need to design something that can be easily extended as the need arises. For that we will try to design this application with extensibility in mind. The easiest way to do that is to follow the general rule of maintaining "separation of concerns (SoC)".

Layers

The easiest way to maintain SoC is to first break major areas of your application into layers. In most applications, this might be broken down into the presentation, business logic, and data access layers.

- **Presentation Layer**: This layer would normally hold anything pertaining to the user interface of your application—the buttons, links, and other controls that a user would click on and interact with while using your application.
- **Business Logic Layer**: This is where the rules of your application would live. This could be as simple as formatting the currency of a price in your product catalogue to something more complex such as enforcing rules regarding data input.
- **Services Layer**: While building **Service Oriented Architecture (SOA)**, services layer is built on top of the business logic layer. Since we are not aiming SOA implementation we will not create this layer. However, in Chapter 13, we will show you how to introduce this layer in the existing design without a lot of changes.
- **Data Access Layer**: The data access layer is responsible for connecting to a data source and interacting with the data that is stored in that location. This could be a database, some XML files, text files, or even a web service.

- **Utility/Components Layer**: Functionalities like mechanisms for caching, logging errors, reading from configuration files, etc. are needed across the application. Such concerns, that cut across application, are referred as cross cutting concerns. To provide implementation to resolve such concerns we create an independent project called Components (also referred as Utility) layer.

In most small applications, just these three layers are good enough as shown in the following screenshot:

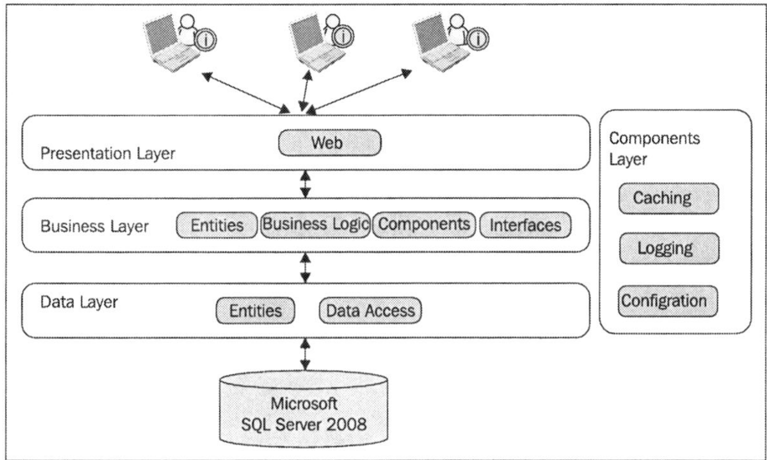

Tiered architecture

While layers are logical separation of concerns, tiers are used for physical separation. In a tiered approach, one or more layers are hosted on to independent machines/boxes to support failover, ensure high availability, and scalability. While architecting an application and planning for growth, this is an essential consideration. We will discuss this in more detail in Chapter 13, when we discuss physical deployment.

Domain-driven Design

Domain-driven Design (DDD) is not a methodology, framework, or technology, but more of a way of thinking practically. It is geared towards making software development move at a faster pace. It puts the focus on the domain and domain logic as it is truly the center of any application. Having a robust application and infrastructure wrapped around poorly designed domain logic is a problem waiting to happen.

The topic of Domain-driven Design is a vast one. To get you started in understanding the high-level concepts, we will outline only the basics here. As we continue to build our framework and application, you will find some of the following principles applied.

For more information about Domain-driven Design check out this website: `http://www.domaindrivendesign.org`.

Important aspects

The important aspects of the Domain-driven Design are as follows:

Ubiquitous language

The concept of **ubiquitous language** is a simple one. It basically states that all individuals involved with a software development project—business owners, project managers, developers, that is, just about everyone—use the same language to describe the aspects of the software being developed. This reduces the confusion, which in turn increases the speed of overall development.

This concept is not just for discussion purposes. It extends to the actual naming of classes, methods, and more. Once this occurs all discussions will sound similar no matter who is involved with the discussion. When this is followed, and everyone is speaking the same language in all conversations, confusion is totally removed and there are no longer islands of expertise.

In the end, the domain and domain logic become more refined. The application is better for it!

Entities

An **entity** is an object in your application that maintains its state for the life of your application. This means that it can be rehydrated from an XML file, saved to a database, later loaded from that database instance, serialized, and sent across the network—resulting in the same object in all the cases. This is performed with the use of a unique ID. This could be anything from an auto-incrementing numeric ID, a GUID or, a **Social Security Number (SSN)**, including anything that would be unique in your system.

An example could be a person in the United States (U.S.). In this case, we could use a person's SSN and each resulting person would be unique. When we look at all the people in the world, the SSN would no longer be considered a good form of unique ID as not all people in the world have one. So in this case, we would probably have to start looking at multiple properties of a person to define their uniqueness. We could take their birth date, last name, country/state, city, and so on. A combination of this information should result in a unique entity in your system. Entities are the most important objects of your domain.

Do all objects in an application need to be unique? Are all objects necessarily entities? Well, the answer is 'No'. In the next section, we will look at value objects as the answer to these questions.

Value objects

A value object is less important than an entity. It does not require an identity, and hence it can be easily created without being concerned to determine its uniqueness. We are more interested in what the item is rather than who it is. A value object should be immutable. If you need to modify the value object, discard it, and create a new one. But if you find that the object is not immutable, or cannot exist without its own identity, it is most likely to be an Entity object.

To extend our person example from the *Entities* section further, we could make an "address" value object rather than have a person with properties of state, city, zip code, street, or any other information pertaining to the address. The value object would then store information about state, city, zip code, street, and so on. This address object could then be part of a person. So you could use it as *person.Address.City*. Technically, this address could be shared for all the people in the same house. We don't care so much for the address itself, but for the fact that it is attached to a specific person.

Why do we need value objects? Value objects are important as they offer a way of grouping bits of information as you saw in the above example. Being "lightweight" objects, they reduce the amount of resources used in an application. They also simplify an application where value objects don't require uniqueness.

Services

The Services term should not be confused with Services from **Service Oriented Architecture** (**SOA**) world.

As we discuss our application using the ubiquitous language, we will quickly end up with a vocabulary of nouns (entities and value objects) and verbs (methods of those objects). However, not all the verbs that we end up with will easily fit into our defined entities and value objects. What do we do with these equally important but homeless verbs? They are obviously needed by the application. Do we stick them into one of our existing objects for lack of a better place to put them? Doing that would create clutter and confuse the objects making them difficult to use. So, the answer to the previous questions is 'No'. We would rather create a service.

A **service** is neither an entity nor a value object. Having said that, we have to create an object of some kind or another considering the fact that we are using an **Object Oriented Programming (OOP)** based language. So we create a service-based object that provides the needed action (verb) for our application. Take an e-commerce application for example. We might have a customer and a vendor wherein one of them needs to contact the other via email. Would it be appropriate to add a method to the customer object to send them an email from the vendor to the customer? Would it be appropriate to add this method to the vendor object? It doesn't quite seem right in either object. So we could create an email service. Now when our customer needs to contact the vendor, or the vendor needs to contact the customer, either one can use the service to take care of the communication.

Modules

Even if you have never heard of or worked with Domain-driven Design, you will easily understand what a module is. A **module** is a group of features and functionality in your application. Modules are a way of organizing large and complex domain logic into smaller and more understandable units. Modules also help in abiding by the principles of high cohesion and low coupling by putting highly cohesive code together.

In this application, we will have accounts, blogs, picture galleries, and many other features. While we could easily create one vast library of code to cover all these features, it would be easier for us to create smaller units of code that specifically describe the features of each module separately. Obviously, we will have some overlap among modules as an account is used in both galleries and blogs. It would also be possible for blogs to reference an image in an image gallery. As you can see, not only do modules make your code easier to understand, they also help keep things decoupled as you have further refined your code into yet another container!

Aggregates

Up to this point we have discussed the idea that we must use a ubiquitous language to define our application's vocabulary. From that definition we will draw out entities and value objects. Where methods don't fit our entities or value objects, we can create services. And all these items can be grouped into modules. Now we are going to move on to how these items can be managed, created, and stored using aggregation, factories, and repositories.

With a complex application, we will have lots of objects to deal with. So far we have tried to reduce the complexity by keeping things easy to understand by way of a well-defined vocabulary and by grouping that vocabulary into smaller containers. Also, we have tried to reduce complexity by stating that some objects need to be able to maintain the state across the application, while others do not.

What we have not yet discussed is how to maintain an object's life cycle. We know that they will be created, stored, passed around, and so on. But what about when it is time to completely erase one of these objects from the system? If we do not closely manage the usage of our objects, we could end up with objects randomly floating about our system for no reason at all. This in turn could create issues for us in the form of memory leaks, buffer overruns, null pointer access, finally resulting in a system crash.

For this reason, it is important that we plan for simplicity in how our objects interact with one another. Rather than have objects spin one another up haphazardly, it would be nice to have gatekeepers, that we have to go through to gain access to other objects. For example, the only way for object Z to gain access to object B is through object A. This way when object Z is done using object A and object B, we can simply remove object A, and object B will go too.

An **aggregation** is a boundary that we can use with our objects. We discussed that our `person` object was an entity object, and that the address information was a value object. Let's extend this example to say that we would also have an object that handles the person's contact information, which could be phone numbers, email addresses, and so on. This too would be a value object. Rather than letting external objects directly access the address and contact information, we could force them to go through the entity object to read this data. Also, if an external object wanted to add a phone number to the list of phone numbers for a person, we could enforce that the only way to do this is through the `person` object rather than through the contact information object.

Following through with this concept further simplifies our domain logic in the form of breaking our class structure down into even smaller buckets of code. It is not only easier to work from a development point of view, but also simpler to manage how objects come and go in our application.

Factories

With all the simplicity that we are striving to achieve in our design, how can we limit the complexity that is involved in the creation of an object? It doesn't make sense to store that logic in the object that we are trying to create. It is one thing to put some simple logic in the constructor of an object and let the object make itself, but quite another when that object is an entity and itself has several value objects as part of its make up (an aggregate). In this case, we would want to stash the creation logic into something called a factory.

As we strive to keep the objects focused on their single concern it makes sense to have a person factory that would create a person, the person's address information, and contact information rather than have the person object know how to do these tasks, as well as how to be a person. To grasp the concept better, take the example of buying a TV. If you wanted a new TV, you would go to the local electronics store and purchase one. You wouldn't expect the vendor to give you a screen, a box, some electronics, a few cables, some plastic, a handful of buttons, and the directions to assemble your TV. You would walk down an aisle, pick a TV, purchase a box with a working TV in it, and go home. We should keep our objects working in the same order. Think of a factory as the electronics store, and your objects as the assembled TV. Your object should do what it does best, act like a person, and not worry about how to read genetic code and assemble cells.

Repositories

Now that we have understood that a factory's sole purpose is the creation of objects, what about the hydration of an already existing object? Perhaps we have a list of people stored in a data store. Should a factory be responsible for retrieving these people? In DDD, it is stated that this is the role of the Repository.

A **Repository** is an object whose purpose is specific to a single Entity object. For example we will have a `PersonRepository` object that would know how to get a person (or many people) based on certain well-defined parameters. It would also know how to persist `person` objects to a data store.

Note that we use 'data store', and not 'database'. A repository works closely with your application's infrastructure code. It should know how to work with all sorts of data stores that your application might know how to work with. This could be a database, a web service, a collection of XML files, or any other data store. While your repository is intelligent enough to work with infrastructure code, the interfaces that it presents to other domain objects should be domain-oriented and should be simple for the other domain objects to use.

Entity Framework

In the earlier section, we discussed Domain-driven Design. Now we will take a look at how we can implement the same concepts. Microsoft ADO.NET Entity Framework provides data access framework to build domain-centric applications needing to solve object relational impendence mismatch. Object relation impedance mismatch happens primarily due to a difference in the structure of underlying relational entities or tables as against the structure of domain/business concepts that are usually modeled in the form of Object Oriented concepts like Class, Aggregation, Inheritance, etc. explained as entities and value objects in the Domain-Driven Design section above.

Entity Framework solves the problem of impedance mismatch by implementing a logical abstraction layer on top of existing Relational or non-Relational data sources called as **Entity Data Model (EDM)** which hosts mapping between entities and relational table. This mapping can be easily changed without changing the data access code written on top of this logical abstraction. Due to this, Entity framework can support connectivity to multiple databases like Microsoft SQL Server, ORACLE, DB2, etc.

Entity framework is an integral part of .NET Framework 4, and builds upon its earlier release through some interesting features like model first approach, support for plain old CLR objects (POCO), etc. Due to the simplicity, flexibility, and increased adoption of Entity Framework, we decided to use it to build our data access layer.

Repository pattern and Entity Framework

Earlier we had a high-level discussion on repositories. Now we are ready to dig in a little deeper. We know that repositories are all about providing a way for our domain logic to access resources in the outside world. We know that they can be used for web services, XML files, and just about anything else. In our case, we will discuss how to access data in a database using the EF.

We haven't really touched upon anything related to the Fisharoo application so far, which means that we don't really have anything in the database for us to play with just yet. For that reason, we created a simple `Person` table for us to work with. It has the following fields: `PersonID`, `FirstName`, `LastName`, and `Email`. We then created four entries in the database for us to work with.

```
CREATE TABLE [dbo].[Person](
   [PersonID] [int] IDENTITY(1,1) NOT NULL,
   [FirstName] [varchar](30) NULL,
   [LastName] [varchar](30) NULL,
   [Email] [varchar](150) NULL
) ON [PRIMARY]
```

This `Person` table will be used later in our .NET solution via the ADO.NET Entity Framework (`.edmx` file).

Building Extensibility using Managed Extensibility Framework (MEF)

To support extensible architecture we need to build several extensibility points that if needed can be easily replaced seamlessly with different implementations. For example, replace one caching implementation with another caching one.

However, this should be achievable with the least overall impact i.e. it should not require code change and recompilation of the application. The replacement should ideally be as trivial as replacing the existing assembly with the new implementation.

There are a few frameworks that help achieve this including Unity framework, Structure Map, Castle Windsor, etc. However, we have decided to use **Managed Extensibility Framework (MEF)** which is an integral part of .NET 4. Visual Studio 2010 itself uses MEF internally to provide extensibility.

We chose MEF over others because of the simplicity it has to offer including aspects like a lot less code to code to achieve the necessary functionality, simple API support with attribute style programming, and no need to maintain any configuration files.

Following are three core concepts associated with MEF:

- **Export(s)** is/are potential candidates in the applications that can be replaced at runtime. It exposes "Contracts" and Contract can be anything like .NET Interface or Class or property.

  ```
  [Export(typeof(ICache))]
  public class Caching: ICache
  {
      public object Get(string cache_key)
      {
         //Specific caching implementation goes here
      }
  }
  ```

- **Imports** are used to consume exported instances. Consuming application will be as:

  ```
  [Import()]
  Private ICache cache;
  ```

- **Catalog** hosts the components that need to be composed:

```
public static void Compose(object o)
{
    var container = new CompositionContainer(
                    new DirectoryCatalog(Path.Combine(
                    AppDomain.CurrentDomain.BaseDirectory,
                    @"bin\MEFBin")));
    var batch = new CompositionBatch();
    batch.AddPart(o);
    container.Compose(batch);
}
```

Composition binds all of them together at runtime to deliver the functionality. In Components layer (described later in this chapter) we will see in more detail how to realize MEF implementation.

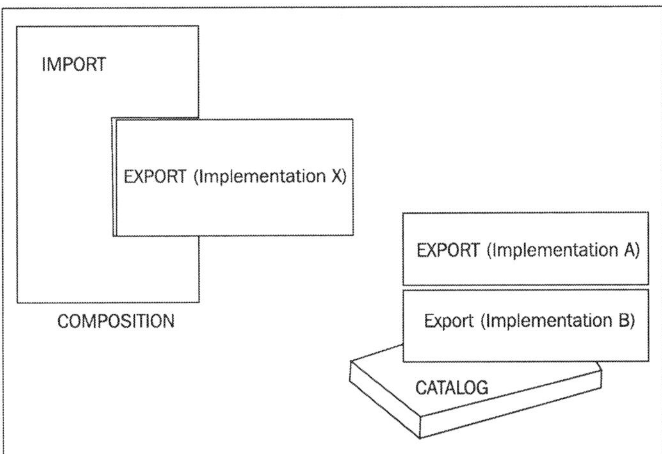

Model View Presenter pattern

> At the time of writing this, Microsoft has also released Model View Controller (MVC) framework (version 2 is currently available as part of .NET 4). We had a discussion on using it for this edition of the book or not and eventually decided against it. See *Appendix A* for a discussion on MVC and why we didn't use it.

Model

The **model** is a direct reference to your domain logic—the business logic layer so to speak. This provides access to the backend data (from the database) and implements additional business logic on it. As when we do authentication for a user, we need to manage encryption and decryption of the password. Such things will be managed by model.

View

The **view** is made up of the `.aspx` and `.cs` files of your webpage. These files are responsible for defining the physical items that a user interacts with in your website. They are also responsible for receiving the various events that a user raises while navigating through your site. The handled events should be immediately passed to the presenter rather than being handled in the view. Doing this ensures that the presenter has all the logic and the application remains testable. It is the responsibility of the presenter to decide how to handle each event. The view is required to pass itself (by reference) to the presenter giving the presenter total control over the view.

Presenter

The **presenter** is a separate class file. There should be one presenter file per webpage. The presenter is ultimately responsible for indirectly handling events fired by the view and directly controlling what the view displays. It is the only part of the presentation layer that can communicate with the domain objects (or the model).

Tests can be wrapped around the presenter object. While this is not a full test of the UI, it is a full test of the logic that the UI interacts with.

How it works

To quickly describe how this works from a programmatic point of view, let's think about loading a list of people. The view would contain something like a GridView or some other form of Repeater. The steps would be as shown in the following screenshot (and described later):

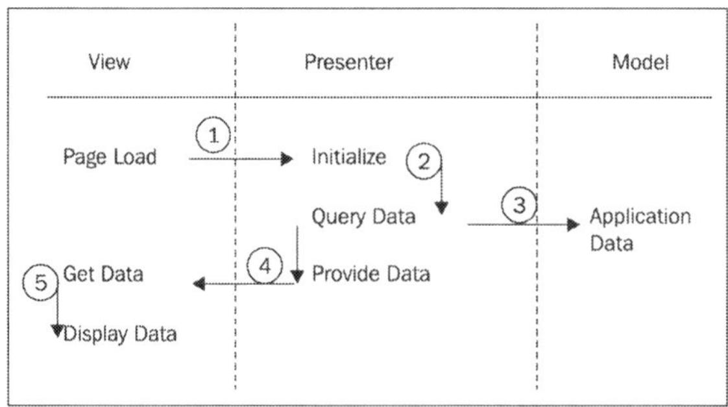

1. On loading, the view would instantiate its presenter. It then passes a reference of itself to that presenter by calling an `init` method in the presenter.
2. This passes the control of the view to the presenter. The presenter is now responsible for initializing the page (loading the initial state of the page).
3. The presenter works with our domain objects (the model) to get a list of people.
4. The presenter then passes the newly acquired list of people to the view by calling appropriate method provided by the view.
5. The view then attaches the list of people to the data source of a repeater and asks the repeater to bind on that list.

If someone were to click on a person in that list, the process would be repeated up through the view, into the presenter, over some domain objects, and back down to the view.

Creating the .NET Solution

So far we have looked at layering, MVP, MEF, and Entity Framework concepts, etc. Let's now start with implementation and for that let's create an empty .NET solution called Fisharoo under which we can start creating various layers designed in the form of .NET projects.

Presentation layer

In the `Fisharoo` solution, create a new ASP.NET web application project, that will act as a presentation layer. We call it `Web`. Once the project is created you will see a structure as shown in following screenshot:

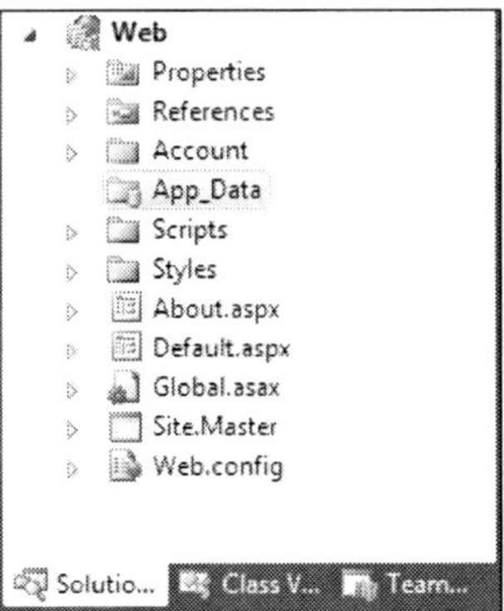

Let's quickly look at this in detail:

- `Account` **folder**: This folder contains the files for user login, user registration, and password change. The user authentication logic uses the `asp.net` membership provider, but we will be replacing this with custom authentication logic.
- `App_Data` **folder**: This folder is to hold any application-specific data files like typically the membership provider's database.
- `Scripts` **folder**: This folder contains jQuery 1.4.1 related files.
- `Styles` **folder**: This folder contains the `Site.css`, the style sheet that contains the various styles that the site uses.
- `Site.Master`: This is the `asp.net` master page that will provide the common look and feel for the web application and all other aspx pages will be content place holders for various sections within this page.
- `Global.asax`: The global application level code that has code for application start and end and session start and end, apart from error handling routine.
- `Default.aspx`: This is the application start page.
- `About.aspx`: This contains the **AboutBox** kind of values for our web application.
- `Web.Config`: This is the standard web configuration file, but in ASP.NET 4 project you will see multiple configuration files, one per build configuration. So you will have `web.config.debug` and `web.config.release` configuration files. Refer to this link for more details: `http://www.drdobbs.com/visualstudio/224201017`

We will alter some of the structure and add/delete files as we go along. For now let's retain everything that we see.

Components layer

At this point in the application, we have not discussed any business logic; however let us discuss common functionalities that are needed across application such as logging, caching, email, etc. Each application will have specific logging and, caching requirements which can be satisfied with specific implementation. Hence it is best to build these points as extensibility points so that the existing implementation can be replaced with different implementation of the same as need be. Such plugin-plugout points in application are referred to as extensibility points. As discussed earlier, we have chosen MEF to build extensibility in our core framework. To achieve this, we have bundled each of the extensibility points e.g. Caching, Email, Configuration, Logging, etc. as Interfaces in **Interfaces** project and implementation for the same in **Components** project, both are of type .NET class library. Let's look at some of the components that we will need in our site.

To get true extensibility, each of the plug-ins (Configuration, Caching, Email, etc.), should be in a respective dedicated class library project, so that we can replace any one component without affecting anything else. However, for our current site this will be an overkill for this application hence we decided to include implementation for all these in one `Components` project.

Configuration

For the configuration utility, we want to create something that is capable of returning a strongly typed item out of our configuration source. Of course, this configuration source will initially be the standard `web.config`. As the `web.config` only holds string values, our configuration object will be responsible for casting out the appropriate type.

```
//Fisharoo/Components/Configuration.cs
using System;
using System.ComponentModel.Composition;
using System.Configuration;
using Fisharoo.Interfaces;

namespace Fisharoo.Components
{
    [Export(typeof(IConfiguration))]
    public class Configuration : IConfiguration
    {
        public object GetConfigurationSetting(Type expectedType,
        string key)
        {
            string value = ConfigurationManager.AppSettings.Get(key);
            if (value == null)
            {
                throw new Exception(string.Format("AppSetting: {0} is
                not configured.", key));
            }

            try
            {
                if (expectedType.Equals(typeof(int)))
                {
                    return int.Parse(value);
                }

                if (expectedType.Equals(typeof(string)))
                {
```

```
                    return value;
                }

                throw new Exception("Type not supported.");
            }
            catch (Exception ex)
            {
                throw new Exception(string.Format("Config key:{0} was
                expected to be of type {1} but was not.", key,
                expectedType), ex);
            }
        }
    }
}
```

As you can see, from the start we have included a MEF attribute above the class definition (`Export`) so that we can easily swap out this for another one if needed. For MEF support, we need to add a reference to `System.ComponentModel.Composition` assembly.

The `Configuration` class currently exposes only a single method `GetConfigurationSetting()` to retrieve application configuration entries in a generic manner. It communicates with the `config` file using the `ConfigurationManager` and gets the string value that was specified by the key that was passed in. Rest of the code is fairly self-explanatory. We test whether the retrieved value is null, and throw an error if it is. We then try to return the expected type by parsing as `int` or `string`. If the expected type is neither `int` nor `string`, then we throw an error stating that the requested type is not supported.

Cache

Continuing on the principles of extensibility, we will build a cache object implementing `ICache` interface. Our cache implementation will wrap the `HttpContext.Current.Cache` object from `System.Web.Caching`. Tomorrow if need be, we can replace this implementation with say **MemCached** or **AppFabric**.

The logic will deal with saving and retrieving items from the cache using a key as reference to identify cached items. Cache will also support time-based caching, where the cached item will expire once the time limit is over. We will also support deleting entries from cache. This could be used to make room for newer entries once the cache starts to fill up or simply to remove an item that is no longer needed by the application. Look up the associated code with this chapter for implementation details of this class.

Session

The session object is another item that is frequently used in most web applications. That being said, it is also something that we can squeeze performance out of down the road. Even if performance wasn't an issue, the session object by itself does not really conform to the most basic of OOP principles. Rather than trying to cast an item out of thin air or the `HttpContext.Current.Session`, it would be much better if we could call an object that returned the appropriate object for us. Here is the basic implementation:

```
//Fisharoo/Components/Session.cs
using System.ComponentModel.Composition;
using System.Web;
using Fisharoo.Interfaces;

namespace Fisharoo.Components
{
    [Export(typeof(IWebContext))]
    public class WebContext : IWebContext
    {
        public void ClearSession()
        {
            HttpContext.Current.Session.Clear();
        }

        public bool ContainsInSession(string key)
        {
            return HttpContext.Current.Session[key] != null;
        }

        public void RemoveFromSession(string key)
        {
            HttpContext.Current.Session.Remove(key);
        }

        private string GetQueryStringValue(string key)
        {
            return HttpContext.Current.Request.QueryString.Get(key);
        }

        private void SetInSession(string key, object value)
        {
            if (HttpContext.Current == null || HttpContext.Current.
            Session == null)
            {
```

```
                return;
            }
            HttpContext.Current.Session[key] = value;
        }

        private object GetFromSession(string key)
        {
            if (HttpContext.Current == null || HttpContext.Current.
            Session == null)
            {
                return null;
            }
            return HttpContext.Current.Session[key];
        }

        private void UpdateInSession(string key, object value)
        {
            HttpContext.Current.Session[key] = value;
        }
    }
}
```

We will continue to extend this object to have specific methods that could handle some of the dirty work. Say we stored a person in the session as the current user. We could have a `GetCurrentUserFromSession()` method defined that would interact with our wrapper methods. It would retrieve the user and cast the object as a person. This is much better OOP-wise. Let's look at the wrapper and for brevity, we will only look at key or new aspects in this code.

Let us look at some of the public method definitions. These are all pretty easy to understand and primarily work with the `HttpContext` object. We have a `ClearSession()` method that simply resets the session. We have a `ContainsInSession()` method that takes a key value. It checks whether that key is present in the session and returns true or false. The `RemoveFromSession()` method that takes in a key and attempts to remove that key from the session.

After our public methods, we have a few private methods, namely, `GetQueryStringValue()`, `SetInSession()`, `GetFromSession()`, and `UpdateInSession()`. Before we discuss these methods, we need you to understand why they are private. We could make all of these public and they would work just fine. However, making them public would also mean that we would scatter the code about our application that directly interacts with the session. Our preference is that we extend this object to provide more specific methods that work with these private methods, that in turn work with the session. This provides us a bit more encapsulation regarding the session interaction.

The GetQueryStringValue() method takes in a key value and retrieves the item from the query string. The SetInSession() method allows you to pass in a key and an object. The object is then stored in the session under that key name. GetFromSession() does just that—it takes a key and retrieves that corresponding object. UpdateInSession() is very similar to SetInSession() with the exception that it assumes that a key already exists and updates the value that is currently stored there. This method will throw an error if a key does not exist. Therefore prior to using this method, you should check that your key exists in the session collection!

Redirection

From an OOP point of view, Response.Redirect is about as useful as the session object is (we're starting to see a trend here). It simply provides a way of sending you from one place to another. It would be nice if we could work with it using methods. It would be even better if we could hide some logic in those methods if need be. Our initial implementation is very easy.

```
//Fisharoo/Components/Redirector.cs
using System.ComponentModel.Composition;
using System.Web;
using Fisharoo.Interfaces;

namespace Fisharoo.Components
{
    [Export(typeof(IRedirector))]
    public class Redirector : IRedirector
    {
        public void GoToHomePage()
        {
            Redirect("~/Default.aspx");
        }

        public void GoToErrorPage()
        {
            Redirect("~/Error.aspx");
        }

        private void Redirect(string path)
        {
            HttpContext.Current.Response.Redirect(path);
        }
    }
}
```

This class, like the others, uses MEF so that it can be stubbed out for testing later. Currently there are two methods—one an example, and another handling redirection. Let's look at the `Redirect()` method. It takes a path parameter and then uses the `HttpContext` object to redirect the user to the appropriate location. An example is the `GoToHomePage()` method. It asks the `Redirect()` method to send the user to the homepage. If the homepage of the application changes later, we need to edit only this method.

Of course, this class can be expanded with as many new methods as needed to redirect for any purpose. We can extend this object to be a bit more versatile too. We can also perform all sorts of logic inside these methods prior to using the redirection, obviously without degrading the overall design and where actually required.

Email

Sending emails is one task that every website has to be capable of. How many emails you plan to send should certainly determine how you go about sending that email. As we do not yet know how many emails we plan to send, we will initially rely upon the tools that are provided in the .NET framework to send our email. For brevity, we will look at the specific methods from this class here.

As with all our objects, we will have the MEF Export attribute in place that makes this a Pluggable class. The class itself inherits from our `IEmail` interface. We will have a couple of constants declared—one for the website's receiving the email account and another for the website's sending the email account. (We could have used one variable for both, but a little flexibility never hurt anyone!) We then jump into our first method:

```
public void SendEmail(string From, string Subject, string Message)
        {
            MailMessage mm = new
            MailMessage(From,TO_EMAIL_ADDRESS);
            mm.Subject = Subject;
            mm.Body = Message;
            Send(mm);
        }
```

This method is one of the various overrides for the `SendEmail()` method. This one is a bit different from the others in that it is used for the site to send email to another site rather than to a user. The user of this method will provide the email address that the message is from, the subject and the message. This method would be used in a 'Contact Us' page or a similar mail form. At the bottom of this method, you will see a `Send()` method call. This method spins up an `SmtpClient` and sends the email message as do each of the other `SendEmail()` methods.

The remaining `SendEmail()` methods are used in various ways for the site to send an email to the users of the site. These allow sending email to a single user (single user for **To**, CC, and **BCC** inputs) or to an array of users (multiple users for **To**, CC, and **BCC** inputs). The `SendIndividualEmailsPerRecipient ()` method accepts multiple user names but sends individual emails per user.

Finally, we get to the `Send()` method that is used by all of the other methods. This method is responsible for actually sending the emails. But before this method performs any action, we need to add the following section to our `web.config` just after the `configuration` tag. It is responsible for telling the .NET framework how to connect to our mail server.

```
<system.net>
  <mailSettings>
    <smtp>
      <network host="localhost" port="25"
           defaultCredentials="true" />
    </smtp>
  </mailSettings>
</system.net>
```

Now, we can define the last method `Send()` as:

```
private void Send(MailMessage Message)
{
    SmtpClient smtp = new SmtpClient();
    smtp.Send(Message);
}
```

This configuration is very flexible in how it sends the email. However, it still requires the webpage to be responsible for sending emails directly. This creates a page with lots of overheads given that there could be a lot of recipients to process, or a lot of network lag involved in the transactions.

The nice thing about having this class is that we can easily create another class that implements the `IEmail` interface but uses a mail queue instead of requiring the page to send the email. This would allow the website to just create mail messages and put them in the queue, which is much faster than actually processing and sending the emails. We could then have a queue processor somewhere that would be responsible for sending our emails. We will look at this further in Chapter 13.

Error handling and logging

We don't think any "enterprise application" can truly be called "enterprise" if it doesn't handle errors well and notify someone to address them. In an ASP.NET site, there are basically two forms of errors—errors that you have caught, and the ones you couldn't. Pretty simple, right? Well, not so fast! Whether you have trapped an error or not, the user of your application is still going to end up with some form of disruption in their surfing experience. So we need a way to not only provide users with a smooth disruption but also to fix the disruption so that it doesn't happen again.

Error handling is the act of doing your best to trap expected or possible errors. It is also the act of not allowing ugly error messages to get in front of your customers. Logging is to capture details of these errors so that we can fix them down the road.

Logging

Logging can either be overly complex, or really easy. As we don't have loads of time on our hands, we usually opt not to reinvent the wheel whenever possible! So in this case, we will be using the `log4net` framework that provides an extensive set of tools for various forms of logging.

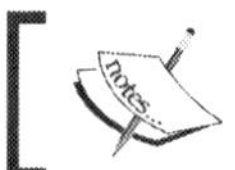

For more information regarding the log4net project look here: `http://logging.apache.org/log4net/`.

To get `log4net` working, you will need to copy the `log4net dll` and the `log4net.xml` files into your `bin` directory in the `Components` project. Once it is there, add a reference to `log4net`. Then you will need to create a `log4net.config` file in the root or `bin` directory of your `Web` project.

For more information about `log4net` configuration look here: `http://logging.apache.org/log4net/release/config-examples.html`.

Now, we can create a class which implements our `ILogger` interface and helps us to interact with what `log4net` provides us. Since this is a routine code, we are not going to discuss it in detail here. You can refer to the code associated with this chapter for the implementation. Once the `logging` class is complete, all we have to do is send something to the log. Let's go back to the `Global.asax.cs` file and add this line at the bottom of the `Application_Error()` method:

```
Log.Error(sender,"Error caught by the Global.asax: " + e.ToString());
```

That should take care of our logging needs!

Error handling

The familiar approach to capture and work with an error that might possibly occur in our code is using `try/catch/finally` syntax. But what about errors that occur outside of the environment? What do you do then to prevent users from seeing some crazy geeked out error message? The easiest thing to do in a web environment is to tap into the `Application_Error` event handler using the `Global.asax` file.

To implement this, let's edit the `Global.asax.cs` file. We will want to take a look at the `Application_Error` method in this file. This is the event that is raised when an unhandled error occurs. We want to do two things in this method:

- We first want to log what happened so that we can fix it
- Then we want to redirect the user to a friendly error page

We will utilize the `log` and `Redirector` class that we built earlier. It is also time now to see how the various MEF compliant implementations that we wrote earlier are consumed in the application. To get started, make sure that you are in the `Global.asax.cs` file. At the top of this file you need to add these `using` statements:

```
using System;
using System.ComponentModel.Composition;
using Fisharoo.Common;
using Fisharoo.Interfaces;
```

At the class level add the following private variable with `Import` attribute. At runtime, MEF engine will search for matching `Export` attribute on a class and instantiate it.

```
[Import]
public IRedirector redir;

[Import]
public ILogger log;
```

We don't need to create the object of Redirector or Log class ourselves. MEF infrastructure takes care of doing that. But before this we do need to dynamically locate the implementation of part (or component) and compose it in the main assembly.

At runtime, we need to pick up the implementation for `IRedirector, ILog` and add it to the container. For this, first you need to create a Catalog for hosting assemblies and then pick up matching implementation for `IRedirector, ILog` from the directory where the assembly for the implementation of `IRedirector, ILog` is residing.

We would need to create the composition logic for composing every part we deal with. For example Log, Cache, Email, Configuration, Redirector, etc. so instead of repeating the composition logic all over the code, we will create a static class to have centralized logic for composition.

```
//Fisharoo/Common/MEFManager.cs
using System;
using System.ComponentModel.Composition;
using System.ComponentModel.Composition.Hosting;
using System.IO;

namespace Fisharoo.Common
{
    public static class MEFManager
    {
        public static void Compose(object o)
        {
            var container = new CompositionContainer(
            new DirectoryCatalog(Path.Combine(
            AppDomain.CurrentDomain.BaseDirectory, "bin")));

            var batch = new CompositionBatch();
            batch.AddPart(o);
            container.Compose(batch);
        }
    }
}
```

To read the assembly from directory, `DirectoryCatalog()` method is used. Once the assembly providing the implementation for `IRedirector` is found, it is picked up by a program and composed in application using `container.ComposeParts()`.

We invoke this composition logic from `Application_Start ()` method.

```
void Application_Start(object sender, EventArgs e)
        {
            // Code that runs on application startup
            MEFManager.Compose(this);
            log.EnsureInitialized();
        }
```

Finally we are back to the `Application_Error ()` method. Let's add the logic to redirect to error page as shown below:

```
void Application_Error(object sender, EventArgs e)
   {
       // Code that runs when an unhandled error occurs

       //Initializing MEF container
       MEFManager.Compose(this);
       log.Error(sender, "Error caught by the Global.asax: " +
       e.ToString());
       redir.GoToErrorPage();
   }
```

We will also add a new method to the `Redirector` class for handling the `GoToErrorPage()` redirection. First we need to edit the `IRedirector` interface to add a new method definition. As we are providing a way to send a user to an error page, we should also create an error page. Add a webform to the root of the Web project named `Error.aspx`. For now, we have included a simple message in the body of the page. We can modify this later to something more explanatory.

```
<%@ Page Title="" Language="C#" MasterPageFile="~/Site.Master"
AutoEventWireup="true" CodeBehind="Error.aspx.cs" Inherits="Fisharoo.
Web.Error" %>
<asp:Content ID="Content1" ContentPlaceHolderID="HeadContent"
runat="server">
</asp:Content>
<asp:Content ID="Content2" ContentPlaceHolderID="MainContent"
runat="server">
    There is an Error
</asp:Content>
```

To simplify our deployment needs, we also added a post-build event for the Components project to copy the output assembly to the bin directory of Web project.

```
copy $(TargetPath) "$(SolutionDir)Web\Bin\."
```

While we are sure that there will be other items that might need extensibility, that we will come across, this small library should be good enough to get us started!

Now, let's move on to creating data access functionality.

Data Access layer

To implement the domain model as discussed in domain driven design section above, we will use the Entity Framework to create the data access layer. For this we need to add a new project to our solution. We will call it `DataAccess`.

In this project, we will create two classes and one `edmx` file. The first class will be our connection object (named `Connection.cs`), and the second file will be called `PersonRepository.cs`. Once you have those class files created, add a new ADO. NET Entity Data Model by right-clicking the `DataAccess` project and select **Add New Item**. From the Data tab select **ADO.NET Entity Data model** as shown in the following screenshot:

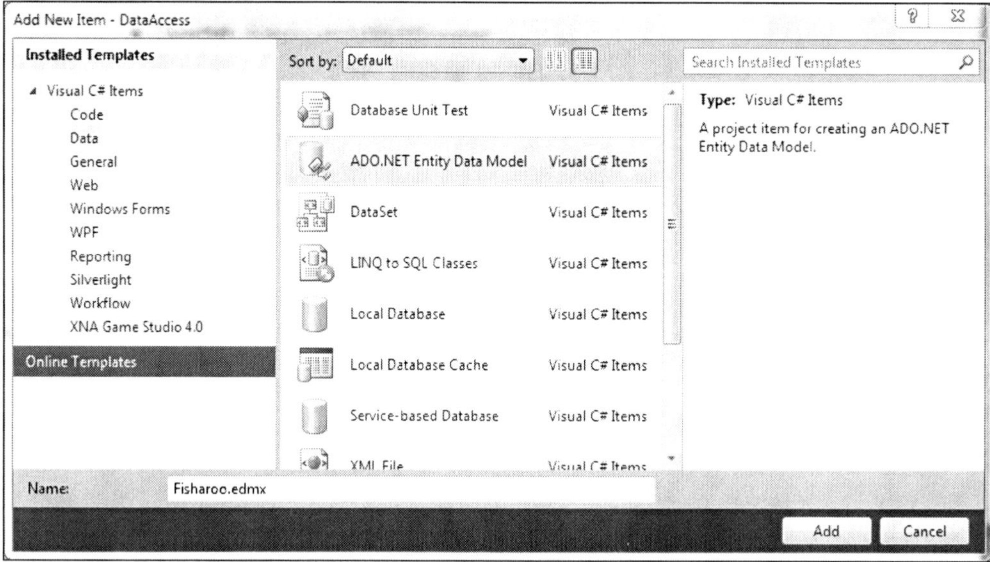

Let's call it `Fisharoo.edmx`. After this the wizard will drive you through various steps as explained below. Since we have already created a table in the database and want our model to be based on that table, we will select **Generate from database** in the first screen and click **Next**. Select appropriate connection string settings and click **Next**.

In the next screen choose your Database objects from **Tables | Person** as follows and provide Model Namespace as **FisharooModel** and click **Finish**.

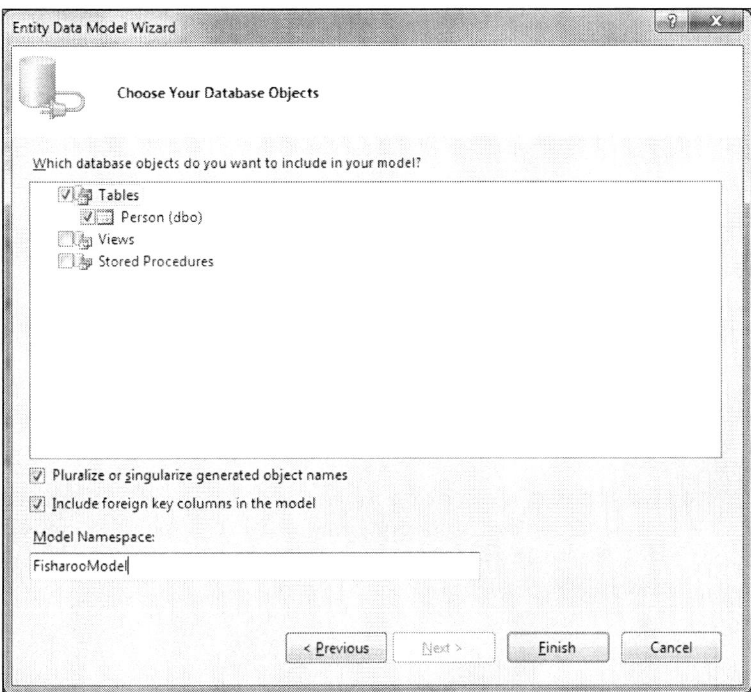

This will complete the creation of `Fisharoo.edmx` under **Data Access** project.

Once you have your table on the `Fisharoo.edmx` design surface, and you hit **Save**, Visual Studio creates a `Fisharoo.Designer.cs` within which is the `FisharooDataContext` class and one class for every table that you have on the design surface. Each class that represents a table will have all the columns of the tables represented as fields and properties for that class. It also creates the entity collection corresponding to each entity as part of `FisharooDataContext` class. This will come in handy when you are using LINQ to perform your queries!

This takes care of the base framework for some demonstrations. Now, let's dig into those two class files that we have created—`Connection.cs` file and the `PersonRepository.cs` file. The `Connection` class gives us a way to encapsulate our `DataContext` creation. It has one method that returns the `FisharooDataContext` object. If we have more data contexts to work with down the road, they could go here too and we can rename the current `GetContext ()` method to a more meaningful name.

```
//Fisharoo/DataAccess/Connection.cs
namespace Fisharoo.DataAccess
{
    public class Connection
    {
        public static FisharooDataContext GetContext()
        {
            FisharooDataContext fdc = new FisharooDataContext(Config
            urationManager.ConnectionStrings["FisharooConnectionStri
            ng"].ToString());
            return fdc;
        }
    }
}
```

Note that we are spinning up a new instance of our `FisharooDataContext` class with a reference to our connection string that we had put in the `web.config` file earlier.

Now, let's move over to the `PersonRepository` class. The `Person` table that we created earlier is only for demonstration purposes, and so is the repository. Here is that class.

```
//Fisharoo/DataAccess/PersonRepository.cs
using System.Collections.Generic;
using System.ComponentModel.Composition;
using System.Linq;
using Fisharoo.Interfaces;

namespace Fisharoo.DataAccess
{
    [Export(typeof(IPersonRepository))]
    public class PersonRepository : IPersonRepository
    {
        public List<string> GetAllNames()
        {
            List<string> names = new List<string>();
```

```
            FisharooDataContext dc = Connection.GetContext();

            var people = from p in dc.People
                         select p;

            foreach (Person p in people)
            {
                names.Add(p.FirstName + " " + p.LastName);
            }

            return names;
        }
    }
}
```

Note that it has an Export attribute so that we can swap the implementation out later if we need to. As with all MEF classes (and for good design reasons) we have also inherited from an `IPersonRepository` interface, which clearly defines this class.

There is only one method in our repository now. It is responsible for simply selecting all the people in the `Person` table and returning a list of the first and the last names of those people. We have a list of type strings for the names collection, which will be returned at the end of the method. We then fetch our `DataContext` for our query. Once we have the `DataContext` defined, we can perform our query.

We declare a local variable with the `var` keyword. This allows us to declare a variable with a dynamic type. In this case, we will be selecting a collection of our Person classes. But we don't really know that for sure! Nor do we really need to know that.

The query we see in the code is to select all the people from the `Person` table and return a collection of those people. It is very much like SQL, however in reverse order, i.e. `from` comes first and `select` comes last. This is how LINQ queries are written and it is due to this ordering that **Visual Studio Intellisense** works with.

Once the query is executed the results are fetched into the `people` variable which is of type `ObjectSet<Person>`. This helps us to iterate over it in a loop. When we created `edmx`, Entity Framework automatically creates `People` ObjectSet as part of `FisharooDataContext` class.

Finally in the code we have a loop, where we concatenate the first name and last name of each person and add them to our `names` collection. Once this is completed, we simply return that collection back to the user of this method.

The demonstration given here is very simple, as we didn't want to overwhelm you. You would get the idea across as to how the Repositories will work in this application. We have also touched upon the basics of LINQ.

At this time, the solution structure is looking like the following screenshot:

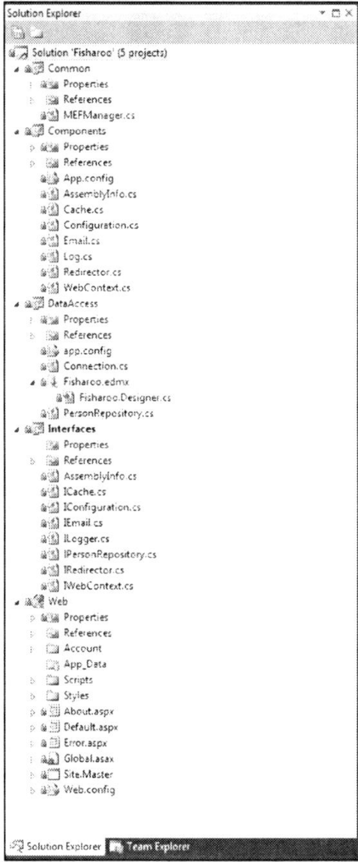

Summary

In this chapter, we have covered creating an enterprise framework to handle the essential needs of most web applications. We have discussed architecture layering, domain driven design, related patterns, and best practices. We also worked through some code to create Components for the basic framework classes that we will be using in our application. We discussed how we will approach our data access using some new technologies and existing patterns. We also looked at how we will use MVP pattern in the presentation layer. This chapter should provide you with a solid foundation on top of which we can now begin to build our application.

3
User Accounts

Without people, your community doesn't exist!

For any community site to be considered successful, it must first have a group of dedicated users. While there are other measures, however in most cases the larger the community's population the more successful it is considered to be. It would then make sense that we create a way for users to come to our site, create an account, and become a part of our community. The following screenshot shows how the registration page will look like:

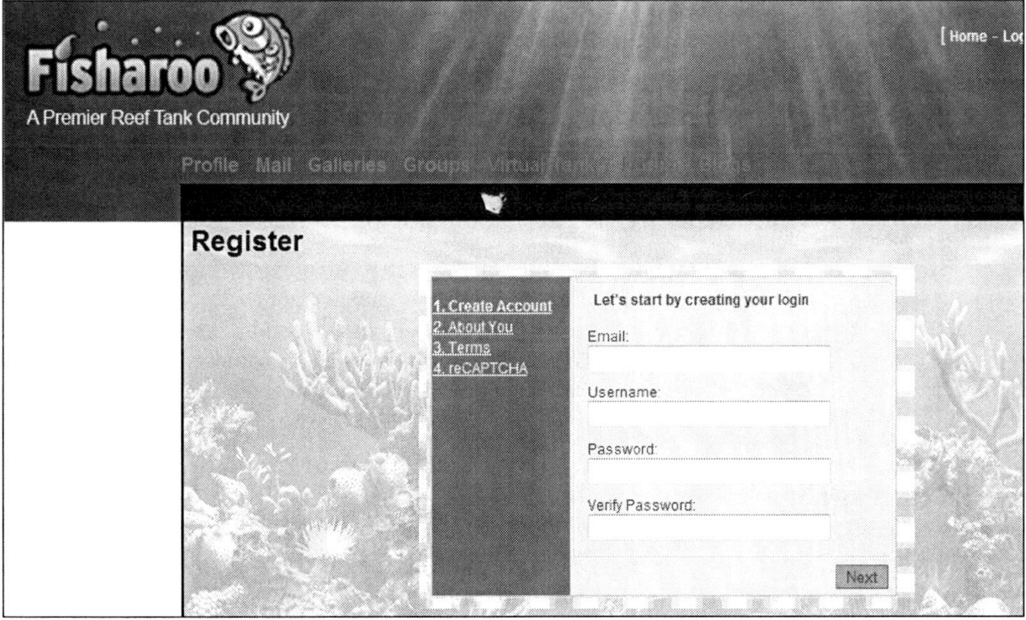

In this chapter, we will discuss many of the common features that are related to user accounts. This will include handling registration, authentication, permissions, and security. We will also go over some basic tools such as password reminders, account administration, and reCAPTCHA. This chapter will provide the foundation for our users upon which we will be able to build all of our other features.

Problem

With most sites these days, regardless of their purpose, you need to know who your users are. You need to know this so that you can restrict how users interact with the site, or you might need this information so that you can provide a dynamic experience to your user. No matter what your reason is, the task of identifying and controlling the users has a few basic requirements.

In order to get to know our users, we will need a way to register them on our site. This would give us a footprint for that user, that we can use each time the user returns. The registration process is fairly straightforward most of the time so that we can easily bring onboard new users. We need to capture the data that we are interested in (such as username, password, email, and so on). We must make sure that we store their password properly so that their identification is safe not only from the other users of the site but also from the administrators and staff of the site. Also, given the amount of fraud and spam on the Internet these days, we need to equip our site with some form of intelligence to guard it from automated registrations. In another attempt to protect the site, we need to make sure that our users are providing us with valid information. We can do this by validating the email provided by them to check if it is a functioning account under their control. As part of the registration process, we also need to inform the user about our current terms and conditions so that they know the rules of our site up-front.

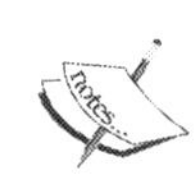

When we refer to automated registrations, we are really describing the act of a bot (or program) that is used to create accounts with the sole purpose of posting advertisements to public areas such as message boards, blogs, and so on.

Once a user has successfully registered, we will need to provide them with tools so that they can identify themselves to us each time they return. This is typically done using a centralized login screen. Upon successful authentication, we can track that user through the site. Knowing that users frequently forget the information that they provided us with, we will need to offer tools to remind the users how to get into our site with a password reminder feature. After the users have authenticated themselves, we would need to define where a user can go and what they can do on our site with some kind of permissions-based system.

Once the users are registered and authenticated, we will need to provide them with a way to administer their account data. In addition to the users being able to administer their own data, the staff that runs the site will also need tools to manage all the users and their data. In addition to managing user data, administrators should be able to control the users' permissions and update the terms and conditions.

Design

In this section, we will discuss the various aspects that are required to implement our new features. Once we are finished, we should have a good idea of what will be required from each area.

Registration

Registration includes the task of acquiring user information, allowing them to pick a username, password, and email verification. In addition, we will require that our users agree to our terms and provide verification that they are human and not a bot by reading our reCAPTCHA image. Once we have all this information, we will create the user account and assign appropriate permissions to the account.

Accounts

While ASP.NET provides various pre-built tools for handling your users via the membership controls, we have decided to explore a custom way to handle our users with regards to logging them in, encrypting their passwords, and so on. The reason for this is to demonstrate that it is fairly simple to build custom authentication logic, and there is sufficient literature available on regular ASP.NET authentication anyway.

To begin with, we need a way to describe our accounts. From the database point of view, it will be fairly simple. All we need is an "Accounts" table where we can hold a username, password, and a few other bits of information.

Password strength

Password strength is not only an issue for the account's security but also for the site owner. The weaker your user's password is, the more likely someone performs a brute force attack on your site. If an account with a high-level permission (such as Administrator) is compromised due to a weak password, you will look pretty silly! It doesn't make much sense on your part to create a secure site in every other way and then allow your users to bypass all your efforts!

Having said that forcing your users to have a strong password, can become an inconvenience to them. Believe it or not, there are many users who would prefer to have a password as "password". While we are not for letting your users become lazy and placing their account at risk, you do need to be aware that there is a chance that you will lose signups due to this requirement. It is up to you to decide how important a secure site is.

Terms and conditions

While terms and conditions are not a necessary requirement for a good site, this section is the place to cover the concept. We will create a simple way to manage your terms and conditions. Terms and conditions are a legal thing. Knowing that terms and conditions can change over time, it is important that you track which version of terms and conditions your users last agreed to. It is also important that you track when they agreed to them.

reCAPTCHA

CAPTCHA, or **Completely Automated Public Turing test to tell Computers and Humans Apart**, is a form of challenge-response test to determine if the user of your site is a computer or human. reCAPTCHA is a CAPTCHA service from Google, that helps in digitizing books, newspapers, and old time radio shows.

reCAPTCHA presents two words to the user and of these two, one is a word that the **Optical Character Recognition (OCR)** process is able to convert from image to text. The other is the word that the OCR cannot translate. The system assumes that if the user provided the right answer for the word for which the translation was known, the other one for which it wasn't known is also translated correctly. The system will then reuse this new word in multiple instances to gain higher confidence in correctness of translation. reCAPTCHA provides plugins for various programming environments and we will be using the one for ASP.NET. For more details check out this website: `http://www.google.com/recaptcha`.

Here is an example of an image that will be generated by our system:

Email confirmation and verification

There are several reasons to use email communications in our community. For example, our site will require registration confirmation and email validation.

When a user signs up at our site, we need to be able to let them know that the registration was completed successfully. This email will usually welcome a user to the site. It may also provide them with some frequently asked questions, a list of benefits received upon registration, and any other pertinent information that a user may need prior to using your site.

In addition to the registration receipt, we need a way to check whether the email address that the user has provided is a valid account (that it actually exists), and one to which the user actually has access. We will validate this by embedding a link in the email that the user will have to click. Once this link is clicked, we will assume that the email address is valid!

Security

Security is obviously one of the most important aspects of building a site. Not only should you be able to provide access to certain areas of your site a specific user, but more important is the ability to deny access to various users of your site. All sites have areas that need to be locked down. For example, one of the most important areas could be the administration section of your site, or paid areas of your site. Therefore, it is very important to make sure that you have some form of security.

Permissions

There are a number of ways to handle permissions (also called as authorization). We could make something really complex by implementing a permission-based system using permissions, roles, groups, and so on. We could even make it as complex as Microsoft's Active Directory system. However, I find that keeping something only as complex as your current requirement is the best thing to do. We can always add to the system as our needs increase.

Our permissions system will simply encompass a name/role (Administrator, Editor, Restricted, and so on). This permission name will then be statically mapped to each page (using the `Sitemap` file that .NET provides us!). As long as we keep our pages to serve a single functionality, this should always suit our needs. As this is a good design practice anyway, we shouldn't have any problems here. Of course, a user can have many permissions tied to their accounts so that they can traverse various sections of our site. Once this is in place, all we need to do is have a system that checks a user's permissions upon entering each page to ensure that they have the permission that the page requires.

We will have a `Permissions` table, that relates to the `Accounts` table through the `AccountPermissions` table. This is a pretty straightforward and simple design.

Password encryption/decryption

When working with passwords, there is an important question to answer. Do we have one way hashing, or do we store encrypted passwords and provide a way to decrypt them? If we don't provide decryption facilities, then we won't be able to send reminder emails to our users who have their passwords. If we were creating a banking system, sending passwords via email would not be acceptable. However, as we are creating something slightly less confidential, the convenience for users to be able to retrieve their passwords without too much hassle is a great reason for decrypting the password and sending it to the user.

Logging in

Once a user has created an account, it is important for them to be able to re-identify themselves to us. For this reason, we will need to provide a way for them to do this. This will come in the form of a page that accepts a username and a password. Once they have authenticated themselves to us, we will need to make sure that they are still allowed to get into our site (if they are valid users).

Password reminder

A user will inevitably forget his/her password. As we require a strong password, and a fair number of users would rather not have a password at all, or would like to use the word "password" as their password, it is highly possible that they forget what they registered with. Not a problem! As we decided to use a two-way encryption, we will be able to decrypt their chosen password and email it to them. This way, our user will never be locked out for too long!

Manage account

In order to keep customer service calls to a minimum, we will need a way for our customers to manage their own accounts. Our customers will need a way to update most of the information they provide us. While we will not allow them to change their username, we will allow them to edit the rest. And when we allow them to change their email address we need to make sure that we force them to validate their new address.

Solution

Now, let's take a look at how we can go about implementing all the new features.

Implementing the database

We will start by implementing our database, and we will work our way up from there.

The Accounts table

The `Accounts` table will store all the base information for a user. Most of this is easy to figure out as they have indicative names (a sign of good design).

Column Name	Data Type	Allow Nulls
AccountID	int	☐
FirstName	varchar(30)	☑
LastName	varchar(30)	☑
Email	varchar(150)	☑
EmailVerified	bit	☐
Zip	varchar(15)	☑
Username	varchar(30)	☑
Password	varchar(50)	☑
BirthDate	smalldatetime	☑
CreateDate	smalldatetime	☑
LastUpdateDate	smalldatetime	☑
Timestamp	timestamp	☐
TermID	int	☐
AgreedToTermsDate	smalldatetime	☑

However, there are a few columns that may not be 100 percent clear at first glance. We will explain those here.

EmailVerified	This is a bit flag to let us know if a user's email address has been verified or not.
CreateDate	This is the date on which the record was created. It has a default value of `GetDate()`.
LastUpdateDate	This is similar to the **CreateDate** with the exception that we should update it every time we update the record. This could be done with a trigger, or done programmatically.
AgreedToTermsDate	This is used to track the date on which the user agreed to the terms and conditions.

The Permissions table

The `Permissions` table primarily acts as a lookup table for the various types of permissions. It holds the name of each permission with a unique ID.

The AccountPermissions table

The `AccountPermissions` table allows us to create a many-to-many type of relationship between our Permissions and our Accounts. It simply holds a reference to a record the end of the relationship.

The Terms table

The `Terms` table is a lookup for our terms and conditions. Also, it provides us with a historical view of the terms our customers have agreed to in the past.

Creating the relationships

First, while you could work in a database without any enforced relationships, we wouldn't advise it. Secondly, if you don't have all your database constraints clearly defined, you might find yourself working with corrupt data.

For this set of tables we have relationships between the following tables:

- `Accounts` and `AccountPermissions`
- `Permissions` and `AccountPermissions`
- `Accounts` and `Terms`

Implementing the data access layer

Now that we have our database defined for all the features required by this chapter, let's take a look at how we go about accessing that data! Keep in mind that this chapter will not have a step that we discussed in an earlier chapter, i.e. telling Entity Framework how to connect to our database so that it can generate Entity classes for us based on our table structure.

Update Model from Database

In Chapter 2, we created `EDMX` and added Person table from Database. In this chapter, so far we have discussed various tables and relationships that we created in SQL Server. Now it's time to get them reflected in our `EDMX`. This can be done by double clicking `Fisharoo.EDMX` (you need to first open the solution in Visual Studio 2010) and it will open it in designer interface. Right click the designer interface and select **Update Model from Database**. In the wizard that comes up (as shown in the following screenshot) select the necessary tables that need to be added.

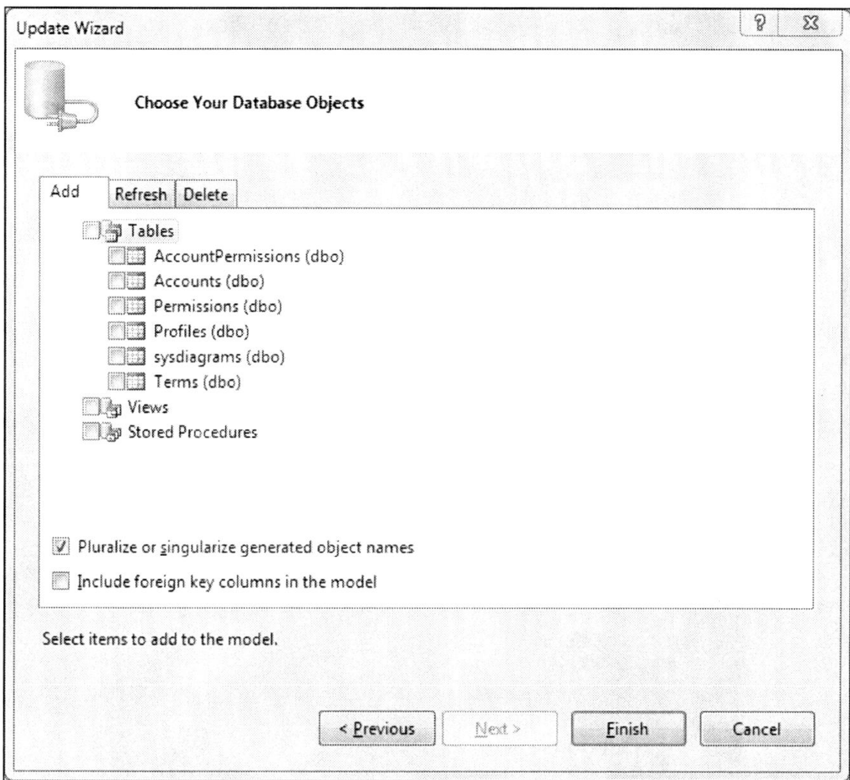

Click **Finish** and the selected tables are added to the EDMX designer as shown in the following screenshot:

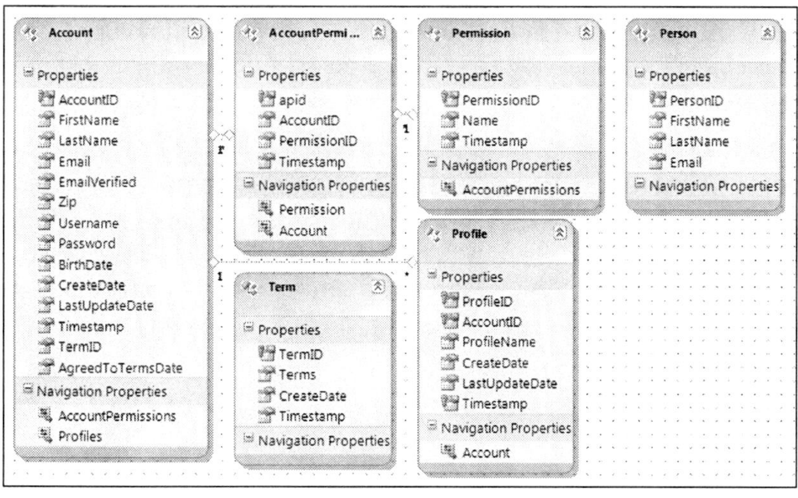

At this time VS 2010 will update `Fisharoo.Designer.cs` and generate Entity classes corresponding to all the tables selected. You won't see these classes as files in your project, but we can see them in the class viewer. Open your class viewer by going into the **View** menu and selecting **Class View**. Then expand the `DataAccess` project.

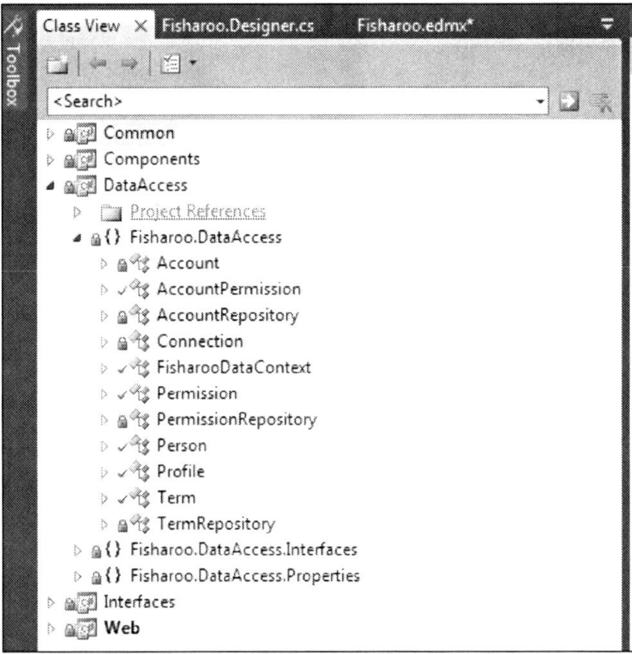

To start with, you should see a class for each table you put on the `Fisharoo.EDMX` design surface. These are partial classes that you can extend by making an additional partial class of the same name in the same namespace (we will do this in a while). Do not edit the generated classes directly as your additions will get lost the next time you generate them!

The only other item here that you should see other than the classes that represent your tables is `FisharooDataContext`. This class handles all the LINQ facilities for your tables and classes. It tracks what changes you have made to your objects, what objects can be worked with, how you can query those objects, and so on. Any time we work with our LINQ classes or data, we will be going through the `FisharooDataContext` class.

A Data Context wrapper

Now that we know `FisharooDataContext` is used by LINQ extensively, let's look at how we can work with this DataContext wrapper in a way that fits our overall design by limiting the knowledge required to use the `FisharooDataContext`. In Chapter 2 we already discussed a `Connection` wrapper that will return the `FisharooDataContext` to the caller without requiring the caller to know what goes into its actual creation.

Building repositories

Once we have a way to get to our DataContext, we can begin to look at how we work with the objects and data stored behind that DataContext. While we could just access our objects and the power of LINQ directly in our code, it would be very helpful down the road if we continued our layered approach by adding a Repository layer. A **Repository** provides us with a single place to go for our data (that doesn't necessarily have to be a database).

The repository layer is responsible for performing data access and data persistence. Each repository will be responsible for data related to a particular entity.

So let's start creating our first repository by looking at the `AccountRepository`. Navigate to `DataAccess` project and create a new class called `AccountRepository.cs`. Here is what the code looks like:

```
//Fisharoo/DataAccess/AccountRepository.cs
namespace Fisharoo.DataAccess
{
    [Export(typeof(IAccountRepository))]
    public class AccountRepository : IAccountRepository
    {
        private Connection conn;

        public AccountRepository()
        {
            conn = new Connection();
        }

        public Account GetAccountByID(int AccountID)
        {
            Account account = null;
            using (FisharooDataContext dc = conn.GetContext())
            {
                account = (from a in dc.Accounts
                           where a.AccountID == AccountID
```

```
                        select a).FirstOrDefault();
            }
            return account;
        }

        public Account GetAccountByEmail(string Email)
        {
            Account account = null;
            using (FisharooDataContext dc = conn.GetContext())
            {
                account = (from a in dc.Accounts
                    where a.Email == Email
                    select a).FirstOrDefault();
            }
            return account;
        }

        public Account GetAccountByUsername(string Username)
        {
            Account account = null;
            using (FisharooDataContext dc = conn.GetContext())
            {
                account = (from a in dc.Accounts
                    where a.Username == Username
                    select a).FirstOrDefault();
            }
            return account;
        }

        public void AddPermission(Account account,
        Permission permission)
        {
            using(FisharooDataContext dc = conn.GetContext())
            {
                AccountPermission ap = new AccountPermission();
                ap.AccountID = account.AccountID;
                ap.PermissionID = permission.PermissionID;
                dc.AccountPermissions.AddObject(ap);
                dc.SaveChanges();
            }
        }


    public void SaveAccount(Account account)
```

```
        {
            using(FisharooDataContext dc = conn.GetContext())
            {
                if(account.AccountID > 0)
                {
                    dc.Accounts.Attach(new Account { AccountID =
                    account.AccountID });
                    dc.Accounts.ApplyCurrentValues(account);
                }
                else
                {
                    dc.Accounts.AddObject(account);
                }
                dc.SaveChanges();
            }
        }

        public void DeleteAccount(Account account)
        {
            using (FisharooDataContext dc = conn.GetContext())
            {
                dc.Accounts.DeleteObject(account);
                dc.SaveChanges();

            }
        }

        public List<Account> GetAllAccounts(Int32 PageNumber)
        {
            IEnumerable<Account> accounts = null;

            using (FisharooDataContext dc = conn.GetContext())
            {
                 accounts = (from a in dc.Accounts
                             orderby a.Username
                             select a).Skip((PageNumber - 1) * 10).
                             Take(10);
            }
            return accounts.ToList();
        }
    }
}
```

The first thing you will notice here is the `Export()` attribute of MEF as well as the `IAccountRepository` interface. As we may want to swap this repository out during testing, these are important. Also, don't forget that the use of MEF allows us to easily ensure that coupling is reduced once we start using the Repository. This means that we could technically swap out the entire repository without requiring a change to our code.

Then in the constructor we initialize the `Connection` object for use throughout the rest of the `AccountRepository` class.

Selecting accounts

Once our Connection object is ready for use, we can look at any of the methods from a generic point of view. Let's start with the `GetAccountByID()` method.

This method is set up to retrieve an account with an ID. We first start out by defining our return variable (`account` in this case) outside the `using` statement. We then retrieve a `FisharooDataContext` inside a `using` statement, that ensures that the DataContext is disposed of once we have finished with it. We then move to the LINQ query itself inside the `using` statement. This looks very much like a standard SQL `SELECT` statement with a twist. We have to define the `from` statement first so that intellisense can interrogate the collection we are working with. This allows us to work with our query as though we were working with any other collection of objects using dot syntax. We then define a `where` clause to restrict what is returned. Finally, we select the object that we want to use.

You will then notice that the entire query is wrapped in parenthesis. This allows us to chain methods on top of the result set. In this case, we are calling the `FirstOrDefault()` function. This restricts our dataset to the first record returned by the query or default value if no element is found. As we know that there can only be one account associated with an ID, this should be acceptable here!

> We could use `var` as the query result if we didn't know what `type` to expect back from our query.
>
> 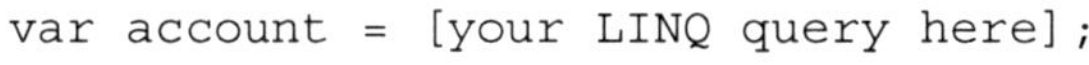
>
> ```
> var account = [your LINQ query here];
> ```
>
> 
>
> `var` is called an anonymous type. It is used heavily by LINQ. The caveat to using an anonymous type is that it can only be used locally. So if your intent is to use the queried objects outside of the scope from which they were retrieved, you will have to do some form of casting, looping, or otherwise, to move them away from their anonymous status.

The `GetAccountByEmail()` and `GetAccountByUsername()` methods are almost identical in the way they function. So we are not going to explain them in detail.

Saving an account

Now that we have a way to select Account objects out of the database in various ways, we now need to consider how we are going to get the data into the database. This brings us to our `SaveAccount()` method. We could have created two methods out of this one method—an `Insert()` and an `Update()` method. However, the only difference is in the one line of code between those two methods. So we chose to roll these two methods up and replace them with the `SaveAccount()` method.

As you will see, with all our Repository methods, we have wrapped the acquisition of the `FisharooDataContext` in a `using` statement. This makes our clean up automatic! (Technically speaking, that is!). Once we have our `DataContext` to work with, we interrogate the object that was passed in to see if it already has an `AccountID`. If the object does have an `AccountID`, it can't be new. If it doesn't have an `AccountID`, it must be new.

A new object is easy to work with. We simply call the `dc.Accounts.AddObject()` method and then we call `dc.SaveChanges()`. This tells the `DataContext` that it needs to persist all the changed data into the database—in our case it needs to save that new Account record.

Our code makes updating data look almost as easy as inserting new data. However, while updating, we first create stand-in Account object by assigning the `AccountId` of the received `Account` and then Apply Values. This is achieved by telling the `DataContext` that the object that is being passed in is the modified version of the current original. In the end we still need to call `dc.SaveChanges()`.

Deleting an account

Now that we have a way to add accounts into the system it only makes sense that we would also want to know a way to delete an account, which is achieved with the `DeleteAccount()` method.

We think deleting an object from the `DataContext` is one of the easiest things to do! Simply locate the collection that you want the object to delete from, pass the object to be deleted to the `DeleteObject ()` method, and then call `dc.SaveChanges()`. It doesn't get any easier than that!

Adding permissions to an account

Shouldn't adding permission go in a `Permission` repository or something? No, not really. In reality, we are not really adding permission. We are creating a record in the non-entity table, `AccountPermissions`, to link a `Permission` to an `Account`. Recall that we had stated that we will not create non-entity repositories so that we can at least try and stick to DDD. So this leaves us to add permissions to accounts in the `Permissions` repository or in the `Accounts` repository. Adding permissions to the Accounts repository makes more sense to us!

The code is also pretty simple as you can see in the `AddPermission()` method (you will find that this is a recurring statement!).

```
public void AddPermission(Account account, Permission permission)
        {
            using(FisharooDataContext dc = conn.GetContext())
            {
                AccountPermission ap = new AccountPermission();
                ap.AccountID = account.AccountID;
                ap.PermissionID = permission.PermissionID;
                dc.AccountPermissions.AddObject(ap);
                dc.SaveChanges();
            }
        }
```

This method is going to simply link an `Account` object to a `Permission` object. To do this, it expects an `Account` and `Permission` object to be passed in. It then creates a new `AccountPermission` object and assigns the `AccountID` and `PermissionID` properties based on the objects that were passed in. This new `AccountPermission` object is then inserted into the `AccountPermissions` collection in the `DataContext`. Finally, the `SaveChanges ()` method is called.

If you think back to our DDD discussions (covered in the Appendices), Entity objects are important enough to recreate and track with a unique ID. Value objects are less important and can't (or shouldn't) exist without a parent Entity object. In this case, the value object, `AccountPermission`, can exist with Permission or an Account as its parent. While this is a true statement, the overall design can be simplified by stating that Accounts can have `AccountPermissions` and that Permissions can't. This makes keeping track of the objects easier when they only have one entry point into the world.

Now, having said that, we can think of a scenario where we might need to be able to say: "For this permission, show me all the related accounts". This might be useful in an Administration console. We will see that when we get there. We could just as easily run a query that says: "Show me all the accounts with this permission".

The other repositories

Now that we have had a fairly detailed look at the `AccountRepository`, we are going to quickly cover the remaining repositories. We will discuss some interesting points here and there, but for the most part, once you have seen one repository, you have seen them all!

Permissions repository

In the `GetPermissionsByAccountID()` method of this repository, you will see an interesting LINQ query.

```
//Fisharoo/DataAccess/PermissionRepository.cs
public List<Permission> GetPermissionsByAccountID(Int32 AccountID)
{
    using (FisharooDataContext dc = conn.GetContext())
    {
        var permissions = from p in dc.Permissions
                          join ap in dc.AccountPermissions on
                          p.PermissionID equals ap.PermissionID
                          join a in dc.Accounts on
                          ap.AccountID equals a.AccountID
                          where a.AccountID == AccountID
                          select p;
        return permissions.ToList();
    }
}
```

This query introduces the concept of joining one set of objects with another set of objects exactly as one would do in SQL. In this case, we need to create a variable to reference each collection of objects.

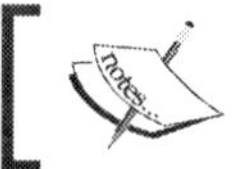

For all you SQL people out there, think of this as a table alias.

Examples of this would be `p in dc.Permissions`, `ap in dc.AccountPermissions`, and `a in dc.Accounts`. Once you have your collections to work with, you can then define the join parameters with `on p.PermissionID equals ap.PermissionID`. This query basically says, "Give me all the `Permissions` related to these `Account-Permissions`, related to these `Accounts`, where the `AccountID` equals the passed in `AccountID`."

Another interesting method to look at is `GetPermissionByName()`, interesting because it uses Lambda expressions. We are sure from the statement itself you would have inferred the benefit of the Lambda expression.

```
//Fisharoo/DataAccess/PermissionRepository.cs public
List<Permission> GetPermissionByName(string Name)
    {
        using (FisharooDataContext dc = conn.GetContext())
        {
```

```
                var permissions = from p in dc.Permissions.Where(
                                  p=>p.Name.Equals(Name))
                                  select p;
                return permissions.ToList();
            }
        }
```

Key advantages with Lambda Expressions over standard query are type inference, simplicity, and increased readability of code.

Lambda Expression consists of a lambda operator '=>' (goes to), left side of which signifies the input parameter (for more than one input parameter, make it comma separated) and right side signifies the expression or statement block to be evaluated. The compiler performs automatic type inference based on the usage of arguments.

Terms repository

In the `GetCurrentTerm()` method of the `TermRepository()`, there is a new LINQ query statement item added.

```
//Fisharoo/DataAccess/TermRepository.cs
public Term GetCurrentTerm()
    {
        using (FisharooDataContext dc = conn.GetContext())
        {
            Term term = (from t in dc.Terms
                        orderby t.CreateDate descending
                        select t).FirstOrDefault();
            return term;

        }
    }
```

Here, you will see that we have an `orderby` clause introduced as well as a `descending` keyword. This allows us to take all the terms ever created and put the most recent ones at the top of the stack.

Implementing the application layer

This layer can be called as application or business logic or components or services layer. In our code, we have called this as **Components**. They are all one and the same. This layer should be relatively thin and lightweight. It is not supposed to hold any business logic or data access logic. It is more of a working layer that is responsible for keeping the business layer easier and cleaner to use. Often, it will combine several items from the business layer and several methods from the data layer to present an easy-to-use interface for a complex task.

An example of this would be our `AccountService`. The `AccountService` provides a few simple methods that utilize several of our more infrastructure-oriented classes. Here is the code:

```
//Fisharoo/Components/AccountService.cs
namespace Fisharoo.Components
{
    [Export(typeof(IAccountService))]
    public class AccountService : IAccountService
    {
        [Import]
        private IAccountRepository _accountRepository;
        [Import]
        private IPermissionRepository _permissionRepository;
        [Import]
        private IUserSession _userSession;
        [Import]
        private IRedirector _redirector;
        [Import]
        private IEmail _email;
        public AccountService()
        {
            MEFManager.Compose(this);
        }
        public bool UsernameInUse(string Username)
        {
            Account account =
             _accountRepository.GetAccountByUsername(Username);
            if(account != null)
                return true;
            return false;
        }
```

```
public bool EmailInUse(string Email)
{
    Account account =
     _accountRepository.GetAccountByEmail(Email);
    if (account != null)
        return true;
    return false;
}
public void Logout()
{
    _userSession.LoggedIn = false;
    _userSession.CurrentUser = null;
    _userSession.Username = "";
    _redirector.GoToAccountLoginPage();
}
public string Login(string Username, string Password)
{
    Password = Password.Encrypt(Username);
    Account account =
       _accountRepository.GetAccountByUsername(Username);

    //if there is only one account returned - good
    if(account != null)
    {
        //password matches
        if(account.Password == Password)
        {
            if (account.EmailVerified)
            {
                _userSession.LoggedIn = true;
                _userSession.Username = Username;
                _userSession.CurrentUser =
                  GetAccountByID(account.AccountID);
                _redirector.GoToHomePage();
            }
            else
            {
                _email.SendEmailAddressVerificationEmail(
                       account.Username, account.Email);
                return @"The login information you provided
                was correct
                but your email address has not yet
                been verified.
                We just sent another email
                verification email to you.
```

```
                                        Please follow the instructions in
                                            that email.";
                        }
                    }
                    else
                    {
                        return " Your Password seems to be incorrect. Try
                        again!";
                    }
                }
                return "Check your Username and try again!";
            }
            public Account GetAccountByID(Int32 AccountID)
            {
                Account account =
                        _accountRepository.GetAccountByID(AccountID);
                List<Permission> permissions =
              _permissionRepository.GetPermissionsByAccountID(AccountID);
                foreach (Permission permission in permissions)
                {
                    account.AddPermission(permission);
                }
                return account;
            }
        }
    }
```

Let's look at the `Login()` method. It expects a username and a password. From there it fetches the users' accounts by their usernames. It makes sure that the password that was provided matches what we have on the file for that account. It then makes sure that the user has verified their email address, and finally logs in the user.

This method can be extended further to use additional repositories or other services for future needs. The signature of the method could still be just as simple without muddying up the design.

Extension methods

As you probably noticed in the `Login()` method just seen, we had our first introduction to the `Cryptography` class. However, this method is called directly from a string. How does that work?

The subject of Cryptography is an extensive one, and is beyond the scope of this book. However, the `Cryptography` class that is included in this project is heavily commented if you want to understand `System.Security.Cryptography.Rijndael` a bit better! You can find that class in the **Common** project.

To start let's look at how we were able to call `Encrypt()` from a `string` variable. To achieve this is actually very simple. Although the `string` class is sealed, meaning that we can't technically extend it in any way that we are used too, we can use the feature of .NET called "extension methods".

```
//Fisharoo/Common/Extensions.cs
namespace Fisharoo.Common
{
    public static class Extensions
    {
        public static string Encrypt(this string s, string key)
        {
            return Cryptography.Encrypt(s, key);
        }
        public static string Decrypt(this string s, string key)
        {
            return Cryptography.Decrypt(s, key);
        }
    }
}
```

An extension method allows us to extend a class without affecting the way that it would normally work. The way to do this is by defining a static method in a static class. The thing to notice is that the first parameter of the method starts with the target type, a `string` in this case. Therefore we have effectively defined an `Encrypt()` and `Decrypt()` method for the `string` class. Note that the only difference between this method and one you would normally write is the `this` reference preceding the first parameter. It's that simple!

Implementing the domain layer

As we are using Entity Framework, it has facilities that are now part of the .NET framework; our business layer has been greatly simplified for us. We can recall that in our previous applications different sorts of data access layers were used, that required us to spend a great deal of time writing SQL in the database, connection logic, providers, and hydration and persistence logic for objects. In addition to all that, we would still need to define business objects. Of those objects, 95 percent of the logic was simply to shuttle data around in a more manageable manner.

With Entity Framework so much of this has gone away! We now have fully generated classes that take care of shuttling our data around. But what happens if we need custom logic? While we could simply add logic to the generated classes, this would not be the best route. The next time we make a change we will have to regenerate our classes. This would resort in the loss of all that custom functionality.

Fortunately for us the classes that are generated are partial classes. This means that we can make a new `partial` class file of the same name within the same namespace and extend our generated classes. Here is our custom `Account` object, which extends the generated `Account` object.

```
//Fisharoo/DataAccess/Account.cs
namespace Fisharoo.DataAccess
{
    public partial class Account
    {
        private List<Permission> _permissions = new
        List<Permission>();
        public List<Permission> Permissions
        {
            get{ return _permissions; }
        }

        public void AddPermission(Permission permission)
        {
            _permissions.Add(permission);
        }

        public bool HasPermission(string Name)
        {
            foreach (Permission p in _permissions)
            {
                if (p.Name == Name)
                    return true;
            }
            return false;
        }
    }
}
```

With this new `partial` class, we can now extend our existing generated `Account` class. We have added a few important features to the `Account` class. We now have methods for adding and checking permissions. We also have a property that returns a list of permissions.

This can easily be done for any partial class in our project!

Implementing the presentation layer

Most of the presentation layer is made up of very standard ASP.NET tools and principles. As this book isn't so much about how a button or label works, we will be focusing more on the non-standard features of our site. We will look at building a scalable UI using the MVP pattern.

Model view presenter

To start with, let's discuss the overall architecture of our presentation layer. We mentioned earlier in Chapter 2 that we will be using the MVP pattern. Information about this pattern can also be found under the separated names of Supervising Controller and Passive View.

The basic reason for this pattern is so that at the end of the day you can wrap a large percentage of your front end code with testing. It also allows you to easily swap out your UI without having to rewrite every aspect of the front end of your application. This can be useful in case we need a new UI or want to target additional devices like mobile. You will also find that this pattern significantly breaks up and compartmentalizes your logic, that makes working on the front end of your application more straightforward.

The MVP pattern in the ASP.NET world basically requires you to have four files (five if you are working in a web application project):

- The design or `.aspx` file
- Your code behind or `.cs` file
- An interface that defines the code behind (another `.cs` file)
- And a class (`.cs`) file called the presenter, that actually controls everything

Of course, the model portion of this pattern is generally referring to your domain objects that will constitute many other files!

The design file of course holds all your display logic such as a repeater, buttons, labels, and so on. It shouldn't have any server-side logic.

The code behind (or the view) is responsible for handling events from the page such as button clicks. It is also allowed to take care of simple display issues. The view also provides methods to the presenter to toggle the state of the various display items. When the page first starts up (generally on page load), the view initializes the presenter and passes a reference to itself, to the presenter. For every event that is triggered on the page, the view is simply responsible for informing the presenter so that it can decide what to do with the event.

The **View** passes a reference of itself to the presenter by way of the interface that defines the view. Using the interface provides us with a decoupled structure. This is what allows us to easily swap out our UI if we so choose. As long as the UI implements the interface appropriately it can use the presenter.

The presenter is the acting controller in this scenario. Once it is spun up and has a reference to the code behind, it can actively decide how to handle events in the front end. The presenter is also the only part of our front end that is capable of interacting with our domain logic (or model).

In the following sections, we will discuss the login process. This is more to illustrate how the MVP pattern works and less about ASP.NET, as the code itself is very simple.

An **Account** folder was created when we created the ASP.NET 4 application (in Chapter 2). It added basic files related to login, user registration, changing the password, etc. along with the code that uses ASP.NET membership services. However, since we wanted to write custom logic for authentication and authorization, we deleted all files in this folder and wrote custom logic as discussed in the following sections.

View

We will start with the front end ASP.NET code. It basically defines a username and password text box and a button to click for login. It also has two link buttons for simple navigational tasks—one to go to the recover password page and another to take you to the registration page.

```
//Fisharoo/Web/Account/Login.aspx
<%@ Page Language="C#" MasterPageFile="~/Site.Master"
AutoEventWireup="true" CodeBehind="Login.aspx.cs"
    Inherits="Fisharoo.Web.Account.Login" %>

<asp:Content ContentPlaceHolderID="Content" runat="server">
    <div class="divContainer">
        <div class="divContainerBox">
            <fieldset class="login">
                <legend>Enter your Username and Password</legend>
                <asp:Table CssClass="tableLogin" runat="server">
                    <asp:TableRow>
                        <asp:TableCell HorizontalAlign="Left">
                            <asp:Panel ID="Panel1"
DefaultButton="btnLogin" runat="server">
                                <p>
                                    <asp:Label ID="UserNameLabel"
```

```
runat="server" AssociatedControlID="txtUsername">Username:</asp:Label>
                                    <br />
                                    <asp:TextBox ID="txtUsername"
runat="server" CssClass="textEntry"></asp:TextBox>
                                </p>
                                <p>
                                    <asp:Label ID="PasswordLabel"
runat="server" AssociatedControlID="txtPassword">Password:</asp:Label>
                                    <br />
                                    <asp:TextBox ID="txtPassword"
runat="server" CssClass="passwordEntry" TextMode="Password"></
asp:TextBox>
                                </p>
                                <p class="submitButton">
                                    <asp:Button ID="btnLogin"
CssClass="loginButton" OnClick="btnLogin_Click" runat="server"
                                        Text="Log In" />
                                </p>
                                <asp:Label runat="server"
ID="lblMessage" BackColor="Wheat" ForeColor="Red"></asp:Label>
                            </asp:Panel>
                        </asp:TableCell>
                        <asp:TableCell HorizontalAlign="Right"
VerticalAlign="Top">
                            <p>
                                <asp:LinkButton ID="lbRecoverPassword"
runat="server" Text="Forgot Password?" OnClick="lbRecoverPassword_
Click" />
                            </p>
                            <p>
                                <asp:LinkButton ID="lbRegister"
runat="server" Text="Register" OnClick="lbRegister_Click" />
                            </p>
                        </asp:TableCell></asp:TableRow>
                </asp:Table>
                <br />
            </fieldset>
        </div>
    </div>
</asp:Content>
```

The login screen will look as shown in the following screenshot:

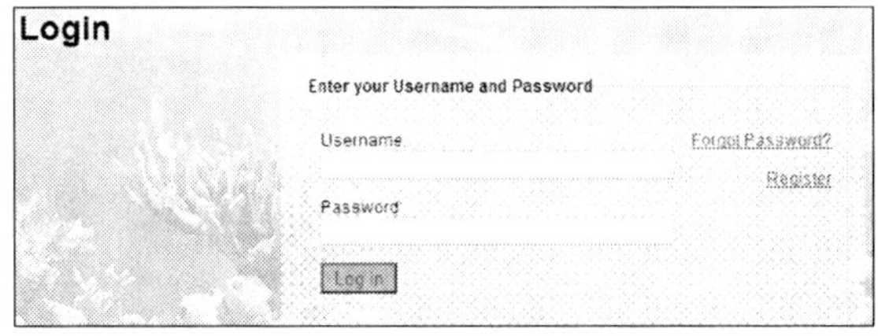

Normally we would not show you the interfaces in our application as they are very simple. But as the interface is very important to this pattern, we will make an exception this first time! This interface is what the code behind has to conform to in order to be able to interact with the presenter:

```
//Fisharoo/Web/Account/Interfaces/ILogin.cs
namespace Fisharoo.Web.Account.Interfaces
{
    public interface ILogin
    {
        void DisplayMessage(string Message);
    }
}
```

Here is the code behind for our application. Notice that it only handles display logic. It does not actually make any decisions. It defers all decision making to the presenter.

```
//Fisharoo/Web/Account/Login.aspx.cs
namespace Fisharoo.Web.Account
{
    public partial class Login : System.Web.UI.Page, ILogin
    {
        private LoginPresenter _presenter;
        protected void Page_Load(object sender, EventArgs e)
        {
            _presenter = new LoginPresenter();
            _presenter.Init(this);
        }
        protected void btnLogin_Click(object sender, EventArgs e)
        {
            _presenter.Login(txtUsername.Text, txtPassword.Text);
        }
        protected void lbRecoverPassword_Click(object sender,
                                               EventArgs e)
        {
            _presenter.GoToRecoverPassword();
        }
        protected void lbRegister_Click(object sender, EventArgs e)
        {
            _presenter.GoToRegister();
        }
        public void DisplayMessage(string Message)
        {
            lblMessage.Text = Message;
        }
    }
}
```

You will notice above that in the `Page_Load()` we initialize our presenter. Once we have the presenter spun up, we immediately pass a reference of the code behind to the presenter in the `_presenter.Init(this)` method call. You should also notice that there is a button-click event captured by the code behind. But all that this method does is notify the presenter that it needs to perform the `Login()` method and passes up the raw username and password values. Lastly, notice that the code behind does implement the interface with its `DisplayMessage()` method. As the presenter has access to the code behind class, it will be able to utilize any public method as it needs to.

Another aspect to note is that when you start writing code, Visual Studio will add a lot of `using` statements on the top of the file. Visual Studio 2010 refactoring support provides for removing unused `using` statements. You may want to try this to keep things organized.

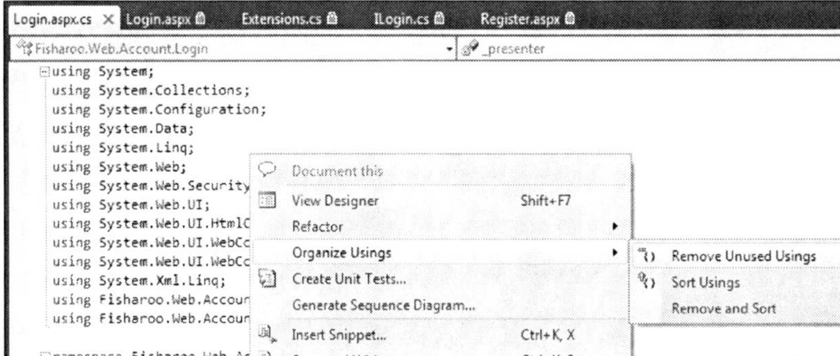

We did it and ended up with only three `using` statements as against an earlier list of fourteen statements.

Presenter

Here is the presenter code:

```
//Fisharoo/Web/Account/Presenters/LoginPresenter.cs
namespace Fisharoo.Web.Account.Presenters
{
    public class LoginPresenter
    {
        private ILogin _view;
        [Import]
        private IAccountService _accountService;
        [Import]
        private IRedirector _redirector;
        public void Init(ILogin view)
        {
            _view = view;
```

```
            MEFManager.Compose(this);
        }
        public void Login(string username, string password)
        {
            string message = _accountService.Login(username,
                                                   password);
            _view.DisplayMessage(message);
        }
        public void GoToRegister()
        {
            _redirector.GoToAccountRegisterPage();
        }
        public void GoToRecoverPassword()
        {
            _redirector.GoToAccountRecoverPasswordPage();
        }
    }
}
```

Note that in the `Init()` method, the presenter sets up the objects that it needs to get its job done by using MEF framework. If a page needs to display data on its initial load, this is where it would happen. Beyond the initialization of the presenter, you will notice that the presenter has three other methods: `Login()`, `GoToRegister()`, and `GoToRecoverPassword()`.

The `Login()` method handles the button-click event that the **View** passes to it. Note that even here we do not have a lot of logic to manage. The presenter is quick to pass off the responsibility of logging the user in to the `AccountService` object that we discussed earlier. It simply expects a friendly message back from the `AccountService` to describe how the login process went. As we know, if it gets a message back, it means that the login failed; otherwise the `AccountService` will redirect the user appropriately. Once the login is complete, the presenter uses the view's `DisplayMessage()` method to inform the user of its status.

The `GoToRegister()` and `GoToRecoverPassword()` methods simply utilize the Redirector object to send the user to the appropriate page on the site. While this may seem a bit extreme, remember that it follows the good design principles. If you follow this across your entire site, you will reap the following three benefits:

1. You can easily swap out the UI and expect the same results with minimum efforts.
2. As your redirection code is in one place, when several links use the same method to redirect to a location, you can change this redirection in that place and impact all the links across your site.
3. This aids the testability of your site!

Here are the added Redirector methods:

```
//Fisharoo/Components/Redirector.cs
...
        public void GoToAccountRegisterPage()
        {
            Redirect("~/Account/Register.aspx");
        }
...
        public void GoToAccountRecoverPasswordPage()
        {
            Redirect("~/Account/RecoverPassword.aspx");
        }
...
```

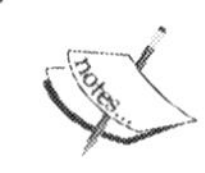

We hope you are noticing that as each file is responsible for a very specific set of tasks, each file is also short and sweet. While this is a complex way of thinking about things, it is very nice to work with!

Registration page

We will admit that using the standard .NET controls to create an account is so much easier! Having said that, it was quite a bit of fun creating the registration page for this site. We ended up using a wizard control to display the various steps of the registration process and also used the out-of-box formatting for it. Our steps are as follows (as the ASPX code takes up lot of space, we have put images of how the screens look instead. For code refer to the code associated with this chapter):

1. We always start by grabbing the email, username, and password of the users. There is validation in place for all of these. We want to validate their email addresses for their authenticity. We also want to make sure that their username conforms to some length rules. Then we allow them to enter their password and require them to re-enter their password to verify that what they have entered is what they meant to enter. And of course, all these fields are required!

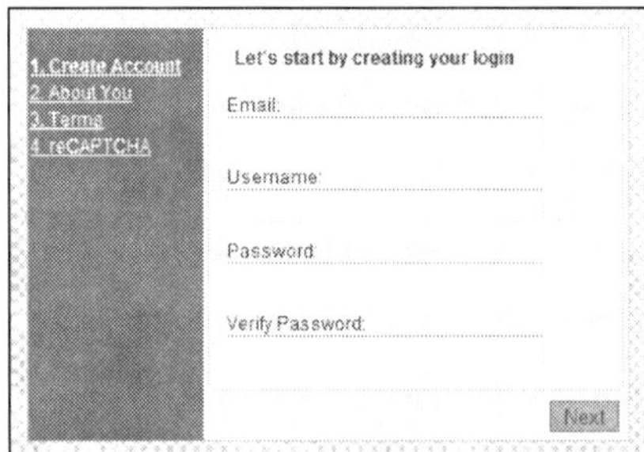

2. The next step is to get some descriptive information about the users such as their first names and last names. When building a community site of any type, it is usually important that you also harvest their birthday and zip code or postal code. This lets you know what is appropriate for them and where in the world they are. There is validation in place to make sure that the date of birth they enter is a valid date (MM/DD/YYYY format) and that the zip code is a valid format for US. Though we have validated for only US zip codes, in a community site you will need to validate based on different formats for different countries. All these fields are also required fields.

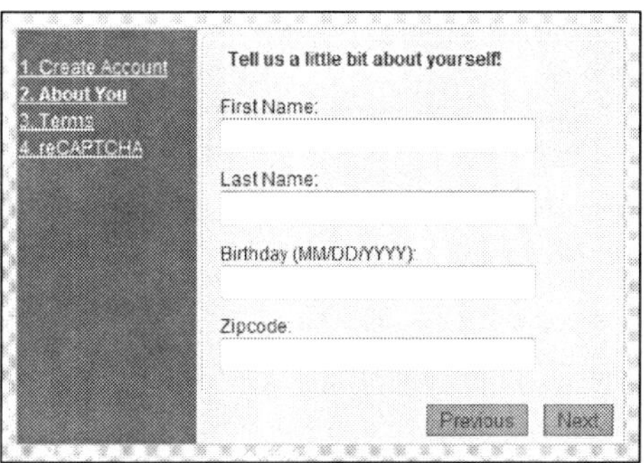

3. The third step presents the terms and conditions. This is the one step that requires you to fetch some data for display. This data is retrieved from the `TermRepository.GetCurrentTerm()` (which we covered earlier). All the user needs to do here is read the terms (most of your users won't do this of course!) and check the box indicating that they agree with your terms (we have kept it checked by default).

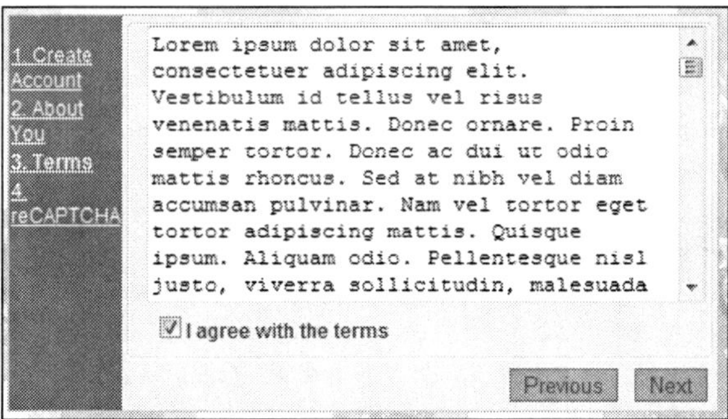

4. Finally, we present the reCAPTCHA step so that we can make sure that the person signing up is a person and not a spam bot! Using reCAPTCHA is fairly straightforward. You need to use the ASP.NET specific control that is provided and get the necessary keys from the reCAPTCHA site (`http://www.google.com/recaptcha/whyrecaptcha`).

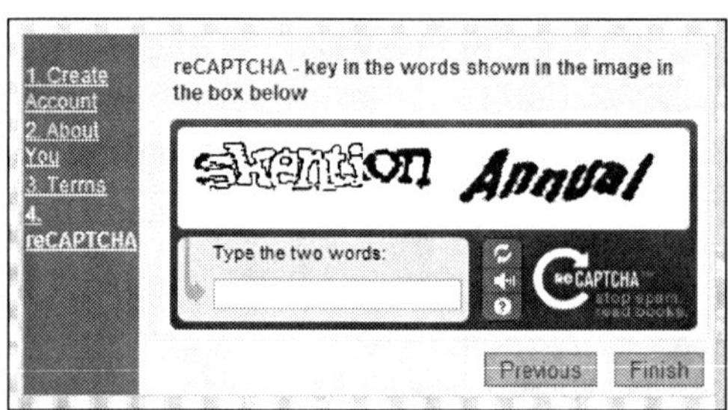

While we have made this entire information mandatory during registration, you can decide based on your specific needs. There is always a balance required of not overdoing the required information during registration as that may put off some users from registering. Users can always go to the profile page to provide more information once they have registered and logged into the site.

Knowing that the code behind is really just a middle man responsible for passing data to and from the presenter, we are going to show you only the relevant code.

```
//Fisharoo/Web/Account/Register.aspx.cs
namespace Fisharoo.Web.Account
{
    public partial class Register : System.Web.UI.Page, IRegister
    {
        . . . .

        protected void wizRegister_FinishButtonClicked(object sender,
                                                        EventArgs e)
        {
            _presenter.Register(
                txtUsername.Text,ViewState["password"].ToString(),
                txtFirstName.Text,txtLastName.Text,txtEmail.Text,
                txtZipcode.Text,Convert.ToDateTime(txtBirthday.Text),
                Page.IsValid, chkAgreeWithTerms.Checked,
                        Convert.ToInt32(lblTermID.Text));
        }


        public void LoadreCaptchaSetting(bool value)
```

```
            {
                recaptcha.SkipRecaptcha = value;
            }

            . . . .

        }
    }
```

The reCAPTCHA validation is integrated with the page validation and hence if `Page.IsValid` returns `true`, we know that the reCAPTCHA validation has succeeded. Also note that for using reCAPTCHA we need to add a new register directive in our ASPX page:

```
<%@ Register TagPrefix="recaptcha" Namespace="Recaptcha"
Assembly="Recaptcha" %>
```

During development we will not want to keep getting the reCAPTCHA validation screen. To prevent this we set the `SkipRecaptcha` property on the control to `false` for the debug configuration. This makes the reCAPTCHA control always return `true` for validation. We will want the control to work properly during final deployment and hence we have used the `web.release.config` file for this purpose. The appropriate tag in that file of interest is:

```
//Fisharoo/Web/Web.Release.Config
    <appSettings>
        <add key="reCaptcha" value="false" xdt:Transform="Replace"
xdt:Locator="Match(key)" />
    </appSettings>
```

As we publish our site with release configuration, the `Replace` transform mentioned above will replace the value from the main `web.config` file.

> We had briefly touched upon multiple configuration files in a previous chapter. This is a new feature for ASP.NET 4 applications with Visual Studio 2010. Appropriate build tasks take care of replacing the values from respective configuration files to the main one. To know more about this read here: `http://msdn.microsoft.com/en-us/library/dd465326.aspx`.

Now we get to the meat and potatoes of this page. Once we have gathered all the data, we need to process it. Enter the presenter (that was fun to say!). We will also focus only on the `Register()` method in the code as that is where most of the action happens.

```
//Fisharoo/Web/Account/Presenters/RegisterPresenter.cs
namespace Fisharoo.Web.Account.Presenters
{
    public class RegisterPresenter
    {
        . . .

        public void Register(string Username, string Password,
            string FirstName, string LastName, string Email,
            string Zip, DateTime BirthDate, bool isCaptchaValid,
            bool AgreesWithTerms, Int32 TermID)
        {
            if (AgreesWithTerms)
            {
                if (isCaptchaValid)
                {
                    Fisharoo.DataAccess.Account acc = new Fisharoo.
                    DataAccess.Account();
                    acc.FirstName = FirstName;
                    acc.LastName = LastName;
                    acc.Email = Email;
                    acc.BirthDate = BirthDate;
                    acc.Zip = Zip;
                    acc.Username = Username;
                    acc.Password = Password.Encrypt(Password);
                    acc.TermID = TermID;
                    //TODO: For development marked as verified already
                    acc.EmailVerified = true;

                    if (_accountService.EmailInUse(Email))
                    {
                        _view.ShowErrorMessage("This email is already
                        in use!");
                        _view.ToggleWizardIndex(0);
                    }
                    else if (_accountService.UsernameInUse(Username))
                    {
                        _view.ShowErrorMessage("This username is
                        already in use!");
                        _view.ToggleWizardIndex(0);
```

```
                    }
                    else
                    {
                        _accountRepository.SaveAccount(acc);

                        List<Permission> permissions
                        = _permissionRepository.
                        GetPermissionByName("PUBLIC");
                        Fisharoo.DataAccess.Account newAccount = _
                        accountRepository.GetAccountByEmail(Email);

                        if (permissions.Count > 0 && newAccount !=
                        null)
                        {
                            _accountRepository.
                            AddPermission(newAccount, permissions[0]);
                        }

                        _email.SendEmailAddressVerificationEmail(acc.
                        Username, acc.Email);

                        _view.ShowAccountCreatedPanel();
                    }
                }
                else
                {
                    _view.ShowErrorMessage("Your entry doesn't match
                    the reCAPTCHA image.  Please try again.");
                }
            }
            else
            {
                _view.ToggleWizardIndex(2);
                _view.ShowErrorMessage("You can't create an account on
                this site if you don't agree with our terms!");
            }
        }
    }
}
```

You will notice that most of this code is just more validation or navigation logic such as "did they agree with the terms?", or "did they enter the correct reCAPTCHA?". Nothing fancy here!

The new thing here, that is somewhat interesting, is the mention of the `Email` object. You may recall when we built the `Email` object a while back. It provides us with the facilities to send an email in various ways. What we have done here is extended the `Email` object so that it also encapsulates the messages that are sent by the system. Here is the new code for the Email object that allows us to send an email verification of the validity and ownership of an email address.

```
//Fisharoo/Components/Email.cs
public void SendEmailAddressVerificationEmail(string Username, string
To)
{
    MEFManager.Compose(this);
    string rootURL = _configuration.GetConfigurationSetting(
                              typeof(string), "RootURL").ToString();
    string encryptedName = Cryptography.Encrypt(Username, "verify");

    string msg = "Please click on the link below or paste it into a
                  browser to verify your email account.<BR><BR>" +
                  "<a href=\"" + rootURL + "Account/VerifyEmail.
                  aspx?a=" +
                  encryptedName + "\">" +
                  rootURL + "Account/VerifyEmail.aspx?a=" +
                  encryptedName + "</a>";

    SendEmail(To, "", "", "Account created! Email verification
    required.", msg);
}
```

Also notice the link that is embedded here encrypts the registrant's username with a salt of "verify". This way we know who we are dealing with after they receive the email and follow the link back to our site (more about this in the next section).

In the Wizard's stepped environment, it is very easy to present small chunks of data like this without having too much coding overhead. While it is not as easy as the .NET membership widgets, we think it is quite a bit more flexible. Also, we can easily test this whole process now.

Email verification

We lightly touched upon this subject in the previous section. Basically, the registration process triggers an email to be sent to the newly registered user asking them to verify their email address. This process usually sends an email to the email address that the user provided us when they signed up. If the user can receive the email on their end, then we know that the email address is valid. If they can click on the link that is embedded in the email, then we know that they have access to the email as well. This doesn't necessarily mean that they own the account, but we can't really verify that, and hence we can't really worry about it.

The item we didn't cover above is the page that receives the click from the link in the email. This series of code is relatively simple. So to start, we are going to list all of the files in order of use (design, code behind, and presenter). Then we can discuss it.

```
//Fisharoo/Web/Account/VerifyEmail.aspx
<%@ Page Language="C#" MasterPageFile="~/Site.Master"
AutoEventWireup="true" CodeBehind="VerifyEmail.aspx.cs"
Inherits="Fisharoo.Web.Account.VerifyEmail" %>
<asp:Content ContentPlaceHolderID="Content" runat="server">
    <asp:Label ID="lblMsg" runat="server" ForeColor="Red"></asp:Label>
</asp:Content>

//Fisharoo/Web/Account/VerifyEmail.aspx.cs
namespace Fisharoo.Web.Account
{
    public partial class VerifyEmail : System.Web.UI.Page,
                                       IVerifyEmail
    {
        private VerifyEmailPresenter _presenter;
        protected void Page_Load(object sender, EventArgs e)
        {
            _presenter = new VerifyEmailPresenter();
            _presenter.Init(this);
        }
        public void ShowMessage(string Message)
        {
            lblMsg.Text = Message;
        }
    }
}

//Fisharoo/Web/Account/Presenters/VerifyEmailPresenter.cs

using System.ComponentModel.Composition;
using Fisharoo.Common;
using Fisharoo.DataAccess.Interfaces;
using Fisharoo.Web.Account.Interfaces;

namespace Fisharoo.Web.Account.Presenters
{
    public class VerifyEmailPresenter
    {
        [Import]
        private IWebContext _webContext;
        [Import]
```

```
        private IAccountRepository _accountRepository;

        public void Init(IVerifyEmail _view)
        {
            MEFManager.Compose(this);
            string username = Cryptography.Decrypt (_webContext.
            UsernameToVerify, "verify");

            Fisharoo.DataAccess.Account account = _accountRepository.
            GetAccountByUsername(username);

            if(account != null)
            {
                account.EmailVerified = true;
                _accountRepository.SaveAccount(account);
                _view.ShowMessage("Your email address has been
                successfully verified!");
            }
            else
            {
                _view.ShowMessage("There appears to be something wrong
                with your verification link!  Please try again.  If
                you are having issues by clicking on the link, please
                try copying the URL from your email and pasting it
                into your browser window.");
            }
        }
    }
}
```

The reason that we listed out the code this way was to show you that all the logic is pretty much lodged in the presenter (as it should be!). Notice that we attempt to get the username from the WebContext (query string in this case) and decrypt it with our "verify" salt. Once we have this username, we attempt to retrieve the Account using `AccountRepository.GetAccountByUsername()`. If we get an account back, we toggle the `Account.EmailVerified` property to `true` and save it back into the repository.

Password recovery

This is another simple page that we can quickly show you the code for.

```
//Fisharoo/Web/Account/RecoverPassword.aspx
<%@ Page Language="C#" MasterPageFile="~/Site.Master"
AutoEventWireup="true" CodeBehind="RecoverPassword.aspx.cs"
    Inherits="Fisharoo.Web.Account.RecoverPassword" %>
```

```
<asp:Content ContentPlaceHolderID="Content" runat="server">
    <div class="divContainerSmall">
        <asp:Panel ID="pnlRecoverPassword" runat="server">
            <fieldset class="recoverPassword">
                <div class="divContainerTitle">
                    Please enter your email address below
                </div>
                <p>
                    <asp:Label ID="EmailLabel" runat="server"
                    AssociatedControlID="txtEmail">Email:</asp:Label>
                    <asp:TextBox CssClass="textRegister" ID="txtEmail"
                    runat="server"></asp:TextBox>
                </p>
                <asp:Button CssClass="recoverPwdButton"
                ID="btnRecoverPassword" Text="Recover Password"
                    runat="server" OnClick="btnRecoverPassword_Click"
/>
            </fieldset>
        </asp:Panel>
        <asp:Panel Visible="false" ID="pnlMessage" runat="server">
            <asp:Label ID="lblMessage" runat="server"
            ForeColor="Red"></asp:Label>
        </asp:Panel>
    </div>
</asp:Content>
```

We will skip the code for `RecoverPassword.aspx.cs` and `IRecoverPassword.cs` as there is nothing to highlight there and jump to the `RecoverPasswordPresenter.cs`.

```
//Fisharoo/Web/Account/Presenters/RecoverPasswordPresenter.cs
namespace Fisharoo.Web.Account.Presenters
{
    public class RecoverPasswordPresenter
    {
        private IRecoverPassword _view;
        [Import]
        private IEmail _email;
        [Import]
        private IAccountRepository _accountRepository;
        public RecoverPasswordPresenter()
        {
            MEFManager.Compose(this);
        }
        public void Init(IRecoverPassword View)
        {
```

```
                _view = View;
            }
            public void RecoverPassword(string Email)
            {
                Fisharoo.DataAccess.Account account =
                _accountRepository.GetAccountByEmail(Email);
                if(account != null)
                {
                    _email.SendPasswordReminderEmail(account.Email,
                          account.Password, account.Username);
                    _view.ShowRecoverPasswordPanel(false);
                    _view.ShowMessage("An email was sent to your
                                      account!");
                }
                else
                {
                    _view.ShowRecoverPasswordPanel(true);
                    _view.ShowMessage("We couldn't find the account you
                                      requested.");
                }

            }
        }
    }
```

This page asks the user to provide their email address. It then looks up the account with that email address. If it finds the account it then uses the `Email.SendPasswordReminderEmail()` method to send the user's decrypted password to their email account.

The `SendPasswordReminderEmail()` method looks like this.

```
//Fisharoo/Components/Email.cs
        public void SendPasswordReminderEmail(string To,
              string EncryptedPassword, string Username)
        {
            string Message = "Here is the password you requested: " +
                    Cryptography.Decrypt(EncryptedPassword, Username);
            SendEmail(To, "", "", "Password Reminder", Message);
        }
```

Edit account

To save a bit of space we are going to forgo showing you the design, the code behind, and interface portion of this code. It is just a basic form with text boxes and the like, and has the same validation requirements as the registration form did. It allows you to change the information and on successfully saving displays an appropriate message and prevents further editing (user can go to another page and come back here to edit again). There are a couple of aspects however in the `UpdateAccount()` method that we describe below.

```
//Fisharoo/Web/Account/Presenters/EditAccountPresenter.cs

namespace Fisharoo.Web.Account.Presenters
{
    public class EditAccountPresenter
    {
        . . .

        public void UpdateAccount(string OldPassword, string
        NewPassword, string Username,
            string FirstName, string LastName, string Email,
            string ZipCode, DateTime BirthDate)
        {
            //verify that this user is the same as the logged in user
            if(OldPassword.Encrypt(OldPassword) == account.Password)
            {
                if (Email != _userSession.CurrentUser.Email)
                {
                    if (!_accountService.EmailInUse(Email))
                    {
                        account.Email = Email;
                        //TODO: for development disable sending
                        emails, so setting the following to true
                        //in production this will be set to false
                        account.EmailVerified = true;
                        _email.SendEmailAddressVerificationEmail(accou
                        nt.Username, Email);
                    }
                    else
                    {
                        _view.ShowMessage(false, "The email your
                        entered is already in our system!", account.
                        UserName);
                        return;
                    }
                }
```

```
                if(!string.IsNullOrEmpty(NewPassword))
                    account.Password = NewPassword.
                    Encrypt(NewPassword);

                account.FirstName = FirstName;
                account.LastName = LastName;

                account.Zip = ZipCode;
                account.BirthDate = BirthDate;

                _accountRepository.SaveAccount(account);
                _view.ShowMessage(true, "Your account has been
                updated!" , account.UserName);
            }
            else
            {
                _view.ShowMessage(false, "The password you entered
                doesn't match your current password!  Please try
                again." , account.UserName);
            }
        }
    }
}
```

One thing to notice with the presenter is that when it is first initialized, it loads the current user's account details and passes that data to the view for initial display. Then once the user edits their data, there are several validation steps that occur. The most important is that of the password and the email.

If the password is not changed, we want to make sure that we do not store an empty value to the system!

For the email, if a user changes it, we want to make sure that we resend the verification email again and flag the account as not having a validated email address.

Beyond that we are simply updating the account object via the `AccountRepository.Save()` method.

Implementing security

Now that we have all of our plumbing in place, we are at a point that we can lock down our site. Up until now someone could go wherever they wanted to on the site and we would not be able to stop them at all!

SiteMap

The primary .NET widget that we will use to lock down our site is the ASP.NET sitemap. This is a wonderful tool that can be used not only for security but also to display breadcrumb trails, your primary navigation, and many other useful page/file-oriented tasks.

A `sitemap` file is made up of several `siteMapNodes`. Each node contains things such as URL, title, description, and roles by default. You can also add your own custom attributes. In our site we will use attributes for identifying links that belong in the `topnav`, the `footer nav`, as well as allowing the `siteMap` to help us with each page's title. Our current `siteMap` looks like this:

```
//Fisharoo/Web/Web.Sitemap
<?xml version="1.0" encoding="utf-8" ?>
<siteMap xmlns="http://schemas.microsoft.com/AspNet/
                       SiteMap-File-1.0" >
    <siteMapNode url="default.aspx" title="Home"  description="Home
                         page" pageTitle="Welcome to Fisharoo.com!"
                         roles="PUBLIC">
<!-- TOP NAV NODES -->
      <siteMapNode url="/account/default.aspx" title="My Account"
            description="" pageTitle="" roles="PUBLIC">
        <siteMapNode url="/account/EditAccount.aspx" title="Edit
            Account" description="" pageTitle="" roles="PUBLIC" />
        <siteMapNode url="/account/Login.aspx" title="Login"
            description="" pageTitle="" roles="PUBLIC" />
        <siteMapNode url="/account/RecoverPassword.aspx"
                   title="Recover Password" description="Recover Your
                   Password" pageTitle="Recover your password"
                   roles="PUBLIC" />
        <siteMapNode url="/account/Register.aspx" title="Register"
                  description="" pageTitle="" roles="PUBLIC" />
        <siteMapNode url="/account/VerifyEmail.aspx" title="Verify
                 Email" description="Verify your email address"
                 pageTitle="Email Verification" roles="PUBLIC" />
        <siteMapNode url="/account/AccessDenied.aspx" title="Access
                 Denied" description="Access Denied"
                 pageTitle="Access Denied" roles="PUBLIC" />
      </siteMapNode>
      <siteMapNode url="/profile/default.aspx" title="Profile"
                description="" topnav="1" pageTitle=""
                roles="PUBLIC"></siteMapNode>
      <siteMapNode url="/friends/default.aspx" title="Friends"
               description="" topnav="1" pageTitle=""
               roles="PUBLIC"></siteMapNode>
      <siteMapNode url="/mail/default.aspx" title="Mail"
```

```
                description="" topnav="1" pageTitle=""
                roles="PUBLIC"></siteMapNode>
        <siteMapNode url="/galleries/default.aspx" title="Galleries"
                description="" topnav="1" pageTitle=""
                roles="PUBLIC"></siteMapNode>
        <siteMapNode url="/groups/default.aspx" title="Groups"
                description="" topnav="1" pageTitle=""
                roles="PUBLIC"></siteMapNode>
        <siteMapNode url="/virtualtanks/default.aspx" title="Virtual
                     Tanks" description="" topnav="1" pageTitle=""
                     roles="PUBLIC"></siteMapNode>
        <siteMapNode url="/forum/default.aspx" title="Forum"
                    description="" topnav="1" pageTitle=""
                    roles="PUBLIC"></siteMapNode>
        <siteMapNode url="/blogs/default.aspx" title="Blogs"
                     description="" topnav="1" pageTitle=""
                     roles="PUBLIC"></siteMapNode>
<!-- /TOP NAV NODES -->
<!-- FOOTER NODES -->
        <siteMapNode url="AboutUs.aspx" title="About Us"
                    description="About Us" footernav="1"
                    pageTitle="" roles="PUBLIC"></siteMapNode>
        <siteMapNode url="Advertisers.aspx" title="Advertisers"
                     description="Click here to learn more about
                     advertising on our site" footernav="1"
                     pageTitle="" roles="PUBLIC"></siteMapNode>
        <siteMapNode url="Help.aspx" title="Help" description="Click
                     here to enter our help section" footernav="1"
                     pageTitle="" roles="PUBLIC"></siteMapNode>
        <siteMapNode url="Privacy.aspx" title="Privacy"
                    description="Click here to learn about our
                    privacy policy" footernav="1" pageTitle=""
                    roles="PUBLIC"></siteMapNode>
        <siteMapNode url="Terms.aspx" title="Terms" description="Click
                     here to learn about our terms and conditions"
                    footernav="1" pageTitle=""
                    roles="PUBLIC"></siteMapNode>
<!-- /FOOTER NODES-->
<!-- NONE NAVIGATION NODES -->
        <siteMapNode url="Search.aspx" title="Search"
                    description="Click here to perform a site
                    search" pageTitle=""
                    roles="PUBLIC"></siteMapNode>
        <siteMapNode url="Error.aspx" title="Error" description="An
                     error has occurred" pageTitle=""
                     roles="PUBLIC"></siteMapNode>
<!-- /NONE NAVIGATION NODES -->
    </siteMapNode>
</siteMap>
```

SiteMap wrapper

As with all of the other controls and classes that .NET exposes to us, it is a good idea to wrap the `SiteMap` class. We did this by creating a `Navigation` class. It not only exposes all the properties that `SiteMap` does, but it also adds a bit more control to the way we interact with our nodes.

```
//Fisharoo/Components/Navigation.cs
namespace Fisharoo.Components
{
    [Export(typeof(INavigation)]
    public class Navigation : INavigation
    {
        [Import]
        private IUserSession _userSession;
        [Import]
        private IRedirector _redirector;
        private Account _account;
        public Navigation()
        {
            MEFManager.Compose(this);
        }

        public List<SiteMapNode> AllNodes()
        {
            List<SiteMapNode> nodes = new List<SiteMapNode>();
            nodes.Add(SiteMap.RootNode);
            foreach (SiteMapNode node in SiteMap.RootNode.ChildNodes)
            {
               nodes.Add(node);
            }
            return nodes;
        }
        public List<SiteMapNode> PrimaryNodes()
        {
            List<SiteMapNode> primaryNodes = new List<SiteMapNode>();
            foreach (SiteMapNode node in AllNodes())
            {
                if (node["topnav"] != null &&
               CheckAccessForNode(node))
                    primaryNodes.Add(node);
            }
            return primaryNodes;
        }
        public List<SiteMapNode> FooterNodes()
        {
            List<SiteMapNode> footerNodes = new List<SiteMapNode>();
            foreach (SiteMapNode node in AllNodes())
            {
                if (node["footernav"] != null &&
```

```
                CheckAccessForNode(node))
                    footerNodes.Add(node);
            }
            return footerNodes;
        }
        private bool CheckAccessForNode(SiteMapNode node)
        {
            if (!node.Roles.Contains("PUBLIC"))
            {
                if (_account != null && _account.Permissions != null
                    && _account.Permissions.Count > 0)
                {
                    foreach (string role in node.Roles)
                    {
                        if (!_account.HasPermission(role))
                            return false;
                    }
                    return true;
                }
                else
                    return false;
            }
            return true;
        }
        public void CheckAccessForCurrentNode()
        {
            bool result = CheckAccessForNode(CurrentNode);
            if(result)
                return;
            else
                _redirector.GoToAccountAccessDenied();
        }
        public SiteMapNode RootNode
        {
            get { return SiteMap.RootNode; }
        }
        public SiteMapNode CurrentNode
        {
            get
            {
                return SiteMap.CurrentNode;
            }
        }
    }
}
```

All nodes

By default the `SiteMap` class doesn't return all nodes so to speak. It provides you with a call to the `RootNode` and a call to its children. As you can see in our first method, we simply created an `AllNodes ()` call that returns "all nodes".

Navigation

Our site will have several navigation sections. Here we have:

- Top navigation
- Primary navigation
- Secondary navigation
- Left navigation
- Footer navigation

If we had to dig through all of the navigation collections, each time we needed them we may find it quite cumbersome. Instead we will add methods to the classes that produce the required sub-selection of nodes.

The `PrimaryNodes()` method is the first example of such a method. It produces a list of nodes that go in the primary navigation section by iterating through all the nodes returned by the `AllNodes()` method looking for each node with a custom `topnav` attribute. You will notice a special filter though in addition to this. With each `topnav` node that is found, a security check is performed to see if the current user should have access to this node. If not, the node is not displayed.

The `FooterNodes()` method is exactly the same as the `PrimaryNodes()` method with the exception that it looks for a `footernav` attribute. This method also checks to make sure that the user has access to a specified collection of nodes.

Checking access

This brings us to the `CheckAccessForNode()` method, that we are using in our other methods. This method looks at the passed in node and checks its `Roles` collection. It first checks to see if the `PUBLIC` role is specified. If so, all remaining checks are not performed. We then move to see if there is an account present, that is, whether any user has logged in. If there is a user, we check their permissions property. If that exists, we check to see if there are any permissions in the permission list. We then iterate through each role specified in the node and check to make sure that the account has that permission. If the account doesn't contain any of the specified permissions we return `false`. If all the permissions are valid then we return `true`.

Security

Up until now we have discussed navigational aspects of this class. But seeing how security is rolled into this so deeply, it makes sense that we would also have something to check the current node for security reasons rather than just displaying links. This brings us to the `CheckAccessForCurrentNode()` method.

The `CheckAccessForCurrentNode()` method wraps the `CheckAccessForNode()` method and passes in the current `SiteMap` node. If there is sufficient access to the current node, no action is performed. However, if access to the current node is denied, then the user is automatically redirected to the access denied page by way of the `Redirector` class.

Implementing navigation and security

With this wrapper in place we now have a way to easily restrict where our users go and what forms of navigation they see. All we have to do is make calls into this class to get a list of nodes for the appropriate navigation section. We also need to make a call into the `CheckAccessForCurrentNode()` method at some global point.

In our case these calls will be made from our master page as it controls both global access and navigational display. So the first thing we will do is add a call to the `CheckAccessForCurrentNode()` in the `Page_Load()` method of the `Site.Master.cs` page.

```
protected void Page_Load(object sender, EventArgs e)
{
    _navigation.CheckAccessForCurrentNode();
    ...
}
```

For navigational purposes (not really covered too much to this point) we have a simple repeater that will iterate over `SiteMapNodes`. In the design view we have a repeater that looks like this:

```
<asp:Repeater ID="repPrimaryNav" OnItemDataBound="repPrimaryNav_
ItemDataBound" runat="server">
    <ItemTemplate>
        <asp:HyperLink ID="linkPrimaryNav" CssClass="PrimaryNavLink"
                   runat="server"></asp:HyperLink>
    </ItemTemplate>
</asp:Repeater>
```

Then for the `Page_Load()` method, we have the following binding code in the Master page's code behind:

```
repPrimaryNav.DataSource = _navigation.PrimaryNodes();
repPrimaryNav.DataBind();
```

If we only had this code, we wouldn't have any navigation. This is where the `OnItemDataBound="repPrimaryNav_ItemDataBound"` property comes in handy. It basically states that the `repPrimaryNav_ItemDataBound()` method will be our `OnItemDataBound` event handler.

This method will be responsible for displaying all the links. It also takes care of formatting the links to properly show which section you are in.

```
protected void repPrimaryNav_ItemDataBound(object sender,
RepeaterItemEventArgs e)
{
    HyperLink linkPrimaryNav = e.Item.FindControl("linkPrimaryNav")
                              as HyperLink;
    SiteMapNode node = (SiteMapNode) e.Item.DataItem;
    linkPrimaryNav.Text = node.Title;
    linkPrimaryNav.NavigateUrl = node.Url;
    if (node == _navigation.CurrentNode || node ==
                                _navigation.CurrentNode.ParentNode)
    {
        linkPrimaryNav.CssClass = "PrimaryNavLinkActive";
    }

     //TODO: For Chapter 3 these links will be kept disabled
    linkPrimaryNav.Enabled = false;
}
```

Summary

In this chapter we implemented user registration. This allowed us to gather data about our users so that they could become a member of our community. In addition to gathering the data, we briefly covered the ways to store some of the more important information. We also created a reCAPTCHA tool to reduce the amount of spam our community would have to deal with. We also provided some tools for the newly registered users so that they could remind themselves of their passwords and edit their account data. Once the registration tools were put in place, we then discussed and implemented an easy way to manage site-wide navigation and security.

With the account creation and management tools in place, we can now move on to other chapters. It was important to get this chapter under our belts as all the following chapters will use many of the features we created here.

4
User Profiles

While user accounts are a requirement for the system to work, user profiles are a must for your community to work. A user profile allows your users to share all sorts of details about themselves. It should be very flexible so that you can easily extend the capabilities of your users' profiles as your community matures and morphs over time.

In this chapter we will discuss the basics of setting up a user profile. This will include collecting various personal tidbits of data about your users, contact information, and so on. We will also go over the concept of allowing your users to upload an **avatar** (an icon or image associated with a user's profile) as well as integrating with a third-party avatar service, **Gravatar**. Part of the uploading of a custom avatar will take us into some image manipulation so that all avatars are of equal size and shape on our site!

With this out of the way we can move on to putting the user's public profile together and discuss how that profile can be accessed with a custom homepage or fancy URL. Once we have collected some data about our users—for other users of our site to see—we will need to discuss giving our users control of their privacy settings and allowing them to lock down the display of that data.

The last part of this chapter will get into the creation of a news feed/alert, that keeps track of what our users are doing. This will be a very important feature once the concept of Friends comes into play in the following chapter.

Problem

We are not going to discuss the profiles capability of .NET for the same reason that we chose not to write about the membership capabilities of .NET. This topic is widely covered in many books and on many of the top blog sites. We thought it might be more interesting to discuss a custom implementation of creating a profile and dynamic attributes so that a member's profile could be expanded with time. Also, this will get us a bit deeper into LINQ and how our framework works.

Another interesting topic that must be discussed absolutely while building profiles is avatars. An avatar is a small icon or image that is associated with each user's profile. This allows you to visually pick a profile out of the group with ease. Generally, an avatar is displayed next to just about everything a user does or interacts with. This could be their blog posts, forum posts, comments, and so on. It provides a sort of virtual face-to-face feeling.

Of course, we could take an easier approach and not allow our users to create custom avatars—certain communities do this. We could just provide a gallery of canned generic avatars for a user to associate with their profile. But the biggest draw to any community site is its ability for the users to have as much free expression as possible. For this reason, we will discuss the other end of the spectrum when it comes to custom avatars.

We need a way for the users to upload their own pictures of just about any size (though we will have a file size constraint! No 10 MB images to process please!). Knowing that an avatar is usually closer to the size of an icon rather than a poster, we will need to tackle resizing an image. Also, as we know that images can come in just about any shape, it would be really cool if we could figure out a UI that allows the user to select a specific section of the uploaded image and constrain that selection to a specific shape. We would prefer a square shape as it is the easiest to work with.

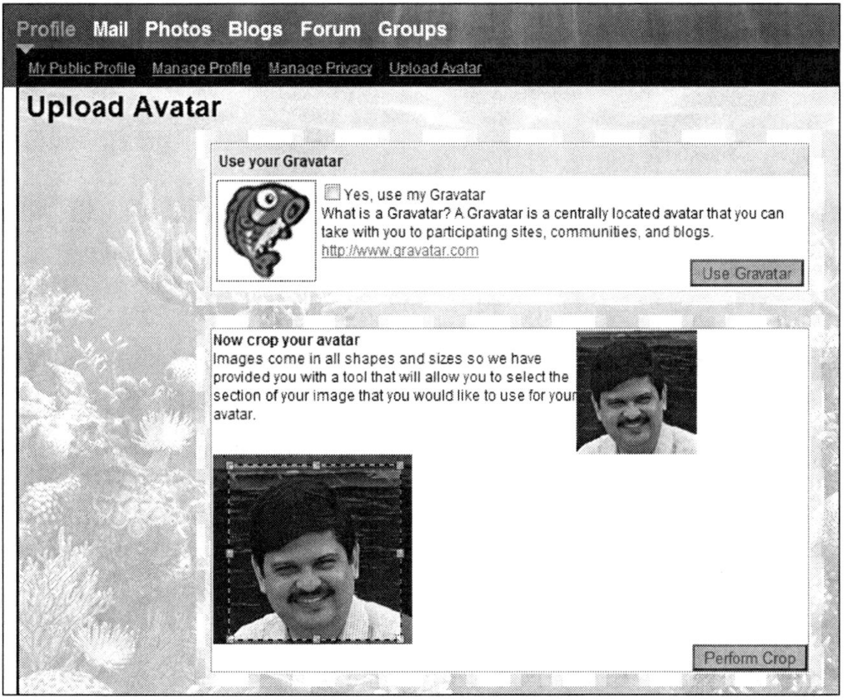

In addition to custom avatars, there are many services available these days that provide centralized avatars. This allows a user to upload and manage their avatars in one place and have them automatically feed out to all the sites that they are a member of. We will take a look at how to use one of the largest and most popular services, Gravatar.

Once we have all the data collection and profile configuration utilities out of the way, we will tackle the issue of displaying that data to our community. A good feature to take on here is the concept of a fancy URL, that will allow our users to have their own personal homepage within our community, something like this: `www.fisharoo.com/profiles/atulgupta`.

A very popular feature of Facebook is the concept of a continuous feed about you, your friends, and activities in the community. This sort of feature has become so popular that MySpace has recently implemented a version. This is an important feature as it gives us something new to look at on a daily basis. The more friends you are tracking (covered in Chapter 6), the more entries you will have to follow. As these feeds or alerts generally go on a user's private homepage, and as it is a major subsystem that many other features will dump into, we should address the underlying framework for this now rather than later.

Design

Let's take a look at what the design for these features would look like.

Profile

Our profiles will collect basic data about a user. Some items that we will collect are:

- Various IM (Instant Messaging) IDs
- The users' post/comments
- Some basic fish-related information such as how many fish tanks they have and how many fishes they have

In addition to this we will allow our profiles to have dynamic attributes. While these could be dynamic from a user's point of view, we will currently restrict this feature to allow only an administrator of the site to add additional attributes. Some examples of dynamic attributes are "about you", "occupation", and "your (reef/aquarium) setup".

Manage profile

As we will have several bits of data to manage, we need to consider how best to present this to the user. Also, we don't want to create a bunch of different screens to manage the profile as it will become a nightmare for us. We will use a simple step-by-step Wizard type interface so that we can break the data collection/management process into logical steps.

Avatar

There are many ways to manage images in a system. The top two methods that have been debated heavily over the years are storing the images in the database or storing them on the file system. For everyday image galleries, we are all for storing them on the file system. However, something that is used as frequently as an avatar (given the diminutive size of an avatar) can be stored directly with the profiles in the database.

Custom avatars

Most of us would think that uploading an image or a file is simple. However, resizing an image in a way that that doesn't make it look all distorted is indeed a challenge. Moreover, we want to upsize and/or crop the image so that it is a perfect square. But we can't squish the user's image into a square. Also we can't just pick out a square portion of the uploaded picture at random! The avatar could end up having just the nose rather than the head. So we need to either create a UI (or find one) that allows the user to specify which section of the uploaded image to use.

Gravatar

`Gravatar.com` and other similar sites have another interesting idea. They allow you to store an avatar in one centralized location and reference it from other sites. This way, if you ever wanted to change your avatar, you could simply go to one location, make the change, and your avatar would be changed across all the sites that reference it. We felt this was something that we should support in our site.

Public profile

As people join the site, they would like to know about other members of the site and interact with them. We need to present a public area for our users to express and share with the world. This will be a major launching pad for our other features in the following chapters.

Custom homepage

Most users of the Internet are used to seeing an URL that looks something like this: `http://www.domain.com/somepage.aspx?id=asduiw892lslcm&t=89889`. While computers can read this easily, it is absolutely meaningless to a human. As we already have a public profile page for each of our users, why not allow an easy way for curious folk to locate that page? More importantly why not provide an easy way for our users to share their public profile? Instead of the previous URL, we will make an URL that looks more like `http://www.fisharoo.com/profiles/YourUsername`.

Privacy

Once we have provided our users with all these tools to enter their personal data, it is very important that we provide them with a way to manage who sees that data. In this chapter, we will focus on creating the base system that we can later extend upon in the following chapters. In this chapter, we will look at how to keep the user's data either public or private. The system that we will create should be flexible enough to allow us to protect a single piece of data, or an entire section of data. An example could be that we want to protect a user's social security data individually (we won't store socials though!) and protect all the users' IM accounts with one flag.

Here the flags are the actual user settings. The flag types are the specific data or areas of data to be protected. As this will be statically defined in the system, this data need not be directly manageable. The visibility level boils down to public, private, and friends-only. With this structure, the end user will be able to configure each flag type independently.

News feed

As we had mentioned earlier, the news feed section is one of our favorite features of any community. We think if this area is created correctly, it will have the most activity and possibly the most value for the users. It essentially allows a user to keep track of other users.

There are several ways in which we can execute this type of functionality. We could keep the data scattered about for all the various types of notifications that we want to track. Or we could centralize it and disconnect it from the relational model. We are opting to keep things simple (as usual). So in our case, when a notification is generated it will be stored in a simple structure that will allow us to be more efficient with regards to getting this data quickly to our users.

Alerts are generated by each user. All these alerts will show up in a user's homepage so that he/she can see what they are up to chronologically.

Solution

Now, let's take a look at how we can go about implementing these new features.

Revisiting the Solution Structure

Before we dig into the details, let's quickly revisit the solution structure. Since this site will become pretty huge by the time we reach the end of the book and cover all the features, a bit of modularization is in order. Also to properly follow the application-layering concept we discussed earlier, it is important that we set things in the correct manner upfront. Our solution structure looks like the following:

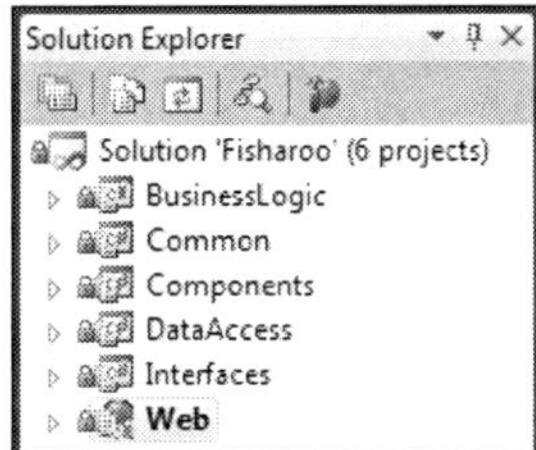

The various projects serve a specific purpose. Let's look at these:

- `Business Logic`: All business-related logic, rules, etc. will be in this project.
- `Common`: This is a common functionality that any layer can use.
- `Components`: These are also common components, but are those that can be replaced by different implementation as need be. Essentially these components implement MEF.
- `Data Access`: This layer is a wrapper on the actual data access and has various repositories that use the entity framework generated entities to work with the database.
- `Interfaces`: These are the interfaces that various classes in the `Components` project implement.
- `Web`: This is the presentation layer and has all the ASPX pages and related logic.

Implementing the database

We will start by implementing our database and work our way up from there. The following screenshot shows the main tables that we will be working with in this chapter.

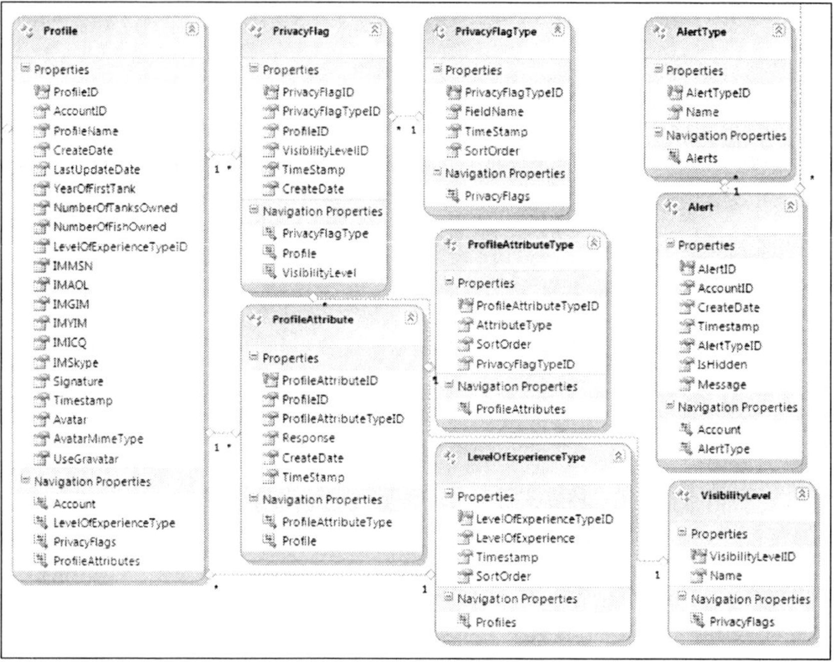

The Profiles table

Before we can really put an interface together, we need to discuss how the data for a profile will be stored. See the previous screenshot for the profiles table. Let's discuss some of the fields that are somewhat less than normal. In this case, we are referring to the **Avatar** storage, that uses **varbinary(MAX)** field. With the MAX size constraint (not much of a constraint!), a person could technically store a DVD in this field. This of course would be ridiculous, so we need to make sure that there are some constraints on the front end so that the file storage size is kept to a minimum. As you will see later, this field is essentially a character array!

Level of experience

Once we have our base profile container in place, we can create some of the surrounding tables. The easiest of which is the level of experience system. This will be used as other features of the site are built. Initially, a user can come in and set up his/her profile and claim a level of experience. Then as the user adds posts to the forum, creates new blog entries, or interacts with our community in any other way, we can adjust the user's level of experience dynamically. This can be based on the medals earned by the user, which we will discuss in Chapter 11.

The Attributes table

The next easiest portion of the profile system is the dynamic attributes system. Recall that this will allow the site administrator to easily extend the data that is collected for each user. There are two tables—`ProfileAttribute` and `ProfileAttributeType`. The first one is for user entered attributes and the second one is for the various attributes that are used in the site.

The Privacy table

Now we can discuss the privacy system. This is simply a one-to-many relationship system with some configuration/lookup tables on the child side of the relationship. We have `PrivacyFlag` for storing the user created values. We then have `PrivacyFlagType` to define what the flag is protecting. And finally, we have the `VisibilityLevel`, which defines who can see the protected data.

The Alerts table

Now, we are on to the tables that will support our news feed or "Alerts" concept on the profile page. This includes the `Alert` table and the `AlertType` table.

An interesting field to discuss here is the **IsHidden** field. We will use this later so that a user can hide an alert from his/her news feed. We can also use it so that the user can hide a whole set of alerts based on its alert type.

Setting up the data access layer

Unlike in the last chapter, our data access layer will be much less involved. All the ground work has already been completed. So from now on, when we speak about setting up the data access layer, all we are really speaking about is opening up the `Fisharoo.edmx` file and adding new tables on to the design surface. Open the `Fisharoo.edmx` file, right click in the designer and select **update model from Database**. This will pop up the **Update Wizard** of Entity Framework, as shown in the following screenshot. We can pick the items we want to add (the selected tables as seen in the following screenshot).

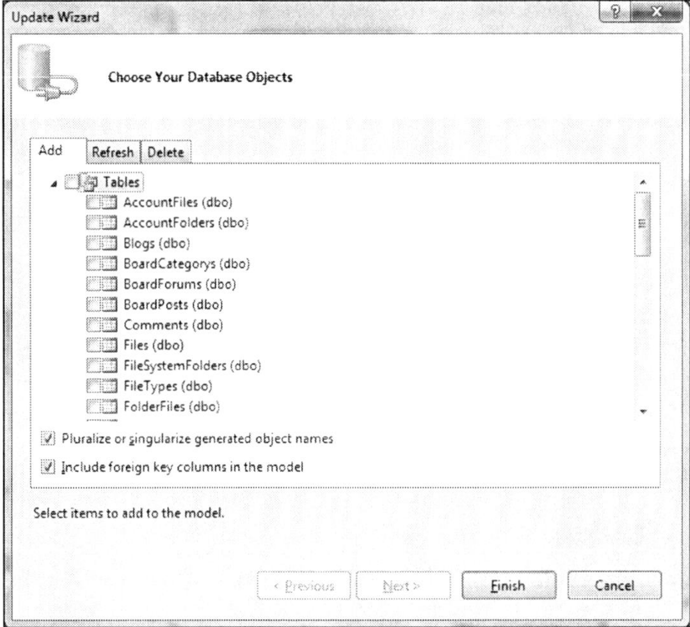

On clicking the **Finish** button in the wizard, the selected tables will get added in the designer (EDMX file). We will follow this procedure of adding respective tables, views, and stored procedures in every chapter.

Entity classes

On expanding the `Fisharoo.Edmx` node, you will see `Fisharoo.Designer.cs` which has namespace `Fisharoo.DataAccess`, and inside it has created Context and Entity classes. All the generated Entity classes are partial classes and correspond to the entity in `EDMX`. The `Context` class inherits from `ObjectContext` and has properties for Object Collection that is generated based on navigational properties in each entity.

In applications where business layer has a significant amount of business logic, independent business entities can be created and transformations applied to and from entities (for example, transformation from DataAccess entity to Business Entity and vice versa). Similarly if the presentation layer demands the entities to have additional properties specific to presentation layer, presentation entities can be created.

Let's extend our `Profile` object by creating a new `Profile` partial class in the `DataAccess` project. In this class, let's add a property to store the list of profile attributes and a property to hold the level of experience for the profile. We don't need to have corresponding scalar properties as these would be available and hence we need not worry about adding them in this partial class. The `Profile` partial class would look like as:

```
//Fisharoo/DataAccess/Profile.cs
namespace Fisharoo.DataAccess
{
    public partial class Profile
    {
        public List<ProfileAttribute> Attributes { get; set; }
        public LevelOfExperienceType levelOfExperienceType { get; set;
}

        public Profile()
        {
            Attributes = new List<ProfileAttribute>();
        }
    }
}
```

Along similar lines, we will create partial Entity classes for `AlertType`, `PrivacyFlagType`, `ProfileAttribute`, and `VisiblityLevel`. Refer to the code provided for Chapter 4 for details on these classes.

Building repositories

With the addition of new tables will come the addition of new repositories to get to the data stored in the tables. We will be creating a few repositories to support our profile needs, namely `ProfileRepository`, `ProfileAttributeRepository`, `PrivacyRepository`, `LevelOfExperienceTypeRepository` and `AlertRepository`.

Each of our repositories will have a method for selecting on the basis of the ID, selecting on the basis of the parent ID, for save and delete. Once you have seen one repository, you have pretty much seen them all. Let's take a look at `ProfileRepository.cs`:

```
//Fisharoo/DataAccess/Respositories/ProfileRepository.cs
namespace Fisharoo.DataAccess.Repositories
{
    [Export(typeof(IProfileRepository))]
    public class ProfileRepository : IProfileRepository
    {
        private Connection conn;
        public ProfileRepository()
        {
            conn = new Connection();
        }

        public Profile GetProfileByAccountID(int AccountID)
        {
            Profile profile;

            using (FisharooDataContext dc = conn.GetContext())
            {
                profile = (from p in dc.Profiles.Include(
                         "ProfileAttributes.ProfileAttributeType")
                           .Include("LevelOfExperienceType")
                           where p.AccountID == AccountID
                           select p).FirstOrDefault();
            }
            if (profile != null)
            {
                foreach (ProfileAttribute item in profile.
                ProfileAttributes)
                {
                    profile.Attributes.Add(item);
                    item.profileAttributeType = item.
                    ProfileAttributeType;
                }
                profile.levelOfExperienceType = profile.
                LevelOfExperienceType;
            }
            return profile;
        }

        public Int32 SaveProfile(Profile profile)
```

```
{
    Int32 profileID = 0;
    Boolean HasAttributeId = false;
    profile.LastUpdateDate = DateTime.Now;
    using (FisharooDataContext dc = conn.GetContext())
    {
        if (profile.ProfileID > 0)
        {
            dc.Profiles.Attach(new Profile { ProfileID =
            profile.ProfileID });
            dc.Profiles.ApplyCurrentValues(profile);
            if (profile.Attributes != null)
            {
                foreach (ProfileAttribute item in profile.
                Attributes)
                {
                    dc.ProfileAttributes.Attach(
                                   new ProfileAttribute
                    {
                        ProfileAttributeID = item.
                        ProfileAttributeID,
                    });
                    dc.ProfileAttributes.
                    ApplyCurrentValues(item);
                }
            }
        }
        else
        {
            profile.CreateDate = DateTime.Now;
            //when working with new profile we don't expect
            attributes to be null, but check anyway
            if (profile.Attributes != null)
            {
                foreach (ProfileAttribute item in profile.
                Attributes)
                {
                    dc.ProfileAttributes.AddObject(new
                    ProfileAttribute
                    {
                        ProfileAttributeID = item.
                        ProfileAttributeID,
                        ProfileAttributeTypeID = item.
                        ProfileAttributeTypeID,
                        ProfileID = item.ProfileID,
```

```
                                Response = item.Response,
                                CreateDate = item.CreateDate,
                                TimeStamp = item.TimeStamp
                            });
                            HasAttributeId = true;
                        }
                    }
                    dc.Profiles.AddObject(profile);
                }
                dc.SaveChanges();
                profileID = profile.ProfileID;
                if (HasAttributeId)
                {
                    var result = from pa in dc.ProfileAttributes.
                                 Include("ProfileAttributeType")
                                 where pa.ProfileID == profileID
                                 select pa;
                    profile.Attributes = result.ToList();
                    foreach (ProfileAttribute item in profile.
                    ProfileAttributes)
                    {
                        item.profileAttributeType = item.
                        ProfileAttributeType;
                    }
                }
            }
            return profileID;
        }

        public void DeleteProfile(Profile profile)
        {

            using (FisharooDataContext dc = conn.GetContext())
            {
                dc.Profiles.DeleteObject(dc.Profiles
                                        .Where(pf => pf.ProfileID.
                                        Equals(profile.ProfileID)).
                                        FirstOrDefault());
                dc.SaveChanges();
            }
        }
    }
}
```

Let's look at some important parts of the above code. In `GetProfileByAccountID()` method, the important thing to note is the various `.Include`. By doing this, for each profile we are fetching `ProfileAttributes` and for each `ProfileAttribute`, its corresponding `ProfileAttributeType`. Another `Include` clause fetches `LevelofExperienceType` for each profile. All this data will be fetched from the database in one shot. This has an advantage of fetching data in batches as against hitting database multiple times.

Before we go further, let's quickly understand a bit more the loading options that Entity framework provides. Entity Framework by default uses lazy loading. This means that navigational objects will not be loaded/queried by default. It will be loaded only when the navigational properties are accessed in code. This means multiple round trips to the database.

Eager loading on the other hand means loading corresponding navigational properties along with loading of the main object. This reduces the number of round trips. This is done by using `Include` clause as shown above.

Both the approaches have their respective pros and cons. Lazy loading will mean a bit of delayed experience when accessing the data for the first time. Eager loading on the other hand can build memory pressure if there are several large-sized nested objects.

For social networking sites, it is important that data is available to users without delays and would be one of the important factors in ensuring overall user experience and hence we have selectively used eager loading in this application.

Back to our code! As mentioned earlier, the navigational objects such as `ProfileAttributes`, `ProfileAttributeType`, and `LevelOfExperienceType` will not be available outside of `DataContext` and hence we will assign them to the property of entity objects by looping through appropriate collection (as seen in `GetProfileByAccountID()` method).

Similarly, while saving `Profile`, we pass the profile object to `SaveProfile()` method where we first check if the passed profile is a newly created profile or update of an existing profile. If the profile has `ProfileID > 0`, it means this is an existing profile and it must be updated in the database. If equal to 0, it is a new profile.

Once this is done, for `Profile` we check for corresponding navigational properties and loop through it and save it by calling respective repository method.

Deleting `Profile` is straightforward; first we locate or load the `Profile` object in the `DataContext`. Once loaded we just delete it and then call `dc.SaveChanges()` to save the changes in `DataContext` to the database. The method uses lambda expression to locate the right `Profile`.

Lambda Expression consists of a lambda operator '=>' (pronounced as goes to), left side of which signifies the input parameter and right side signifies the expression or statement block to be evaluated. The main advantages of these over standard query are type inference, simplicity, and increased readability of code.

Other repositories are built on similar lines and we will not be showing the code here. You can check out the code associated with this chapter for more details.

Implementing the services/application layer

Once all the repositories are built for single-serving purposes, we can begin creating the service layer. Service layer will be consumed by Presentation layer project. The Repository classes (except entities) will never be accessed directly in Presentation layer project and will be always accessed only in BusinessLogic project. This will help maintain the coupling and cohesion between various layers in the application. Not only this, it also helps in establishing the design principle of "separation of concerns" that means each layer will only perform dedicated activities expected from it.

We will create some services, namely `ProfileService`, `PrivacyService`, `AlertService`, `ProfileAttributeService`, `LevelOfExperienceTypeService`, and `PermissionService`.

In addition to the above services, we will also need to modify a couple of services.

ProfileService

Now we can look at building our `ProfileService`. Create a new class in the `BusinessLogic project` called `ProfileService`.

```
//Fisharoo/BusinessLogic/ProfileService.cs
namespace Fisharoo.BusinessLogic
{
    //CHAPTER 4
    [Export(typeof(IProfileService))]
    public class ProfileService : IProfileService
    {
        [Import]
        private IProfileRepository _profileRepository;
        [Import]
        private IAlertService _alertService;
        [Import]
```

```
        private IProfileAttributeRepository _
        profileAttributeRepository;
        [Import]
        private IUserSession _userSession;
        [Import]
        private ILogger _log;

        public ProfileService()
        {
            MEFManager.Compose(this);
        }

        public Profile LoadProfileByAccountID(Int32 AccountID)
        {
            Profile profile = null;
            profile = _profileRepository.GetProfileByAccountID(Accoun
            tID);
            return profile;
        }

        public void SaveProfile(Profile profile)
        {
           _profileRepository.SaveProfile(profile);
           _userSession.CurrentUser.Profile = profile;
        }
    }
}
```

As you can see, this class has methods for `LoadProfileByAccountID()` and `SaveProfile()`. They are pretty straightforward to understand as they are just calling the corresponding DataAccess Layer methods and passing appropriate parameters.

We are not directly accessing the repository classes by creating instance in the `ProfileService` class but use them through interface to DataAccess Repository (`IProfileRepository`) using MEF, as explained in the earlier chapter.

Account service

Now that we have our ProfileService created, let's extend our AccountService to take advantage of our new features. Note that we are loading Profiles and AccountPermissions along with Account in AccountRepository.cs and hence these will be available as navigational properties with account object. Let's start by extending our Login method in the AccountService.cs file. When the user attempts to log in, we get their account with the method that we just extended (GetAccountByID). This means that we now have their profile as well! We can now make a decision as to whether we have a user with a fully created profile or not and redirect them accordingly. Let's update the AccountService.cs Login() method with the following code:

```
//Fisharoo/BusinessLogic/AccountService.cs
if (account.EmailVerified)
{
    _userSession.LoggedIn = true;
    _userSession.Username = Username;
    _userSession.CurrentUser = GetAccountByID(account.AccountID);
    if(_userSession.CurrentUser.Profile != null &&
     _userSession.CurrentUser.Profile.ProfileID > 0)
        _redirector.GoToProfilesDefault();
    else
        _redirector.GoToProfilesManageProfile();
}
```

Of course, this means that we need to add these new methods to our Redirector class! Here is the code:

```
//Fisharoo/Components/Redirector.cs
public void GoToProfilesProfile()
{
    Redirect("~/Profiles/Profile.aspx");
}

public void GoToProfilesDefault()
{
    Redirect("~/Profiles/Default.aspx");
}
```

Privacy service

The privacy service is currently solely responsible for determining if a piece of data or a section that displays multiple types of data can be displayed or not. It has a method named ShouldShow() that returns a Boolean value.

```
//Fisharoo/BusinessLogic/PrivacyService.cs
public bool ShouldShow(Int32 PrivacyFlagTypeID,
    Account AccountBeingViewed,
    Account Account,
    List<PrivacyFlag> Flags)
{
    bool result;

    //CHAPTER 5 - come back to this when we start friends
    bool isFriend = false;
    //flag marked as private test
    if(Flags.Where(f => f.PrivacyFlagTypeID == PrivacyFlagTypeID &&
    f.VisibilityLevelID == (int)VisibilityLevel.VisibilityLevels.
    Private).FirstOrDefault() != null)
        result = false;
    //flag marked as friends only test
    else if (Flags.Where(f => f.PrivacyFlagTypeID ==
                        PrivacyFlagTypeID && f.VisibilityLevelID ==
                        (int)VisibilityLevel.VisibilityLevels
                        Friends).
            FirstOrDefault() != null && isFriend)
        result = true;
    else if (Flags.Where(f => f.PrivacyFlagTypeID ==
                        PrivacyFlagTypeID && f.VisibilityLevelID ==
                        (int)VisibilityLevel.VisibilityLevels.Public)
            .FirstOrDefault() != null)
        result = true;
    else
        result = false;
    return result;
}
```

Note that we are using enum rather than record numbers to test against. In order to use these enum values represented by the `VisibilityLevel.VisibilityLevels`, we will have to create a new partial `VisibilityLevel` class. Navigate to `DataAccess` and create a new class file named `VisibilityLevel.cs`. In there, enter the following code:

```
public enum VisibilityLevels
{
    Private = 1,
    Friends = 2,
    Public = 3
}
```

Back to the `ShouldShow` method! This method may look complex but is really just checking many different relationships. This method bears into mind the account that is being viewed, the account doing the viewing, the `PrivacyFlagType` that is being viewed, and a list of `PrivacyFlags` for the account being viewed.

The method then checks to see if the data is flagged as private, in which case no one but the owner can see it. It then checks to see if the account being viewed and the account doing the viewing are friends, and whether or not the data is marked viewable by friends. As we have not yet implemented Friends, we left a note so that we can come back and rework this section when we get to this concept in Chapter 5. And finally, we check to see if the data is marked as public in which case everyone can view it.

Alert service

The `AlertService` boils down to a wrapper for saving alerts into the system and getting them back out again. Rather than having the client code format a new alert message, we will add new custom alert wrappers such as `AddAccountModifiedAlert()`. This will not only give us a place to manage how alerts are formatted and stored in our system, but it will also give us a place to modify when we want to extend the system to handle new concepts such as the ability of Friends to get subscribed to your alerts.

```
//Fisharoo/BusinessLogic/AlertService.cs
private void Init()
{
    account = _userSession.CurrentUser;
    alert = new Alert();
    alert.AccountID = account.AccountID;
    alert.CreateDate = DateTime.Now;
}
...
public void AddAccountModifiedAlert()
{
    Init();
    alertMessage = "<div class=\"AlertHeader\">" +
    GetProfileUrl(account.Username) +
                  " modified their account.</div>";
    alert.Message = alertMessage;
    alert.AlertTypeID = (int) AlertType.AlertTypes.AccountModified;
    SaveAlert(alert);
}
...
private void SaveAlert(Alert alert)
{
    _alertRepository.SaveAlert(alert);
}
```

Other services

- **Profile Attribute service**: This service is responsible for assembling a `ProfileAttribute` with its corresponding `ProfileAttributeType` based on the `ProfileAttributeTypeID` that is stored with the `ProfileAttribute`. This is pretty straightforward to implement as it simply makes a call into the `ProfileAttributeRepository` to get a list of `ProfileAttributes` by the specified `ProfileID`. We have just implemented this from a code completion perspective. This service may not be invoked or used as we are already loading all the `ProfileAttribute` with each Profile in `ProfileRepository.cs`
- **Level of Experience type service**: This is a simple wrapper service that invokes the `LevelOfExperienceTypeRespository` to get the list of all levels of experience types. This is written to avoid the presentation layer directly invoking the repository classes.
- **Permission service**: This is similar to `LevelOfExperienceTypeService` and invokes method on `PermissionRepository` to get the permissions associated with names as used in the `Web.sitemap`.

Check out the code associated with this chapter to look at the details of these services.

Implementing the presentation layer

Now that the entire backend is created and ready to go, let's move on to discussing how we will make the presentation work for us. While the privacy features could just as easily be implemented after everything else, we think it will be easiest if we get it ready first. Then as we build the other areas out, we can sew in our privacy checking where it is needed.

Privacy

Now, let's implement the privacy feature.

Manage privacy

As with all the other types of data we will be collecting from our users, we need to provide a way for our users to manage their privacy—which is not really about data entry though. In this case, we will be providing a way for our user to check who can see a certain section of their data, and who has access to their entire data. We will create a page that is dynamically built based on the `PrivacyFlagTypes` that are defined in the database.

As the view always gets us started, let's take a look at the code there first. As a good chunk of this page is built on the fly, the mark-up for this page is relatively simple. It consists of some instructions explaining what each visibility type is, and a placeholder for our dynamic form elements.

//Profiles/ManagePrivacy.aspx

```
<%@ Page Language="C#" MasterPageFile="~/Site.Master"
AutoEventWireup="true" CodeBehind="ManagePrivacy.aspx.cs"
    Inherits="Fisharoo.Web.Profiles.ManagePrivacy" %>

<asp:Content ContentPlaceHolderID="Content" runat="server">
    <div class="divContainer">
        <fieldset class="formFields">
            <div class="divContainerTitle">
                Set the visibility of each section below: </div>
            <div align="left">
                Private: Only you can see it <br />
                Friends Only: Only you and your friends can see it <br
/>
                Public: Everyone can see it <p />
```

```
                <asp:PlaceHolder ID="phPrivacyFlagTypes"
runat="server"></asp:PlaceHolder> </div>
            <div class="divContainerFooter">
                <asp:Label ID="lblMessage" runat="server"
ForeColor="Red"></asp:Label>
                <asp:Button CssClass="loginButton" ID="btnSave"
runat="server" Text="Save Privacy Settings" OnClick="btnSave_Click" />
            </div> </fieldset> </div>
</asp:Content>
```

This then brings us to our code behind. Of course, it inherits from an interface so that we can pass a reference from this page to our `ManagePrivacyPresenter` class. As with most **Model View Presenter (MVP)** pages, we have to set up our presenter class. To get started we pass a reference of this page to the presenter in `Page_Load`.

```
//Fisharoo/Web/Profiles/ManagePrivacy.aspx.cs
namespace Fisharoo.Web.Profiles
{
   public partial class ManagePrivacy : System.Web.UI.Page,
   IManagePrivacy
    {
        private ManagePrivacyPresenter _presenter;

        protected void Page_Load(object sender, EventArgs e)
        {
            _presenter = new ManagePrivacyPresenter();
            _presenter.Init(this);
        }

        public void ShowPrivacyTypes(List<PrivacyFlagType>
        PrivacyFlagTypes,
            List<VisibilityLevel> VisibilityLevels,
            List<PrivacyFlag> PrivacyFlags)
        {
            foreach (PrivacyFlagType type in PrivacyFlagTypes)
            {
                //Add the field name to the display
                phPrivacyFlagTypes.Controls.Add(new
                LiteralControl("<p>"));
                Label lbl = new Label();
                lbl.Text = type.FieldName + ":";
                lbl.Width = 100;
                phPrivacyFlagTypes.Controls.Add(lbl);

                //Create the visibility drop down
```

```
                DropDownList ddlVisibility = new DropDownList();
                ddlVisibility.ID = "ddlVisibility" +
                                 type.PrivacyFlagTypeID.ToString();
                foreach (VisibilityLevel level in VisibilityLevels)
                {
                    ListItem li = new ListItem(level.Name,
                    level.VisibilityLevelID.ToString());
                    if(!IsPostBack)
                        li.Selected = _presenter.IsFlagSelected(
                                      type.PrivacyFlagTypeID,
                                      level.VisibilityLevelID,
                                      PrivacyFlags);
                    ddlVisibility.Items.Add(li);
                }
                phPrivacyFlagTypes.Controls.Add(ddlVisibility);
                phPrivacyFlagTypes.Controls.Add(new LiteralControl("</
                p>"));
            }
        }

        protected void btnSave_Click(object sender, EventArgs e)
        {
            lblMessage.Text = "";
            foreach (PrivacyFlagType type in
                                    _presenter.GetPrivacyFlagTypes())
            {
                DropDownList ddlVisibility =
                    phPrivacyFlagTypes.FindControl("ddlVisibility" +
                    type.PrivacyFlagTypeID.ToString()) as
                    DropDownList;
                if(ddlVisibility != null)
                    _presenter.SavePrivacyFlag(
                                type.PrivacyFlagTypeID,Convert.
                                ToInt32(
                                ddlVisibility.SelectedValue));
            }
            lblMessage.Text = "Your privacy settings were saved
            successfully!";
        }

        public void ShowMessage(string Message)
        {
            lblMessage.Text += Message;
        }
    }
}
```

The thing to note here is that as with all presenter-controlled pages, the view calls an `Init()` method, which is a method in the presenter responsible for loading the page. The presenter calls into the `LoadPrivacyTypes()` to load privacy data using the appropriate service and then calls into `ShowPrivacyTypes()` method in the view passing in what is needed to dynamically build the UI. The `ShowPrivacyTypes()` method then iterates through all the values of the passed in lists to add drop-downs to the place holder in the `.aspx` page. While loading the UI, it also attempts to locate the current value for each menu to load.

We then have the `btnSave_Click()` event handler that is responsible for extracting the current selections and passing those values upstream to the presenter to persist the data to the database.

Finally, we have a `ShowMessage()` method, that allows the presenter to pass messages back to the user of this page.

The presenter, `ManagePrivacyPresenter`, provides us with various methods to load and handle events from the `ManagePrivacy` page. Here is the code:

```
//Profiles/Presenters/ManagePrivacyPresenter.cs
namespace Fisharoo.Web.Profiles.Presenters
{
    public class ManagePrivacyPresenter
    {
        [Import]
        private IPrivacyService _privacyService;
        [Import]
        private IUserSession _userSession;

        private Account account;
        int profileID;

        private List<PrivacyFlagType> privacyFlagTypes;
        private List<VisibilityLevel> visibilityLevels;
        private List<PrivacyFlag> privacyFlags;
        private IManagePrivacy _view;

        public void Init(IManagePrivacy View)
        {
            _view = View;
            MEFManager.Compose(this);
            account = _userSession.CurrentUser;
            profileID = account.Profile.ProfileID;

            LoadPrivacyTypes();
```

```
        }

        private void LoadPrivacyTypes()
        {
            privacyFlagTypes = _privacyService.GetPrivacyFlagTypes();
            visibilityLevels = _privacyService.GetVisibilityLevels();
            privacyFlags = _privacyService.GetPrivacyFlagsByProfileID(
                                                               profileID
);

_view.ShowPrivacyTypes(privacyFlagTypes,visibilityLevels,privacyFlags
);
        }

        public List<PrivacyFlagType> GetPrivacyFlagTypes()
        {
            return privacyFlagTypes;
        }

        public void SavePrivacyFlag(Int32 PrivacyFlagTypeID,
        Int32 VisibilityLevelID)
        {
            foreach (PrivacyFlag flag in privacyFlags)
            {
                if (flag.PrivacyFlagTypeID == PrivacyFlagTypeID)
                {
                    flag.VisibilityLevelID = VisibilityLevelID;
                    _privacyService.SavePrivacyFlag(flag);
                    return;
                }
            }

            //not in collection?  Add a new one
            PrivacyFlag newFlag = new PrivacyFlag();
            newFlag.PrivacyFlagTypeID = PrivacyFlagTypeID;
            newFlag.VisibilityLevelID = VisibilityLevelID;
            newFlag.ProfileID = profileID;
            newFlag.CreateDate = DateTime.Now;
            privacyFlags.Add(newFlag);
            _privacyService.SavePrivacyFlag(newFlag);
        }

        public bool IsFlagSelected(Int32 PrivacyFlagTypeID,
                    Int32 VisibilityLevelID, List<PrivacyFlag>
                    PrivacyFlags)
        {
```

```
                List<PrivacyFlag> result = privacyFlags.FindAll(
                        pf => (pf.PrivacyFlagTypeID.
                        Equals(PrivacyFlagTypeID))
                        && (pf.VisibilityLevelID.
                        Equals(VisibilityLevelID)));
                if (result.Count > 0)
                {
                    return true;
                }
                return false;
            }
        }
    }
```

We have the `Init()` method, that simply captures the view reference and uses MEF to load the required services. It then calls the `LoadPrivacyTypes()` to initialize the calling page's UI. This method gets a list of privacy flag types, visibility levels, and the current privacy flags for the current user. The `ShowPrivacyTypes()` is then called in the view to display the UI.

The `GetPrivacyFlagTypes()` method is called from the view when saving the data so that we can iterate over the UI in the same way that we built it. We use a list of `PrivacyFlagTypes` to build the UI so it is only fitting that we also use it to destroy the UI!

This then brings us to the `SavePrivacyFlag()` method, which is responsible for interacting with the save button click event in the view. This method simply iterates over the passed-in `PrivacyFlags` and saves them to the database.

With all this done, we are now free to call into the `PrivacyService` class to see if an area should be shown or not. Although we have private data to work with, determining if we should show something or shouldn't won't currently do us any good, as there is no way to add profile data at this time! Let's add a profile management page. But before we do that, do note that all pages follow the similar MVP pattern and hence some part of the code will be similar. We will henceforth show only the relevant and important parts of the code. For the complete code, you can always refer to the code associated with this chapter.

Manage profile

As we know that this area has a big chance of growing and expanding as the site grows, we have decided to build this page using a series of wizard steps. The code for the UI is not difficult by any means, but it is longer than we want to show here in the text! So we will only show the steps for the wizard.

Here, we collect some attributes about the user's fish tank as shown in the following screenshot.

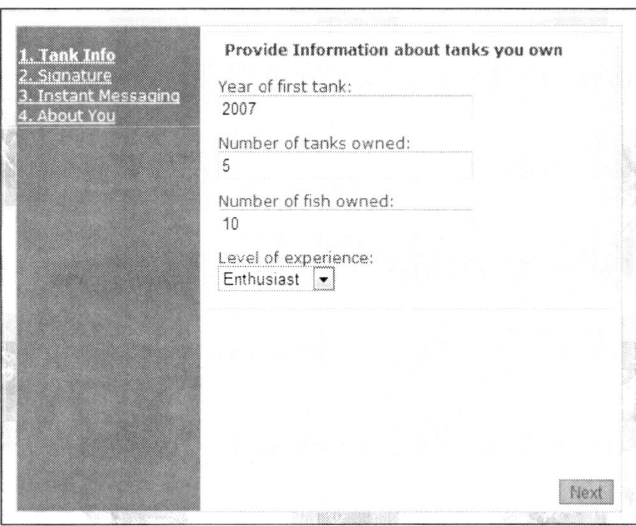

Then, we gather the user's signature (which we can use for any postings to the forum or other features) as shown in the following screenshot:

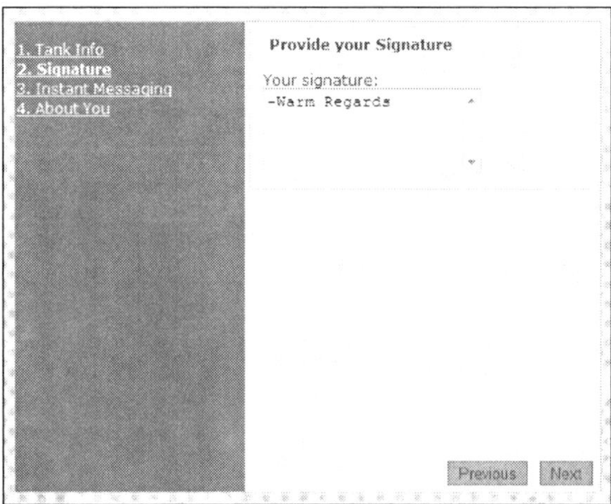

Next we collect all of the user's methods to communicate with other users in the site. We focus on collecting their Instant Messaging client IDs here.

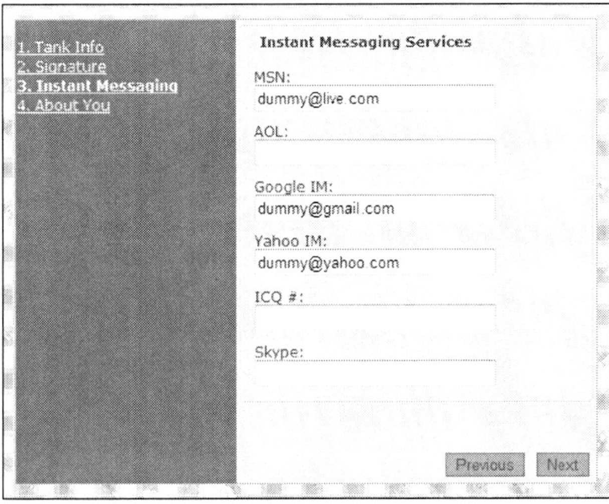

Finally, we have some attributes about the user that we can display on their profile page.

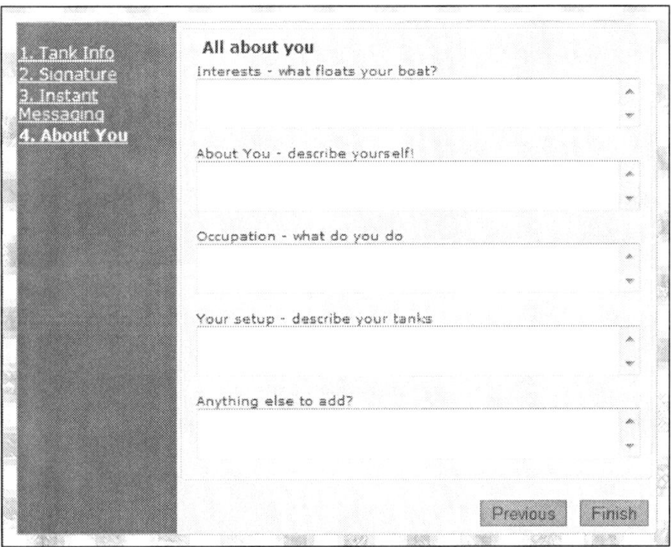

The only steps that are a bit different from the norm are the first and the last steps. The first step's **level of experience** menu and all the inputs in the last step are dynamically generated.

During initialization, the presenter initiates the UI with a couple of previously discussed service methods.

```
//Fisharoo/Web/Profiles/Presenters/ManageProfilePresenter.cs
public void Init(IManageProfile view, bool IsPostback)
{
    . . .
    _view.LoadLevelOfExperienceTypes(
        _levelOfExperienceTypeService.
        GetAllLevelOfExperienceTypes());
        _view.LoadProfileAttributeTypes(GetProfileAttributeTypes());

    if (!IsPostback)
    {
        _view.LoadProfile(GetProfile());
    }
}
```

The presenter then feeds the data back to the UI to dynamically create the required controls, appropriately format them, and finally display the output.

```
//Profiles/ManageProfile.aspx.cs
public void LoadProfileAttributeTypes(List<ProfileAttributeType>
types)
{
    foreach (ProfileAttributeType type in types)
    {
        Label lbl = new Label();
        lbl.ID = "lblAttribute" + type.ProfileAttributeTypeID.
        ToString();
        lbl.Text = type.AttributeType;
        lbl.CssClass = "formLabel";

        Label lblAttributeTypeID = new Label();
        lblAttributeTypeID.ID = "lblAttributeTypeID" + type.
        ProfileAttributeTypeID.ToString();
        lblAttributeTypeID.Text = type.ProfileAttributeTypeID.
        ToString();
        lblAttributeTypeID.Visible = false;

        Label lblProfileAttributeID = new Label();
        lblProfileAttributeID.ID = "lblProfileAttributeID" + type.
        ProfileAttributeTypeID.ToString();
        lblProfileAttributeID.Visible = false;
```

```
            TextBox tb = new TextBox();
            tb.ID = "txtProfileAttribute" + type.ProfileAttributeTypeID.
            ToString();
            tb.TextMode = TextBoxMode.MultiLine;
            tb.Columns = 40;
            tb.Rows = 2;

            CustomValidator cv = new CustomValidator();
            cv.ControlToValidate = "txtProfileAttribute" + type.
            ProfileAttributeTypeID.ToString();
            cv.ClientValidationFunction = "MaxLength2000";
            cv.ErrorMessage = "This field can only be 2000 characters
            long!";
            cv.Text = "*";
            cv.ForeColor = System.Drawing.Color.Red;


            phAttributes.Controls.Add(lblAttributeTypeID);
            phAttributes.Controls.Add(lblProfileAttributeID);
            phAttributes.Controls.Add(lbl);
            phAttributes.Controls.Add(new LiteralControl("<br />"));
            phAttributes.Controls.Add(tb);
            phAttributes.Controls.Add(cv);
            phAttributes.Controls.Add(new LiteralControl("<br />"));
        }
    }
```

Once the UI is created, the rest is a simple matter of plumbing and UI upkeep. Each time someone clicks the **Next** button, we clear the error message label. And when the **Finish** button is clicked, we extract the data from the UI and pass it to the presenter to be saved to the database.

Avatar

Now let's look at creating the user's Avatar, that will be displayed next to all his/her interactions with the site.

Upload avatar

Pretty much all the work for this feature occurs in the presenter. The UI presents a file upload box with a standard browse button and an additional button to submit the selected file. When the **Submit** button is clicked, the view passes the `PostedFile` to the `UploadFile()` method of the presenter.

```
//Fisharoo/Web/Profiles/Presenters/UploadAvatarPresenter.cs
public void UploadFile(HttpPostedFile File)
{
    string extension = Path.GetExtension(File.FileName).ToLower();
    string mimetype;
    byte[] uploadedImage = new byte[File.InputStream.Length];
    switch (extension)
    {
        case ".png":
        case ".jpg":
        case ".gif":
            mimetype = File.ContentType;
            break;
        default:
            _view.ShowMessage("We only accept .png, .jpg, and
                               .gif!");
            return;
            break;
    }
    if (File.ContentLength / 1000 < 1000)
    {
        File.InputStream.Read(uploadedImage, 0,
                              uploadedImage.Length);
        profile.Avatar = uploadedImage;
        profile.AvatarMimeType = mimetype;
        profile.UseGravatar = 0;
        _profileRepository.SaveProfile(profile);
        _view.ShowCropPanel();
    }
    else
    {
        _view.ShowMessage("The file you uploaded is larger than the
           1mb limit.  Please reduce the size of your file and try
           again.");
    }
}
```

This method is responsible for receiving the file and performing some basic checks on the file. We first get the extension of the file being uploaded and check to make sure that the file that was uploaded is an image that we support. If not, we show a message stating the issue.

Once we make it past that check, we check to make sure that the file size is not too large. If the file is in an acceptable size, we read the file into the `uploadedImage` byte array. We then pass the byte array into the current profile's `Avatar` property along with its mimetype (we also set the `UseGravatar` flag to `0`, which we will discuss shortly). Finally, we save this data to the user's profile and update the display to show the cropping UI. Alternatively, if the file size was too large, we show an error message.

Image manipulation

To start with, the entire UI for this image-cropping tool is located at: `http://www.defusion.org.uk/code/javascript-image-cropper-ui-using-prototype-scriptaculous/`. This is an open source JavaScript tool that provides us with all the fancy interface options that can be dragged and resized. It uses prototype (`http://www.prototypejs.org/`), scriptaculous (`http://script.aculo.us/`), and some fancy footwork from Dave Spurr. To implement this script, download the source from the defusion site above and include the references to the prototype, scriptaculous, and cropper files in the `UploadAvatar.aspx`.

```
//Fisharoo/Web/Profiles/UpdateAvatar.aspx
<script type="text/javascript" src="/js/cropper/lib/prototype.js"
       language="javascript"></script>
<script type="text/javascript"
              src="/js/cropper/lib/scriptaculous.js?
              load=builder,dragdrop" language="javascript"></script>
<script type="text/javascript" src="/js/cropper/cropper.js"
        language="javascript"></script>
```

Once you have the JavaScript side plugged in, you need to add some items to your ASPX page to get this widget factory working. To start with, we need to add an image control that will load the image that we want to operate on.

```
<asp:Image ImageUrl="~/images/ProfileAvatar/ProfileImage.aspx"
id="imgCropImage" runat="server"/>
```

Note that this Image control has an `ImageUrl` reference to a page rather than an image. The `images/ProfileAvatar/ProfileImage.aspx` page displays a user's avatar depending on the current configuration of his/her profile. If it doesn't have an avatar, it shows a default avatar. If it is decided to use the Gravatar service instead (discussed shortly) it shows the avatar stored on Gravatar.

This is optional, but the cropper script provides us with a preview of what we are doing. To implement this, we need to have a location for the preview to output in the form of a `div` tag.

```
<div id="previewWrap"></div>
```

We then need to add a JavaScript function that hooks up the cropper scripts to our UI. This script sets some of the basic properties such as what the image's ID is, where to stash the output for the preview, the minimum height and width, a fixed ratio (forcing the cropper to be a square in our case), and what to do when the cropping is complete. Also note that the name of the image control (`Content_imgCropImage`) is unlike what you would have typically seen working with earlier versions of ASP. NET. With ASP.NET 4, the control name is much simpler to get to and no longer uses the `ctl00` prefix.

```
<script type="text/javascript" language="javascript">
    Event.observe( window, 'load', function() {
        new Cropper.ImgWithPreview(
           'Content_imgCropImage',
           {
               previewWrap: 'previewWrap',
               minWidth: 100,
               minHeight: 100,
               ratioDim: {x: 100,y: 100},
              displayOnInit: true,
              onEndCrop: onEndCrop
          }
        );
    } );
</script>
```

We want the cropper to store some of the data that is captured in some hidden fields so that we can work with it on the server side. We then need to add a function that handles the `onEndCrop` event that is fired off by the cropper. This will actually handle storing the data into the `HiddenField` controls. We skip showing this part of the code as it is fairly trivial.

Moving on, once a user has selected the area of the image that he/she would like to use for the avatar and submits that selection to the server, we have what we need to perform an image crop. The presenter's `CropFile()` method will handle this task.

```
//Fisharoo/Web/Profiles/Presenters/UploadAvatarPresenter.cs
public void CropFile(Int32 X, Int32 Y, Int32 Width, Int32 Height)
{
    byte[] imageBytes = profile.Avatar.ToArray();
```

```
    using (MemoryStream ms = new MemoryStream(imageBytes, 0,
                                              imageBytes.Length))
    {
        ms.Write(imageBytes, 0, imageBytes.Length);
        System.Drawing.Image img =
             System.Drawing.Image.FromStream(ms, true);
        Bitmap bmpCropped = new Bitmap(200, 200);
        Graphics g = Graphics.FromImage(bmpCropped);
        Rectangle rectDestination = new Rectangle(0, 0,
                                bmpCropped.Width, bmpCropped.Height);
        Rectangle rectCropArea = new Rectangle(X,Y,Width,Height);
        g.DrawImage(img, rectDestination, rectCropArea,
                    GraphicsUnit.Pixel);
        g.Dispose();
        MemoryStream stream = new MemoryStream();
        bmpCropped.Save(stream,
                       System.Drawing.Imaging.ImageFormat.Jpeg);
        Byte[] bytes = stream.ToArray();
        profile.Avatar = bytes;
        _profileRepository.SaveProfile(profile);
    }
    _view.ShowApprovePanel();
}
```

This method expects the X and Y coordinates of where the crop is to start as well as the width and height of the crop. This gives us the location of the square that we plan to extract from our uploaded image.

We then load the image that is currently stored in the profile into the `imageBytes` byte array. Once we have the data stored in the array, we load it into the memory. Note that we perform this task inside a `using` statement. This ensures that all the resources are released once we complete our operation.

We then load the memory stream into an Image. Now, we create a new `Bitmap` object, `bmpCropped` with the size of the avatar that we wish to achieve. This will store our completed avatar. We then create a `Graphics` object, `g`, that will actually carry out the cropping on the `bmpCropped Bitmap`. We are now ready to actually perform the surgery on our image! We will start by creating two rectangles—one rectangle to hold our final image, and the other to hold the image to be cropped from our original image. We then call the `DrawImage()` method on our `Graphics` object and pass in our `Image`, the destination coordinates, the crop coordinates, and the unit of measure—pixels in this case. This results in the `bmpCropped` image having the appropriately cropped portion of our originally uploaded image.

Now, we pass that new image back into memory. We then convert it into a byte array, and finally save it back to our profile.

Gravatar

As we discussed earlier, Gravatar is a service that allows you to store your avatars in a central place. It allows you to associate an avatar to your email address so that other sites (like ours) can reference it later. This is great for a user who has profiles scattered all over the Internet!

In order for our users to use the Gravatar service, all they have to do is check the box on the initial page of the upload avatar screen. When they hit **submit**, we set the `UseGravatar` property of their `Profile` to `1`. Then whenever we call the `ProfileImage.aspx` page to display the avatar, we must use the Gravatar instead of the locally stored avatar.

In order to make a call into the Gravatar service, we have to create an URL with a properly formatted email address in the form of a hexadecimal `MD5` hash. We created a method in our `Cryptography` class to perform this conversion for us.

```
public static string CreateMD5Hash(string StringToHash)
{
    MD5 md5Hasher = MD5.Create();
    byte[] data =
      md5Hasher.ComputeHash(Encoding.Default.GetBytes(StringToHash));
    StringBuilder sBuilder = new StringBuilder();
    for (int i = 0; i < data.Length; i++)
    {
        sBuilder.Append(data[i].ToString("x2"));
    }
    return sBuilder.ToString();
}
```

We then created a simple extension method that handles the conversion for us in a more simplified manner than calling into the `Cryptography` suite directly.

```
public static string ToMD5Hash(this string s)
{
    return Cryptography.CreateMD5Hash(s);
}
```

With this background let's see the method.

```
//Fisharoo/Web/Images/ProfileAvatar/ProfileImage.aspx.cs
public string GetGravatarURL()
{
    defaultAvatar = Server.UrlPathEncode(_webContext.RootUrl +
                                "/images/ProfileAvatar/Male.jpg");
    gravatarURL = "http://www.gravatar.com/avatar.php?";
    gravatarURL += "gravatar_id=" + account.Email.ToMD5Hash();
```

```
        gravatarURL += "&rating=r";
        gravatarURL += "&size=80";
        gravatarURL += "&default=" + defaultAvatar;
        return gravatarURL;
    }
```

The properties that we discussed are fairly easy to figure out. However, you can get a full listing of how to work with the Gravatar service here: `http://site.gravatar.com/site/implement#section_1_1`.

Public profile

Now that we have figured out privacy, provided a way for our users to manage their profile data, and allowed them to upload and appropriately format their avatar, we need to provide our users with a page that displays all their data.

For the most part this is simply another "plumbing page", meaning that we are just displaying the data here. Nothing overly complex! So we will skip most of the legwork and get right to the nitty gritty, which is how our privacy stuff is handled.

In the `Profile.aspx` page, we have stored everything within the panels such as this:

```
//Fisharoo/Web/Profiles/Profile.aspx
<asp:Panel ID="pnlPrivacyAccountInfo" runat="server">
    <fieldset>
        <div class="divContainerTitle"> Account Info</div>
        <table class="profileInfo">
            <tr> <td>Email: </td>
                <td><asp:Literal ID="litEmail" runat="server" /></td>
            </tr>
            <tr> <td>Zip:</td>
                <td><asp:Literal ID="litZip" runat="server" /></td>
            </tr>
            <tr> <td>Birthday: </td>
                <td><asp:Literal ID="litBirthDate" runat="server" /></
                td>
            </tr>
            <tr> <td>Updated: </td>
                <td><asp:Literal ID="litLastUpdateDate" runat="server"
                />
                </td> </tr>
        </table> </fieldset>
</asp:Panel>
```

This allows us to easily lock down an area of data as needed (to hide for example). In the presenter for this page, we have a `TogglePrivacy()` method.

```
//Fisharoo/Web/Profiles/Presenters/ProfilePresenter.cs
private void TogglePrivacy()
{
    _view.pnlPrivacyIMVisible(_privacyService.ShouldShow((int)
    PrivacyFlagType.PrivacyFlagTypes.IM,_accountBeingViewed, _account,
    _privacyFlags));
    _view.pnlPrivacyAccountInfoVisible(_privacyService.
    ShouldShow((int)PrivacyFlagType.PrivacyFlagTypes.AccountInfo,_
    accountBeingViewed,
    _account, _privacyFlags));
    _view.pnlPrivacyTankInfoVisible(_privacyService.ShouldShow((int)
    PrivacyFlagType.PrivacyFlagTypes.TankInfo,_accountBeingViewed,
    _account, _privacyFlags));
}
```

This method makes a call to the `PrivacyService.ShouldShow()` method, that returns a Boolean value of whether or not the item should be displayed. This Boolean value is directly set to the `Panel.Visible` property in the view that effectively shows or hides the data in question.

Custom homepage

When we say "custom homepage", we are really referring to the public profile page in an easy to get manner. This is really a fancy URL, something like `http://www.fisharoo.com/profiles/atulgupta`. We could even take it as far as `http://atulgupta.fisharoo.com` or something along those lines! We will however stick with the first example in our case.

To implement this we will use ASP.NET Routing support. ASP.NET 4 improves on its URL routing feature in a number of ways. These are now SEO-friendly URLs and ASP.NET 4 MVC relies heavily on this feature. At the very core, URL routing is a feature that allows your application to accept URLs that do not map to physical files. The friendly URL that we mentioned above (`http://www.fisharoo.com/profiles/atulgupta`) doesn't map to a physical file on the server, yet our application is capable of serving it.

Implementation logic for this is fairly straightforward. We need to first define an URL pattern that we would like to accept as valid for our application. This is added to a `RouteTable`. The entry in the table also specifies which page to redirect to in case the pattern matches. Finally in the specific page, we query for the values that were passed in to the page (similar to query string parameters) and then go ahead and process in the way we want to. The `RouteTable` entry is added to the `Global.asax.cs` file in `Application_Start` method.

```
void Application_Start(object sender, EventArgs e)
{
    . . .// Code that runs on application startup
    RegisterRoutes(RouteTable.Routes);
}

public static void RegisterRoutes(RouteCollection routeCollection)
{
    //profile URL - //http://appname/profiles/username
    routeCollection.MapPageRoute("ProfileRoute", "profiles/
    {username}", "~/Profiles/Profile.aspx");
}
```

The key part is the call to `MapPageRoute` method of `RouteCollection` object. We are passing three parameters to this method:

- The first parameter is a name that we are giving to this route (`ProfileRoute`) and can be used later to query back this particular route's details.
- The second parameter is the URL pattern that we want to match (`profiles/{username}`). A few points to note here: the URL pattern is specified by excluding the server name and the application name. Any place holder values like in query string, are mentioned within the curly brackets {}. In our case the username is like a variable and will have the value as specified in the URL. So if you enter an URL like `http://www.fisharoo.com/profiles/atulgupta`, the value of `username` will be `atulgupta`.
- The third parameter is the path to the actual `aspx` page that will handle this request. In this case it is `Profile.aspx` which is inside `Profiles` folder.

Once this is done, we then need to add the necessary processing logic to `Profile.aspx.cs` page in its `Page_Load` method.

```
//Fisharoo/Web/Profiles/Profile.aspx.cs
protected void Page_Load(object sender, EventArgs e)
{
    _presenter = new ProfilePresenter();
     string username = Page.RouteData.Values["username"] as string;
    _presenter.Init(this, username);
}
```

The values from the routed URL are added to the `RouteData` collection and are accessible from the `Page` class. We extract this value, cast it is as string and then pass it to our presenter to take further action based on this value. The specific part of the presenter's `Init()` method, which is of interest here is as follows:

```
if (string.IsNullOrEmpty(username))
    _accountBeingViewed = userSession.CurrentUser;
else
    _accountBeingViewed = accountService.
    GetAccountByUsername(username);
```

If the passed in username is valid then we query for that account and display it. That's all there is to URL routing and getting it to support our fancy URL requirement.

In case you are wondering won't a direct call to the `Profile.aspx` page (`http://www.fisharoo.com/profiles/profile.aspx`) match the URL route we have defined and the `username` parameter being set to `profile.aspx`, the answer is **No**. The routing engine by default excludes all calls that match to physical files.

News feed/Alerts

The last concept that we will cover in our discussion about building profiles is news feed (or alerts). A news feed allows us to see what we have been doing with our account, friends, our photos, and any other changes in the system. More importantly, it will allow us to see what our friends have been doing with all their data such as when they add a new photo.

This system will be built on the alerts system that we have already discussed. Any time we want to add a new alert to the system based on an action performed by our user or the system, we simply make a call into the `AlertService` and select the appropriate method such as `AddNewAvatarAlert()`. Once the site is peppered with the addition of alerts to the system we will have fairly active news feed to follow. Now, we just need a place to read this feed!

Knowing that this news feed will easily be one of the most active pages on our site, we should put it on the users' homepage so that they can see it as soon as they log in. To implement this, all we need is a repeater with a label in it, on the homepage, which we can hook up to a list of alerts for the current user. See the code for `//Fisharoo/Web/Profiles/Default.aspx` page.

Then from the presenter, we need to pass the view, the appropriate data to bind to. We get the list of alerts, convert them into a list of strings and pass it to the view to display.

```
//Fisharoo/Web/Profiles/Presenters/Defaultpresenter.cs
private void ShowDisplay()
{
    List<string> msgs = new List<string>();
    List<Alert> alerts = _alertService.GetAlertsByAccountID(
                              _userSession.CurrentUser.AccountID);
    foreach (Alert item in alerts)
    {
        msgs.Add(item.Message);
    }
    _view.ShowAlerts(msgs);
}
```

Once we get into the concept of *Friends*, this page will be much more active as users can see their alerts as well as their friends!

Summary

We have covered a lot of ground in this chapter. We have discussed the concept of a profile and a way for our users to manage their data. We have also built a way for our users to manage their privacy regarding their profile data. We have also created tools for our users to manage a custom avatar as well as a way to hook up to their centrally stored Gravatar. With all of these features out of the way, we have created a public profile for our users. And finally, we also created a default landing page for users where they can see their alerts.

5
Friends

The subject of this chapter is the key to the success of any community. Your friend features will be the main reason for people to interact with your community. It is also the biggest drive for your users to advertise for you. "Hey Peter, come and check this out. I love it, so will you!"—a friend in a community site, like in life, is someone who you have something in common with, enjoy the company of, or turn to when you have something to discuss. A circle of friends can be thought of as a sub-community within a community.

This chapter will show you how to take advantage of people's nature to congregate around things that they enjoy, find useful, or that intrigue them. We will start this chapter by extending the framework to allow for relationships to be built between our users. We will then add some features that allow our users to locate all of their existing friends, as well as make new friends. Then we will have a discussion about providing real time status updates in the form of a micro blog so that all of our friends can stay in touch with everything we are doing.

Problem

There are many aspects to building relationships in any community—real or virtual. First and foremost is initiating contact with the people whom you will eventually call your friends. The easiest way to locate someone who you might want to call a friend is to directly invite the people who you already know as a friend. We will do this in a few ways.

1. First, we will provide a way for our users to search the site for friends who are also the members.

2. Second, we will create a form that allows you to enter your friends' email IDs and invite them directly.

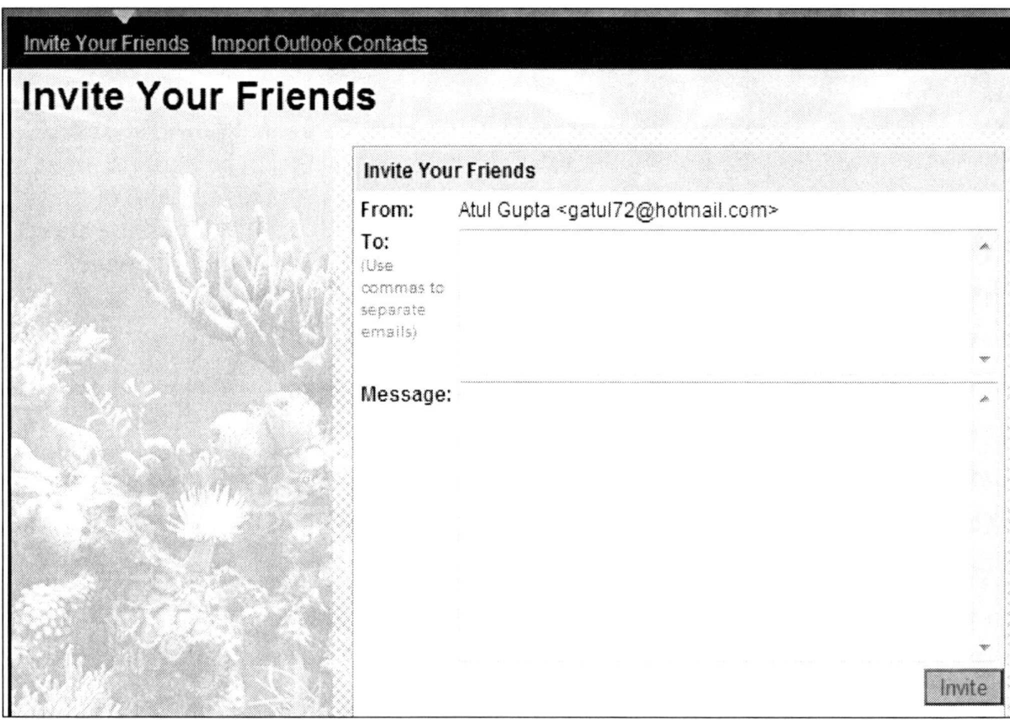

3. Third, we will create a form that allows you to import all of your contacts from the Outlook.

All of these methods of inviting a friend into the system would of course generate an email invite (and eventually a system-based message—see next chapter). The user will have the ability to then follow the link into the system and either sign up or log in to accept the request. Once the user has clicked on the link in their email, he/she will be taken to a page displaying the request.

Once we have a way for our users to attach friends to their profile, we need to start integrating the concept of friends into the fabric of our site. We will need a way for our users to view all of their friends. We will also need a way for our users to remove the relationships (for those users who are no longer friends!).

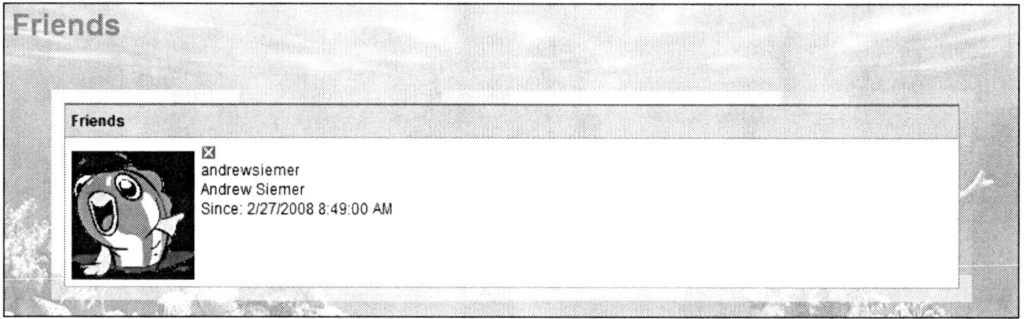

Finally we will need to add friends to our user's public profile.

While this is a good first pass at integrating the concept of friends into our site, there are a couple more steps for true integration. We need to add a friend request and friend confirm alerts. We also need to modify the alert system so that when users modify their profile, change their avatar, or any other alert that is triggered by users of our system, all of their friends are notified via alerts.

In the current world, anyone who has an online presence is also typically active on Twitter. It is a micro-blogging platform and mostly gets used by people for:

- What they are currently doing
- Where they are or
- What they are thinking about
- Or just about anything they want to write about

We will build a similar platform for our community site as shown in the following screenshot. Users can update this and the updates will be sent to their friends as alerts.

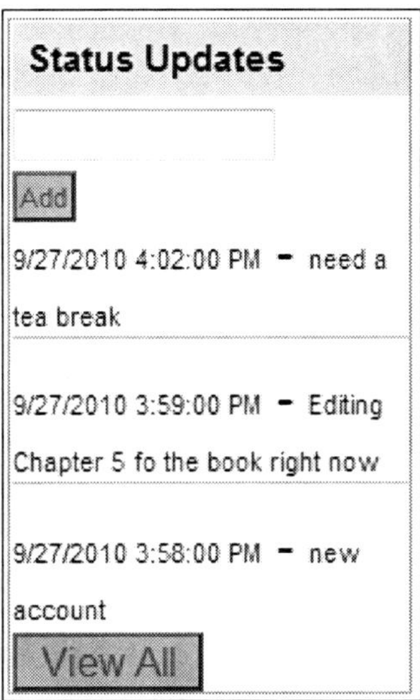

The box in the preceding screenshot is where the user can enter his/her **Status Updates**. Each of these updates will also be shown on the updates view and in their alerts view.

Such alerts/notifications keep the people aware of what their friends are up to and keep them involved with their friends.

Design

Now let's talk about the design of these features.

Friends

This chapter is an attempt to throw light on the infrastructure needs and more heavily focus on the UI side for creating and managing relationships. That being said, there is always some form of groundwork that has to be in place prior to adding new features.

In this case we need to add the concept of a friend prior to having the ability to create friendships. This concept is a relatively simple one as it is really only defining a relationship between two accounts. We have the account that requested the relationship and the account that accepted the relationship. This allows an account to be linked to as many other accounts as they wish.

Finding friends

The Friends feature will not go anywhere if there is no way for people to find friends. For that reason the various ways to locate and invite someone to be your friend is our first topic.

Searching for a friend

The easiest way to locate friends who might be interested in the same site as you are is to search through the existing user base. For that reason we will need to create a simple keyword search box that is accessible from any page on the site. This search feature should take a look at several fields of data pertaining to an account and return all possible users. From the search results page we should be able to initiate a friend request.

Inviting a friend

The next best thing to locating friends who are already members of the site is to invite people who you know out of the site. The quickest way to implement this is to allow a user to manually enter an email address or many email addresses, type a message, and then submit. This would be implemented with a simple form that generates a quick email to the recipient list. In the body of the email will be a link that allows the recipients to come in to our site.

Importing friends from external sources

An obvious extension of the last topic is to somehow automate the importing process of contacts from an email management tool. We will show how the user can export their contacts from Outlook and import them via a web form. The user should then be able to select the contacts that they want to invite.

Sending an invitation

With all three of the above methods we will end up sending out an invitation email. We could simply send out an email with a link to the site. However, we need to maintain:

- Who has been invited?
- Who initiated the invitation? and
- When this occurred?

In the email, rather than just inviting people in, we want to assign the user a key so that we can easily identify them on their way in. We will use a system-generated GUID to do this. In the case of inviting an existing user, we will allow him/her to log in to acknowledge the new friendship. In the case of a non-member user who was invited, we will allow him/her to create a new account. In both cases we will populate the invitation with the invited user's Account ID so that we have some history about the relationship.

Adding friend alerts

Once we have the framework in place for inviting and accepting friendship requests, we need to extend our existing system with alerts. These alerts should show up on the existing user's Alerts page to show that they sent an invitation. For existing users, we should have alerts showing that they have been invited. Once a user has accepted a friendship we should also have a related alert.

Interacting with your friends

Now let's discuss some of the features that we need to interact with our friends.

Viewing your friends

Friends are only good if a user can interact with them. The first stop along this train of thought is to provide a page that allows a user to see all the friends he/she has. This is a jumping off point for a user to view the profile of friends. Also, as the concept of a user's profile grows, more data can be shown about each friend in an at-a-glance format.

In addition to an all **Friends** page, we can add friends' views to a user's public profile so that other users can see the relationships.

Managing your friends

Now that we can see into all the relationships we can finally provide the users with the ability to remove a relationship, in our initial pass this will be a permanent deletion of the relationship.

Following your friends

We can extend the alert system so that when alerts are generated for a user, such as updating their profile information, uploading a new photo, or any other user-specific task, all the user's friends are also notified via their Alerts page.

Providing status updates to your friends

We have briefly touched on this already in earlier sections. Users can write a short message as their status update/micro blob and this will show up on the Alerts page of all the user's friends. This feature creates a lot of dynamic content on an end user's homepage, which keeps things interesting.

Solution

Now let's look at our solution.

Implementing the database

Let's look at the tables that are needed to support these new features.

The friends table

As the concept of friends is our base discussion for this chapter, we will immediately dive in and start creating the tables around this subject. As you have read previously this is a very straightforward table structure that simply links one account to the other.

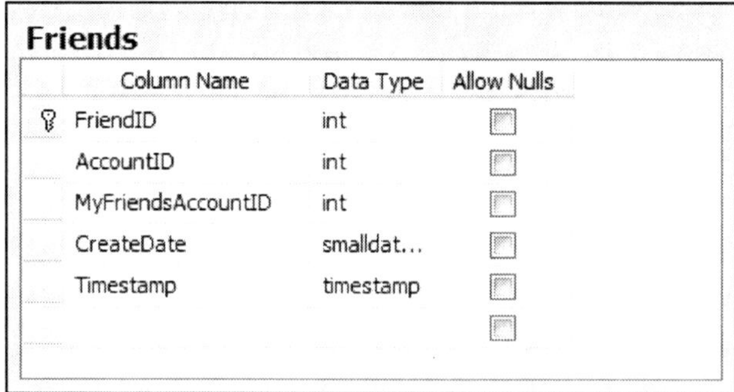

Friends

Column Name	Data Type	Allow Nulls
FriendID	int	
AccountID	int	
MyFriendsAccountID	int	
CreateDate	smalldat...	
Timestamp	timestamp	

Friend invitations

This table is responsible for keeping track of who has been invited to the site, by whom, and when. It also holds the key (**GUID**) that is sent to the friends so that they can get back into the system under the appropriate invitation. Once a friend has accepted the relationship, their **AccountID** is stored here too, so that we can see how relationships were created in the past.

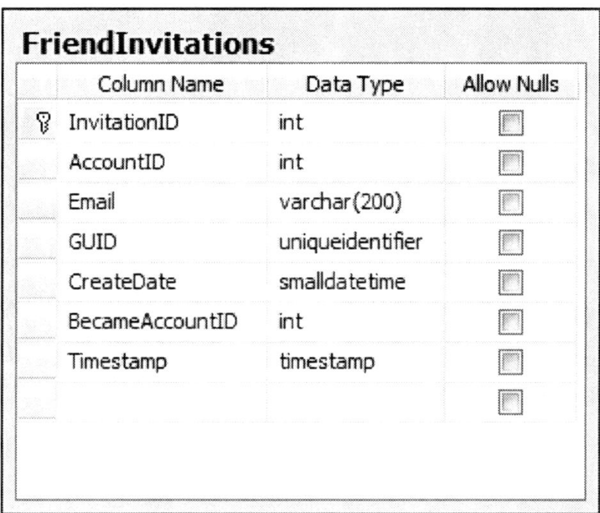

FriendInvitations

	Column Name	Data Type	Allow Nulls
🔑	InvitationID	int	☐
	AccountID	int	☐
	Email	varchar(200)	☐
	GUID	uniqueidentifier	☐
	CreateDate	smalldatetime	☐
	BecameAccountID	int	☐
	Timestamp	timestamp	☐
			☐

Status updates

Status Updates allow a user to tell their friends what they are doing at that time. This is a micro blog so to speak.

A **micro blog** allows a user to write small blurbs about anything. Examples of this are Twitter and Yammer. For more information take a look here at: `http://en.wikipedia.org/wiki/Micro-blogging`.

The table needed for this is also simple. It tracks who said what, what was said, and when.

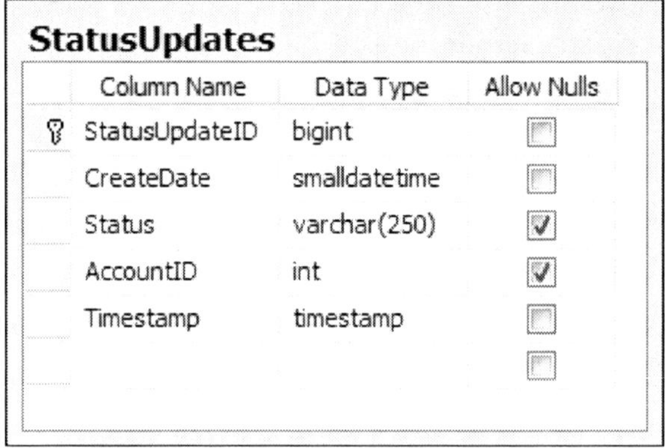

StatusUpdates

	Column Name	Data Type	Allow Nulls
🔑	StatusUpdateID	bigint	☐
	CreateDate	smalldatetime	☐
	Status	varchar(250)	☑
	AccountID	int	☑
	Timestamp	timestamp	☐
			☐

Creating the relationships

Here are the relationships that we need for the tables we just discussed:

- `Friends` and `Accounts` via the owning account
- `Friends` and `Accounts` via the friends account
- `FriendInvitations` and `Accounts`
- `StatusUpdates` and `Accounts`

Setting up the data access layer

Let's extend the data access layer now to handle these new tables that we just discussed. Open your `Fisharoo.edmx` file and add these three new tables. Once you hit **Save** we should have three new classes to work with.

Building repositories

As always, with these new tables will come new repositories. The following repositories will be created:

- `FriendRepository`
- `FriendInvitationRepository`
- `StatusUpdateRepository`

In addition to the creation of the above repositories, we will also need to modify the `AccountRepository`. Let's look at each of these repositories one by one.

FriendRepository

Our repositories will always follow the same design. They provide a way to get at one record, many records by a parent ID, save a record, and delete a record.

This repository however differs slightly from the norm when it is time to retrieve a list of friends. It has two sides of the relationship to look at—on one side where it is the owning account of the friend relationship, and on the other side the relationship is owned by another account. Here is that method:

```
//Fisharoo/DataAccess/Repositories/FriendRepository.cs
public List<Friend> GetFriendsByAccountID(Int32 AccountID)
{
    List<Friend> result = new List<Friend>();
    using (FisharooDataContext dc = conn.GetContext())
    {
        //Get my friends direct relationship
        IEnumerable<Friend> friends = (from f in dc.Friends
                                       where f.AccountID == AccountID
                                       &&
                                       f.MyFriendsAccountID !=
                                       AccountID
                                       select f).Distinct();
                                       result = friends.ToList();


        ////Get my friends indirect relationship

        IEnumerable<Friend> friends2 = (from f in dc.Friends
               where f.MyFriendsAccountID == AccountID &&
               f.AccountID != AccountID  select f).Distinct();

        foreach (Friend f in friends2)
        {
            if (f != null)
            {
                var tempFriendsAccountId = f.MyFriendsAccountID;
                var tempAccountId = f.AccountID;
                f.AccountID = tempFriendsAccountId;
                f.MyFriendsAccountID = tempAccountId;
                result.Add(f);
            }
        }
    }
    return result;
}
```

This method queries all friends that are owned by this account. Note that the LINQ to Entity query returns `IEnumerable<T>`, where `T` is the class. We want to return `List<Friend>` which is achieved by calling `friends.ToList()`.

It then queries for the reverse relationship where this account is owned by another account. Then it adds the second query to the first and returns that result.

Here is the method that gets the Accounts of our Friends.

```
//Fisharoo/DataAccess/Repositories/FriendRepository.cs
public List<Account> GetFriendsAccountsByAccountID(Int32 AccountID)
{
    List<Friend> friends = GetFriendsByAccountID(AccountID);
    List<int> accountIDs = new List<int>();
    foreach (Friend friend in friends)
    {
        accountIDs.Add(friend.MyFriendsAccountID);
    }

    List<Account> result = new List<Account>();
    using(FisharooDataContext dc = conn.GetContext())
    {
        IEnumerable<Account> accounts = from a in dc.Accounts
                     where accountIDs.Contains(a.AccountID)  select
                     a;
        result = accounts.ToList();
    }
    return result;
}
```

This method first gathers all the friends (via the first method we discussed) and then queries all the related accounts and returns the result.

FriendInvitationRepository

Like the other repositories this one has the standard methods and we don't list them here. Refer to the code associated with this chapter for details. In addition to those we also need to be able to retrieve an invitation by **GUID** or the invitation key that was sent to the friend.

```
//Fisharoo/DataAccess/Repositories/FriendInvitationRepository.cs
public FriendInvitation GetFriendInvitationByGUID(Guid guid)
{
    FriendInvitation friendInvitation;
    using(FisharooDataContext dc = conn.GetContext())
    {
```

```
            friendInvitation = dc.FriendInvitations.Where(fi => fi.GUID
                                               == guid).FirstOrDefault();
        }
        return friendInvitation;
    }
```

This is a very straightforward query matching the **GUID** values. In addition to the above method we will also need a way for invitations to be cleaned up. For this reason we have the following method:

```
//Fisharoo/DataAccess/Repositories/FriendInvitationRepository.cs
public void CleanUpFriendInvitationsForThisEmail(FriendInvitation
friendInvitation)
{
    using (FisharooDataContext dc = conn.GetContext())
    {
        IEnumerable<FriendInvitation> friendInvitations
                        = from fi in dc.FriendInvitations
                        where fi.Email == friendInvitation.Email &&
                        fi.BecameAccountID == 0 &&
                        fi.AccountID == friendInvitation.AccountID
                        select fi;
        foreach (FriendInvitation invitation in friendInvitations)
        {
            dc.FriendInvitations.DeleteObject(invitation);
        }
        dc.SaveChanges();
    }
}
```

This method is responsible for clearing out any invitations in the system that are sent from account A to account B and have not been activated (account B never did anything with the invite). Rather than checking if the invitation already exists when it is created, we will allow them to be created time and again (checking each invite during the import process of 500 contacts could really slow things down!). When account B finally accepts one of the invitations all of the others will be cleared. Also, in case account B never does anything with the invites, we will need a database process that periodically cleans out old invitations.

StatusUpdateRepository

The method of interest in this repository is the one that gets `topN StatusUpdates` for use on the profile page.

```
//Fisharoo/DataAccess/Repositories/StatusUpdateRepository.cs
public List<StatusUpdate> GetTopNStatusUpdatesByAccountID(Int32
AccountID, Int32 Number)
{
    List<StatusUpdate> result;
    using (FisharooDataContext dc = conn.GetContext())
    {
        IEnumerable<StatusUpdate> statusUpdates = (from su in
                                    dc.StatusUpdates
                                    where su.AccountID ==
                                    AccountID
                                    orderby su.CreateDate descending
                                    select
                                    su).Take(Number);
        result = statusUpdates.ToList();
    }
    return result;
}
```

This is done with a standard LINQ to Entity query with the addition of the `Take()` method, that translates into a `TOP` statement in the resulting SQL.

AccountRepository

With the addition of our search capabilities we will require a new method in our `AccountRepository`. This method will be the key for searching accounts.

```
public List<Account> SearchAccounts(string SearchText)
{
    List<Account> result = new List<Account>();
    using (FisharooDataContext dc = conn.GetContext())
    {
        IEnumerable<Account> accounts = from a in dc.Accounts
                where(a.FirstName + " " +
                a.LastName).Contains(SearchText) ||
                a.Email.Contains(SearchText) ||
                a.Username.Contains(SearchText)
                select a;
        result = accounts.ToList();
    }
    return result;
}
```

This method currently searches through a user's first name, last name, email address, and username. This could of course be extended to their profile data and many other data points (all in good time!).

- Implementing the services/application layer

Now that we have the repositories in place we can begin to create the services that sit on top of those repositories. We will be creating one service per repository added and in addition to that we will also be extending these services:

- `AlertService`
- `PrivacyService`

FriendService

The `FriendService` currently has a couple of duties. We will need it to tell us whether or not a user is a `Friend` or not so that we can extend the `PrivacyService` to consider friends (recall that we currently only understand public and private settings!). In addition to that we need our `FriendService` to be able to handle creating `Friends` from a `FriendInvitation`.

```
//Fisharoo/BusinessLogic/FriendService.cs
public bool IsFriend(Account account, Account accountBeingViewed)
{
    if(account == null)
        return false;
    if(accountBeingViewed == null)
        return false;
    if(account.AccountID == accountBeingViewed.AccountID)
        return true;
    else
    {
        Friend friend =
                  _friendRepository.GetFriendsByAccountID
                  (accountBeingViewed.AccountID).
                  Where(f => f.MyFriendsAccountID ==
                  account.AccountID).FirstOrDefault();
        if(friend != null)
            return true;
    }
    return false;
}
```

This method needs to know who (user account) is making the request as well as to whom the request is made to made to? It then verifies that both of the accounts are valid so that we can use them down the road and returns `false` if either of them is invalid. We then check to see if the user that is doing the viewing is the same user as is being viewed. If so we can safely return `true`. Then comes the fun part—currently we are using the `GetFriendsByAccountID` method found in the `FriendRepository`. We iterate through that list to see if our friend is there in the list or not. If we locate it, we return `true`. Otherwise the method has failed to locate a result and returns `false`.

> Keep in mind that this way of doing things could quickly become a major performance issue. If someone had 500 friends this would not be acceptable. As our goal is for people to have lots of friends, we generally would not want to follow this way. Your best bet then is to create a LINQ query in the `FriendsRepository` to handle this logic directly only by returning `true` or `false`. An alternative will be to use caching.

Now comes our `CreateFriendFromFriendInvitation` method, which as the name suggests creates a friend from a friend invitation.

```
//Fisharoo/BusinessLogic/FriendService.cs
public bool CreateFriendFromFriendInvitation(Guid InvitationKey,
Account InvitationTo, bool ExistingMember)
{
    //update friend invitation request
    FriendInvitation friendInvitation = _friendInvitationRepository.Ge
    tFriendInvitationByGUID(InvitationKey);
    //validate if the friend request is for the same person who has
    logged in
    //however if this is a new member (new registration), then don't
    validate as the
    //person may use a different email during registration
    if(ExistingMember && (friendInvitation.Email != InvitationTo.
Email))
        return false;

    friendInvitation.BecameAccountID = InvitationTo.AccountID;
    _friendInvitationRepository.SaveFriendInvitation(friendInvitati
    on);
    _friendInvitationRepository.CleanUpFriendInvitationsForThisEmail(f
    riendInvitation);

    //create friendship
    Friend friend = new Friend();
    friend.AccountID = friendInvitation.AccountID;
    friend.MyFriendsAccountID = InvitationTo.AccountID;
```

```
        _friendRepository.SaveFriend(friend);

        Account InvitationFrom = _accountRepository.
        GetAccountByID(friendInvitation.AccountID);
        _alertService.AddFriendAddedAlert(InvitationFrom, InvitationTo);
        return true;
    }
```

This method expects the `InvitationKey` (in the form of a system-generated GUID) and the `Account` that is wishing to create the relationship. It then gets the `FriendInvitation` and updates the `BecameAccountID` property of the new friend. We then make a call to flush any other friend invites between these two users. Once we have everything cleaned up we add a new alert to the system (covered shortly) letting the account that initiated this invitation know that the invitation was accepted.

Notice that we will also need to add something here to send a message via the messaging system (covered in the next chapter!).

AlertService

The alert service is essentially a wrapper to post an alert to the user's profile. All the plumbing for this was covered in a previous chapter. So the additional methods that we have added are very similar to what was done previously. We will not describe these methods here. You can look up the `AddStatusUpdateAlert()`, `AddFriendRequestAlert()` and `AddFriendAddedAlert()` methods in the `AlertService` class (available as part of the code associated with this Chapter).

PrivacyService

Now that we have a method to check if two people are friends or not, we can finally extend our `PrivacyService` to account for friends. Remember that up to this point we are only interrogating whether something is marked as private or public. There is only a minor change in the code.

```
//Fisharoo/BusinessLogic/PrivacyService.cs
public bool ShouldShow(Int32 PrivacyFlagTypeID,
    Account AccountBeingViewed, Account Account, List<PrivacyFlag>
Flags)
{
    bool result;

    bool isFriend = _friendService.IsFriend(Account,AccountBeingView
    ed);
    . . .
    //rest of the code is as is
}
```

All we did here is pointed the `isFriend` variable at the result of the new `IsFriend()` method in the `FriendService`. Everything else was handled previously!

Implementing the Presentation layer

Now that we have the base framework in place we can start discussing what it will take to put it all together. Like we said earlier, this chapter is less about framework and more about the UI that utilizes the new and existing framework!

Searching for friends

Let's see what it takes to implement a search for friends.

SiteMaster

Let's begin with searching for friends. We haven't covered too much regarding the actual UI and nothing regarding the master page of this site. We don't want this to be about design! So we will simply say that we have added a text box and a button to the master page to take in a search phrase.

When the button is clicked the site redirects to `Search.aspx` page, passing the search phrase along with it.

Search

The `Search.aspx` page has no interface. It expects a value to be passed in from the previously discussed text box in the master page. With this text phrase we hit our `AccountService` and perform a search using the `Contains()` operator. The returned list of `Accounts` is then displayed on the page.

For the most part, this page is all about MVP plumbing. We are going to assume that you are up to speed with MVP, from this point on stick to only the fun stuff. Here is the repeater that displays all our data.

```
//Fisharoo/Web/Search.aspx
<%@ Register Src="~/UserControls/ProfileDisplay.ascx"
TagPrefix="Fisharoo" TagName="ProfileDisplay" %>
...
<asp:Repeater ID="repAccounts" runat="server"
                  OnItemDataBound="repAccounts_ItemDataBound">
    <ItemTemplate>
        <Fisharoo:ProfileDisplay ShowDeleteButton="false"
                       ID="pdProfileDisplay" runat="server" />
    </ItemTemplate>
</asp:Repeater>
```

The following screenshot shows how the search results get displayed:

The fun stuff in this case comes in the form of the `ProfileDisplay` user control that was created so that we have an easy way to display concise profile data in various places with one chunk of reusable code that will allow us to make global changes.

You should see that we have `<Fisharoo:ProfileDisplay ... />`. You will also notice that our tag has custom properties that are set in the tag definition. In this case you see `ShowDeleteButton="false"`.

All the logic and display is very standard. You have the MVP plumbing, which makes up most of it. The `ProfileDisplay` control also has a `LoadDisplay()` method responsible for loading the UI for that control. This is invoked in the `Search` page in the `repAccounts_ItemDataBound()` method.

```
//Fisharoo/Web/Search.aspx.cs
protected void repAccounts_ItemDataBound(object sender,
                                         RepeaterItemEventArgs e)
{
    if(e.Item.ItemType == ListItemType.Item || e.Item.ItemType ==
                          ListItemType.AlternatingItem)
    {
        ProfileDisplay pd = e.Item.FindControl("pdProfileDisplay") as
                             ProfileDisplay;
        pd.LoadDisplay((Account)e.Item.DataItem);
        if(_webContext.CurrentUser == null)
            pd.ShowFriendRequestButton = false;
    }
}
```

Let's look at `ProfileDisplay` user control code in order of display, code behind, and the presenter (omitting the interface of the view as usual).

```
//Fisharoo/Web/UserControls/ProfileDisplay.ascx
<%@ Control Language="C#" AutoEventWireup="true"
CodeBehind="ProfileDisplay.ascx.cs"
```

```
    Inherits="Fisharoo.Web.UserControls.ProfileDisplay" %>
<div style="height: 116px; float: left;">
    <table>
        <tr>
            <td style="width: 102px">
                <%--NavigateURL and Image's URL will be set in code--
                %>
                <asp:HyperLink ID="imageLink" runat="server"
                Width="100" Height="100">
                    <asp:Image Style="padding: 5px; width: 100px;
                    height: 100px;" ImageAlign="Left" Width="100"
                        Height="100" ID="imgAvatar" ImageUrl="~/
                        Images/ProfileAvatar/ProfileImage.aspx"
                        runat="server" />
                </asp:HyperLink>
            </td>
            <td style="padding: 2px 2px 2px 15px; text-align: left;"
            valign="top">
                <asp:ImageButton ImageAlign="AbsMiddle"
                ID="ibInviteFriend" runat="server"
                AlternateText="Become Friends"
                    OnClick="lbInviteFriend_Click" ImageUrl="~/Images/
                    icon_friends.gif" ToolTip="Add As Friend">
                </asp:ImageButton>
                <asp:ImageButton ImageAlign="AbsMiddle" ID="ibDelete"
                runat="server" OnClick="ibDelete_Click"
                    ImageUrl="~/Images/icon_close.gif" ToolTip="Delete
                    Friend" /><br />
                <asp:HyperLink ID="linkUsername" runat="server" /><br
                />
                <asp:Label ID="lblFirstName" runat="server"></
                asp:Label>
                <asp:Label ID="lblLastName" runat="server"></
                asp:Label><br />
                Since:
                <asp:Label ID="lblCreateDate" runat="server"></
                asp:Label><br />
                <asp:Label ID="lblFriendID" runat="server"
                Visible="false"></asp:Label>
            </td>
        </tr>
    </table>
</div>
```

We will look at only the important methods in the code behind:

```
//Fisharoo/Web/UserControls/ProfileDisplay.ascx.cs
namespace Fisharoo.Web.UserControls
{
    public partial class ProfileDisplay : System.Web.UI.UserControl,
    IProfileDisplay
    {
        . . .

        public void LoadDisplay(Account account)
        {
            _account = account;
            ibInviteFriend.Attributes.Add("FriendsID",
                                         _account.AccountID.
                                         ToString());
            ibDelete.Attributes.Add("FriendsID",
                                         _account.AccountID.
                                         ToString());
            lblLastName.Text = account.LastName;
            lblFirstName.Text = account.FirstName;
            if (account.CreateDate.HasValue)
                lblCreateDate.Text = account.CreateDate.Value.
                ToShortDateString();
            imgAvatar.ImageUrl += "?AccountID=" +
                                          account.AccountID.
                                          ToString();
            linkUsername.Text = account.Username;
            //navigation URL will follow the URL routing pattern
            string url = Page.GetRouteUrl("ProfileRoute",
                                     new { username = account.Username
                                     });
            linkUsername.NavigateUrl = url;
            imageLink.NavigateUrl = url;
            lblFriendID.Text = account.AccountID.ToString();
        }
    }
}

//Fisharoo/Web/UserControls/Presenters/ProfileDisplayPresenter.cs
namespace Fisharoo.Web.UserControls.Presenters
{
    public class ProfileDisplayPresenter
    {
        . . .
```

```
            public void SendFriendRequest(Int32 AccountIdToInvite)
            {
                _redirector.GoToFriendsInviteFriends(AccountIdToInvite);
            }

            public void DeleteFriend(Int32 FriendID)
            {
                if (_userSession.CurrentUser != null)
                {
                    _friendService.DeleteFriendByID(_
                                userSession.CurrentUser.AccountID,
                                FriendID);
                    HttpContext.Current.Response.Redirect(
                                HttpContext.Current.Request.RawUrl);
                }
            }
        }
    }
```

The `ProfileDisplay` control also has a couple of properties—one to show/hide the delete friend button and the other to show/hide the invite friend button. These buttons are not appropriate for every page that the control is used in. In the search results page we want to hide the **Delete** button as the results are not necessarily friends. We would want to be able to invite them in that view. However, in a list of our friends the **Invite** button (to invite a friend) would no longer be appropriate as each of these users would already be a friend. The **Delete** button in this case would now be more appropriate.

Clicking on the **Invite** button makes a call to the `Redirector` class and routes the user to the `InviteFriends` page. An important point to note is the construction of the URL in the `LoadDisplay()` method, which takes you to the user's profile page.

You will recall that we had defined the `ProfileRoute` in previous chapter to support fancy URL directly linking to user's profile page. In order to create the link, we use the `GetRouteURL` helper method. This is useful if we end up changing our route pattern, as defined in `Global.asax.cs`, we don't need to make the changes to regenerate the URL. The `GetRouteURL` method will use the current route definition and return a valid URL.

Invite your friends

This page allows us to manually enter email addresses of friends that we want to invite. It is a standard **From**, **To**, **Message** format where the system defaults the sender (to you), and you specify who to send to and the message that you want to send.

This is a simple page so the majority of the code for it is the MVP plumbing. The only important part in the code behind is the call to the presenter to send the invitation when the **Invite** button is clicked. We will skip looking at the ASPX and the code behind file and directly jump to the presenter code.

```
//Fisharoo/Web/Friends/Presenters/InviteFriendsPresenter.cs
namespace Fisharoo.Web.Friends.Presenters
{
    public class InviteFriendsPresenter
    {
        . . .

        public void Init(IInviteFriends view)
        {
            _view = view;
            MEFManager.Compose(this);

            _account = _userSession.CurrentUser;

            if (_account != null)
            {
                _view.DisplayToData(account.FirstName + " " +
                                    _account.LastName + " &lt;" + _
                                     account.Email + "&gt;");

                if (_webContext.AccoundIdToInvite > 0)
                {
                    _accountToInvite = _accountService.
                    GetAccountByID(_webContext.AccoundIdToInvite);

                    if (_accountToInvite != null)
                    {
                        SendInvitation(_accountToInvite.Email,
                                       _account.FirstName + " " +
                    _account.LastName + " would like to be your
                    friend!");
                        _view.ShowMessage(_accountToInvite.Username +
                                          " has been sent a friend
                                          request!");
                        _view.TogglePnlInvite(false);
                    }
                }
            }
```

```
        }

        public void SendInvitation(string ToEmailArray, string
        Message)
        {
            string resultMessage = "Invitations sent to the following

            recipients:<BR>";
            Account account = _userSession.CurrentUser;
            resultMessage += _email.SendInvitations(account.AccountID,
            account.FirstName, account.LastName, ToEmailArray,
            Message);
            _view.ShowMessage(resultMessage);
            _view.ResetUI();
        }
    }
}
```

The UI is initialized based on the current user details. Once the user fills in the emails to be invited, the `SendInvitation()` method is invoked, that takes in the comma delimited array of emails and the message to be sent in the invitation. It then makes a call to the `Email.SendInvitations()` method.

```
//Fisharoo/Components/ Email.cs
public string SendInvitations(int accID, string FirstName, string
LastName, string ToEmailArray, string Message)
{
    string resultMessage = Message;
    foreach (string s in ToEmailArray.Split(','))
    {
        FriendInvitation friendInvitation = new FriendInvitation();
        friendInvitation.AccountID = accID;
        friendInvitation.Email = s;
        friendInvitation.GUID = Guid.NewGuid();
        friendInvitation.BecameAccountID = 0;
        _friendInvitationRepository.SaveFriendInvitation(

        friendInvitation);
        //add alert to existing users alerts
        Account account = _accountRepository.GetAccountByEmail(s);
        if (account != null)
        {
            _alertService.AddFriendRequestAlert(_
                                  userSession.CurrentUser, account,
                                    friendInvitation.GUID, Message);
        }
```

```
            SendFriendInvitation(s, FirstName, LastName,
                                 friendInvitation.GUID.ToString(),
                                 Message);
            resultMessage += "• " + s + "<BR>";
        }
        return resultMessage;
    }
```

This method is responsible for parsing out all the emails, creating a new `FriendInvitation`, and sending the request via email to the person who was invited. It then adds an alert to the invited user if they already have an `Account`.

Outlook CSV importer

The **Import Contacts** page is responsible for allowing our users to upload an exported contacts file from Microsoft Outlook into our system. Once they have imported their contacts the user is allowed to select which email addresses are actually invited into our system.

Importing contacts

This page is made up of a couple of views, which are created using panels. This allows us to easily show or hide an entire set of controls within a panel. In the initial view we let the user upload a CSV file, which is an exported list of Microsoft Outlook contacts. There are instructions on the page that help the user with the export operations (see the following screenshot).

There is a method in our presenter that handles the submission of CSV file from the view.

```
//Fisharoo/Web/Friends/Presenters/OutlookCsvImporterPresenter.cs
public void ParseEmails(HttpPostedFile file)
{
    using (Stream s = file.InputStream)
    {
        StreamReader sr = new StreamReader(s);
        string contacts = sr.ReadToEnd();
        _view.ShowParsedEmail(_email.ParseEmailsFromText(contacts));
    }
}
```

This method is responsible for handling the upload process of the `HttpPostedFile`. It puts the file reference into a `StreamReader` and then reads the stream into a string variable (named `contacts`). Once we have the entire list of contacts we can then call our `Email` class and parse all the emails out.

```
//Fisharoo/Components/Email.cs
public List<string> ParseEmailsFromText(string text)
{
    List<string> emails = new List<string>();
    string strRegex = @"\w+([-+.]\w+)*@\w+([-.]\w+)*\.\w+([-.]\w+)*";
    Regex re = new Regex(strRegex, RegexOptions.Multiline);
    foreach (Match m in re.Matches(text))
    {
        string email = m.ToString();
        if(!emails.Contains(email))
            emails.Add(email);
    }
    return emails;
}
```

This method expects a string that contains some email addresses that we want to parse. It then parses the emails using a regular expression. We then iterate through all the matches in the `Regex` and add the found email addresses to our list, provided they aren't already present. Once we have found all the email addresses, we will return the list of unique email addresses.

The presenter then passes that list of parsed emails to the view.

Selecting contacts

Once we have handled the upload process and parsed out the emails, we then need to display all the emails to the user so that they can select the ones they want to invite. This is another view/panel in the ASPX page.

We essentially have a checkbox list in our panel. This checkbox list is bound to the list of email addresses returned post-parsing in the presenter class.

```
//Fisharoo/Web/Friends/OutlookCsvImporter.aspx.cs
public void ShowParsedEmail(List<string> Emails)
{
    pnlUpload.Visible = false;
    pnlResult.Visible = false;
    pnlEmails.Visible = true;
    cblEmails.DataSource = Emails;
    cblEmails.DataBind();
}
```

The user can go through the list and select the ones that they want to invite into our system. Once they are through selecting the emails that they want to invite, they can click on the **Invite** button.

We then iterate through all the items in the checkbox list to locate the selected items.

```
//Fisharoo/Web/Friends/OutlookCsvImporter.aspx.cs
protected void btnInviteContacts_Click(object sender, EventArgs e)
{
    string emails = "";
    foreach (ListItem li in cblEmails.Items)
    {
        if(li != null && li.Selected)
            emails += li.Text + ",";
    }
    emails = emails.Substring(0, emails.Length - 1);
    _presenter.InviteContacts(emails);
}
```

Once we have gathered all the selected emails we pass them to the presenter to run the invitation process.

```
//Fisharoo/Web/Friends/PresentersOutlookCsvImporterPresenter.cs
public void InviteContacts(string ToEmailArray)
{
    string result = _email.SendInvitations(_userSession.CurrentUser,
                                            ToEmailArray, "");
    _view.ShowInvitationResult(result);
}
```

The presenter promptly passes the selected items to the `Email` class to handle the invitations. This is the same method that we used in the last section to invite users.

We then output the result of the emails that we invited into the third view/panel, that is a simple message that displays the emails to which the invitation was sent.

Confirm friendship

Having covered all these ways to invite someone into our site, we now need to look at what the invited user sees in the invitation. Let's start with what they would see in their inbox. The user gets an email in their inbox telling them that someone has invited them to become part of the Fisharoo community.

Once they open that email they can see the link that they can follow to the site to take advantage of the invitation. Clicking the link brings them to `server/appname/Friends/ConfirmFriendshipRequest.aspx` with a GUID for an invitation key. There are two screens that the user might see after this point.

The first screen is for the users who are already members and are currently logged into the site. It asks them to log in again to confirm the friendship.

The other screen is for the users who aren't members, or the users who aren't logged in.

The only real logic in the `ConfirmFriendshipRequest.aspx` page is to check the GUID that is passed in to make sure that it is valid. This happens in the presenter of this page.

```
//Fisharoo/Web/Friends/Presenters/ConfirmFriendshipRequestPresenter.cs
public void Init(IConfirmFriendshipRequest view)
{
    _view = view;
    if (!string.IsNullOrEmpty(_webContext.FriendshipRequest))
    {
        FriendInvitation friendInvitation =
            _friendInvitationRepository.GetFriendInvitationByGUID(new
                                Guid(_webContext.FriendshipRequest));
        if(friendInvitation != null)
        {
            if (_webContext.CurrentUser != null)
                LoginClick();

            Account account =
                        _accountRepository.GetAccountByID
                        (friendInvitation.AccountID);
            _view.ShowConfirmPanel(true);
            _view.LoadDisplay(_webContext.FriendshipRequest,
                         account.AccountID, account.FirstName,
                        account.LastName, _configuration.SiteName );
        }
        else
        {
            _view.ShowConfirmPanel(false);
            _view.ShowMessage("There was an error validating your
                              invitation.");
        }
    }
}
```

Either we can load a friendInvitation from the GUID or not. If we can, then we check to see if the user is already a member of the system and logged in. If they are logged in we automatically redirect them to the login screen. Otherwise we prompt them to log in or create an account. If the friendInvitation can't be loaded properly then we show an error explaining that.

The real magic occurs for the invitation process in the login and registration pages.

Login

In the login presenter we have added some logic to the Init method to recognize if we have a friendship request or not.

```
//Fisharoo/Web/Accounts/Presenters/LoginPresenter.css
public void Init(ILogin view)
{
    _view = view;
    . . .
    if(!string.IsNullOrEmpty(_webContext.FriendshipRequest))
        _view.DisplayMessage("Login to add this friend!");
}
```

This logic lets the user know that by logging in they will be accepting the friend request.

Then in the AccountService.cs file we have added some additional logic. If the login is a success and if there is a friend request, we confirm the request and make these two users friends, via the FriendService we discussed earlier. However, before making friends, we need to validate if the friend request is really meant for the account that has been logged into. If not we display appropriate error message and don't allow the user to log in.

```
//Fisharoo/BusinessLogic/AccountService.cs
public string Login(string Username, string Password)
{
    ...
            if (account.EmailVerified)
            {
                _userSession.LoggedIn = true;
                _userSession.Username = Username;
                _userSession.CurrentUser = account

                if(!string.IsNullOrEmpty(_webContext.
                                 FriendshipRequest))
                {
```

```
                    If(!_friendService.
                    CreateFriendFromFriendInvitation(
                    new Guid(_webContext.FriendshipRequest),
                    _userSession.CurrentUser, true))
                   {
                         return @"The Friend invitation is not meant
                         for the account you are logging in with.
                         Kindly login with the right account";
                    }
                }
                ...
}
```

Registration

If the invited friend is not already a user of the site, then we allow them to walk through the registration site as normal. Once the registration is complete, we not only register them but we also create the friendship.

```
//Fisharoo/Web/Accounts/Presenters/RegisterPresenter.css
public void Register(string Username, string Password,
                    string FirstName, string LastName, string Email,
                    string Zip, DateTime BirthDate, bool
                    isCaptchaValid,
                    bool AgreesWithTerms, Int32 TermID)
{
    ...
                //if this registration came via a friend request...
                if(friendInvitation != null)
                {
                    _friendService.CreateFriendFromFriendInvitation(n
                    ew Guid(_webContext.FriendshipRequest),newAccount,
                    false);
                }
...
}
```

Show friends

Now that we have everything we need to invite and accept a friend, we need the ability to see our friends. For this we will add to our Friends section landing page (`Default.aspx`) a list of all our friends. This will be actually quite easy as we will use our `ProfileDisplay` user control that we created earlier for our `Search` page.

This page will simply consist of a repeater with our `ProfileDisplay` control. We set the `ShowFriendRequestButton` to `false` as these are already our friends.

Our presenter then loads the display with all the current user's friends by calling into the `FriendService` and passing that collection down to the view.

```
//Fisharoo/Web/Friends/Presenters/DefaultPresenter.cs
public void LoadDisplay()
{
    _view.LoadDisplay(
                _friendService.GetFriendsAccountsByAccountID
                                    (_userSession.CurrentUser.
                                    AccountID));
}
```

The view then hooks up the repeater's data source. On each `ItemDataBound` of the repeater we spin up the `ProfileDisplay` user control

```
//Fisharoo/Web/Friends/Default.aspx.cs
protected void repFriends_ItemDataBound(object sender,
                                        RepeaterItemEventArgs e)
{
    if(e.Item.ItemType == ListItemType.Item || e.Item.ItemType ==
       ListItemType.AlternatingItem)
    {
        ProfileDisplay pdProfileDisplay =
            e.Item.FindControl("pdProfileDisplay") as ProfileDisplay;
          pdProfileDisplay.LoadDisplay(((Account)e.Item.DataItem));
    }
}
```

We then end up with the output as shown in the following screenshot:

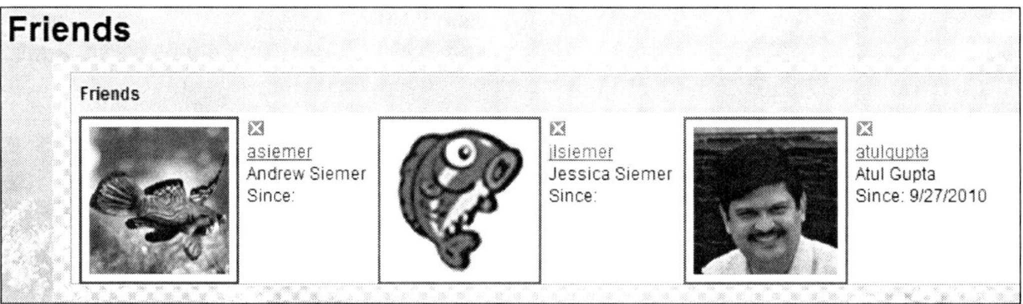

We have not done it yet, but down the road we are most likely to have some form of pagination implemented here too!

Friends on profile

After having a page that shows all of our friends, it should be easy to update our public profile to show a handful of friends. To do this we will open the `Profile.aspx` page and add to it a bit.

We are simply going to add the same sort of repeater to the profile page as we did in the case of the `Friends/Default.aspx` page.

```
//Fisharoo/Web/Profiles/Profile.aspx
<asp:Repeater ID="repFriends" runat="server"
                  OnItemDataBound="repFriends_ItemDataBound">
    <ItemTemplate>
        <Fisharoo:ProfileDisplay ShowFriendRequestButton="false"
                  ShowDeleteButton="false" ID="pdProfileDisplay"
                             runat="server" />
    </ItemTemplate>
</asp:Repeater>
```

Then in our `ProfilePresenter.cs` file we have added a line that loads that repeater.

```
//Fisharoo/Web/Profiles/Presenters/ProfilePresenter.aspx
public void Init(IProfile View)
{
    _view = View;
    . . . .
    _view.LoadFriends(
            _friendService.GetFriendsAccountsByAccountID(
            _accountBeingViewed.AccountID));
    . . . .
}
```

And in the `Profile.aspx.cs` file we have added an event handler for `repFriends_ItemDataBound()` that takes care of loading each `ProfileDisplay` control.

```
//Fisharoo/Web/Profiles/Profile.aspx.cs
protected void repFriends_ItemDataBound(object sender,
                                        RepeaterItemEventArgs e)
{
    if(e.Item.ItemType == ListItemType.Item || e.Item.ItemType ==
                          ListItemType.AlternatingItem)
    {
        ProfileDisplay pdProfileDisplay =
            e.Item.FindControl("pdProfileDisplay") as ProfileDisplay;
            pdProfileDisplay.LoadDisplay(((Account)e.Item.DataItem));
    }
}
```

Status updates

Status updates (our micro blog) are very simple to implement at this point. We will need to open the master page and add a small section to take in and display a top listing of these updates.

In our master page we will add a panel to our global display. It will be responsible for taking in new updates as well as displaying the most recent updates.

```
//Fisharoo/Web.Site.master
<%@ Import Namespace="Fisharoo.Web.HelperClasses" %>
. . . .
<asp:Panel ID="pnlStatusUpdate" runat="server">
    <fieldset>
        <div class="divContainerTitle">
            Status Updates</div>
        <asp:TextBox Width="85" Style="font-size: 9px; padding-left:
        0px; padding-right: 0px;"
            ID="txtStatusUpdate" runat="server"></asp:TextBox>
        <br />
        <asp:Button CssClass="SiteButton" Style="font-size: 9px;
        padding-left: 1px; padding-right: 1px;"
            ID="btnAddStatus" runat="server" Text="Add"
            OnClick="btnAddStatus_Click" /><br />
        <asp:Repeater runat="server" ID="repStatus">
            <ItemTemplate>
                <asp:Label ID="Label1" Text='<%# ((PEStatusUpdate)
                Container.DataItem).CreateDate.ToString() %>'
                    runat="server" Style="font-size: 9px;"></
                    asp:Label>
                -
                <asp:Label ID="Label2" Text='<%# ((PEStatusUpdate)
                Container.DataItem).Status %>'
                    runat="server" Style="font-size: 9px;"></
                    asp:Label>
            </ItemTemplate>
            <SeparatorTemplate>
                <div class="divContainerSeparator">
                </div>
            </SeparatorTemplate>
        </asp:Repeater>
        <br />
        <asp:Button CssClass="SiteButton" ID="btnShowAllStatusUpdates"
        runat="server" Text="View All"
            OnClick="btnShowAllStatusUpdates_Click" />
    </fieldset>
</asp:Panel>
```

An important point to note here is the introduction of a new class `PEStatusUpdate`. Instead of directly binding the entity object to the UI, we create this new value object (explained in Chapter 2) which essentially is a sub-set of the `StatusUpdate` entity object and has only the relevant fields as required by the UI. It can be called as presentation entity. To create this, we also added a new helper class `Translator` that manages the conversion. The code for these two classes is as below:

```
//Fisharoo/Web/HelperClasses/PEStatusUpdate.cs
namespace Fisharoo.Web.HelperClasses
{
    public class PEStatusUpdate
    {
        public DateTime CreateDate { get; set; }
        public string Status { get; set; }

        public PEStatusUpdate(DateTime dt, string msg)
        {
            CreateDate = dt;
            Status = msg;
        }
    }
}

//Fisharoo/Web/HelperClasses/Translator.cs
namespace Fisharoo.Web.HelperClasses
{
    public class Translator
    {
        public static List<PEStatusUpdate> StateUpdateToPEStatusUpdate
        (List<StatusUpdate> stList)
        {
            List<PEStatusUpdate> peList = new List<PEStatusUpdate>();
            foreach (StatusUpdate item in stList)
            {
                peList.Add(new PEStatusUpdate(item.CreateDate, item.
                Status));
            }
            return peList;
        }
    }
}
```

Once the display is in place, we need to add a method to capture our button clicks so that we can add new updates.

```
//Fisharoo/Web/Site.master.cs
protected void btnAddStatus_Click(object sender, EventArgs e)
{
    StatusUpdate su = new StatusUpdate();
    su.CreateDate = DateTime.Now;
    su.AccountID = _userSession.CurrentUser.AccountID;
    su.Status = txtStatusUpdate.Text;
    _statusService.SaveStatusUpdate(su);
    _alertService.AddStatusUpdateAlert(su);
    //refresh the status listing on the UI
    LoadStatus();
}
```

This method spins up a new `StatusUpdate` and passes it to the `StatusUpdateService` to be added to the database.

This then takes us to displaying our top `StatusUpdates` in the master page. To do this we need to add the method that gets the top N `StatusUpdates`.

```
//Fisharoo/Web/Site.master.cs
protected void LoadStatus()
{
    List<PEStatusUpdate> statusMsgs =
             Translator.StateUpdateToPEStatusUpdate(
             _statusService.GetTopNStatusUpdatesByAccountID(
             _userSession.CurrentUser.AccountID, 5));

    repStatus.DataSource = statusMsgs;
    repStatus.DataBind();
}
```

With this in place we need to update the `Page_Load()` method of the master page so that the status updates are loaded when a user logs into the site.

```
//Fisharoo/Web/Site.master.cs
protected void Page_Load(object sender, EventArgs e)
{
    ...
    if (_userSession.CurrentUser != null)
    {
        LoadStatus();
        pnlStatusUpdate.Visible = true;
```

```
        }
        else
            pnlStatusUpdate.Visible = false;
    }
```

Now that we have a way to capture new status updates as well as a way to display the most recent updates, we need to provide a way for our user to see all of their updates. We will do this with a page dedicated to showing this data. As this is similar to Alerts, we add this to the `Profile` pages.

```
//Fisharoo/Web/Profiles/StatusUpdates.aspxProfiles
<%@ Page MasterPageFile="~/Site.Master" Language="C#"
AutoEventWireup="true" CodeBehind="StatusUpdates.aspx.cs"
Inherits="Fisharoo.Web.Profiles.StatusUpdates" %>
<%@ Import Namespace="Fisharoo.Web.HelperClasses" %>

<asp:Content ContentPlaceHolderID="Content" runat="server">
    <div class="divContainer" style="width:90%">
        <fieldset style="text-align:left;padding-left:5px">
            <div class="divContainerTitle">Status Updates</div>
            <asp:Repeater ID="repStatusUpdates" runat="server">
                <ItemTemplate>
                    <%# ((PEStatusUpdate)Container.DataItem).
                    CreateDate.ToString() %>
                    <%# ((PEStatusUpdate)Container.DataItem).Status %>
                </ItemTemplate>
                <SeparatorTemplate>
                    <div class="divContainerSeparator"></div>
                </SeparatorTemplate>
            </asp:Repeater>
        </fieldset>
    </div>
</asp:Content>
```

This page of course has the same plumbing issues as the others. But it basically boils down to calling into the `StatusUpdateService` and gets all the `StatusUpdates` for a given `Account`. The only difference between this and showing the **TopN** `StatusUpdates`, as we did on the master page, is that we will show all the updates here.

This is another page that will eventually benefit from having pagination implemented.

Summary

This chapter was certainly less about building the framework and more about reworking some existing items so that they could be more friends-oriented. We have provided various methods to locate and invite friends to join us. We also extended some systems so that our friends could stay in touch with us and what we are doing on the site in the form of alerts and status updates. We now have a site that allows us to connect with and interact with others. This is the first among many chapters that has really helped us put the community feeling into our community.

6
Messaging

Given that our site's focus is to gather people together so that they can interact with each other, we need a way for them to interact. The primary way for people to interact with one another is through direct communication. We will build a system to perform this communication in a way that is similar to sending an email from a standard email client such as Outlook or Hotmail.

We will provide a way for our users to create and send messages via the Xinha WYSIWYG editor.

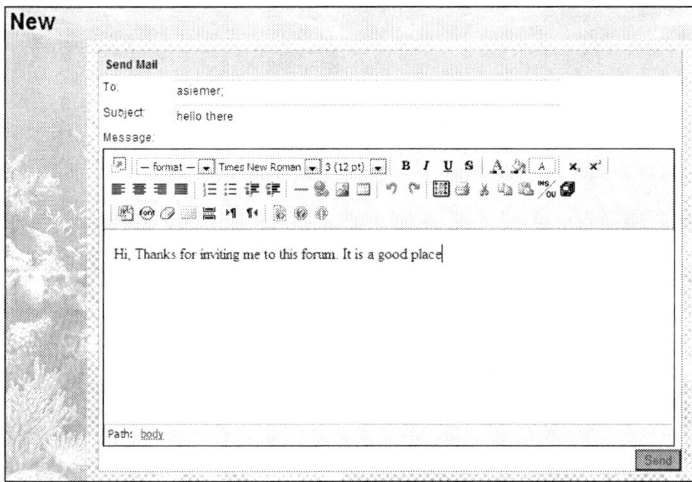

Once a user can create and send messages, we will then create a way for other users to receive and read those messages. The emails will queue up in their inbox, and from there they will be able to read their messages.

Once we have this messaging subsystem in place we can hook up our other features in a way that they too can send messages—such as when a user accepts a friend request we can show the acceptance of that request in the friend's `Inbox`.

Problem

A basic messaging system should be able to manage messages, senders and recipients, folders that contain the messages, and email notifications. In our case, we are going to try and keep things simple where it makes sense to do so, but in one area, we will do things in a more complicated way simply because it will result in less wear and tear on the overall system. This is how the messages will be delivered to the users.

Rather than following a standard email messaging system where each person gets a physical copy of a message, we are going to build our system in the same way that the MS Exchange server works. We are going to make one copy of a message and subscribe users to that message. So rather than have 50 messages for 50 recipients, we will have one message and 50 recipient subscriptions.

The next problem lies in building a WYSIWYG (what you see is what you get) messaging editor. For this feature, there are many open source WYSIWYG editors; we will use one of those to save us a bit of time. We will be using one of the popular editors—XINHA. This editor can be downloaded for free here at `http://xinha.webfactional.com/`. You may have seen this editor already as it is widely used across many popular community sites.

Design

Let's take a look at the design of these features.

Messages

Messages are the core of any messaging system. Generally, a message would contain details like the sender of the message, receiver of the message, and other metadata like time sent, server from where it was sent, etc. and the message, subject, and body. In our case, the message will contain the sender, subject, body, and the data sent. It will also contain one additional field, i.e. the type of message (message, friend request, and so on).

We will need to create a page that allows a user to compose a new message (as seen in the image at the start of this chapter). This interface should also allow a user to add his/her friends easily rather than force them to remember everyone. Also, this interface should allow a user to quickly snap together some HTML without ever having to look at HTML. This can be accomplished with a WYSIWYG editor.

Recipients

As we have already discussed that we are going to move some of the complexity away from the message, following a subscription model instead, you will find that most of the complexity of this system lies around the recipient concepts.

In this case, the recipient subscription is what will be contained in a folder and will have a read status. With this design, we will remove some of the burden from the database. The overhead of doing this of course means that we now need to manage our data closely, as it is kept in many pieces.

A more simple design that would result in more copies of data to be managed would be to create one message for each recipient. This is easier as each message can easily be deleted and moved around without having to worry about the copies of that message of the other recipients. Having said that, if the message is quite large, and more importantly if we were to allow file attachments, all the copies of the messages would be identical for each recipient. This would quickly bloat your database!

Solution

Now let's take a look at our solution.

Implementing the database

First let's take a look at what tables are needed:

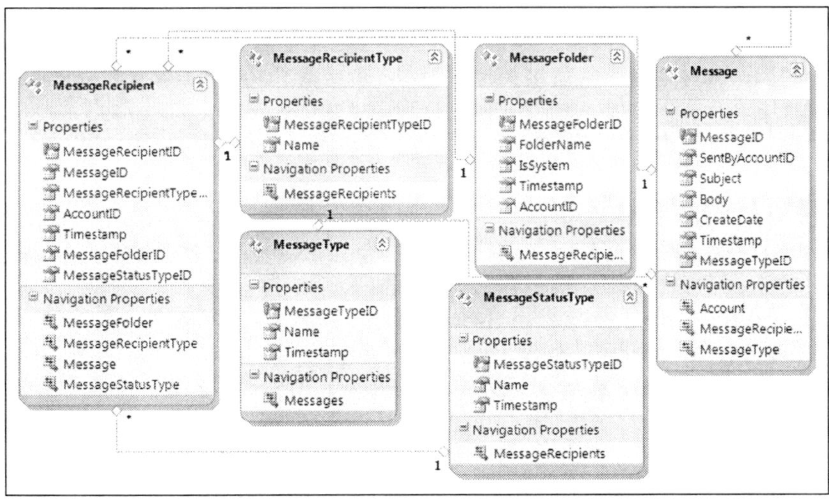

Messages

A message will primarily be made up of the subject and its body. In addition to that we will need to know what type of message we are sending so that we can do some more fancy things in the UI down the road. In addition to this, we are going to maintain who owns/created the message at this level.

There aren't really any major complexities to note here other than the fact that the **Body** is made up of a **varchar(MAX)** data type. If you feel this is too large for your system, feel free to make it anything you are comfortable with. The value you eventually use will drive the message for your system.

MessageTypes

Message Types allows us to assign a type to our messages. This is purely a lookup table that will allow us to know what the types are during queries. We will keep a list of enums in the code to make the lookups easier from that end.

MessageRecipients

A message recipient is simply the receiving party to the message. But as we try to minimize the data that we manage in our system, the message recipient is also a very important part of the message. In our case, it is the receiving party as well as all the things that the receiving party does with their subscription of that message. We will use this subscription to denote which folder the receiver is keeping the message in, and whether the receiver has read the message or not. Also, if the receiver chooses to delete the message, he/she can just delete the subscription to a message (unless they are the last subscription, in which case we will delete the message as well).

The SQL for this subscription is actually quite straightforward. It tracks a relationship to the message, a relationship to the receiver, which folder the subscription is currently in, and the status of the message for this receiver.

MessageRecipientTypes

The message recipient type allows us to track the receiver of this message addressed in the **TO**, **CC**, or **BCC** fields. Initially, our interface will only have a **TO** field. We should add this bit of metadata though just in case we want to expand our capabilities down the road! This is another example of a lookup table that we might need to use in the SQL queries. In our case, we will have an enum defined that maintains this lookup for us on the code side.

MessageStatusTypes

`MessageStatusTypes` allows us to track what a recipient is doing with his/her copy of the message, whether they have read the message, replied to the message, and so on. This is primarily so that we can change the UI to reflect its status to the recipient. However, we could also create a dashboard down the road for the senders of the messages to know whether their message was read or not and by whom (think of all the big brother things one could do...but probably should not do!).

MessageFolders

`MessageFolders` in our first round of implementation will simply hold copies of new messages in the `Inbox` and copies of sent messages in the `Sent` folder. We will also have a `trash` folder and a `spam` folder. That said, we always wanted to build a system with the future in mind if it doesn't require a lot of extra work, and so we have also baked in the concept of a user being able to create and manage his/her own folders.

Therefore, rather than just see the `MessageFolders` table as another lookup table, you will see that there is an **IsSystem** flag to denote which folders are to be seen system-wide. And you will see an **AccountID** column for custom folders so that we know who owns which folders.

Creating the relationships

Once all the tables are created, we can create the relationships.

For this set of tables, we have relationships between the following tables:

- `Messages` and `MessageRecipients`
- `Messages` and `Accounts`
- `Messages` and `MessageTypes`
- `MessageRecipients` and `MessageRecipientTypes`
- `MessageRecipients` and `MessageFolders`
- `MessageRecipients` and `MessageStatusTypes`

Setting up the data access layer

The data access layer in this case is very straightforward. Open up your `Fisharoo.edmx` file and add all of your new message-oriented tables.

Once you save this, you should now have a list of new domain objects in your arsenal (see the previous screenshot).

Building repositories

With these new tables come some additional repositories. We will create the following repositories.

- `MessageRepository`
- `MessageRecipientRepository`
- `MessageFolderRepository`

As we have gone over the creation of repositories in the previous chapters, we will not cover all the details again. We will create a method for selecting a single entity by ID, a group of entities by their parents, saving entities, and deleting entities.

Having said that, there are a couple of methods that have something special in the set of repositories. As we are using message subscriptions, we don't necessarily want to delete recipients haphazardly. We may want to delete a recipient, and if that recipient is the last recipient with a subscription to a message, we may also want to delete the message. On the other end of the spectrum, if we do delete a message, we may also want to remove all the recipient subscriptions.

In addition to these different ways of deleting data, we will also run into a scenario where selecting a single entity from our repositories won't be quite good enough. So in this case, we have created an aggregate class that will allow us to select several entities at once for use in our inbox scenarios.

MessageRepository

When we think of a standard inbox, we know that we need to see the messages that we have, who sent them, when they were sent, and at least the subject of their message. In this case, we have discussed two different entities here. When we think about the fact that we also need to know who they were sent to, we have added a third entity. While we could run three separate queries for this data, it would be better for us to run one query (as we would have done in the old days) and return the data that we need in one shot.

What do we do? In this case, we need to create an aggregate. This is a class that contains other entities. We will therefore create a `MessageWithRecipient` class that will contain the sender's account info, the message, and the recipient. This should provide us with enough data to represent messages in our inbox view later.

Before we write any queries, we first need to create the aggregate.

```
//Fisharoo/DataAccess/MessageWithRecipient.cs
namespace Fisharoo.DataAccess
{
```

```
        public class MessageWithRecipient
        {
            public Account Sender { get; set; }
            public Message Message { get; set; }
            public MessageRecipient MessageRecipient{ get; set; }
        }
    }
```

With this aggregate in place we can now turn our attention to the repository that will get all this data for us.

```
//Fisharoo/DataAccess/Repositories/MessageRepository.cs
public List<MessageWithRecipient> GetMessagesByAccountID(Int32
AccountID, Int32 PageNumber, MessageFolders Folder)
{
    List<MessageWithRecipient> result = new
    List<MessageWithRecipient>();
    using(FisharooDataContext dc = conn.GetContext())
    {
          IEnumerable<MessageWithRecipient> messages =
          (from r in dc.MessageRecipients
          join m in dc.Messages on r.MessageID equals m.MessageID
          join a in dc.Accounts on m.SentByAccountID equals a.AccountID
          where r.AccountID == AccountID &&
          r.MessageFolderID == (int)Folder
          orderby m.CreateDate descending
          select new MessageWithRecipient()
          {
          Sender = a,
          Message = m,
          MessageRecipient = r
          }).Skip((PageNumber - 1)*10).Take(10);
        result = messages.ToList();
    }
    return result;
}
```

This is a fun method! This method involves selecting a list of our `MessageWithRecipient` aggregate objects. The LINQ query is joining all the tables that we need and selecting a new instance of the `MessageWithRecipient` aggregate, that is then populated with the three classes that we need in the aggregate. Additionally, we have introduced some paging logic with the `.Skip` and `.Take` methods to produce a subset of the `MessageWithRecipient` objects.

In addition to the selection method above, we also need to discuss the delete method for this repository. As we have the data holding a subscription to our message data, it is important that we first remove all the subscriptions prior to removing the message itself.

```
//Fisharoo/DataAccess/Repositories/MessageRepository.cs
public void DeleteMessage(Message message)
{
    using (FisharooDataContext dc = conn.GetContext())
    {
        IEnumerable<MessageRecipient> recipients =
        dc.MessageRecipients
        .Where(mr => mr.MessageID == message.MessageID);
        foreach (MessageRecipient mr in recipients)
        {
            dc.MessageRecipients.DeleteObject(mr);
        }
        dc.Messages.DeleteObject(message);
        dc.SaveChanges();
    }
}
```

This is easily accomplished by retrieving all the `MessageRecipients` for the needed `MessageID` from the `MessageRecipients` in `DataContext`. Once we have the list, we iterate over each recipient and remove it from DataContext's `MessageRecipients` list. Finally, we delete the message and save changes

MessageRecipientRepository

The message recipient repository is considerably easier. It simply has an altered delete statement to adjust for the fact that if we delete the last subscription to a message, it will amount to deleting the message.

```
//Fisharoo/DataAccess/Repositories/MessageRecipientRepository.cs
public void DeleteMessageRecipient(MessageRecipient messageRecipient)
{
    using (FisharooDataContext dc = conn.GetContext())
    {

        dc.MessageRecipients.DeleteObject(dc.MessageRecipients.Where
        (mr=> mr.MessageRecipientID.Equals
        (messageRecipient.MessageRecipientID))
        .FirstOrDefault());
        //if the last recipient was deleted
        //...also delete the message
```

```
            int RemainingRecipientCount =
            dc.MessageRecipients.Where(mr => mr.MessageID ==
            messageRecipient.MessageID).Count();
            if (RemainingRecipientCount == 0)
             {
                 dc.Messages.DeleteObject(dc.Messages.Where(m
                 => m.MessageID == messageRecipient.MessageID).
                 FirstOrDefault());
             }
             dc.SaveChanges();
        }
    }
```

In this method, we delete the recipient in question. We then get a count of the remaining recipients for the message, which has the last recipient removed. If that count is zero, then there are no more recipients remaining for that message. In that case we perform a delete on that message and remove it from the system as well.

Implementing the services/application layer

Once all the repositories are built for single serving, we can begin to create the services layer. Again, this layer is responsible for assembling aggregates and performing complex actions with our entities. We will create only one service for this chapter. We will also extend a couple of services.

- `MessageService`
- `Email`
- `AlertService`
- `FriendService`

MessageService

The `MessageService` will help us in one way—sending messages. Keep in mind that to send a message, we will need to create a `Message` then create a `MessageRecipient` for the sender's copy, and then create one-to-many `MessageRecipients` for the receivers of the message. While this is not a complex task, it is a very appropriate series of tasks for a service object!

```
public void SendMessage(string Body, string Subject, string[] To)
{
    Message m = new Message();
    m.Body = Body;
    m.Subject = Subject;
    m.CreateDate = DateTime.Now;
```

```
        m.MessageTypeID = (int)MessageTypes.Message;
        m.SentByAccountID = _userSession.CurrentUser.AccountID;
        Int64 messageID = _messageRepository.SaveMessage(m);

        //create a copy in the sent items folder for this user
        MessageRecipient sendermr = new MessageRecipient();
        sendermr.AccountID = _userSession.CurrentUser.AccountID;
        sendermr.MessageFolderID = (int) MessageFolders.Sent;
        sendermr.MessageRecipientTypeID = (int) MessageRecipientTypes.TO;
        sendermr.MessageID = messageID;
        sendermr.MessageStatusTypeID = (int)MessageStatusTypes.Unread;
        _messageRecipientRepository.SaveMessageRecipient(sendermr);

        //send to people in the To field
        foreach (string s in To)
        {
            Account toAccount = null;
            if (s.Contains("@"))
                toAccount = _accountRepository.GetAccountByEmail(s);
            else
                toAccount = _accountRepository.GetAccountByUsername(s);

            if(toAccount != null)
            {
                MessageRecipient mr = new MessageRecipient();
                 mr.AccountID = toAccount.AccountID;
                mr.MessageFolderID = (int)MessageFolders.Inbox;
                mr.MessageID = messageID;
                mr.MessageRecipientTypeID = (int) MessageRecipientTypes.
                TO;
                mr.MessageStatusTypeID = (int)MessageStatusTypes.Unread;
                _messageRecipientRepository.SaveMessageRecipient(mr);
                Account acc = _userSession.CurrentUser;
                _email.SendNewMessageNotification(acc.FirstName, acc.
                LastName, toAccount.Email);
            }
        }
```

This should be very straightforward to follow. The first thing we do is spin up a new instance of the `Message` that we are sending. We then save it via the `MessageRepository` and get back the new `MessageID` to work with down the line.

The next task is to make sure that we paste a copy of the message in the sender's `Sent Items` folder. We do this by creating a `MessageRecipient` object and tying it to the sender's account. You will notice that we have assigned it to the `Sent Items` folder using an enum named `MessageFolders`, which has IDs that map to the `MessageFolders` lookup table. This enum is stored next to a new domain object named `MessageFolder`. Check the `MessageFolder.cs` file for details on this enum.

The next item in the `MessageService` is assigning the `MessageRecipientTypeID` to the sender's copy. The `MessageRecipientType` is to let the display know whether to show the `MessageRecipient` as a `TO`, `CC`, or `BCC` recipient. This is another enum value that maps back to a lookup table in the database and is in the `MessageRecipientType.cs` file.

We then move into a `foreach` loop in the `MessageService`, that is responsible for determining whether we are looking up a recipient via an email address or a username. It does this by testing the **To** value of the `MessageRecipients` to see if it has an ampersand or not, which would correspond to an email address.

Depending on whether the `TO` value is an email address or a username, we get a copy of an `Account` object. Once we have a valid `Account` object to work with, we move on to creating a new `MessageRecipient` for that `Account`. You should note that in this implementation of the `MessageRecipient`, we are placing the `Message` subscription into the `Inbox` instead of the `Sent Items` folder. This `MessageRecipient` is also of `MessageRecipientType` `TO`.

Email

Once the `MessageRecipient` is successfully created and persisted to the database, we then move on to sending an email notification to the `MessageRecipient`. The most important thing to note about the additional method of `SendNewMessageNotification()` is that we are sending a notification—not the whole message!

We mention this because we feel it is important to note that one of the quickest ways to get your sites' IP addresses banned is to be determined to be a sender of spam. Since you are entirely responsible for the content that goes out in your messages, you can't directly control what your users type in a message. So don't risk your reputation by sending the entire contents of their messages!

```
//Fisharoo/Components/Email.cs
public void SendNewMessageNotification(string FirstName, string
LastName, string ToEmail)
{
    foreach (string s in ToEmail.Split(new char[] {',',';'}))
```

```
        {
            string message = FirstName + " " + LastName +
            " has sent you a message on " + _configuration.SiteName + "!
             Please log in at " + _configuration.SiteName +
            " to view the message.<HR>";
            SendEmail(s, "", "", FirstName + " " + LastName
                    +
                " has sent you a message on " +
                _configuration.SiteName + "!", message);
        }
    }
```

This method breaks down all the `TO` recipients and creates a new email notification using our existing subsystem telling the recipients that they have a new message waiting for them in their `Inbox`.

AlertService

We created a placeholder in one of the previous chapters in our `AlertService` to allow us to insert an URL in our alerts that would allow the receiver of an alert to easily click into sending a message to the sender of that alert. At the time we created this, it was purely a placeholder as we didn't have any tools to send from. We will now create these tools, so that we can fill this placeholder out.

```
//TODO: MESSAGING - point to send message URL
private string GetSendMessageUrl(Int32 AccountID)
{
    return "<a href=\"[rootUrl]/mail/newmessage.aspx?AccountID=" +
       AccountID.ToString() + "\">Click here to send message</a>";
}
```

This method is responsible for creating a link to the new message page passing in the user you want to send a message to. This method is already called from several of our existing `AlertService` methods.

FriendService

We now need to extend our `FriendService.CreateFriendFromFriendInvitation()` method. Remember that this method is responsible for creating a friend from an accepted invitation. We now want to add some logic to this so that when a friend request is accepted, we are able to send a new Message to the creator of that friend request letting them know that their request was accepted.

```
//Fisharoo/BusinessLogic/FriendService.cs
public bool CreateFriendFromFriendInvitation(Guid InvitationKey,
Account InvitationTo, bool ExistingMember)
{
    //update friend invitation request
    FriendInvitation friendInvitation = _friendInvitationRepository.Ge
    tFriendInvitationByGUID(InvitationKey);
    //validate if the friend request is for the same person who has
    logged in
    //however if this is a new member (new registration), then don't
    validate as the
    //person may use a different email during registration
    if (ExistingMember && (friendInvitation.Email != InvitationTo.
    Email))
        return false;

    friendInvitation.BecameAccountID = InvitationTo.AccountID;
    _friendInvitationRepository.SaveFriendInvitation(friendInvitati
    on);
   _friendInvitationRepository.CleanUpFriendInvitationsForThisEmail(fr
   iendInvitation);

    //create friendship
    Friend friend = new Friend();
    friend.AccountID = friendInvitation.AccountID;
    friend.MyFriendsAccountID = InvitationTo.AccountID;
    _friendRepository.SaveFriend(friend);

    Account InvitationFrom = _accountRepository.
    GetAccountByID(friendInvitation.AccountID);
    _alertService.AddFriendAddedAlert(InvitationFrom, InvitationTo);
    return true;
    //CHAPTER 6
    //TODO: MESSAGING - Add message to inbox regarding new friendship!
}
```

This additional code is going through the motions of creating a new message and a recipient for that message. In this case though, we are giving this message the `MessageTypeID` of `MessageTypes.FriendConfirm` (or a friend confirmation). Other than that, this code is straightforward.

Implementing the presentation layer

Now that our framework has been updated to handle the new concept of messaging, let's start creating some UI features so that we can use our new tools. We are going to need at least three pages to really utilize our messaging features. We will need a way to create and send a new message, a way to receive and view the messages, and a way to read an individual message. In addition to the creation of a message, we will need a way to easily choose from our list of friends, the recipients of our new messages. Also, while viewing our list of messages, we will need a way of drilling into different folders of messages. Let's get started!

New message

The UI for the new message page is trivial. It consists of a **To** field, a **Subject** field, a message field, and a button to signify that we are ready to send the message. Where things are significantly different in the use of the Xinha WYSIWYG editor! This is a JavaScript library that allows you to transform a multiline text box into a full-featured editor.

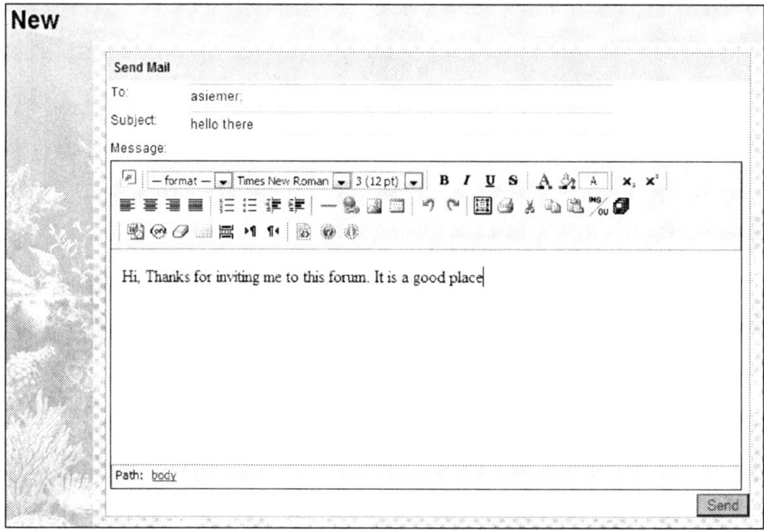

To get started with the integration of Xinha, we will first need to get the latest code base. This can be acquired from the code base of this book or by going to `http://xinha.webfactional.com/wiki/DownloadsPage`. Install this code base into a new Xinha directory off the root of the site.

Then open the `Site.Master` page. Add the following JavaScript directly after the body:

```
<script type="text/javascript">
    xinha_editors = null;
    xinha_editors = xinha_editors ? xinha_editors : [];
</script>
```

This code is not part of the standard installation process. What it does is allow us to spin up multiple instances of the editor all throughout a single page. You will see this later.

Then further down in our master page, just before the ending body tag, we will insert another huge blob of JavaScript. As this is a very large blob we are not going to show it here. Please open the existing master page from this chapter to see it.

You will see that this blob is responsible for setting the vast amount of configuration options that Xinha exposes. This code is heavily commented and so should be understandable. Also, the configuration of this package is covered extensively on the net!

The only thing, but definitely the special one, we added to in this configuration is the very first line that sets the base URL of the site. In this case, we changed it to point to the path where XINHA files are installed.

```
...
_editor_url = "/Scrits/Xinha";
...
```

This brings us back to our `NewMessage.aspx` page. Now that we have Xinha installed, we can add a line below our page UI that effectively ties our multiline text box control to the Xinha library. This is done with a snippet of JavaScript.

```
<script type="text/javascript">
    xinha_editors[xinha_editors.length] = 'Content_txtMessage';
</script>
```

Note that this is using the same `xinha_editors` variable that we defined initially in the Master page! What we have done here is inserted this new control into an array of Xinha editors. Note the `ClientID` of the text box that we want associated as an editor. This is different than what we are used to in the previous versions of ASP. NET (as discussed earlier in Chapter 4).

Now, we will move on to the presenter of this page. This page has three primary tasks:

- To send a message
- To preload a recipient of a message (if linked to from an `Alert`) and
- To send a reply to a message

This is really the same thing with the exception that to send a reply to a message, we would first have to load that reply. We will get to that down the road!

To send a message, we have to bubble up the button click event through our code behind and into our presenter. As we have covered this concept of MVP extensively in earlier chapters, we will not cover it here. So, in the presenter, we have added a method called `SendMessage()`, that takes in the **Subject**, **Message**, and an array of **To** entries.

```
//Fisharoo/Web/Mail/Presenters/NewMessagePresenter.cs
public void SendMessage(string Subject, string Message, string[] To)
{
    _messageService.SendMessage(Message,Subject,To);
}
```

This method then calls the `MessageService.SendMessage()` method and sends the message.

The preloading of a recipient is handled in the `Init()` method of the presenter. It checks to see if we have an `AccountID` in the QueryString (via our `WebContext` wrapper). If so, it gets the `Accounts Username` property and adds that to the **To** field in the UI.

Loading a reply message into the UI is very similar to loading a username. The `Init()` method checks the `WebContext` to see if we have a `MessageID` in the QueryString and loads the previous Message details into the UI. This is done if the page request isn't a post back request.

```
//Fisharoo/Web/Mail/Presenters/NewMessagePresenter.cs
public void Init(INewMessage view, bool IsPostBack)
{
    _view = view;
    if(!IsPostBack)
    {
        if(_webContext.MessageID != 0)
        _view.LoadReply(_messageService.GetMessageByMessageID(_
        webContext.MessageID,_userSession.CurrentUser.
        AccountID));
```

```
        }
        if(_webContext.AccountID != 0)
            _view.LoadTo(_accountService.GetAccountByID(
                              _webContext.AccountID).Username);
    }
```

Friends control

The other important feature that we have as part of the `NewMessage.aspx` page is the ability to easily select a friend from a list of friends as the recipient of a message—similar to the idea of a contacts book. To achieve this, we will create a user control that lists our friends.

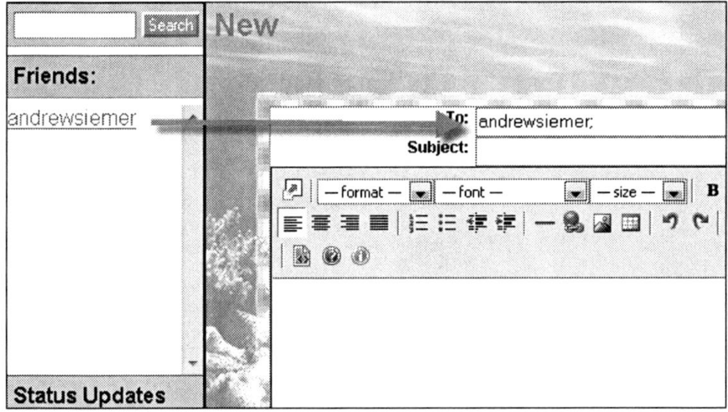

The UI for this control is just a simple `Repeater` object that outputs a friend's username. So let's take a look at what populates the UI. In the `Init()` method in the `FriendPresenter.cs` file, we load all the users' friends and bind to the repeater control in the UI.

```
//Fisharoo/Web/Mail/UserControls/Presenters/FriendsPresenter.css
public void Init(IFriends view)
{
     _view = view;
      List<Account> accounts =
                _friendService.GetFriendsAccountsByAccountID(
                                     _userSession.CurrentUser.
                                     AccountID);
      view.LoadFriends(Translator.AccountsToUserNames(accounts));
}
```

The `Translator.AccountsToUserNames` is taking in the accounts collection and returning a string of usernames of those accounts, which is what is finally bound to the repeater in the UI.

In the code behind for our friend control, we insert a snippet of JavaScript to allow us to click on a friend and carry his/her username into our **To** field in our NewMessage UI.

```
//Fisharoo/Web/Mail/UserControls/Friends.aspx.cs
public void repFriends_ItemDataBound(object sender,
                                    RepeaterItemEventArgs e)
{
    if(e.Item.ItemType == ListItemType.Item || e.Item.ItemType ==
                          ListItemType.AlternatingItem)
    {
        HyperLink linkFriend = e.Item.FindControl("linkFriend") as
                               HyperLink;
        linkFriend.Attributes.Add("OnClick",
                               "javascript:document.forms[0].
                                Content_txtTo.value += '" +
                                e.Item.DataItem + ";';");
    }
}
```

Note that we are adding an attribute for the `OnClick` event of our link that will call a JavaScript to move the username to our **To** field with a semicolon delimiter.

This gives us a list of friends, but how do we tie that back into our UI? Open the `NewMessage.aspx` page. We will need to register the new control in the page and then add a reference to it in the page.

Just below the Page directive add the following code:

```
<%@ Register Src="~/Mail/UserControls/Friends.ascx"
                TagPrefix="Fisharoo" TagName="Friends" %>
```

Then add a new Content section to our page where the friends control will live:

```
<asp:Content ContentPlaceHolderID="LeftNavTop" runat="server">
    <Fisharoo:Friends ID="friends1" runat="server" />
</asp:Content>
```

This inserts the friends control into our left navigation bar as defined in the master page!

Default (or Inbox)

Now that we can successfully send a message, we need a way to receive those messages. This is done in folder view of our messages. This is really just a page that shows a list of messages, who sent them, and when. We can either click on the sender to go to their profile page, or can click on the message to view it. We can also navigate through pages of messages with a list of page navigation links and we will have the ability to delete one or many selected messages. Additionally, we will create a `Folders` control that will allow us to navigate through our various folders to see the messages in those containers.

The UI for this page has just a repeater that iterates through the `MessageWithRecipient` collection that is passed to it. So let's take a look at the presenter, which actually populates our list of messages. As always this is accomplished in the `Init()` method of the presenter.

```
//Fisharoo/Web/Mail/Presenters/DefaultPresenter.cs
public void Init(IDefault view)
{
    _view = view;
    if (_userSession.CurrentUser != null)
    {
        List<MessageWithRecipient> list =
             messageService.GetMessagesByAccountID(
                  userSession.CurrentUser.AccountID, webContext.Page,
                  (MessageFolders)_webContext.FolderID);
                  _view.LoadMessages(
                  Translator.MessageWithRecipientToPEMessage(list));
        view.DisplayPageNavigation(messageService.GetPageCount(
                  (MessageFolders)webContext.FolderID,
                  userSession.CurrentUser.AccountID),
                  (MessageFolders) _webContext.FolderID, webContext.
                  Page);
    }
}
```

We first check to see that the user of the page is actually logged in. We then get a list of messages by the user's `AccountID`. As done in previous chapter, we have a presentation entity `PEMessage` (`HelperClasses` folder) that we have defined which has only those fields that we want to show in the UI. We also get a page count (the number of pages of messages that we have to navigate through).

Loading messages into the UI is simply a matter of binding the `DataSource` to the repeater.

```
public void LoadMessages(List<PEMessage> Messages)
{
    repMessages.DataSource = Messages;
    repMessages.DataBind();
}
```

As this requires no further explanation, let's jump right into how we go about building our page navigation. Recall that in the `Init()` of our presenter we had a call into `_view.DisplayPageNavigation()`, which received the `PageCount` of the folder we were working with, and the current page we were viewing. Here is that method:

```
public void DisplayPageNavigation(Int32 PageCount, MessageFolders
folder, Int32 CurrentPage)
{
    if(PageCount == CurrentPage)
        linkNext.Visible = false;
    if (CurrentPage == 1)
        linkPrevious.Visible = false;
    linkNext.NavigateUrl = "~/mail/default.aspx?folder=" + ((int)
                          folder).ToString() + "&page=" +
                          (CurrentPage + 1).ToString();
    linkPrevious.NavigateUrl = "~/mail/default.aspx?folder=" + ((int)
                              folder).ToString() + "&page=" +
                              (CurrentPage - 1).ToString();
    for(int i = 1; i<=PageCount;i++)
    {
        HyperLink link = new HyperLink();
        link.Text = i.ToString();
        link.NavigateUrl = "~/mail/default.aspx?folder=" +
                ((int)folder).ToString() + "&page=" + i.ToString();
        phPages.Controls.Add(link);
        phPages.Controls.Add(new LiteralControl(" "));
    }
}
```

This chunk of code interacts with three controls in our UI—two hyperlinks, one that displays **Previous** and one displaying **Next**, and a `PlaceHolder` control that will hold the individual page numbers of all the pages for this data set.

This method initially determines if we should show the **Next** or **Previous** links based on our current page and our total page count. We then hook up the navigation property of each of those links to take us to the next page or the previous page of data. After that we use a `for` loop to iterate through all the possible pages, from 1 to `PageCount`, making a new hyperlink for each iteration that contains the location of that page.

The other feature of this page is the ability to delete messages—as many or as few as we like. This is primarily achieved with a helper function in the code behind of the view that extracts all the messages that are selected, that can be called from within the presenter. This allows the presenter to remain in control!

```
public List<Int32> ExtractSelectedMessages()
{
    List<Int32> result = new List<Int32>();
    foreach (RepeaterItem item in repMessages.Items)
    {
        if(item.ItemType == ListItemType.Item || item.ItemType ==
           ListItemType.AlternatingItem)
        {
            CheckBox chkMessage = item.FindControl("chkMessage") as
                                  CheckBox;
            Int32 messageID =
                 Convert.ToInt32(chkMessage.Attributes["MessageID"]);
            if(chkMessage.Checked)
                result.Add(messageID);
        }
    }
    return result;
}
```

This method iterates through all the check boxes to see if they are selected or not. If they are, then it extracts the `MessageID` from an attribute that was created when we loaded the display. A collection of `MessageIDs` is then returned to the caller.

This then brings us to the `Delete` method in the presenter. It is called from a button click event that is bubbled up to the presenter, which then calls into the view to get a list of selected `MessageIDs`. Then using the `MessageService` we get a copy of that message. With the copy, we then call into the `MessageRecipientService.DeleteMessageRecipient()` method and delete each selected message.

Folders

Let's now look at the UI for the Folders user control. This UI is also made up of a `Repeater` that displays the bound data. In this case, we are displaying folders as hyperlinks, which then link to the same `Default.aspx` page, but additionally pass in the folder that we are interested in viewing.

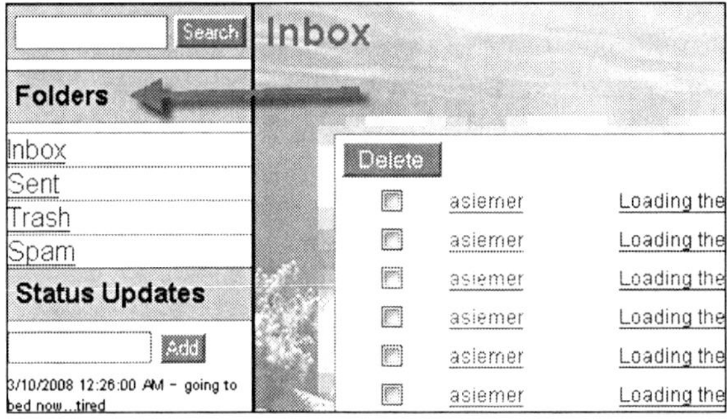

Let's quickly look at the presenter code.

```
//Fisharoo/Web/Mail/UserControls/Presenters/FolderPresenter.cs
public void Init(IFolders view)
{
    _view = view;
    MEFManager.Compose(this);
    _view.LoadFolders(_
                messageFolderservice.GetMessageFoldersByAccountID(
                _userSession.CurrentUser.AccountID));
}
```

In this case, we are calling into the `MessageFolderService` to get a list of folders for this user. We bind that directly to the UI through our view. The view then iterates through the data in our repeater. In our `ItemDataBound` method—in the code behind of the view—we update each hyperlink in the UI.

```
//Fisharoo/Web/Mail/UserControls/Folders.ascx.cs
protected void repFolders_ItemDataBound(object sender,
RepeaterItemEventArgs e)
{
    if (e.Item.ItemType == ListItemType.Item || e.Item.ItemType ==
       ListItemType.AlternatingItem)
    {
        HyperLink linkFolder = e.Item.FindControl("linkFolder") as
                               HyperLink;
        linkFolder.Text =
       ((MessageFolder)e.Item.DataItem).FolderName;
```

```
            linkFolder.NavigateUrl = "~/Mail/Default.aspx?folder=" +
           ((MessageFolder) e.Item.DataItem).MessageFolderID.ToString();
            linkFolder.Attributes.Add("FolderID",
            ((MessageFolder)e.Item.DataItem).
            MessageFolderID.ToString());
        }
    }
```

This creates a list of folders for us in a control. But how do we get it into our UI? To do this, we have to go back to our `Default.aspx` page. This will be done exactly the same way we did for our friends control in our new message page. Open the default page so that we can add the `Folders` control.

```
<%@ Register Src="~/Mail/UserControls/Folders.ascx"
           TagPrefix="Fisharoo" TagName="Folders" %>
<asp:Content ContentPlaceHolderID="LeftNavTop" runat="server">
    <Fisharoo:Folders id="Folders1"
             runat="server"></Fisharoo:Folders>
</asp:Content>
```

Read message

Reading a message is not that difficult at all. We are just loading a message into a static UI based on the `MessageID` that is passed into the page. Let's first discuss the UI (which could easily be made more complex down the road!). This UI will consist of a **From** Label, a **Subject** Label, a **Message** Label, and a **Reply** button.

Here is the message view:

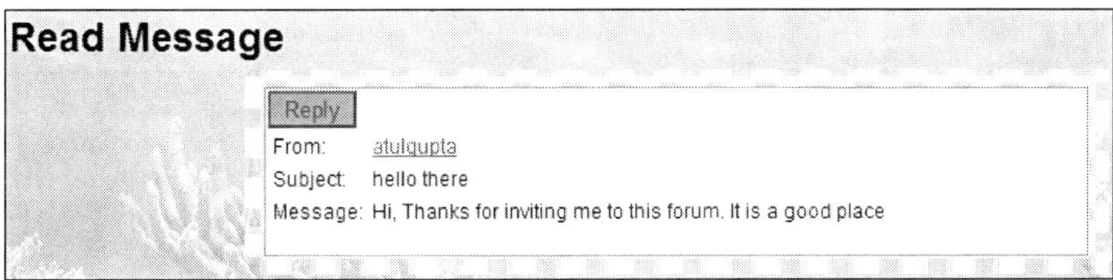

And here is what will be seen after replying to the message:

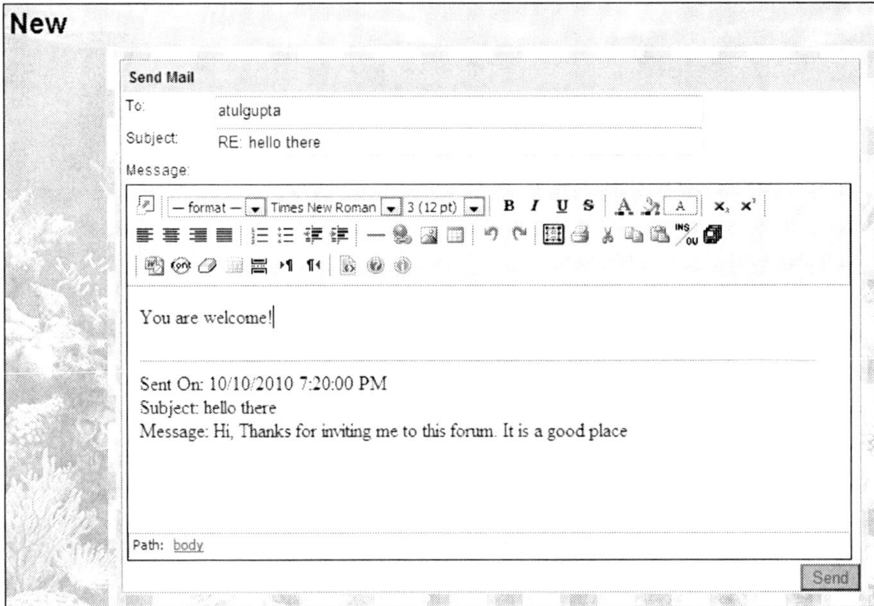

As usual, as all the leg work is done in the presenter, let's jump straight to it.

```
//Fisharoo/Web/Mail/Presenters/ReadMessagePresenter.cs
public void Init(IReadMessage view)
{
    _view = view;
    _view.LoadMessage(_messageService.GetMessageByMessageID(_webContex
                t.MessageID,_userSession.CurrentUser.AccountID));
}
```

As you can see here, we are populating the UI by getting the message based on the ID and then passing it to the view for display.

For the **Reply** button, we will bubble up the click event into the presenter. The presenter then makes a call to the `Redirector` class that passes the current `MessageID` to the `NewMessage` page.

Summary

In this chapter, we have built an entire messaging facility. This section has gone over extending the framework to allow for the creation and retrieval of messages and all the related items of a message. We then covered creating a UI to allow users to create and send messages to the other users of the system. Next, we covered how to receive and read those messages.

This chapter will not only allow our users to send messages to each other but also provide our system with a way to communicate with our user base efficiently. This is not only a good feature to have in your community site but also a basic requirement for it.

7
Media Galleries

In this chapter we will go over the concept of allowing people to share files. We will be specifically focused on sharing images, but we will build the system so that we can easily set it up to share videos, audio files, resumes, or any other type of binary file. In addition to that, we will build the concept of having user-specific sets of files as well as content that can be shared among many users.

In order to create the file management software for our website, we need to consider topics such as a single or multi-file upload, file system management, and image manipulation in the case of photos. In addition to this we will cover creation of pages for displaying the user's photo albums, their friends' photo albums, as well as a few data management pages. This chapter will create a basic framework from which you can easily grow to suit the file management needs of just about any community site.

Problem

Apart from the standard infrastructure issues that we have to consider when building a system such as this, one of the core issues in any web-based file management system is file upload. As we all know, most server side technologies allow only one file to be uploaded at a time and ASP.NET is no different. And while we could easily buy a third-party plug-in to handle multiple files at once, we decided to provide for options to upload the files either via Silverlight or via Flash.

Once we get our file upload process working we are only one-third of the way there! As we are going to be mostly concerned with uploading images, we need to consider that we will need to provide some image manipulation. With each file that is uploaded to our system we need to create a handful of different sizes of each image to be used in various scenarios across our site. To start with, we will create thumbnail, small, medium, large, and original size photos.

Now while creating different size files is technically working with the file storage system, we wanted to take an extra breath with regards to the file storage concepts. As we discussed in the earlier chapters, we could choose to store the files on the file system or in a database. For avatars it made sense to store each with the profile data whereas for image galleries it makes more sense to store the file on the file system. While storing files to the file system we need to be very cautious as to how the file structure is defined and where and how the individual files are stored. In our case we will use system-generated GUIDs as our file names with extensions to define the different sizes that we are storing. We will dig into this more as we start to understand the details of this system.

Once we have uploaded the files to the server and they are ready for our use across the system, we will take up the concept of user files versus system files. If we build the system with some forethought regarding this topic we can have a very generic file management system that can be extended for future use. We will build a personal system in this chapter. But as you will see with some flags in just the right places, we could just as easily build a system file manager or a group file manager.

Design

Let's take a look at the design for this feature.

Files

For our site, as we are not storing our files in the database, we need to take a closer look at what actually needs to be managed in the database so as to keep track of what is going on in the file system. In addition to standard file metadata, we need to keep a close eye on where the file actually lives—specifically which file system folder (directory on the hard drive) the file will reside in. We also need to be able to maintain which accounts own which files, or in the case of system files, which files can be viewed by anyone.

Folders

You may be wondering why we have a separate section regarding folders when we just touched upon the fact that we will be managing which file system folder we will be storing files in. In this section we are going to discuss folder management from a site perspective rather than a file system perspective—user folders or virtual folders if you desire.

Very similar to file storage, we will be storing various metadata about each folder. We will also have to keep track of who owns which folder, who can see which folder, or in the case of system folders whether everyone can see that folder. And of course as each folder is a virtual container for a file, we will have to maintain the relationship between folders and files.

File upload

The file upload process will be handled by a Silverlight/Flash client. While this is not really a book about either Silverlight or Flash, we will show you how simple it is to create this Flash client, that is really just providing a way to store many files that need to be uploaded, and then uploading them one at a time in a way that the server can handle each file. For the Silverlight option, we are using code from Codeplex—`http://silverlightfileupld.codeplex.com/`.

File system management

Managing the file system may seem like a non-issue to begin with. However, keep in mind that for a community site to be successful we will need at least 10,000 or so unique users. Given that sharing photos and other files is such a popular feature of most of today's community sites, this could easily translate into a lot of uploaded files.

While you could technically store a large number of files in one directory on your web server, you will find that over time your application becomes more and more sluggish. You might also run into files being uploaded with the same name using this approach. Also, you may find that you will have storage issues and need to split off some of your files to another disk or another server.

Many of these issues are easily handled if we think about and address them up front. In our case we will use a unique file name for each uploaded file. We will store each file in subdirectories that are also uniquely named based on the year and month in which the file was uploaded. If you find that you have a high volume of files being uploaded each day, you may want to store your files in a folder with the year and month in the name of the folder and then in another subdirectory for each day of that month.

In addition to a good naming convention on the file system, we will store the root directory for each file in the database. Initially you may only have one root for your photos, one for videos, and so on. But storing it now will allow you to have multiple roots for your file storage—one root location per file. This gives you a lot of extensibility points over time meaning that you could easily relocate entire sections of your file gallery to a separate disk or even a separate server.

Data management screens

Once we have all of the infrastructure in place we will need to discuss all the data management screens that will be needed—everything from the UI for uploading files to the screens for managing file metadata, to screens for creating new albums. Then we will need to tie into the rest of the framework and allow users to view their friends' uploaded file albums.

Solution

Let's take a look at our solution.

Implementing the database

First let's take a look at the tables required for these features (see the following screenshot).

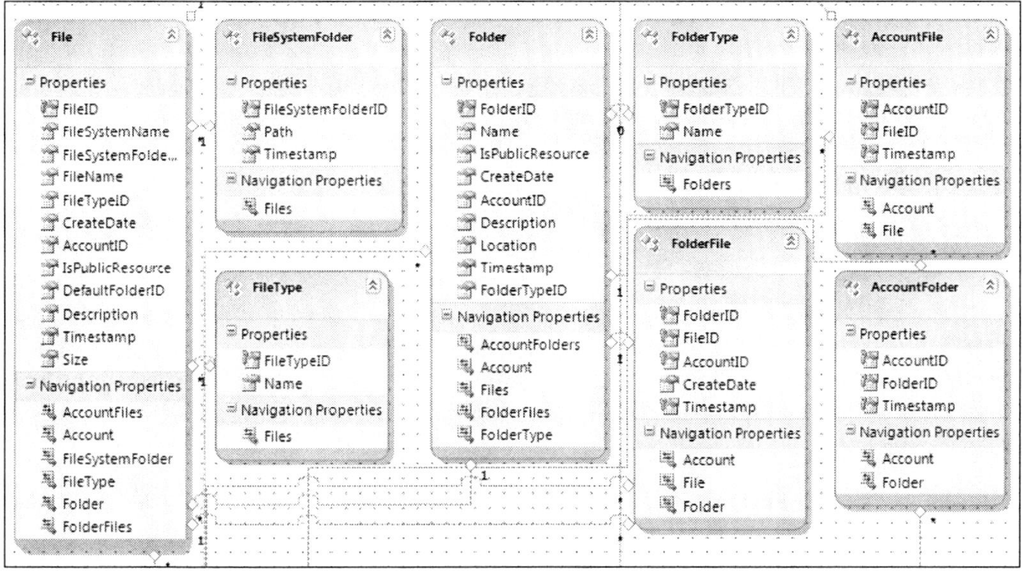

Files

The most important thing to consider storing while in the database is of course our primary interest files. As with most other conversations regarding a physical binary file we always have to consider if we want to store the file in the database or on the file system. In this case we think it makes sense to store the file (and in the case of a photo, its various generated sizes) on the file system. This means that we will only be storing metadata about each file in our database.

The most important field here to discuss is the **FileSystemName**. As you can see this is a GUID value. We will be renaming uploaded files to GUIDs in addition to the original extension. This allows us to ensure that all the files in any given folder are uniquely named. This removes the need for us to have to worry about overwriting other files.

Then we see the **FileSystemFolderID**. This is a reference to the `FileSystemFolders` table, that lets us know the root folder location where the file is stored.

Next on our list of items to discuss is the **IsPublicResource** flag. By its name it is quite clear that this flag will set a file as public or private and can therefore be seen by all or by its owner (**AccountID**).

We then come to a field that may be somewhat confusing: **DefaultFolderID**. This has nothing to do with the file system folders. This is a user created folder. When files are uploaded initially they are put in a virtual folder. That initial virtual folder becomes the file's permanent home. This doesn't mean that it is the file's only home. As you will see later we have the concept that files can live in many virtual folders by way of subscription to the other folders.

File system folders

As mentioned previously, the `FileSystemFolders` table is responsible for letting us know where our file's root directory is. This allows us to expand our system down the road to have multiple roots, that could live on the same server but different disks, or on totally different servers. The fields in the table are **Key**, **Path** (URL), and a **Timestamp**.

File types

The `FileTypes` table will help us to keep track of what sort of files we are storing and working with. This is a simple lookup table that tells us the extension of a given file.

Folders

Folders are virtual in this case. They provide us with a way to specify a container of files. In our case we will be containing photos, in which case folders will act as photo albums. The only field worth explaining here is the flag **IsPublicResource**, which allows us to specify whether a folder and its resources are public or private, that is, viewable by all or viewable only by the owner.

Folder types

The `FolderTypes` table allows us a way to specify the type of folder. Currently this will simply be Name, photos, movies, and so on. However, down the road you may want to specify an icon for each folder type in which case this is the place where you would want to assign that specification.

Account folders

In the `AccountFolders` table we are able to specify additional ownership of a folder. So in the case that a folder is a public resource and external resources can own folders, we simply create the new ownership relationship here. This is not permanent ownership. It is still specified with the `Folders` table's **AccountID**. This is a temporary ownership across many Accounts.

As you can see in the previous screenshot we have the owner (**AccountID**) and the folder that is to be owned (**FolderID**).

Account files

Similar to the `AccountFolders` table, the `AccountFiles` table allows someone to subscribe to a specific file. This could be used for the purposes of **Favorites** or similar concepts. The makeup of this table is identical to `AccountFolders`. You have the owner and the file being owned.

Folder files

The `FolderFiles` table allows an Account to not only subscribe to a file, similar to the Favorites concept, but it also allows a user to take one of my files and put it into one of their folders as though the file itself belonged to them.

As you can see in the previous screenshot this is primarily a table that holds the keys to the other tables. We have the **FolderID**, **FileID**, and **AccountID** for each file. This clearly specifies who is taking ownership of what and where they want it to be placed.

Creating the relationships

Once all the tables are created we can then create all the relationships.

For this set of tables we have relationships between the following tables:

- `Files` and `FileSystemFolders`
- `Files` and `FileTypes`
- `Files` and `Folders`
- `Files` and `Accounts`
- `Folders` and `Accounts`
- `Folders` and `FolderTypes`
- `AccountFolders` and `Accounts`
- `AccountFolders` and `Folders`
- `AccountFiles` and `Accounts`
- `AccountFiles` and `Files`
- `FolderFiles` and `Accounts`
- `FolderFiles` and `Folders`
- `FolderFiles` and `Files`

Setting up the data access layer

The data access layer can be set up in a similar manner as done in earlier chapters. We need to open `Fisharoo.edmx` file, right-click and select **Update Model from Database**, and select the new tables. Save the file and you now have the domain objects to work with for this chapter.

Building repositories

With the addition of new tables will come the addition of new repositories so that we can get the data stored in those tables. We will be creating the following repositories to support our needs.

- `FileRepository`
- `FolderRepository`

Each of our repositories will generally have a method for selecting by ID, select all by parent ID, save, and delete. Once you have seen one repository you have pretty much seen them all. Review previous chapters, the appendices, or the included code for examples of a standard repository. Here we will discuss anything that varies from the standard!

FileRepository

Other than the normal methods that all the `XRepository` classes have, the `FileRepository` also has a couple of additional more interesting methods.

- `UpdateDescriptions`
- `DeleteFilesInFolder`
- `DeleteFileFromFileSystem`

The `UpdateDescriptions()` method is an interesting concept. This method is the first example of performing multiple updates all at once rather than doing them one at a time. This obviously will be much more performance-oriented than individual update executions.

```
//Fisharoo/DataAccess/Repositories/FileRepository.cs
public void UpdateDescriptions(Dictionary<int,string>
fileDescriptions)
{
    using(FisharooDataContext dc = conn.GetContext())
    {
        List<Int64> fileIDs = fileDescriptions.Select(f => Convert.
        ToInt64(f.Key)).Distinct().ToList();
        IEnumerable<File> files = dc.Files.Where(f => fileIDs.
        Contains(f.FileID));
```

```
            foreach (File file in files)
            {
          file.Description = fileDescriptions.Where(f=>f.Key==file.FileID)
          .Select(f=>f.Value).FirstOrDefault();
            }
            dc.SaveChanges();
        }
    }
```

As you can see, this method accepts a `Dictionary` collection, that contains a list of `FileIDs` and `fileDescriptions`. We then open up the DataContext. Then from the `Dictionary` collection we get a list of unique `FileIDs`. We then make one trip to the database to get all of the File objects we need using the `Contains()` method of the `FileID` collection. With the collection of appropriate files in hand we can then iterate through each of them setting the description to the value passed in via the `Dictionary` collection. Once all this leg work is done, we can call the `SaveChanges` method. Keep in mind that we have one working DataContext for this entire operation. It is why this method of updation works!

```
//Fisharoo/DataAccess/Repositories/FileRepository.cs
public void DeleteFilesInFolder(string filePath, Folder folder)
        {
            using (FisharooDataContext dc = conn.GetContext())
            {
                List<File> files = GetFilesByFolderID(folder.
                FolderID);
                foreach (File file in files)
                {
                    DeleteFileFromFileSystem(filePath, folder, file);
                }
                //Entity Framework 4 does not support any method to
                bulk delete, hence only way is to iterate through
                resultset
                //and delete one by one, another way is to use
                dc.ExecuteStoreQuery() and pass SQL String
                //dc.ExecuteStoreQuery() is efficient but does not use
                LINQ syntax
                var ListOffiles = dc.Files.Where(f =>
                f.DefaultFolderID == folder.FolderID).ToList();
                foreach (File f in ListOffiles)
                {
                    dc.Files.DeleteObject(f);
                }
                dc.SaveChanges();
            }
        }
```

The next method that is not a normal Repository method is the `DeleteFilesInFolder`. This method takes in a `Folder` object. With this `folder` object in hand we get a collection of related files. We then iterate over each file and call the `DeleteFileFromFileSystem` method. We then retrieve all the files for the specific FolderID and then iterate through the list of files and call the `DeleteObject` method to delete the `File` records. We then call `SaveChanges` to execute the changes.

Having mentioned the `DeleteFileFromFileSystem`, you probably understood what that method is responsible for. Essentially, it is responsible for removing the physical files that are stored on the file system. This is important as we have just allowed the data to be deleted, so we could end up with huge file stores of random unwanted files.

```
//Fisharoo/DataAccess/Repositories/FileRepository.cs
private void DeleteFileFromFileSystem(string filePath, Folder folder,
File file)
{
    string path = "";
    switch (file.FileTypeID)
    {
        case 1:
        case 2:
        case 7:
            path = "Photos\\";
            break;
        case 3:
        case 4:
            path = "Audios\\";
            break;
        case 5:
        case 8:
        case 6:
            path = "Videos\\";
            break;
    }
    string fullPath = filePath + "Files\\" + path +
                       folder.CreateDate.Year.ToString() +
                       folder.CreateDate.Month.ToString() + "\\";

    if (Directory.Exists(fullPath))
    {
        if (System.IO.File.Exists(fullPath + file.FileSystemName +
        "__o." + file.Extension))
            System.IO.File.Delete(fullPath + file.FileSystemName +
            "__o." + file.Extension);
```

```
            if (System.IO.File.Exists(fullPath + file.FileSystemName +
            "__t." + file.Extension))
                System.IO.File.Delete(fullPath + file.FileSystemName +
                "__t." + file.Extension);
            if (System.IO.File.Exists(fullPath + file.FileSystemName +
            "__s." + file.Extension))
                System.IO.File.Delete(fullPath + file.FileSystemName +
                "__s." + file.Extension);
            if (System.IO.File.Exists(fullPath + file.FileSystemName +
            "__m." + file.Extension))
                System.IO.File.Delete(fullPath + file.FileSystemName +
                "__m." + file.Extension);
            if (System.IO.File.Exists(fullPath + file.FileSystemName +
            "__l." + file.Extension))
                System.IO.File.Delete(fullPath + file.FileSystemName +
                "__l." + file.Extension);

            if(Directory.GetFiles(fullPath).Count() == 0)
                Directory.Delete(fullPath);
        }
    }
```

This method starts off first by attempting to identify the `FileType` that we are dealing with, which gets us the root folder for that type of file.

Keep in mind that if you want to store files at multiple locations and use the `FileSystemFolders`, then this will need to be tweaked a bit. The concept shown here is for a single root file folder!

Another point worth noting is that the file deletion may run into issues if the file is locked. If you run into issues, you can possibly create an entry into a separate table and have a job running that regularly scans the table and deletes the files.

With the root path identified we then create the `fullPath`. This variable is created by making a call into our `WebContext` class, that determines the root path on the server. We then add `Files`, which is the files' root folder. Then comes the path that we just configured. The next portion may seem odd at the moment. When we upload files (coming later) we upload to a directory with the name of the folder's creation date, year, and month.

With the `fullPath` configured appropriately we then check to make sure that the directory actually exists. Now we can step through each file that we created. We check to see if the file exists at the specified location and then call `System.IO.File.Delete`. We do this for each type of file we create in our upload process. Keep in mind that the upload and delete processes are fairly tied at the hip. So if we change something on one end we need to make the changes at the other end too!

With the files deleted we take the file system beautification one step further. We need to check to see if the folder is now empty. If it is, then we delete the folder too!

FolderRepository

There are a couple of methods in the `FolderRepository` that are worth covering.

- `GetFoldersByAccountID`
- `GetFriendsFolders`

The `GetFoldersByAccountID` does just what it says! It takes in an `AccountID` and performs a search to get all the folders by the passed in `AccountID`. It does go a bit beyond that. It then iterates through each folder in the resulting list and generates the file system path for the folder's cover image. This determination is then assigned to the `FullPathToCoverImage`. If there is no cover image found then the default image is assigned. Once we have this taken care of, we return the list of folders.

```
//Fisharoo/DataAccess/Repositories/FolderRepository.cs
public List<Folder> GetFoldersByAccountID(Int32 AccountID)
{
    List<Folder> result = new List<Folder>();
    using(FisharooDataContext dc = conn.GetContext())
    {
        var account = dc.Accounts.Where(a => a.AccountID ==
        AccountID).FirstOrDefault();

        IEnumerable<Folder> folders = (from f in dc.Folders
                                       where f.AccountID == AccountID
                                       orderby f.CreateDate
                                       descending
                                       select f);
        foreach (Folder folder in folders)
        {
            var fullPath = (from f in dc.Files.Include("FileType")
                            join ft in dc.FileTypes
                            on f.FileTypeID equals ft.FileTypeID
                            where f.DefaultFolderID == folder.FolderID
                            select f).FirstOrDefault();
            if (fullPath != null)
            {
                 String FullPathToCoverImage = fullPath.CreateDate.
                 Year.ToString() + fullPath.CreateDate.Month.
                 ToString() + "/" + fullPath.FileSystemName.ToString()
                 + "__S." + fullPath.FileType.Name;
                 folder.FullPathToCoverImage = FullPathToCoverImage;
            }
```

```
            else
                folder.FullPathToCoverImage = "default.jpg";
            if(account != null)
                folder.Username = account.Username;
        }
        result = folders.ToList();
    }
    return result;
}
```

The next interesting method in this repository is the `GetFriendsFolders`. This method introduces a new LINQ concept—**Union**. The Union takes all the items from one collection and merges it with another collection of items. The items that are the same in both the lists are merged so that the resulting list of items is unique.

```
//Fisharoo/DataAccess/Repositories/FolderRepository.cs
public List<Folder> GetFriendsFolders(List<Friend> Friends)
{
    List<Folder> result = new List<Folder>();
    foreach (Friend friend in Friends)
    {
        if (result.Count < 50)
        {
            List<Folder> folders =
                    GetFoldersByAccountID(friend.MyFriendsAccountID);
                    IEnumerable<Folder> result2 = result.
                    Union(folders);
                    result = result2.ToList();
        }
        else
            break;
    }
    return result;
}
```

In our method we take in a list of our `Friends`. We then iterate over this collection and with each pass we check to see if we have less than `50` folders (we chose a random number of items to show on our album homepage). If we have less than `50`, then we get all the folders for the current friend and merge it into our result list using the `Union` method. We continue to do this until we are either out of `Friends` or have `50` folders to show on the homepage.

This method could be made better in a couple of ways. Firstly we could move the `50` to a configuration file or administration panel. Also, this method should return the folders that are the latest, or contain the latest files from our friends. If we really want to be flexible this method should take into account that the user may have more friends than the current limitation. In this case we should really create pagination functionality allowing our user to see all their friends and their friends' folders. We can do all this later though!

Now that we have a place for our data and ways to interact with it, let's move out one more layer closer to the UI. We will now discuss the services' layer to help us get the data out to the front of the application.

Implementing the services/application layer

Once all the repositories are built for a single serving purpose, we can begin to create the services' layer. Again, this layer is responsible for assembling aggregates and performing complex actions with our entities. The only main service to look at here is the `FolderService`.

FolderService

This service is fairly simple. Its sole responsibility for the time being is to interact with various repositories to get the list of `Friend`'s folders for display on the album homepage for our users. Check the code associated with this chapter for implementation details.

That's it! We move on to the presentation layer.

Implementing the presentation layer

With the entire backend created and ready to go let's turn our attention to getting the presentation up and running. We will get started with building the file upload section first as it will be difficult to get the other sections to run successfully without uploaded files.

File upload

As you may already know ASP.NET is very handy at browsing a file, selecting it, and then uploading it. There are very few modifications that need to be made to your application to enable this functionality, such as you need to alter the form to include `enctype="multipart/form-data"`, add a file browse box to your page, and handle the uploaded file. Done!

As stated earlier we will be building a Flash-based file upload client. This client will be responsible for selecting a group of files on the local file system. It will then pass the files one at a time to our server side receiving page. When we discuss photo files (JPG, GIF, and so on) we will also look at some basic image processing concepts. We will also provide a Silverlight upload control as an alternate option and will reuse the control already available on codeplex (`http://silverlightfileupld.codeplex.com/`) for this. There are other options like AJAX-based controls as well, but we wanted to bring in a bit of **Rich Internet Application (RIA)** flavor and hence the use of Flash and Silverlight.

Multiple file upload

Our file receiver will be able to receive multiple files at any one time. In our case we will be primarily concerned with receiving image files. But we will set it up to receive other files as well. The receiver in our case (`ReceiveFiles.aspx.cs`) will be housed inside a webpage in our `Files` directory. We will explain the code here, but will only show the relevant parts here and not the entire code.

The beginning of our receiver will be responsible for spinning up some variables and objects. The only interesting thing to note here is the `sizesToMake` collection. This will hold all the sizes, which we will generate further down the line. If we want to add an additional size or modify one of our existing sizes we would do that here.

```
Dictionary<string,int> sizesToMake = new Dictionary<string,int>();
```

Then in the `Page_Load()` method we have the initialization of our objects and our sizes collection. We then interrogate a query string value to see what sort of file we are dealing with. In our case we will be working with photos, but we might deal with something else later.

```
//determine save-to folder
switch (_webContext.FileTypeID)
{
    case 1:
        saveToFolder = "Photos/";
        break;
    case 2:
        saveToFolder = "Videos/";
       break;
    case 3:
        saveToFolder = "Audios/";
        break;
}
```

Once we have decided which folder we are working with, we would then need to check to make sure that folder is actually on the file system. If not, then we may want to create it.

```
//make sure the directory is ready for use
saveToFolder += DateTime.Now.Year.ToString() +
                DateTime.Now.Month.ToString() + "/";
if (!Directory.Exists(Server.MapPath(saveToFolder)))
    Directory.CreateDirectory(Server.MapPath(saveToFolder));
```

We then have a few other variables that we want to set up. We need to get the Account that we are working with. We also need to receive the uploaded files. And finally, we will need to obtain the full path to the folder that we are saving our files to.

```
Account account = _accountService.GetAccountByID(
  _webContext.AccountID);
HttpFileCollection uploadedFiles =  Request.Files;
string Path = Server.MapPath(saveToFolder);
```

Now that we have a collection of uploaded files we need to work with each file one at a time. To do this we will start a `for` loop. At the top of each iteration we will need to get a single file that we want to process.

```
for(int i = 0 ; i < uploadedFiles.Count ; i++)
{
    HttpPostedFile F = uploadedFiles[i];
```

We then need to initialize some more variables to be set up where the files will be stored and how we will do it. We will get the folder ID from the query string. Notice that we are currently assuming that we are playing with image files with a static `fileType` of `1`. If we were to create another page to upload say audio files, we would want to pass in the `fileType`. Next we attempt to get the `uploadedFileName` by parsing the end of the file name of the uploaded file. Once we have the file name we get the file extension. As we will be saving the files to the file system, we run the risk of overwriting files if we do not ensure that the file has a unique name. To do this, we create a new GUID string that will act as our file system's file name. With all this data in place we then have enough to create the final file name. We then create the domain object file.

```
string folderID = _webContext.AlbumID.ToString();
string fileType = "1";
string uploadedFileName =
             F.FileName.Substring(F.FileName.LastIndexOf("\\") + 1);
string extension =
   uploadedFileName.Substring(uploadedFileName.LastIndexOf(".") + 1);
```

```
Guid guidName = Guid.NewGuid();
string fullFileName = Path + "/" + guidName.ToString() + "__o." +
  extension;
bool goodFile = true;
//create the file
File file = new File();
```

Next, we look at the `fileType` that was set and determine the `File` object's `FileTypeID`. This is an enum that was set up in the File's partial class. Note that at the end of each inner switch statement we are setting a flag for `goodFile` to determine if we have successfully found our `FileTypeID`. Do note that this isn't a foolproof method as corrupt files can still be uploaded with these valid extensions. However, we will trust our users and keep things simple for now.

```
#region "Determine file type"
switch (fileType)
{
    case "1":
        file.FileSystemFolderID =
                         (int)FileSystemFolder.Paths.Photos;
        switch (extension.ToLower())
        {
            case "jpg":
                file.FileTypeID = (int)File.Types.JPG;
                break;
            case "gif":
                file.FileTypeID = (int)File.Types.GIF;
                break;
            case "jpeg":
                file.FileTypeID = (int)File.Types.JPEG;
                break;
            default:
                goodFile = false;
                break;
        }
        break;
    case "2":
        file.FileSystemFolderID = (int)FileSystemFolder.Paths.Videos;
        switch (extension.ToLower())
        {
            case "wmv":
                file.FileTypeID = (int)File.Types.WMV;
                break;
            case "flv":
                file.FileTypeID = (int)File.Types.FLV;
```

```
                    break;
                case "swf":
                    file.FileTypeID = (int)File.Types.SWF;
                    break;
                default:
                    goodFile = false;
                    break;
            }
            break;
        case "3":
            file.FileSystemFolderID = (int)FileSystemFolder.Paths.Audios;
            switch (extension.ToLower())
            {
                case "wav":
                    file.FileTypeID = (int)File.Types.WAV;
                    break;
                case "mp3":
                    file.FileTypeID = (int)File.Types.MP3;
                    break;
                case "flv":
                    file.FileTypeID = (int)File.Types.FLV;
                    break;
                default:
                    goodFile = false;
                    break;
            }
            break;
    }
```

Next, we attempt to populate the domain `File` object with all its properties such as the size of the uploaded file, the account that it belongs to, its file system name, and so on.

```
    file.Size = F.ContentLength;
    file.AccountID = account.AccountID;
    file.DefaultFolderID = Convert.ToInt32(folderID);
    file.FileName = uploadedFileName;
    file.FileSystemName = guidName;
    file.Description = "";
    file.IsPublicResource = false;
```

Now we are ready to start the work. If the goodFile flag is still true then we can commit our file object to the database. We then save the actual uploaded file to the file system with its new file name. And finally if the fileType is a Picture, we scrub the file against our Resize() method to generate the various sizes of files we want to end up with.

```
if (goodFile)
{
    _fileService.SaveFile(file);
    F.SaveAs(fullFileName);
    if(Convert.ToInt32(fileType) == ((int)Folder.Types.Photo))
    {
        Resize(F,saveToFolder,guidName,extension);
    }
}
```

To get into the Resize() method we have to pass in the uploaded file that we are working with, the folder that we want to save the files to, the generated GUID for the file system name, and the extension of the uploaded file. Once in the Resize() method, we can create all the size variations that we need for our uploaded photo. We start off by setting up a foreach loop that will iterate through the dictionary in the class wide sizesToMake collection.

```
public void Resize(HttpPostedFile F, string SaveToFolder, Guid
                  SystemFileNamePrefix, string Extension)
{
    //Makes all the different sizes in the sizesToMake collection
    foreach (KeyValuePair<string, int> pair in sizesToMake)
    {
```

Inside of our loop we will start up a new System.Drawing.Image and we will initialize it from the uploaded files input stream. We then move to creating a new Bitmap that is initialized from the newly created Image. With the Bitmap we can then create new variations on the size of that uploaded image. First we look to see if the file that was uploaded is longer on the top or on the side so that we know how to appropriately determine the ratio of the image's height and width.

```
using(System.Drawing.Image image =
     System.Drawing.Image.FromStream(F.InputStream))
//determine the thumbnail sizes
using(Bitmap bitmap = new Bitmap(image))
{
    decimal Ratio;
    if(bitmap.Width > bitmap.Height)
    {
        Ratio = (decimal) pair.Value / bitmap.Width;
```

```
            NewWidth = pair.Value;
            decimal Temp = bitmap.Height * Ratio;
            NewHeight = (int)Temp;
        }
        else
        {
            Ratio = (decimal) pair.Value / bitmap.Height;
            NewHeight = pair.Value;
            decimal Temp = bitmap.Width * Ratio;
            NewWidth = (int)Temp;
        }
    }
```

Once we have our sizes determined we can resize it and save it to the file system. We do this by again setting a reference to the uploaded file and reconstructing a new `Bitmap`. With this in hand we can then save the bitmap to the file system with its new dimensions. Do note though that in this case when we save the file to the file system, we are not adding a section to the name using the key name from the dictionary. This results in a file name that is made up of `{GUID}__{key}.{extension}`. This means that every file will be unique and will have uniquely named files of various sizes.

```
using(System.Drawing.Image image =
            System.Drawing.Image.FromStream(F.InputStream))
using(Bitmap bitmap = new Bitmap(image, NewWidth, NewHeight))
{
    bitmap.Save(Server.MapPath(SaveToFolder + "/" +
                            SystemFileNamePrefix.ToString() + "__"
                          + pair.Key + "." + Extension),
                            image.RawFormat);
}
```

We continue to loop through all the different file sizes in our dictionary creating new files for each one. Once complete we will move to the next file that was uploaded. Let's now write a test page to test our receiving page.

```
Receiving files with Flash uploader
```

Now that we have a way of receiving uploaded files, let's create the UI to upload a handful of files. This is a Flash-based UI. You can either download a trial copy of Flash or look at alternatives in a product such as Swish or Flex.

As this is not so much a Flash book, we will skim over this topic quickly. We will create a simple Flash UI that has a browse box, a couple of dynamic text boxes, and some labels. We will build the entire UI on one frame and the UI looks something as shown in the following screenshot:

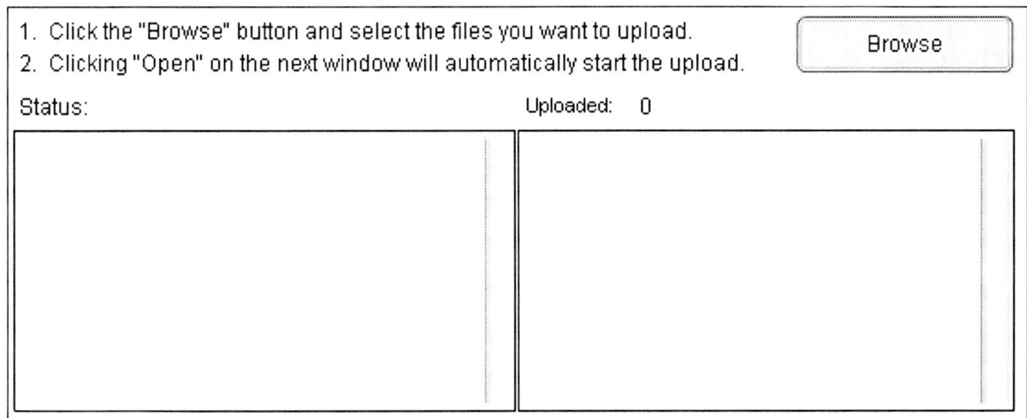

Once we have the UI done, we will need to plug the Flash uploader onto a page. To do this, we will need to add the following code on a page that will house the Flash uploader.

```
//Fisharoo/Web/Photos/AddPhotos.aspx
<object classid="clsid:d27cdb6e-ae6d-11cf-96b8-444553540000"
codebase="http://fpdownload.macromedia.com/pub/shockwave/cabs/flash/
swflash.cab#version=8,0,0,0"
    width="550" height="510" id="FileUpload">
    <param name="allowScriptAccess" value="sameDomain" />
    <param name="movie" value="../Files/FileUpload.
    swf?SiteRoot=<%Response.Write(ctx.RootUrl);%>&AlbumID=<%Response.
    Write(ctx.AlbumID); %>&FileType=<%Response.Write(ctx.FolderType);
    %>&AccountID=<%Response.Write(ctx.AccountID); %>" />
    <param name="quality" value="high" />
    <param name="bgcolor" value="white" />
    <embed src="../Files/FileUpload.swf?SiteRoot=<%Response.
    Write(ctx.RootUrl);%>&AlbumID=<%Response.Write(ctx.
    AlbumID); %>&FileType=<%Response.Write(ctx.FolderType);
    %>&AccountID=<%Response.Write(ctx.AccountID); %>"
        quality="high" bgcolor="#ffffff" width="550" height="220"
        name="FileUpload" align="middle"
        allowscriptaccess="sameDomain" type="application/x-
        shockwave-flash" pluginspage="http://www.macromedia.com/go/
        getflashplayer" />
</object>
```

Once you have the UI showing on our upload page and have the appropriate variables plugged in you should be good to go. Similar to Flash UI, we will also provide for a Silverlight UI, which as mentioned earlier is a control that we have taken from the codeplex site.

Receiving files with Silverlight uploader

The UI when integrated with the application looks as shown in the following screenshot. There are three files currently selected for upload (`desert.jpg`, `jellyfish.jpg` and `penguins.jpg`). We can enable thumbnail previews while the files are being uploaded, but it will slow down the upload process. The code for file upload control (as taken from `http://silverlightfileupld.codeplex.com/`) can be found in `Fisharoo/FileUpload` and `Fisharoo/SilverlightFileUpload` folders.

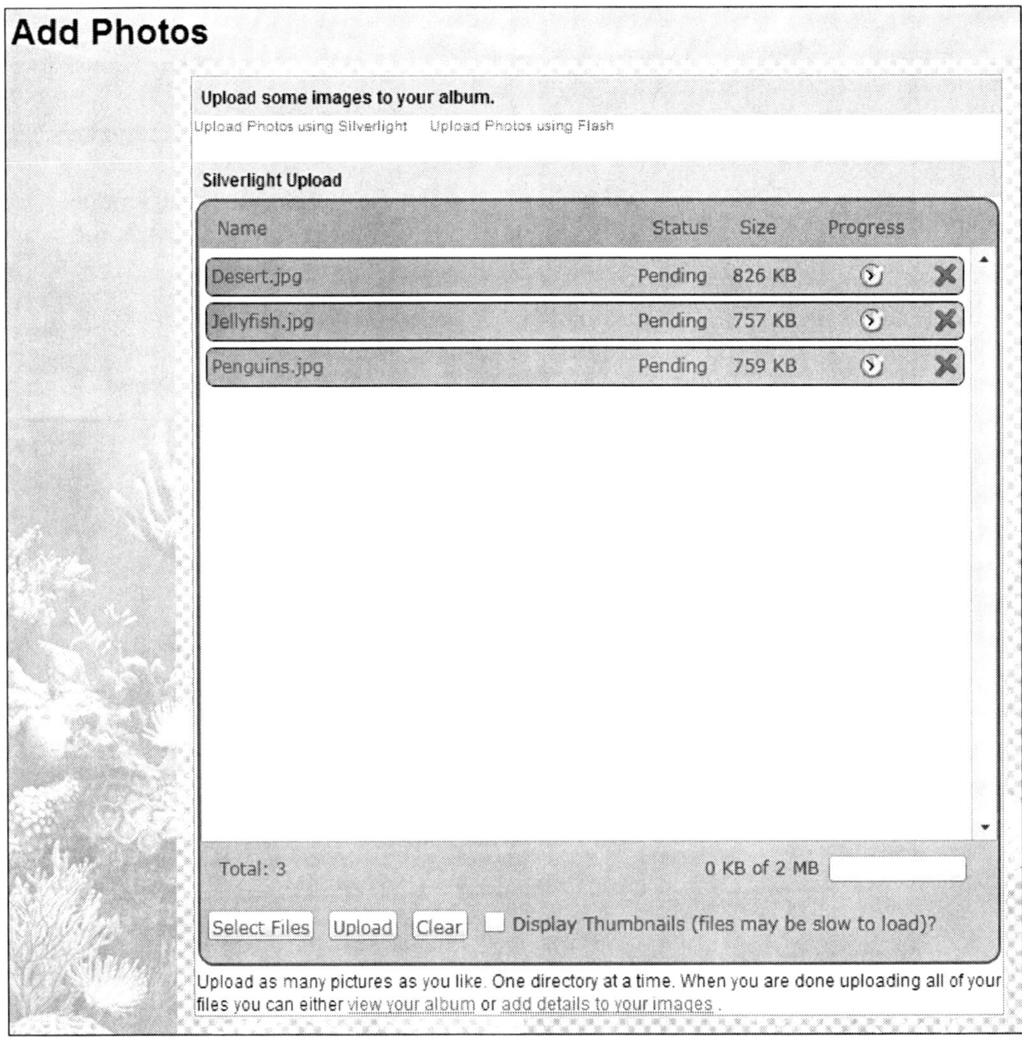

The code to include the Silverlight XAP package in the UI is:

```
//Fisharoo/Web/Photos/AddPhotos.aspx
<object data="data:application/x-silverlight-2," type="application/x-silverlight-2" width="550" height="510">
    <param name="source" value="/ClientBin/FileUpload.xap" />
    <param name="onError" value="onSilverlightError" />
    <param name="background" value="white" />
    <param name="minRuntimeVersion" value="4.0.50401.0" />
    <param name="autoUpgrade" value="true" />
    <param name="initParams" value="UploadPage=/Handlers/
    FileUpload.ashx?AlbumID=<%Response.Write(ctx.AlbumID);
    %>&FileTypeID=<%Response.Write(ctx.FolderType);
    %>&AccountID=<%Response.Write(ctx.AccountID); %>,Filter=Images
    (*.jpg)|*.jpg" />
    <a href="http://go.microsoft.com/fwlink/?LinkID=149156
    &v=4.0.50401.0" style="text-decoration: none">
        <img src="http://go.microsoft.com/fwlink/?LinkId=161376"
        alt="Get Microsoft Silverlight"
            style="border-style: none" />
    </a>
</object>
```

Most of this is the standard code that is used in any Silverlight application while including a Silverlight control in the application. The only main point of interest is the `initParams` parameter, to which we pass the value of the `httpHandler` that will help with the file upload. The code for this handler can be found in `Fisharoo/Web/Handlers/Fileupload.ashx.cs` file. Usually `httpHandlers` need to be registered in the `web.config` file, however since we have the handler as an `.ashx` file, it is managed automatically by the ASP.NET runtime and we don't need to explicitly register it.

This handler hands over the processing to `FileProcessor` class (`Web/HelperClasses/FileProcessor.cs`) that manages the GUID creation, creation of the various sized images, and appropriate entries in the backend. The code here is similar to that already discussed in earlier section: **Multiple file upload**.

Now that we are uploading files, let's move on to discussing the display of those photos.

Photo albums

There are many things we can do now as we have the files uploaded to the server in various sizes! We are going to show you the `MyPhotos` page, which will list all the galleries for the logged in account and link to the `ViewAlbum` page. This should demonstrate how to work with the photo albums and the photos. You can look at other pages that are in the code to see how to create albums, link to the file uploader, and so on—basically all the data management tasks that surround the photo album concepts.

MyPhotos

In this page we will display all the photo albums that an account has. We will use a `ListView` to do this.

```
//Fisharoo/Web/Photos/MyPhotos.aspx
<asp:ListView id="lvAlbums" runat="server"
                 OnItemDataBound="lbAlbums_ItemDataBound">
    <LayoutTemplate>
        <ul class="albumsList">
            <asp:PlaceHolder ID="itemPlaceholder"
                             runat="server"></asp:PlaceHolder>
        </ul>
    </LayoutTemplate>

    <ItemTemplate>
        <li>
            <asp:HyperLink CssClass="albumsActionLink"
                           ID="linkEditAlbum" NavigateUrl="
                          ~/Photos/EditAlbum.aspx" Text="Edit"
                          runat="server"></asp:HyperLink>
            <asp:HyperLink CssClass="albumsActionLink"
                           ID="linkViewAlbum" NavigateUrl=
                            "~/Photos/ViewAlbum.aspx" Text="View"
                            runat="server"></asp:HyperLink>
            <asp:LinkButton CssClass="albumsActionLink"
                            ID="linkDeleteAlbum" Text="Delete"
                            OnClick="linkDeleteAlbum_Click"
                            runat="server"></asp:LinkButton><br />
            <asp:Label CssClass="albumsTitle" ID="lblName"
                       Text='<%#((PEFolder)Container.DataItem).Name
                       %>'
                       runat="server"></asp:Label><br />
            <img src="<%#_webContext.RootUrl
                %>files/photos/<%#((PEFolder)
                Container.DataItem).FullPathToCoverImage %>" /><br />
```

```
            <asp:Label CssClass="albumsLocation" Text="in - "
                           runat="server"></asp:Label>
            <asp:Label CssClass="albumsLocation" ID="lblLocation"
                    Text='<%#((PEFolder)Container.DataItem).Location
                    %>'
                    runat="server"></asp:Label><br />
            <asp:Label CssClass="albumsDescription"
                              ID="lblDescription" Text='<%#
                          ((PEFolder)Container.DataItem).Description
                           %>'
                           runat="server"></asp:Label>
            <asp:Literal Visible="false" ID="litFolderID"
                             Text='<%#((PEFolder)Container.DataItem).
                             FolderID.ToString() %>'
                            runat="server"></asp:Literal>
        </li>
    </ItemTemplate>

    <EmptyDataTemplate>
        Sorry, you don't seem to have any albums at this time!
    </EmptyDataTemplate>
</asp:ListView>
```

Note that the `ListView` has an `OnItemDataBound="lbAlbums_ItemDataBound"` event hooked up. This will become important later on as it controls how we handle each item that is bound to the `ListView`. Also note the use of `PEFolder` class, which is a presentation entity (a concept we have already discussed in earlier chapters) and is bound to the various controls inside the `ListView` template.

The first item you will see inside of the `ListView` is the `LayoutTemplate`. This template defines the iterating items. In our case we have chosen to use an unordered list to display our albums. With some CSS we have full control over how each list item is rendered.

Inside the list you will see that we have a `PlaceHolder` defined with an ID of `itemPlaceholder`. You must use this ID as you see it here! This `PlaceHolder` is responsible for holding everything in the `ItemTemplate` as we do our iteration.

The next section you will see is the `ItemTemplate`. This template actually defines what goes into each item of our list. In our case we have some metadata about each album, the default image for the album, and some link to other functionalities.

Finally we have the `EmptyDataTemplate`. This template is responsible for showing something when there is no data to iterate through. In our case we are displaying a message stating that there are no albums to be displayed.

We can now turn to the code behind this page (keep in mind that we are still using the MVP pattern). Most of our code behind is driven by our presenter file. In our code behind we have the `LoadUI` method, which is passed a list of `Folder` (Albums). This is the key `DataSource` for our `ListView` control.

```
//Fisharoo/Web/Photos/MyPhotos.aspx.cs
public void LoadUI(List<PEFolder> folders)
{
    if (!IsPostBack)
    {
        lvAlbums.DataSource = folders;
        lvAlbums.DataBind();
    }
}
```

Next we have the `lbAlbums_ItemDataBound`. This is the method that we were hooked up to in the `ListView` to handle each item as it is bound to our `ListView`. In this method we are referencing the controls in our `ItemTemplate` so that we can work with them. We make sure that the `Album`'s description is not too long. If it is, we concatenate it to fit our current display. Then we are constructing our links so that they work as expected for each `Album` that we are binding.

```
//Fisharoo/Web/Photos/MyPhotos.aspx.cs
protected void lbAlbums_ItemDataBound(object sender,
                                     ListViewItemEventArgs e)
{
    if (e.Item.ItemType == ListViewItemType.DataItem)
    {
        HyperLink linkEditAlbum = e.Item.FindControl("linkEditAlbum")
                                as HyperLink;
        LinkButton linkDeleteAlbum =
                e.Item.FindControl("linkDeleteAlbum") as LinkButton;
        HyperLink linkViewAlbum = e.Item.FindControl("linkViewAlbum")
                                as HyperLink;
        Literal litFolderID = e.Item.FindControl("litFolderID") as
                            Literal;
        Label lblDescription = e.Item.FindControl("lblDescription")
                             as Label;
        if (lblDescription.Text.Length > 150)
        {
            lblDescription.Text = lblDescription.Text.Substring(0,
                                                                149);
            lblDescription.Text += "...";
        }
        linkEditAlbum.NavigateUrl += "?AlbumID=" + litFolderID.Text;
```

```
            linkDeleteAlbum.Attributes.Add("OnClick","javascript:return(co
            nfirm('Are you sure you want to delete this album?'));");
            linkDeleteAlbum.Attributes.Add("FolderID",litFolderID.Text);
            linkViewAlbum.NavigateUrl += "?AlbumID=" + litFolderID.Text;
        }
    }
```

And finally, we have a method to handle our delete link's click event. This method calls into our presenter to handle the deletion of an `Album`.

```
//Fisharoo/Web/Photos/MyPhotos.aspx.cs
protected void linkDeleteAlbum_Click(object sender, EventArgs e)
{
    LinkButton linkDeleteAlbum = sender as LinkButton;
    _presenter.DeleteFolder(Convert.ToInt64(linkDeleteAlbum.Attributes
                    ["FolderID"]));
}
```

ViewAlbum

The `ViewAlbum` page is exactly the same as the `MyPhotos` page in that it uses the `ListView` to handle its rendering of the data. The only difference is that we use `PEFile` instead of `PEFolder`.

In the code behind we have a similar layout as the `MyPhotos` code behind. We load the photos for the given album. We also load some details about the album itself so that we can show things like the album's description and the like. There are a few button controls that we have our events hooked to so that we can handle things like navigation via the `redirector` class. We are showing only the main parts of the code below:

```
//Fisharoo/Web/Photos/ViewAlbum.aspx.cs
protected void lvAlbum_ItemDataBound(object sender,
                                   ListViewItemEventArgs e)
{
    if(e.Item.ItemType == ListViewItemType.DataItem)
    {
        HyperLink linkImage = e.Item.FindControl("linkImage") as
                              HyperLink;
        Literal litImageName = e.Item.FindControl("litImageName") as
                               Literal;
        Literal litFileExtension =
                e.Item.FindControl("litFileExtension") as Literal;
        string pathToImage = "~/files/photos/" +
               linkImage.NavigateUrl + "/" + litImageName.Text;
        linkImage.NavigateUrl = pathToImage + "__o." +
                litFileExtension.Text;
```

```
            linkImage.ImageUrl = pathToImage + "__s." +
                    litFileExtension.Text;
        }
        if(e.Item.ItemType == ListViewItemType.EmptyItem)
        {
            HyperLink linkAddPhotos = e.Item.FindControl("linkAddPhotos")
                                          as HyperLink;
            linkAddPhotos.NavigateUrl =
                                        "~/photos/AddPhotos.aspx?AlbumID=" +
                                        _webContext.AlbumID.ToString();
        }
    }

    public void LoadAlbumDetails(Folder folder)
    {
        lblAlbumName.Text = folder.Name;
        lblLocation.Text = folder.Location;
        lblDescription.Text = folder.Description;
        lblCreateDate.Text = folder.CreateDate.ToString();
        if(folder.AccountID != _userSession.CurrentUser.AccountID)
        {
            btnEditPhotos.Visible = false;
            btnEditAlbum.Visible = false;
            btnAddPhotos.Visible = false;
        }
    }

    public void LoadPhotos(List<PEFile> files)
    {
        lvGallery.DataSource = files;
        lvGallery.DataBind();
    }
```

Take a look in the photos folder of the website project. There are many other pages for editing photos, editing albums, and so on that demonstrate additional functionality with regards to interacting with our files and photo album data.

Summary

In this chapter we looked at the infrastructure and decisions that go into a media management application. We focused heavily on processing and storing images. But most of the principles that we looked at apply to all sorts of different file types. The only real part that would need to be tweaked is how the file is processed once it is stored on the server. In the case of audio and video files you would most likely want to transfer them to a Flash format from a WAV or WMV format so that they become more accessible to your web users or you can use Silverlight along with IIS Smooth Streaming options to stream WMV files. One aspect to keep in mind will be the content growth and space management along with it. You may want to look up some content distribution network.

This chapter has added the ability to create photo albums. We then discussed the ability to upload and manipulate photos. We also discussed how to handle multiple file uploads and the most appropriate way to store them on the file system. Finally, we created a way for our users to interact with their albums and uploaded files.

8
Blogs

People join a community to either look for or provide information on a pre-specified topic. Often this is performed by way of a blog. A blog allows people to freely express themselves by way of providing stories, articles, or quick blurbs generally on any topic with the community.

Building this key feature into your community is actually one of the easiest things to do. Having built so many features to this point, snapping in the blog module and its required components will go quite smoothly. We will cover not only creating a blog but also how to add friendly URLs to our blog posts. Once this is in place we will follow it up by attaching our blogging system to our alerts system.

Problem

In this chapter we will add the blogging feature to our site. This will handle creating and managing a post. It will also handle sending alerts to your friends' alert page. And finally we will handle creating a friendly URL for your blog posts.

Here we are making our first post to our blog.

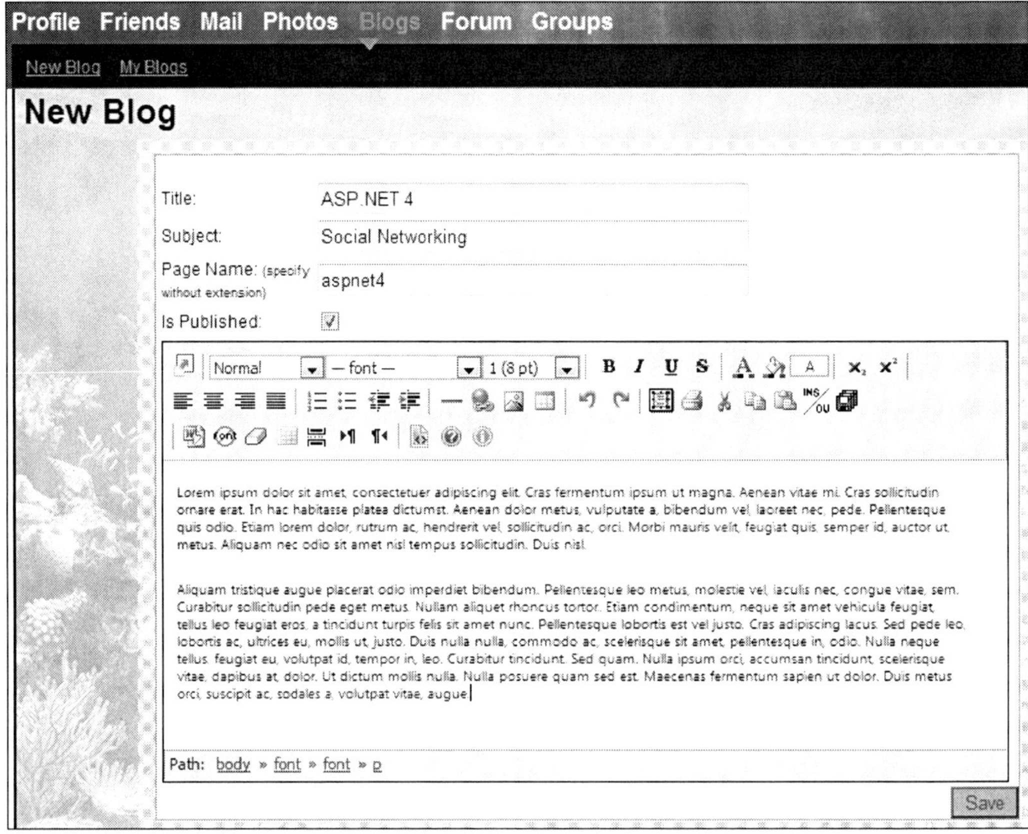

Once our post is created, we will then see it on the Blog's homepage and the **My Blogs** section. From here, we can edit the post or delete it. We can also click into the post to view what we have seen so far.

The following screenshot shows what one will see when he/she clicks on the post:

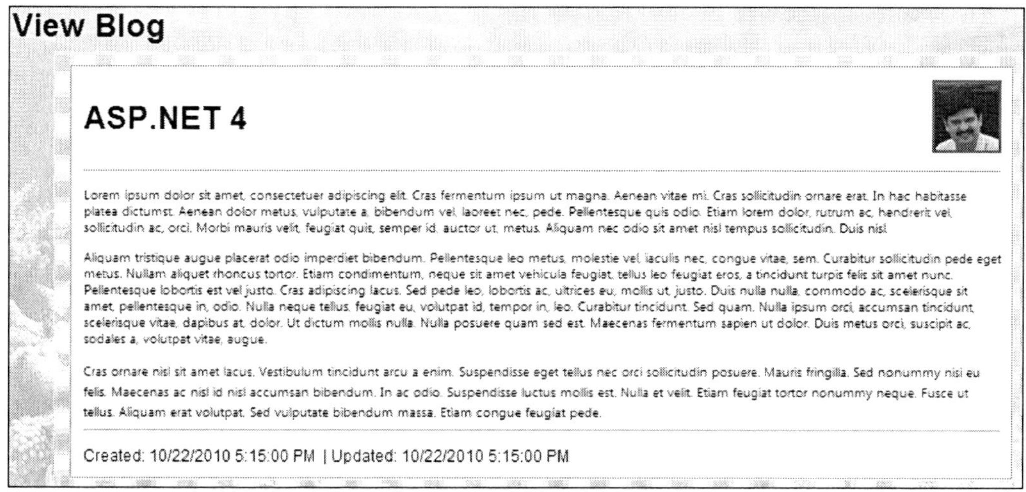

We have the blog post set up to show the blogger's avatar. This is a feature that you can easily add to or remove. Most of your users want to be able to see who the author of the blog they are currently reading is!

Also, we will add a friendly URL to our blog post's pages. You can see in the following screenshot that the blog is being accessed using its name as part of the URL (.../`aspnet-4.aspx`).

Design

We will only need one table to hold our blog posts. After that we need to hook our blog system into our existing infrastructure.

Blogs

In order for us to store our blog, we will need one simple table. This table will handle all the standard attributes of a normal blog post to include the title, subject, page name, and the post itself. It has only one relationship out to the `Accounts` table so that we know who owns the post down the road. That's it!

Solution

Let's take a look at the solution for this set of features.

Implementing the database

Let's take a look at the tables required by our solution.

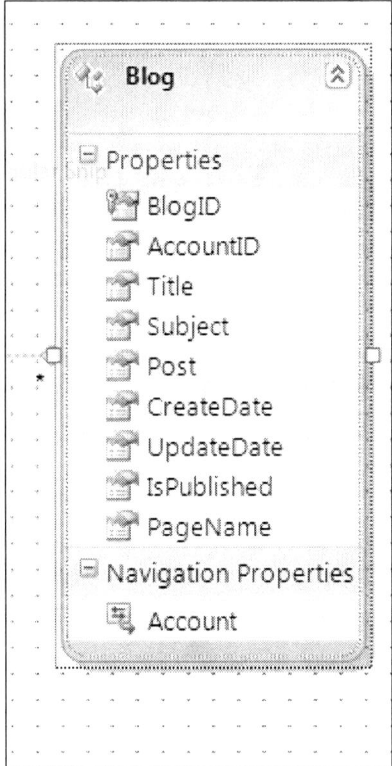

Blogs

The blogs table has the same attributes as the Blog entity above. We have discussed most of this under this section.

The one thing that is interesting here is the **Post** column. Notice that we have this set to a **varchar(MAX)** field. This may be too big for your community, so feel free to change it. For our community we can work with this data type. We can always add a UI restriction without impacting the database design using a validation control. After that we will look at the **IsPublished** flag. This flag tells the system whether or not to show the post in the public domain. Next to that we will also be interested in the **PageName** column. This column is what we will display in the browser's address bar. As it will be displayed in the address bar, we need to make sure that the input is clean so that we don't get hit with SQL injection attacks or parsing issues (responsible for causing data type exceptions). We will handle that on the input side in our presenter later.

Creating the relationships

Once all the tables are created we can then create all the relationships. We have created relationships between the `Blogs` and `Accounts` tables:

Setting up the data access layer

To set up the data access layer follow the steps mentioned next:

1. Open the `Fisharoo.edmx` file and include the new Blog table as described in Chapter 3.
2. Hit **Save** and you should now have the Blog domain object to work with!

Building repositories

With the addition of new tables will come the addition of new repositories so that we can get at the data stored in the corresponding table. We will be creating the `BlogRepository` repository at `Fisharoo\DataAccess\Repositories` to support our needs.

Our repository will generally have a method for selecting by ID, select all by parent ID, save, and delete. Once you have seen one repository you have pretty much seen all of them. Review previous chapters, the appendices, or the included code for examples of a standard repository. We will discuss anything that varies from what is considered standard!

We will start with a method that will allow us to get at a blog by its page name, that we can capture from the browser's address bar.

```
//Fisharoo/DataAccess/Repositories/BlogRepository.cs
public Blog GetBlogByPageName(string PageName, Int32 AccountID)
      {
          Blog result = new Blog();
          using (FisharooDataContext dc = _conn.GetContext())
          {
              result = dc.Blogs.Include("Account").Where(b =>
              b.PageName == PageName && b.AccountID == AccountID).
              FirstOrDefault();
              //we can do this since there will be only one result
              result.account = result.Account;
          }
          return result;
      }
```

Notice that for this system to work we can only have one blog with one unique page name. If we force our entire community to use unique page names, we would eventually have some upset users. We want to make sure to enforce unique page names across users only for this purpose. To do this, we require an `AccountID` to be passed in with the page name, which gives our users more flexibility with their page name overlaps! We will show you how we get the `AccountID` later. Other than that we are performing a lambda expression to select the appropriate blog out of the collection of blogs in the data context.

Next we will discuss a method to get all the latest blog posts via the `GetLatestBlogs()` method. This method will also get and attach the appropriate Account for each blog. Before we dive into this method we will need to extend the `Blog` class to have an `Account` property.

To extend the `Blog` class we will need to create a public partial class under the `DataAccess` project.

```
namespace Fisharoo.DataAccess
{
    public partial class Blog
    {
        public Account account { get; set; }
    }
}
```

Now we can look at the `GetLatestBlogs()` method.

```
public List<Blog> GetLatestBlogs()
      {
          List<Blog> result = new List<Blog>();
```

```
            using (FisharooDataContext dc = _conn.GetContext())
            {
                IEnumerable<Blog> blogs = (from b in dc.Blogs
                                           where b.IsPublished
                                           orderby b.UpdateDate
                                           descending
                                           select b).Take(30);
                IEnumerable<Account> accounts =
                    dc.Accounts.Where(a => blogs.Select(b =>
                    b.AccountID).Distinct().Contains(a.AccountID));
                foreach (Blog blog in blogs)
                {
                    blog.Account = accounts.Where(a => a.AccountID ==
                    blog.AccountID).FirstOrDefault();
                    blog.account = blog.Account; //this is done to
                    access account outside ObjectContext
                }
                result = blogs.ToList();
            }
            return result;
        }
```

The first expression in this method gets the top N blogs ordered by their `UpdateDate` in descending order. This gets us the newest entries. We then add a `where` clause looking for only those blogs that are published.

We then move to getting a list of Accounts that are associated with our previously selected blogs. We do this by selecting a list of `AccountID`s from our blog list and then doing a `Contains` search against our `Accounts` table. This gives us a list of accounts that belong to all the blogs which we have in hand.

With these two collections in hand we can iterate through our list of blogs and attach the appropriate Account to each blog. This gives us a full listing of blogs with accounts.

As we discussed earlier, it is very important for us to make sure that we keep the page names unique on a per user basis. To do this we need to have a method that allows our UI to determine if a page name is unique or not. To do this we will have the `CheckPageNameIsUnique()` method.

```
    public bool CheckPageNameIsUnique(Blog blog)
        {
            blog = CleanPageName(blog);
            bool result = true;
            using (FisharooDataContext dc = _conn.GetContext())
            {
```

```
                int count = dc.Blogs.Where(b => b.PageName == blog.
                PageName && b.AccountID == blog.AccountID).Count();
                if (count > 0)
                    result = false;
            }
            return result;
        }
```

This method looks at all the blog entries except itself to determine if there are other blog posts with the same page name that are also by the same Account. This allows us to effectively lock down our users from creating duplicate page names. This will be important when we start to discuss our user-friendly URLs.

Next, we will look at a private method that will help us clean up these page name inputs. Keep in mind that these page names will be displayed in the browser's address bar and therefore need not have any characters in them that the browser would want to encode. While we can decode the URL easily this conversation is more about keeping the URL user-friendly so that the user and the search engine spiders can easily read where they are at. When we have characters in the URL that are encoded, we will end up with something like `%20` where `%20` is equivalent to a space. But to read `my%20blog%20post` is not that easy. It is much easier to read my-blog-post. So we will strip out all of our so called special characters and replace all spaces with hyphens. This method will be the `CleanPageName()` method.

```
private Blog CleanPageName(Blog blog)
{
    blog.PageName = blog.PageName.Replace(" ", "-").Replace("!", "")
        .Replace("&", "").Replace("?", "").Replace(",", "");
    return blog;
}
```

You can add to this as many filters as you like. For the time being we are replacing the handful of special characters that we have just seen in the code.

Next, we will get into the service layers that we will use to handle our interactions with the system. Unlike other chapters this chapter will not introduce any new service layers—we will add to the existing one.

Implementing the services/application layer

Once all the repositories are built for single serving purposes we can begin creating the services layer. We will not be creating any new services for this component but will need to add to the existing `AlertService` residing under `//Fisharoo/BusinessLogic`.

AlertService

The `AlertService` as we know from the previous chapters is responsible for sending out notifications to our users via their filter page. This is the page that shows new activity amongst your profile and your friends' profiles.

For blogs we added two methods to our `AlertService` class—one method to send out alerts for new blog posts and the other for alerts while updating our blog posts.

```
public void AddNewBlogPostAlert(Blog blog)
    {
        alert = new Alert();
        alert.CreateDate = DateTime.Now;
        alert.AccountID = _userSession.CurrentUser.AccountID;
        alert.AlertTypeID = (int)AlertType.AlertTypes.NewBlogPost;
        alertMessage = "<div class=\"AlertHeader\">" +
        GetProfileImage(_userSession.CurrentUser.AccountID) +
                        GetProfileUrl(_userSession.CurrentUser.
                        Username) + " has just added a new blog
                        post: <b>" +
                        blog.Title + "</b></div>";
        alert.Message = alertMessage;
        SaveAlert(alert);
        SendAlertToFriends(alert);
    }
```

If you have already read Chapter 4 that included the `AlertService` you will know what goes into adding alerts. For those who are not aware, we will quickly take a look at this `AddNewBlogPostAlert()` method.

This method will take in the new Blog that was posted so that we can use some information about it in our alert. As soon as we get into the body of our method, we want to initialize a new Alert. We will then fill out some of the initial properties.

One of the properties that we will need to extend is the `AlertType` class that has the `AlertTypes` property. You will see that this `AlertTypes` property is really a representation of the record IDs we have stored in the `AlertTypes` table in the database. Open up the `AlertType` class and add a couple of new entries for the `NewBlogPost` and `UpdatedBlogPost`.

Refer to code at `//Fisharoo/DataAccess/AlertType.cs`.

Then go into the `AlertTypes` table and create two new records `NewBlogPost` and `UpdatedBlogPost`. If the record IDs that are generated do not correspond to the numbers you see above, update the numbers you see in the enum to the ones that were created in the table.

Now we can look at the message that we want to show in our alert. This can consist of any standard HTML as it will be displayed on the alerts page or "the filter" as we will call it. Once the Alert is fully configured we can then save the Alert to the database. And in this case (but not all cases) we want this alert to show up on all of our friends' filters as well, to let them know that a new blog post was just created.

Here is the method for the updated blog post, that is almost identical to the one seen for updating the blog post:

```
public void AddUpdatedBlogPostAlert(Blog blog)
{
    alert = new Alert();
    alert.CreateDate = DateTime.Now;
    alert.AccountID = _userSession.CurrentUser.AccountID;
    alert.AlertTypeID = (int)AlertType.AlertTypes.NewBlogPost;
    alertMessage = "<div class=\"AlertHeader\">" +
                   GetProfileImage(_userSession.CurrentUser.AccountID)
                   + GetProfileUrl(_userSession.CurrentUser.Username)
                   + " has updated the <b>" + blog.Title +
                   "</b> blog post!</div>";
    alert.Message = alertMessage;
    SaveAlert(alert);
    SendAlertToFriends(alert);
}
```

With the repository and service layers completed we can now take a look at our UI.

Implementing the presentation layer

The presentation for this chapter is almost as modest as the infrastructure is. We will have a **Blog** link in the top navigation. When you click on this link you will be taken to a page where you see a list of the latest blog posts. From the Blog section you can then choose to either view a blog from the latest blogs page or you can choose to view your blogs or create a new blog. In addition to these four pages we will also address how user-friendly URLs come into play in the view post page. You can also look at providing RSS feed for the blogs so that other users can get it delivered in their client applications like Outlook instead of explicitly visiting the site.

Latest blog posts

Viewing the latest blog posts is a single call to the `BlogService`. In order for our UI to get to any service, it first has to hand off its control of all display interactions. It does this by initializing an instance of the `DefaultPresenter` and then passing a reference to itself into the `Init()` method of the presenter. Once in the `Init()` method of the presenter we can then make the call into the service to get the latest blogs. The `Blog` entity is translated to `PEBlog`, which is a presentation entity and has only those fields that are relevant for the UI.

```
//Fisharoo/Web/Blogs/Presenters/DefaultPresenter.cs
public class DefaultPresenter
{
    private IDefault _view;
    [Import]
    private IBlogService _blogService;

    public DefaultPresenter()
    {
        MEFManager.Compose(this);
    }

    public void Init(IDefault View)
    {
        _view = View;
        List<Blog> list = _blogService.GetLatestBlogs();
        _view.LoadBlogs(Translator.BlogToPEBlog(list));
    }
}
```

With the latest blogs in hand we are then able to pass them into the UI's code behind where the blogs are bound in the `Default.aspx` page. The only method of interest here is `ItemDataBound()` method that handles each item that is bound to a list view control.

```
//Fisharoo/Web/Blogs/Default.aspx.cs
public void lvBlogs_ItemDataBound(object sender, ListViewItemEventArgs
e)
{
    Literal litBlogID = e.Item.FindControl("litBlogID") as Literal;
    HyperLink linkTitle = e.Item.FindControl("linkTitle") as
    HyperLink;
    Literal litPageName = e.Item.FindControl("litPageName") as
    Literal;
    Literal litUsername = e.Item.FindControl("litUsername") as
    Literal;
    //navigation URL will follow the URL routing pattern
    linkTitle.NavigateUrl = Page.GetRouteUrl("BlogRoute", new {
    username = litUsername.Text, blogpage = litPageName.Text });
}
```

This will allow us to configure all the controls in the UI for each set of objects. Notice in particular that at the very end of our method, we are configuring the `NavigateUrl` property to display user-friendly URLs. This is created using the appropriate routing table entry (`BlogRoute`). This will be important to remember when we start our discussion about the `ViewPost.aspx` page.

Out in the UI side we can see how all the data sections are bound to the container's blog items.

```
//Fisharoo/Web/Blogs/Default.aspx
<asp:ListView ID="lvBlogs" runat="server" OnItemDataBound="lvBlogs_
ItemDataBound">
    <LayoutTemplate>
        <ul class="blogsList">
            <asp:PlaceHolder ID="itemPlaceholder" runat="server"></
            asp:PlaceHolder>
        </ul>
    </LayoutTemplate>
    <ItemTemplate>
        <li>
            <h2 class="blogsTitle">
                <asp:HyperLink ID="linkTitle" runat="server"
                Text='<%#((PEBlog)Container.DataItem).Title %>'></
                asp:HyperLink></h2>
            <p class="blogsDescription">
                Created:
                <%#((PEBlog)Container.DataItem).CreateDate%><br />
                By:
                <%#((PEBlog)Container.DataItem).Username%><br />
                Subject:
                <%#((PEBlog)Container.DataItem).Subject%><asp:Literal
                ID="litBlogID" runat="server"
                    Text='<%#((PEBlog)Container.DataItem).BlogID
                    %>'></asp:Literal>
                <asp:Literal ID="litPageName" runat="server"
                Visible="false" Text='<%#((PEBlog)Container.DataItem).
                PageName %>'></asp:Literal>
                <asp:Literal ID="litUsername" runat="server"
                Visible="false" Text='<%#((PEBlog)Container.DataItem).
                Username %>'></asp:Literal>
            </p>
        </li>
    </ItemTemplate>
    <EmptyDataTemplate>
        Sorry, there are no blogs posted yet!
    </EmptyDataTemplate>
</asp:ListView>
```

If we have data in the system we would now see a list of the latest blogs!

My Blogs

The **My Blogs** section is identical to the latest blogs post with the exception that they load their list of Blog objects via a different call into the same `BlogService`. In this case we get a list of Blogs by calling the `GetBlogsByAccountID()` method.

This method will get a list of our blog posts sorted by their create date, other than that they are identical.

Fancy URL support

Now that we have both the recent blog posts and the **My Blogs** pages created and out of the way we need to discuss handling the pretty URLs which our UIs are currently displaying. At the moment we are sending people to `domain.com/blogs/username/pagename.aspx`. As you may have guessed, this is a path to a resource that does not actually exist. In order to handle the unknown resources we will again use the URL routing logic explained earlier in Chapter 4. First we add a new routing entry to the routing collection in `RegisterRoutes()` method in `Global.ascx.cs` file.

```
//Fisharoo/Web/Global.ascx.cs
routeCollection.MapPageRoute("BlogRoute", "blogs/{username}/
{blogpage}.aspx", "~/Blogs/ViewPost.aspx");
```

As shown in the above code, the username and the blog's page name are the values used to build this particular URL and while displaying the same values will be extracted and pulled out to get the right blog entry from our database, as we will see the next section.

View post

The `ViewPost.aspx` page is an amazingly straightforward page to build. It extracts the page to be viewed from the URL by way of the routed URL, that contains the username and blog page name to get to the correct blog.

```
//Fisharoo/Web/Blogs/ViewPost.aspx.cs
protected void Page_Load(object sender, EventArgs e)
{
    _presenter = new ViewPostPresenter();
    string username = Page.RouteData.Values["username"] as string;
    string blogpage = Page.RouteData.Values["blogpage"] as string;
    _presenter.Init(this, username, blogpage);
}
```

We get the user name and the blog page name from the routed data collection and then pass it to the `ViewPostPresenter` via the `Init()` method.

Before we look at those details, here is the UI that we are loading:

```
//Fisharoo/Web/ViewPost.aspx
<table style="vertical-align: top" width="100%">
    <tr>
        <td align="left">
                <asp:Label ID="lblTitle" runat="server" Font-
                Bold="True" Font-Size="X-Large"></asp:Label>
        </td>
        <td align="right">
            <asp:HyperLink ID="linkProfile" runat="server"
            CssClass="">
                <asp:Image Width="50" Height="50" ID="imgAvatar"
                runat="server"
                    ImageUrl="/images/profileavatar/profileimage.aspx"
                    />
            </asp:HyperLink>
        </td>
    </tr>
    <tr>
        <td colspan="2" align="left">
            <hr />
            <asp:Label ID="lblPost" runat="server"></asp:Label>
            <hr />
        </td>
    </tr>
    <tr>
        <td align="left" colspan="2">
            Created:
            <asp:Label ID="lblCreated" runat="server"/>
             | Updated:
            <asp:Label ID="lblUpdated" runat="server"/>
        </td>
    </tr>
</table>
```

The thing to pay attention to, as we mentioned before, is that all the paths are in a fixed format at the root of the site. This way no matter where we are at, we know where to go to gain access to the specified resource. Let's also quickly look at the relevant part of the presenter code. Using the user name we get the `Account` details and then using the `AccountID` and the blog's page name we get the specific blog entry details.

```
//Fisharoo/Web/Blogs/Presenters/ViewPostPresenter.cs
public void Init(IViewPost View, string username, string blogpage)
{
    _view = View;
```

```
        Account account = _accountService.GetAccountByUsername(username);
        _view.LoadPost(_blogService.GetBlogByPageName(blogpage, account.
        AccountID));
    }
```

Create or edit post

With all of this working our way we can now turn our attention to the work of creating the actual blog post. This page will actually serve two purposes. We need to use it to create our blog post. But we will also repurpose the UI to edit the already existing posts as well. Let's look at the presenter for this page.

```
//Fisharoo/Web/Blogs/PostPresenter.cs
public void Init(IPost View, bool IsPostBack)
{
    _view = View;
    if (!IsPostBack)
    {
        if (_webContext.BlogID > 0)
        {
            _view.LoadPost(_blogService.GetBlogByBlogID(_webContext.
            BlogID));
        }
    }
}

public void SavePost(Blog blog)
{
    bool result = true;
    if (blog.BlogID == 0)
    {
        //if blog already saved once, the ID will be > 0
        result = _blogService.CheckPageNameIsUnique(blog);
    }
    if (result)
    {
        blog.AccountID = _webContext.CurrentUser.AccountID;
        long blogID = _blogService.SaveBlog(blog);
        _view.UpdateID(blogID);
        _view.ShowError("Blog is saved!");
    }
    else
    {
        _view.ShowError("The page name you have chosen is in use.
        Please choose a different page name!");
    }
}
```

In the first section of the `Init` method we are checking the `WebContext.BlogID` property to see if we have something to work with. If we do then we load the UI with the appropriate blog. If not, it means it is a new blog entry we are creating. The next item you see is the `SavePost` method that takes care of passing a loaded/newly created blog into the `BlogService` to be saved.

Next, we will take a look at the code behind that the presenter works with. Here we will see the `LoadPost` and `btnSave_Click` methods. There is nothing fancy to follow here. But the one aspect to pay attention to is that we keep track of the `BlogID` in the page so that we know what we are working with later.

```
protected void btnSave_Click(object sender, EventArgs e)
{
    Blog blog = new Blog();
    if (litBlogID.Text != "")
        blog.BlogID = Convert.ToInt64(litBlogID.Text);
    blog.IsPublished = chkIsPublished.Checked;
    blog.PageName = txtPageName.Text;
    blog.Post = txtPost.Text;
    blog.Subject = txtSubject.Text;
    blog.Title = txtTitle.Text;
    _presenter.SavePost(blog);
}
public void LoadPost(Blog blog)
{
    txtTitle.Text = blog.Title;
    txtSubject.Text = blog.Subject;
    txtPost.Text = blog.Post;
    txtPageName.Text = blog.PageName;
    chkIsPublished.Checked = blog.IsPublished;
    litBlogID.Text = blog.BlogID.ToString();
}
```

This takes care of the details of data inputs and outputs. However, let's now take a look at what we need to do make the UI usable. You may recall that we used the Xinha WYSIWYG editor before. We will use it here too. All that is required to hook this up is a multiline text box control and a single line of JavaScript.

```
...
<asp:TextBox TextMode="MultiLine" ID="txtPost"
                runat="server"></asp:TextBox>
...
<script type="text/javascript">
    xinha_editors[xinha_editors.length] = 'Content_txtPost';
</script>
...
```

With this in place we should be ready to create a blog post!

Summary

We now have a great way for our community members to share information with one another. This content will serve several purposes. It will not only provide a large repository of information for our community members to see the value in our relationship but also a food source for our search engine spiders.

In this chapter we covered the creation of blog posts. We also went over the pages that are needed for people to see other users' posts as well as their own. And of course we provided a page to actually read a post. In addition to this we covered the concept of fancy or pretty URLs that are more user as well as search engine-friendly. Finally, we added more usability to our UI in the form of the Xinha WYSIWYG.

9
Forums

In this chapter we will be discussing forums. A **forum** is a place where users can post messages to the community in a way that all the responses will be viewable no matter how much time passes between each post—think of it as a long running conversation. As the threads or topics and their posts get older, newer content will start to bury the older content. This makes this section of the site a very dynamic area that many users will want to watch. This is considered a somewhat sticky feature! Given the topic of our community—salt water fish—a forum is a perfect feature for our site. It will allow a user to post an issue that they are having with their aquarium in a way that the entire community can then read and interact with that user's issue. Over time your community will bubble up certain users as subject matter experts on specific topics. And eventually (you hope) your site's forum will become the place to go for your specific type of information. If nothing else, our dear friends Google and Bing will lead people your way.

Problem

To get started we should first discuss the proper terminology. A forum is really a set of containers for storing data. We will have the ability to first create categories. A **category** is the highest level of container and therefore will have a very generic topic. Each category can hold as many forums as is needed. The forum is related to the top level category's subject but is slightly more specific. In each forum we can have a number of threads. Each thread is a very specific subject that users can discuss. The discussion is performed with posts that are simply replies to the containing thread or a post on the thread.

Here is our landing page, that lists each category and its forums:

Forum Name	Forum Description	Threads	Posts	Last Post by	Last Post on
Reef Tank Care	**How to take care of your reef tank**	**5**	**4**	**Suds123**	**5/5/2008**
Filtration	Everything to know about proper filtration	4	0	Suds123	5/15/2008
Lighting	Everything to know about lighting	1	0	Suds123	5/15/2008
Plants	Everything to know about plants	0	0	Suds123	5/15/2008
Salt Water Fish Compatibility	**Which fish go with which fish**	**0**	**0**	**Suds123**	**5/5/2008**
Anenomes	Anenome compatibility	0	0	Suds123	5/15/2008
Star Fish	Star Fish compatibility	0	0	Suds123	5/15/2008
Group Forums	**Houses the group forums**	**3**	**2**	**asiemer**	**5/5/2008**
hello world	hello world	0	0	Suds123	7/3/2008
A really great group	A really great group	0	0	Suds123	7/3/2008
my really really cool group	my really really cool group	0	0	Suds123	7/3/2008
Lion Fish	Lion Fish	0	0	Suds123	7/7/2008
Damsel Fish	Damsel Fish	0	0	Suds123	7/7/2008
Sea Horses	Sea Horses	1	0	andrewsiemer	7/7/2008
Crastaeans	Crastaeans	0	0	andrewsiemer	7/7/2008

Here is our forum page, that lists all of the available threads for that forum:

Here is a thread that would also have a list of its posts:

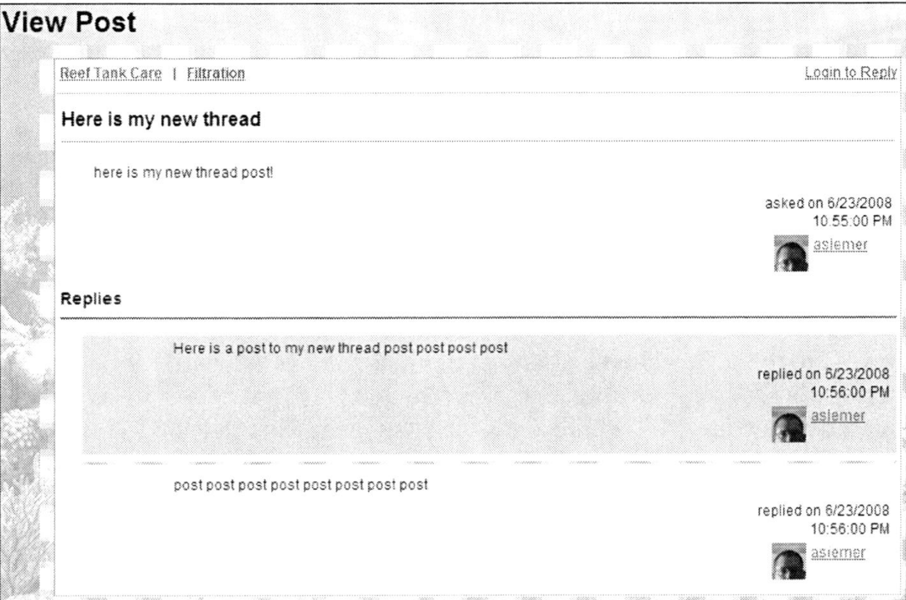

As you may have guessed, the topic of forums is a very large one and you can evaluate and integrate any off the shelf that party message board if you find it a good fit. However, we will go about explaining some of the key constituents of forums such as while creating we will go over the basics of creating categories, forums, threads, and posts. Each of these sections will be able to keep count of how much data lives beneath it. And all of the content will have the ability to be linked to in an SEO-friendly manner (meaning will support friendly URLs). Friendly URLs are also easier for our users to remember and work with. We will also tie in the ability to add alerts to our filters and our friends' filters so that they know when we have new content available.

SEO (**Search Engine Optimization**) is generally defined as the process that optimizes organic search traffic. This generally translates to building your site in a search engine-friendly manner that presents your site and its content in a way that makes the search engine's job easier to index your pages. Generally a long ugly query string such as `default.aspx?userid=324568` is less friendly than `domain.com/atulgupta` would be. More information can be found on the topic here: `http://en.wikipedia.org/wiki/Search_engine_optimization`.

Obviously there are many features that are not yet supported by our application such as hot topics, private threads, ratings, and moderation. We will focus on building a solid framework in this chapter to which we can add these other features down the road.

Design

Let's take a look at the design for this feature.

Categories

Categories are the highest level container of posts that we have in our system. It is responsible for grouping forums together in such a way that makes it easy for a user to locate what they are most interested in. At this level we will keep a count of how many threads and posts we have as well as who made the last post and when. The reason we maintain counts at this level is to remove the need for us to perform the count each time we display the category data.

Forums

A **forum** is a container of threads. It is responsible for grouping together a more specific set of posts. This too keeps a count of thread and post counts so that we can see at this level how much data lies within, again without needing to sum the actual post and thread counts.

Threads and posts

Threads and posts are technically identical with the exception that a post is not a container of anything. A **thread** is the next level container of data below a forum. It is a **post** that is marked as a thread and will act as the parent to many other posts. In simpler terms the initial question asked by a user is a thread. For the same performance reasons we will keep a reply count and a view count. Notice that we have a reference from **ThreadID** to **PostID**. All the posts in the system will have a parent post, that we will refer to as a Thread.

Friendly URLs

If you paid close attention to the previous tables, you must have noticed that there is a **PageName** in each table. In this system we will implement heavy use of friendly URLs. This will allow people to find the information not only in each post but also from the surrounding site as well. In addition to this it makes sharing information easier too.

Alerts

Finally, we will extend our system to use our pre-existing alert system so that each time someone makes a post or creates a new thread; we will see an alert on both the creator's filter as well as one on the friends'. This will help us to promote the new content across the site.

Solution

Let's take a look at our solution.

Implementing the database

Let's start our solution by first discussing the implementation of our database.

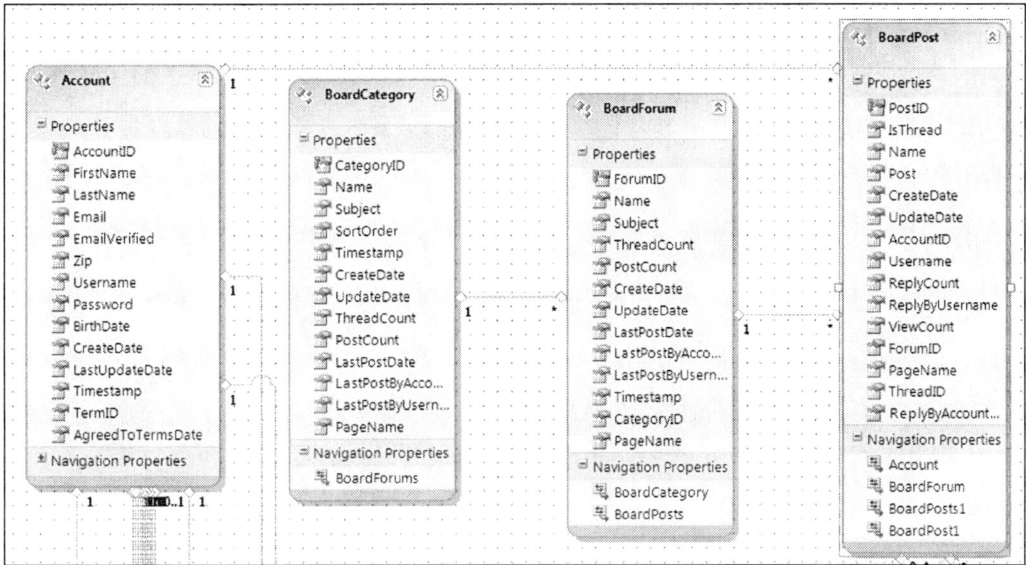

Categories

As we discussed before, the concept of a category is our top level container of data. Let's take a look at the table structure for categories:

The **SortOrder** field is in charge of setting the display order in case we have multiple categories on one page. We already discussed the count fields earlier. The last X fields are to control who made the last post and when. **PageName** controls the friendly URLs that our system will use later.

Forums

Forums are the next level container that holds our entire individual user created threads.

Similar to categories we maintain the counts of our low level posts and threads. We also maintain who created the last post and when. Notice that we have a foreign key reference to the `BoardCategorys` table.

Posts

As we have stated earlier, the `BoardPosts` table is really a dual purpose table containing both posts and threads. We did this primarily because for most part each item has the same data in it with the exception of the parent **ThreadID** column.

The field to note here is the **IsThread** field. This is the easiest way to know when a post is also a Thread. In addition to that we have the **ThreadID**, that also denotes the difference between a post and a thread where a thread won't have a **ThreadID**—a thread is never a part of a thread (at least not yet!). Also notice here that we have a foreign key for the forum that this thread is part of in the form of the **ForumID** foreign key. For threads, we also store the number of times it was viewed as well as how many replies it has.

A nice side effect of this post/thread structure is that any run-of-the-mill post can easily be moved off and treated as its own thread. Often a moderator will find that a post within a thread is generating more traffic than the initial thread itself. In this case that post can easily be promoted to a thread in its own right!

Creating the relationships

Once all the tables are created we can then create all the relationships.

For this set of tables, we have relationships between the following tables:

- `BoardForums` and `BoardCategories`
- `BoardPosts` and `Accounts`
- `BoardPosts` and `BoardForums`
- `BoardPosts` and `BoardPosts` (for post to thread reference)

Setting up the data access layer

To set up the data access layer follow the steps mentioned next:

- Open the `Fisharoo.edmx` file and add the Database tables we have discussed in this chapter by following the guidelines mentioned in the earlier chapter.
- Hit **Save** and you should have the above discussed domain objects to work with!

Your design surface should have all the same items as you see in the previous screenshot (though perhaps in a different arrangement!).

Building repositories

With the addition of new tables will come the addition of new repositories so that we can get at the data stored in those tables. We will be creating the following repositories to support our needs.

- `BoardCategoryRepository`
- `BoardForumRepository`
- `BoardPostRepository`

Each of our repositories will generally have a method for selecting by ID, select all by parent ID, save, and delete. Once you have seen one repository you have pretty much seen them all. Review previous chapters, the appendices, or the included code for examples of a standard repository. We will, however, discuss anything that varies from the standard approach we are following so far!

BoardCategoryRepository

One of the most important features of our message board that may be a bit different from other message boards is that it is very important for us to support friendly URLs. This means that we will need a method in each of our repositories to get the object by page name. Here is the method for this repository:

```
public BoardCategory GetCategoryByPageName(string PageName)
{
    BoardCategory category;
    using(FisharooDataContext dc = _conn.GetContext())
    {
        category = dc.BoardCategories.Where(bc => bc.PageName ==
                                        PageName).FirstOrDefault();
    }
    return category;
}
```

This is a fairly straightforward method that gets a board category by its page name.

BoardForumRepository

The `BoardForumRepository` also has a `GetForumByPageName` method but it is exactly the same as the previous method `BoardCategoryRepository`.

BoardPostRepository

Now this repository is full of interesting items to cover! To start, as our users will be creating posts and threads but will not be allowed to create forums or categories, we need to be able to make sure that they don't create page names that are not unique. It is no good to try to get a thread by its name and end up getting several different threads instead of just the one we expected.

```
//Fisharoo/DataAccess/Repositories/BoardPostRepository.cs
public bool CheckPostPageNameIsUnique(string PageName)
{
    bool result;
    using(FisharooDataContext dc = _conn.GetContext())
    {
        BoardPost bp = dc.BoardPosts.Where(p => p.PageName ==
                                    PageName).FirstOrDefault();
        if(bp != null)
            result = false;
        else
            result = true;
    }
    return result;
}
```

In this method we attempt to load a post by the `PageName` that was specified. If we return a null object then we know that the `PageName` is unique and we can return a true response. Otherwise we have to return a false result. Not fancy, but it gets the job done.

The next method is responsible for getting all the posts for a given thread. This by itself is not that interesting. But as we know that we are only using this method on the page where a thread is viewed, we can insert some logic to increment the number of times a thread has been viewed.

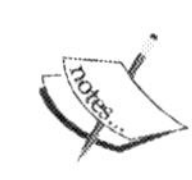

> Keep in mind that this method will only be appropriate if we only use it for getting posts for a given thread and then displaying them. If we start to use this method for other tasks then our view count will be totally skewed!

```
public List<BoardPost> GetPostsByThreadID(Int64 ThreadID)
        {
            List<BoardPost> result;
            using (FisharooDataContext dc = _conn.GetContext())
            {
                //increment the view count for this thread
                BoardPost thread = dc.BoardPosts.Where(p => p.PostID
                == ThreadID).FirstOrDefault();
                if (thread != null)
                    thread.ViewCount += 1;
                dc.SaveChanges();

                IEnumerable<BoardPost> posts = dc.BoardPosts.Where(p
                => p.ThreadID == ThreadID && !p.IsThread)
                .OrderBy(p => p.CreateDate);
                result = posts.ToList();
            }
            return result;
        }
```

We perform this task by getting the thread (really a board post) by its ID and then increment its `ViewCount` property. We then submit the changes on the DataContext to make sure that it is pushed back to the database.

We then move to get all the posts for that thread by its ID.

The next method, `SavePost`, is not only responsible for saving new posts and updating existing posts but also for taking care of incrementing counts at both the Forum and Category levels.

```
        public Int64 SavePost(BoardPost boardPost)
        {
            using (FisharooDataContext dc = _conn.GetContext())
            {
                if (boardPost.PostID > 0)
                {
                    dc.BoardPosts.Attach(new BoardPost { PostID =
                    boardPost.PostID });
                    dc.BoardPosts.ApplyCurrentValues(boardPost);
                }
                else
                {
                    //get the parent containers when a new post is
                    created
                    //  to update their post counts
```

```
                BoardCategory bc = (from c in dc.BoardCategorys
                                    join f in dc.BoardForums
                                    on c.CategoryID equals
                                    f.CategoryID
                                    where f.ForumID == boardPost.
                                    ForumID
                                    select c).FirstOrDefault();
                BoardForum bf = (from f in dc.BoardForums
                                 where f.ForumID == boardPost.
                                 ForumID
                                 select f).FirstOrDefault();

                //update the thread count
                if (boardPost.IsThread)
                {
                    bc.ThreadCount = bc.ThreadCount + 1;
                    bf.ThreadCount = bf.ThreadCount + 1;
                }
                //update the post count
                else
                {
                    bc.PostCount = bc.PostCount + 1;
                    bf.PostCount = bf.PostCount + 1;

                    //update post count on thread
                    BoardPost bThread = null;
                    if (boardPost.ThreadID != 0)
                    {
                        bThread = (from p in dc.BoardPosts
                                   where p.PostID == boardPost.
                                   ThreadID
                                   select p).FirstOrDefault();
                    }
                    if (bThread != null)
                    {
                        bThread.ReplyCount = bThread.ReplyCount +
                        1;
                    }
                }
                dc.BoardPosts.AddObject(boardPost);
            }
            dc.SaveChanges();
        }
        return boardPost.PostID;
    }
```

Notice that the first part of this method is just like every other save method. If the ID of the object being saved is greater than zero, we reattach the object to the data context as a new version of that object. We then call the `SaveChanges()` method and persist it back to the database.

This is where everything else changes. If the item is a new post or thread then we have a whole bunch of things to do. The first thing that we want to do is get the parent objects. We get the `BoardCategory` and `BoardForum` off the post's related `ForumID`. We then check to see if the new post is also a thread. If it is, then we update the `ThreadCount` for our parent objects.

If the post is just a post then we update the `PostCount` for the parent objects. We also get that post's parent thread. With the parent thread in hand we update the reply count. We then perform the task that we are used to and insert the object. Finally we call the `SaveChanges` method on the data context.

Finally, we come to the `DeletePost` method. Remember that a post can also be a thread which means that it can have children. We can't delete a thread that has children as this will create a referential integrity issue (also called dirty data) for us.

```
public void DeletePost(BoardPost boardPost)
  {
      using (FisharooDataContext dc = _conn.GetContext())
      {
          dc.BoardPosts.Attach(boardPost);
          //if this is a thread then we need to delete all of
          it's children
          if (boardPost.IsThread)
          {
              IEnumerable<BoardPost> posts = dc.BoardPosts.
              Where(bp => bp.ThreadID == boardPost.PostID).
              ToList();
              foreach(BoardPost bp in posts)
              {
                  dc.BoardPosts.DeleteObject(bp);
              }
          }
          dc.BoardPosts.DeleteObject(boardPost);
          dc.SaveChanges();
      }
  }
```

So, in order for us to address this issue, we have to test the post that is up for deletion to see if it is also a thread with its `IsThread` property. If there is, then we iterate through the BoardPost and delete by calling `DeleteObject()` on the `BoardPosts` collection.

Implementing the Services/Application layer

Once all the repositories are built for single serving purposes we can begin to create the services layer. Again, this layer is responsible for assembling aggregates and performing complex actions with our entities. We will create the following services:

- `BoardService`
- `AlertService`

BoardService

Our `BoardService` is actually not overly complex. It is responsible for providing us a way to get out the `BoardCategory` with an already hydrated list of `BoardForum` items. Before we look at the `BoardService`, we need to extend the `BoardCategory` object to contain a list of `BoardForum` objects. We do this by adding a `BoardCategory` class to our `Domain` directory. Then make this class a public partial class and finally add a generic list of `BoardForum` objects.

```
public partial class BoardCategory
{
    public List<BoardForum> Forums { get; set; }
}
```

With this class extended we can now look at the `BoardService`.

```
namespace Fisharoo.BusinessLogic
{
    [Export(typeof(IBoardService))]
    public class BoardService : IBoardService
    {
        [Import]
        private IBoardCategoryRepository _categoryRepository;
        [Import]
        private IBoardForumRepository _forumRepository;

        public BoardService()
        {
            MEFManager.Compose(this);
        }

        public List<BoardCategory> GetCategoriesWithForums()
        {
            List<BoardCategory> categories = _categoryRepository.
            GetAllCategories();
            List<BoardForum> forums = _forumRepository.GetAllForums();
```

```
            for(int i = 0;i<categories.Count();i++)
            {
                categories[i].Forums = forums.Where(f => f.CategoryID
                == categories[i].CategoryID).ToList();
            }
            return categories;
        }
    }
}
```

The first thing to notice is that this class, like all others in our solution, is marked up with attributes for MEF. Next, we declare our `BoardCategoryRepository` and `BoardForumRepository`. In the constructor for this class we compose the MEF container.

This then brings us to the `GetCategoriesWithForums()` method. This is an optimized method that our message board homepage calls to get a list of categories and their forums. We are then able to iterate through each list and its child list without making a bunch of separate calls.

This method first gets a list of all Categories. It then gets a list of all the forums in the system. The method then iterates through all the Categories and selects a list of forums from the primary list of forums into the `BoardCategory.Forums` collection. It then returns the complete list of categories.

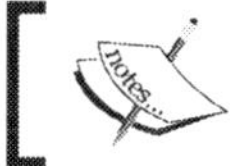

This would be a great method to add to caching as both categories and forums are going to be a fairly static list of data in your site!

AlertService

The alert service is pretty much complete from an infrastructure point of view. It is simply a matter of adding new service messages as we need additional functionality. In this case we want to post alerts when a new post or thread is created. Both of the methods that we want to add are very similar in that they initialize an alert, set the alert type, create a message, save the alert to the alert repository, and finally send the alert off to all of the user's friends.

```
public void AddNewBoardPostAlert(BoardCategory category,
BoardForum forum, BoardPost post, BoardPost thread)
 {
     Init();
     alert.AlertTypeID = (int)AlertType.AlertTypes.
     NewBoardPost;
```

```
    alertMessage = "<div class=\"AlertHeader\">" +
    GetProfileImage(_userSession.CurrentUser.AccountID) +
                GetProfileUrl(_userSession.CurrentUser.
                Username) + " has just added a new post to:
                <b>" +
                post.Name + "</b></div>";

    alertMessage += "<div class=\"AlertRow\"><a href=\"" + _
    webContext.RootUrl + "forums/" + category.Name +
                "/" + forum.Name + ".aspx/" + thread.PostID
                + "\">" + _webContext.RootUrl +
                "forums/" + category.Name + "/" + forum.
                Name + ".aspx/" + thread.PostID + "</a></
                div>";
    alert.Message = alertMessage;
    SaveAlert(alert);
    SendAlertToFriends(alert);
}

public void AddNewBoardThreadAlert(BoardCategory category,
BoardForum forum, BoardPost post)
{
    Init();
    alert.AlertTypeID = (int)AlertType.AlertTypes.
    NewBoardThread;
    alertMessage = "<div class=\"AlertHeader\">" +
    GetProfileImage(_userSession.CurrentUser.AccountID) +
                GetProfileUrl(_userSession.CurrentUser.
                Username) + " has just added a new thread
                on the board: <b>" +
                post.Name + "</b></div>";

    alertMessage += "<div class=\"AlertRow\"><a href=\"" + _
    webContext.RootUrl + "forums/" + category.Name +
                "/" + forum.Name + ".aspx/" + post.PostID +
                "\">" + _webContext.RootUrl +
                "forums/" + category.Name + "/" + forum.
                Name + ".aspx/" + post.PostID + "</a></
                div>";
    alert.Message = alertMessage;
    SaveAlert(alert);
    SendAlertToFriends(alert);
}
```

Implementing the Presentation layer

Now let's discuss the implementation of our presentation layer.

Default.aspx

With the entire infrastructure completed, we can now move on to the more interesting part—displaying the data. We will start by looking at the homepage. This page will be responsible for displaying all of the categories and all of the forums for each category as shown in the first screenshot of this chapter.

Other than the normal plumbing that is required by the **Model View Presenter (MVP)** pattern, this page is primarily made up of two repeaters—the first repeater displaying all the categories in the list of categories and the inner one displaying all the forums for each category.

The list of categories is loaded in the presenter for this page. The relevant method is

```
//Fisharoo/Web/Forums/Presenters/DefaultPresenter.cs
public void Init(IDefault View)
{
_view = View;
 List<BoardCategory> list = _boardService.GetCategoriesWithForums();
_view.LoadCategories(Translator.BoardCategoryToPEBoardCategory(list));
}
```

Once the page's code behind passes control from itself to the presenter by way of calling the presenter's `init` method, the presenter then passes a list of categories and forums (from the `BoardService`) back to the code behind via the `LoadCategories` method. Note also the usage of `PEBoardCategory` presentation entity. We have discussed presentation entities in Chapter 5, so we will skip the explanation here.

The code behind then loads the data source of the first repeater and binds it.

```
//Fisharoo/Web/Forums/Default.aspx.cs
    public partial class Default : System.Web.UI.Page, IDefault
    {
        private DefaultPresenter _presenter;
        protected void Page_Load(object sender, EventArgs e)
        {
            _presenter = new DefaultPresenter();
            _presenter.Init(this);
        }

        public void LoadCategories(List<PEBoardCategory> Categories)
        {
            repCategories.DataSource = Categories;
            repCategories.DataBind();
        }
```

```
        public void repCategories_ItemDataBound(object sender,
        RepeaterItemEventArgs e)
        {
            if (e.Item.ItemType == ListItemType.Item || e.Item.
            ItemType == ListItemType.AlternatingItem)
            {
                if (((PEBoardCategory) e.Item.DataItem).Forums !=
                null)
                {
                    Repeater repForums = e.Item.
                    FindControl("repForums") as Repeater;
                    repForums.DataSource = ((PEBoardCategory) e.Item.
                    DataItem).Forums;
                    repForums.DataBind();
                }
            }
        }

        public void repForums_ItemDataBound(object sender,
        RepeaterItemEventArgs e)
        {
            HyperLink linkForum = e.Item.FindControl("linkForum") as
            HyperLink;
            linkForum.NavigateUrl = Page.GetRouteUrl("ForumRoute", new
                                    {
                                    categoryname = ((PEBoardForum)
                                    e.Item.DataItem).CategoryName,
                                    forumname = ((PEBoardForum)e.Item.
                                    DataItem).Name
                                    });
        }
    }
```

In each iteration of the `repCategories_ItemDataBound` method, we then load the `repForums` repeater with the list of forums for the given category (`PEBoardForum`) and bind it. This continues until the list of categories and forums is thrown on the page.

Also notice that when each forum item is bound, we set the appropriate URL to the hyperlink control's `NavigateUrl` property. This is the friendly URL and will take us to the specific forum page.

URL routing

In order to support our user-friendly URLs we will once again use the URL routing feature. Our additional code will be inserted in the `RegisterRoute()` method in `Global.ascx.cs`. There are four different URL patterns that we will support for our forums. Let's quickly look at each pattern:

- An URL like `http://server/appname/forums/categoryname/forumname.aspx` is used to access a particular forum within a particular category. This request will be serviced by `ViewForum.aspx`.
- A URL like `http://server/appname/forums/categoryname/forumname/postid` is used to access a particular post/thread within a forum. This request will be serviced by `ViewPost.aspx`.
- A URL like `http://server/appname/forums/categoryname/forumname.aspx/new` is used to create a new thread in a forum. This request will be serviced by `Post.aspx`.
- A URL like `http://server/appname/forums/categoryname/forumname.aspx/reply` is used to create a new thread in a forum. This request will be serviced by `Post.aspx`.

You can look at the code to see how these patterns are formed and added to the route collection.

ViewForum.aspx

The view forum page is responsible for displaying a single forum and all of its threads as shown in the second screenshot of this chapter.

The view forum page first extracts the category name and the forum name from the routed data collection and passes it to the presenter. The presenter returns the collection of all the threads in the particular forum. With this collection in hand the view then populates the display of the page. Upon each iteration of a forum the `repTopics_ItemDataBound` method loads the `NavigateUrl` property of the `linkViewTopic HyperLink` control, which is the fancy path to the `particular post` page. Part of this path is the `IsThread=1` variable. The reason for this is that this is a dual purpose page for both creating a post and a thread.

```
//Fisharoo/Web/Forums/ViewForum.aspx.cs
public partial class Forum : System.Web.UI.Page, IViewForum
{
    private ViewForumPresenter _presenter;

    protected void Page_Load(object sender, EventArgs e)
    {
```

```
        _presenter = new ViewForumPresenter();
        string categoryname = Page.RouteData.Values["categoryname"] as
        string;
        string forumname = Page.RouteData.Values["forumname"] as
        string;
        _presenter.Init(this, categoryname, forumname);
    }

    public void LoadDisplay(List<PEBoardPost> Threads, string
    CategoryName, string ForumName, Int32 ForumID)
    {
        //forum can be viewed by anyone but for posting one needs to
        login
        if (_presenter.IsUserLoggedIn())
        {
            //navigation URL will follow the URL routing pattern
            linkNewThread.NavigateUrl = Page.
            GetRouteUrl("NewThreadRoute", new
            {
                categoryname = linkCategoryName.Text,
                forumname = litForumName.Text,
            });
        }
        else
        {
            linkNewThread.Text = "Login to post to forums";
            linkNewThread.NavigateUrl = "/Accounts/Login.aspx";
        }
        repTopics.DataSource = Threads;
        repTopics.DataBind();
    }

    protected void repTopics_ItemDataBound(object sender,
    RepeaterItemEventArgs e)
    {
        if (e.Item.ItemType == ListItemType.Item || e.Item.ItemType ==
        ListItemType.AlternatingItem)
        {
            HyperLink linkViewTopic = e.Item.
            FindControl("linkViewTopic") as HyperLink;
            //navigation URL will follow the URL routing pattern
            linkViewTopic.NavigateUrl = Page.
            GetRouteUrl("ThreadRoute",
                         new
                        {
```

```
                                categoryname = linkCategoryName.Text,
                                forumname = litForumName.Text,
                                postid = ((PEBoardPost)e.Item.DataItem).
                                PostID
                            });
            }
        }
    }
```

Something that you might not expect this page to do is that it loads the navigation for each thread's `HyperLink` directly. We do not pass through the `Redirector` class. The reason for this is performance. This way we avoid doing a postback to the same page, then using the redirector class to do a `Response.Redirect` and then load the page. Rather we use our user-friendly URL and directly jump to the post page.

ViewPost.aspx

The view post page extracts the category name, forum name, and the thread ID and using this displays the thread and all of its posts as displayed in the third screenshot of this chapter.

```
//Fisharoo/Web/Forums/ViewPost.aspx.cs
public partial class ViewPost : System.Web.UI.Page, IViewPost
{
    private ViewPostPresenter _presenter;

    protected void Page_Load(object sender, EventArgs e)
    {
        _presenter = new ViewPostPresenter();
        string categoryname = Page.RouteData.Values["categoryname"] as
        string;
        string forumname = Page.RouteData.Values["forumname"] as
        string;
        int postID = Convert.ToInt32(Page.RouteData.Values["postid"]);
        _presenter.Init(this, IsPostBack, categoryname, forumname,
        postID);
    }

    public void LoadData(PEBoardPost Thread, List<PEBoardPost> Posts,
    string CategoryName, string ForumName)
    {
        linkForumName.NavigateUrl = Page.GetRouteUrl("ForumRoute", new
        {
```

```
                categoryname = CategoryName,
                forumname = ForumName
            });

            linkUsername.Text = Thread.Username;
            linkUsername.NavigateUrl = "~/" + Thread.Username;
            lblCreateDate.Text = Thread.CreateDate;
            lblThreadTitle.Text = Thread.Name;

            lblPost.Text = Thread.Post;
            imgProfile.ImageUrl = "/images/profileavatar/profileimage.
            aspx?AccountID=" + Thread.AccountID.ToString();
            //to reply one needs to login
            if (_presenter.IsUserLoggedIn())
            {
                linkReply.Text = "Reply";
                linkReply.NavigateUrl = Page.
                GetRouteUrl("ReplyThreadRoute", new
                {
                    categoryname = CategoryName,
                    forumname = ForumName,
                    postid = Thread.PostID.ToString()
                });
            }
            else
            {
                linkReply.Text = "Login to Reply";
                linkReply.NavigateUrl = "/Accounts/Login.aspx";
            }

            repPosts.DataSource = Posts;
            repPosts.DataBind();
        }
    }
```

In the `Page_Load()` method we extract the routed data values and pass to the presenter to get us the thread and related posts.

The returned Thread and Post details are bound to the UI elements in the `LoadData()` method. Note that the `linkForumName hyperlink` control has its `NavigateUrl` property set to take us back to the forums page. Notice that we also have a reply link next to everything. In our implementation they all do the same thing—navigate the user to the `Post.aspx` page (via the user friendly URL) to create a post or a reply. However, the option to reply will be available only if the user is logged in. Otherwise the user will be redirected to the login page.

Finally, let's quickly look at one important part of the ViewPost.aspx page where we load the category and forum names directly from the routed data collection.

```
<asp:Hyperlink ID="linkCategoryName" Text="<%$RouteValue:categoryname
%>" NavigateUrl="~/Forums/Default.aspx" runat="server" />
  |  
<asp:Hyperlink ID="linkForumName" Text="<%$RouteValue:forumname %>"
runat="server" />
```

Also note that linkCategoryName hyperlink control links back to the forum's default page.

Post.aspx

The post page is the one page that the forums actually require you to be logged into so that you can interact with it. Once logged in you are able to create a new thread or reply to an existing thread or post.

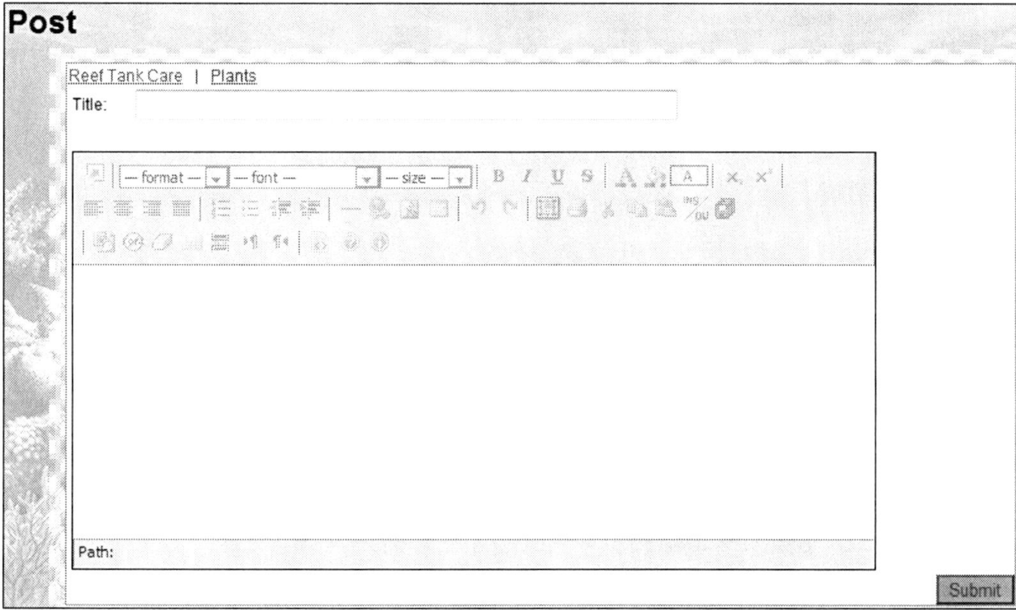

The only thing you might miss about this page is that it is dual purpose. This means that we need to be able to handle creating threads and posts. The difference here is that a post has its title prepopulated as per the thread's title, and you cannot edit it.

Once all of the UI is functioning correctly we then need to wire up the **Save** button. This is done to some degree in the code behind with the `btnSubmit_Click` method where we capture all the data from the UI. We then attempt to pass the data in the form of a `BoardPost` to the presenter to actually persist the data into the database.

```
//Fisharoo/Web/Forums/Post.aspx.cs
protected void btnSubmit_Click(object sender, EventArgs e)
{
    BoardPost post = new BoardPost();
    post.Name = txtName.Text;
    post.Post = txtPost.Text;
    _presenter.Save(post);
}
```

Now the `Save` method in the presenter is something a bit heftier than the rest of this code has been.

```
//Fisharoo/Web/Forums/Presenters/PostPresenter.cs
public void Save(BoardPost post, string forumName, long postID)
{
    BoardForum forum = _forumService.GetForumByName(forumName);
    Boolean newPost = false;
    //is new thread
    if (postID == 0)
    {
        post.ForumID = forum.ForumID;
        post.IsThread = true;
        newPost = true;
    }
    //is reply post
    else
    {
        BoardPost postToReplyToo = _postService.GetPostByID(postID);
        if (postToReplyToo.IsThread)
            post.ThreadID = postToReplyToo.PostID;
        else
            post.ThreadID = postToReplyToo.ThreadID;

        post.ForumID = postToReplyToo.ForumID;
    }
    post.CreateDate = DateTime.Now;
    post.UpdateDate = DateTime.Now;
    post.AccountID = _webContext.CurrentUser.AccountID;
    post.Username = _webContext.CurrentUser.Username;
    post.ReplyCount = 0;
```

```
        post.ViewCount = 0;

        post.PostID = _postService.SavePost(post);

        Account act = _accountService.GetAccountByID(_webContext.
        CurrentUser.AccountID);

        if (!newPost)
        {
            _accountService.SaveAccount(act);
        }

        BoardCategory category = _categoryService.
        GetCategoryByCategoryID(forum.CategoryID);
        BoardPost thread;
        if (post.IsThread)
            thread = _postService.GetPostByID(post.PostID);
        else
            thread = _postService.GetPostByID((long)post.ThreadID);

        //add an alert to the filter
        if (post.IsThread)
            _alertService.AddNewBoardThreadAlert(category, forum, thread);
        else
            _alertService.AddNewBoardPostAlert(category, forum, post,
            thread);

        RouteValueDictionary values = new RouteValueDictionary
                                    {
                                        {"categoryname", category.
                                        Name},
                                        {"forumname", forum.Name},
                                        {"postid", thread.PostID}
                                    };
        VirtualPathData vpd = RouteTable.Routes.GetVirtualPath(null,
        "ThreadRoute", values);
        _redirector.GoToForumsViewPost(vpd.VirtualPath);
    }
```

This method initially looks to determine if we are working with a post or a thread. If we are working with a new thread then we have to set the `ForumID` and `IsThread` properties.

If we are working with a post instead of a thread, then we get the post that we are replying to. With this in mind, we check to see if it is a thread or is just a simple post as well. If it is a thread then we set our new post's `ThreadID` property to that post's `PostID`. Otherwise we set our post's `ThreadID` to that post's `ThreadID`. We also set the `ForumID` from the `postToReplyToo's ForumID` property.

With these determinations made and initial values set, we can then continue setting additional properties such as the create date, update date, accountID, and so on. We finally save the post and get the newly-created post's `PostID`.

With the post created, we then need to determine what type of alert to send out to our friends. If it is a thread then we send out a new thread alert. Otherwise we send out a new post alert.

Finally we create the user-friendly URL that will redirect the user to see their new post.

Summary

In this chapter we created the core features for managing forums—categories, forums, threads, and posts. Along with these features we have also heavily implemented friendly URLs to help our content be more SEO-friendly. This should feed the various search engine spiders effectively. In order to spread the word about our new content we have also integrated our forum section into our alert service. This takes each new post and broadcasts its arrival to homepages of friends of each of the posting users'.

As discussed earlier, the subject of forums is a large one. While we implemented a great foundation this section is by no means feature complete. If you look at the many options for forums and message boards in the market you will quickly notice that there are many other features that you could implement on top of what we built. Voting and medals are two important features that make forums a lot richer. We will look at extending our implementation in a later chapter to support these. This is a great start though!

10
Groups

What are Groups? In the social network context, **Groups** allow users of your community to interact with each other around a common topic. Groups start bringing together our other, already created concepts. Items such as forums, blogs, images, and many other features can be better utilized from the group point of view.

Take forums for example. As a user of our community you can interact with the pre-created forums and you are able to post topics or replies to any public forum in the system. You hope that other users who have similar interests as you, or those who have an answer for your posted question, will stumble upon your post. Many people will see your post, some will reply. There is no guarantee that the right person will see it and even less guarantee that the right person will give you the response that you are seeking. If you are able to post your topic to a forum that is somewhat related to your interest, then your chances go up a bit.

On the other hand, with a group-owned forum you know that there is a specific community, within the global community, paying extra close attention to your forum posts. In addition to that, when you post to a group-owned forum, you know that the entire user base of that group will be made aware of your post (typically via appropriate notifications). This increases your odds of getting to the information that you are seeking. And you know that the majority of people looking at your post most likely have the information you are interested in.

Think of groups as sub-communities with special interests. Because they are sub-communities, they have the same life as a user in the system with the exception that they act on behalf of many users. By becoming part of a group you have taken on many new friends with common interests. You gain access to special interest forums and you could get to see the hidden image galleries!

Here is an example of what we will be building:

Problem

Given that there are so many features in our example site it is impossible for us to integrate them all with our group feature. However, when you read through this chapter, keep in mind that just about anything that applies to a person in our community can be morphed to apply to a group of people. In this chapter, we will focus on creating the core framework for a group.

The framework we are building will allow us to create a group that will have both public and private presence in our site. A group will also be able to have a dedicated group page.

Here is the interface that will be built for group creation:

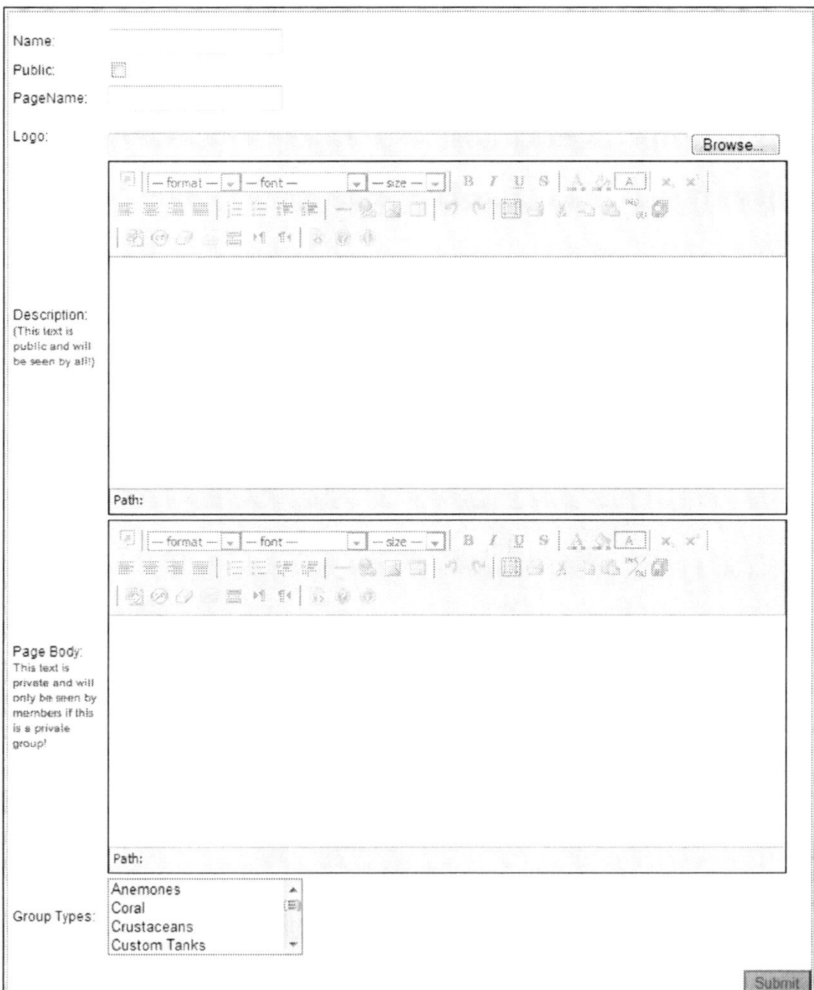

As we have the concept of private groups, we will need to provide a way for people to join a group and be approved by the owner of the group. We will have a **Request Membership** link as shown in the following screenshot:

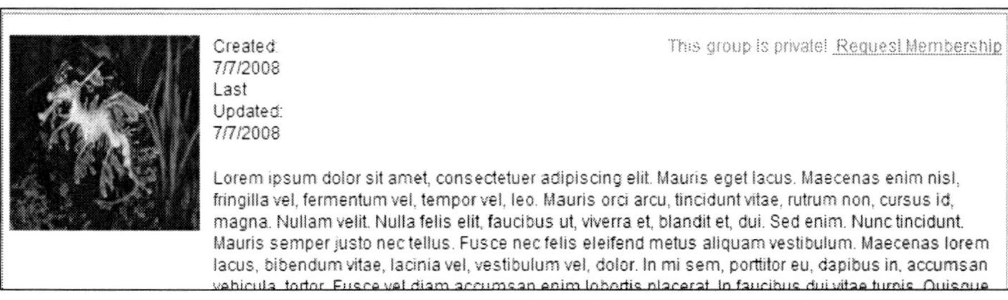

In addition to membership of a group, we will provide a way to have some of those members be considered owners or administrators of a group.

Once the foundation is in place, we will start to connect to some of our other features. We will allow each group to have its own forum. This forum will have some differences in that when a user posts to the forum, the forum will not send alerts to their friends, but instead will send alerts to all the members of that group.

Down the road, we could also extend the group feature to have its own filter to catch user alerts to an account in a similar manner. We could also have related blog posts show up on the homepage of the group. We could also show the latest forum posts on the group's homepage. We could show the latest uploaded images. And many other things could be done off the group foundation.

Design

Let's take a look at the design for this feature.

Groups

In the same way that the `Accounts` table is the core hub for many items in our system, the `Groups` table could be built out to be an additional hub. For that reason, we will address the creation of this feature first. The table structure for a group is not overly complex.

You are probably getting used to seeing the counts bubbled up at the parent level. We will explain again that we are doing this to remove the need to run aggregate queries. Instead, when we load the object we will automatically have the count in hand already.

Something else that you are probably used to seeing is the concept of a page name. As the group page will become a major center of information, we want to make sure that as far as Google or other search engine spiders are concerned, this is a true page rather than some server-generated page. We do this in the hope of getting those cherished SEO points. Also it is much easier for the user to know where they are and it allows our user to send a human readable URL to their friends, which promotes sharing!

The last thing of importance to note is the `IsPublic` flag that we have in our group entry. This will be the key to tell us whether or not anyone can gain access to this group or only group members. We will touch upon this requirement a bit more later.

GroupMembers

Generally in a group there is more than one user who will help operate the group. We will therefore have an `AccountID` in the group, which will help us identify the owner of the group. But we will also need a method to track all the members of the group as well as the members who are also administrators.

You can see from the structure in the screenshot that we are going to track the `GroupID` and the `AccountID` to create the relationship between `Groups` and `Accounts`. In addition to that information, we are also going to keep track of when the member requested the membership, whether they are approved or not (`IsApproved`) and whether the account is also an administrator (`IsAdmin`). This gives us everything we need to create the members for our groups.

GroupTypes

We will eventually have many different groups in our system. As an added feature we want an easy way for our users to locate groups that they may have some interest in. In order to provide this functionality, we will have a system to track what type a group is. Down the road we could use this system for searching groups or grouping them. This system will also allow us to make the statement: "If you like this group you might also be interested in these related groups".

As you can see from the relationships in the screenshot, groups can be associated with many group types (and vice versa). The structure itself is very straightforward.

GroupForums

As we have covered earlier, when a user creates a group they also get a group-owned forum. In order to accomplish this, we have to create a link between the group and a new forum.

This is a simple many-to-many relationship that allows us to technically have many forums and many groups related to one another. We don't like to introduce limitations by design though. So just in case we need to have multiple forums for a group or one group with many forums, we can.

Solution

Now let's take a look at our solution.

Implementing the database

Let's take a look at what we need to implement the database. The following screenshot shows the relevant tables.

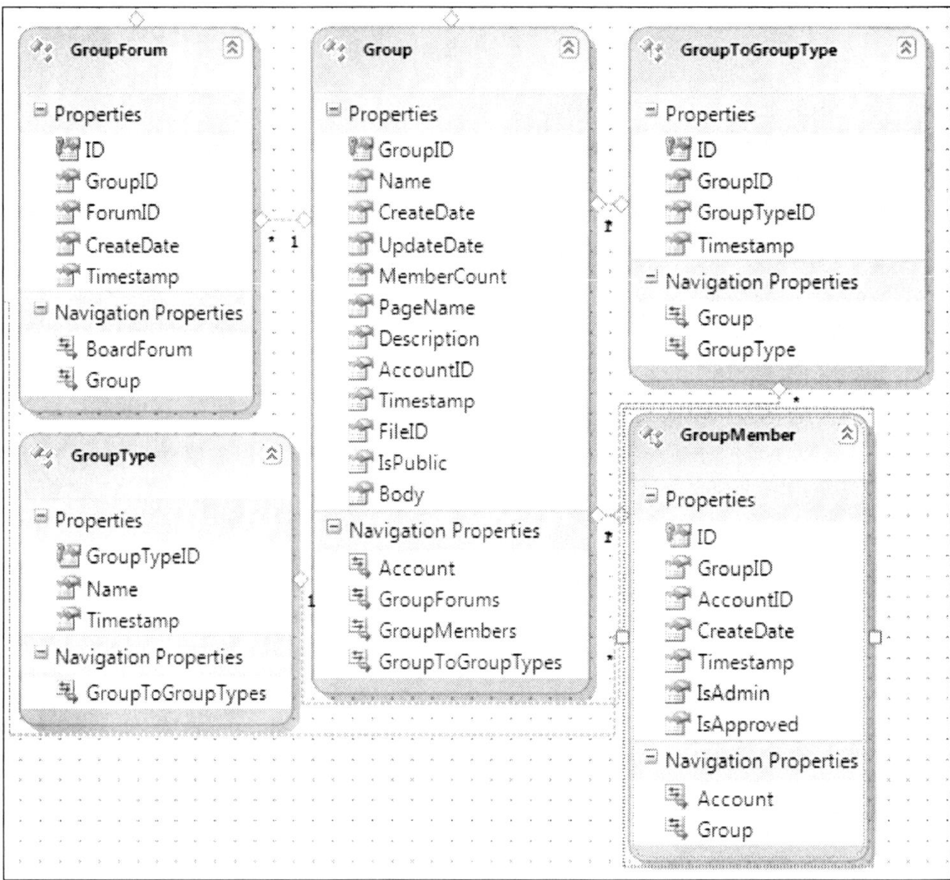

Groups

Refer to the `Groups` table structure in the previous screenshot. The majority of this table is self-explanatory. However, one thing to be very aware of is the **Body** field, which is **varchar(MAX)** here. This means that people could technically put any amount of text that they want here. If this is not the functionality that you want to provide, either make this field smaller or put some form of client-side validation on this field to restrict its size.

You may also be wondering why we have a large **Description** field and an even larger **Body** field. The primary reason for this is so that we have public and private fields of text. A description could simply be the first paragraph of the groups' page text, or it could be a brief synopsis. This totally depends on how you structure your output. We have set it up so that the description and body show up together, with the description on top.

Another item worth noting is that we are tracking a **FileID** with each group. This reference will allow us to upload a photo to the system to be used as the group's avatar or logo.

GroupMembers

The `GroupMembers` table allows us to define who can be our group members. In addition to defining membership, this table will allow us to accept or reject members. Once we have members, we can also use this structure to define additional administrators in the group.

GroupTypes

This table allows us to define the different group types that we want provided by our system. If you wanted to allow your users to provide their own group type, you could add an additional field to define whether it should be system-defined or user-defined. We would probably call this flag `IsSystemType`. This will help us to define our initial library.

Once we have the `GroupTypes` table created, we can then turn our attention to capturing relationships between groups and their type(s). Keep in mind that the users will be able to associate their groups with more than one type, if appropriate.

This is a simple many-to-many relationship definition table that tracks both the **GroupID** and **GroupTypeID**.

GroupForums

This table, like many of the others described earlier, is simply a many-to-many relationship table. This table allows each of our groups to also have a forum. We do this by tracking the **GroupID** and the **ForumID**.

Creating the relationships

Once all the tables are created, we can then create all the relationships.

For this set of tables, we have relationships between the following tables:

- `Groups` to `Accounts`
- `GroupMembers` and `Accounts`
- `GroupMembers` and `Groups`
- `GroupToGroupTypes` and `Groups`
- `GroupToGroupTypes` and `GroupTypes`
- `BoardForums` and `GroupForums`
- `GroupForums` and `Groups`

Setting up the data access layer

To set up the data access layer, we follow the steps as already done in earlier chapters. Open the `Fisharoo.edmx` file and add all the above mentioned tables that we have discussed in this chapter.

Building repositories

With the addition of new tables will come the addition of new repositories so that we can get to the data stored in those tables. We will be creating or modifying the following repositories to support our needs:

- `GroupRepository`
- `GroupToGroupTypeRepository`
- `GroupMemberRepository`
- `GroupForumRepository`
- `GroupTypeRepository`
- `AccountRepository`

Each of our repositories will generally have a method for select by ID, select all by parent ID, save, and delete. Once you have seen one repository you have pretty much seen them all. Review previous chapters, the appendices, or the included code, for example, of a standard repository. However, in this chapter, we will discuss anything that varies from standard!

GroupRepository

The `GroupRepository` is possibly one of our largest repositories so far in the number of methods it provides.

For the most part the methods are standard as in earlier chapters. We will pick a couple of example methods though they demonstrate common tasks.

GetGroupByForumID

This group is responsible for going through the linking table `GroupForums` to get a Group by the passed in `ForumID`. This is performed by joining the `Groups` and `GroupForums` table on the `GroupID` field in each table. We then perform a `where` clause to get the appropriate group for this forum.

```
//Fisharoo/DataAccess/Repositories/GroupRepository.cs
public Group GetGroupByForumID(int ForumID)
{
    Group result = null;
    using(FisharooDataContext dc = conn.GetContext())
    {
        result = (from g in dc.Groups
                  join f in dc.GroupForums on g.GroupID equals
                  f.GroupID
                  where f.ForumID == ForumID
                  select g).FirstOrDefault();
    }
    return result;
}
```

Considering that our table structure technically allows multiple groups for multiple forums, you may need to pay attention if you add the logic that allows the user to create many relationships. The interface that we will create will allow only one forum to be created when a group is initially created. The restriction is strictly enforced through the limitation of the UI. If you intend to use the many-to-many structure on purpose, you will want to change the return type of this method to a `List<Group>`.

IsOwner

The `IsOwner` method is responsible for determining if the passed in `AccountID` is the owner of the group that is associated with the passed in `GroupID`. This is performed on the DataContext groups collection with a `where` clause to determine if we have ownership. If the item returned is not null, then we know that the user is indeed an owner; otherwise he/she is not.

```
//Fisharoo/DataAccess/Repositories/GroupRepository.cs
public bool IsOwner(int AccountID, int GroupID)
{
    bool result = false;
    using(FisharooDataContext dc = conn.GetContext())
    {
        if (dc.Groups.Where(g => g.AccountID == AccountID &&
                      g.GroupID == GroupID).FirstOrDefault() != null)
            result = true;
    }
    return result;
}
```

CheckIfGroupPageNameExists

This method is very important as it determines if a Group's page name is in use yet or not.

```
//Fisharoo/DataAccess/Repositories/GroupRepository.cs
public bool CheckIfGroupPageNameExists(string PageName)
{
    bool result = false;
    using (FisharooDataContext dc = conn.GetContext())
    {
        Group group = dc.Groups.Where(g => g.PageName ==
                                 PageName).FirstOrDefault();
        if(group == null)
            result = false;
    }
    return result;
}
```

GroupToGroupTypeRepository

Keep in mind that this particular repository is supporting an overly simple table structure—a lookup table so to speak. For this reason, the repository is fairly lightweight too. We will discuss only one method from this repository.

SaveGroupTypesForGroup

This method is of interest in that it addresses a common problem that we have with lookup tables of this nature. The initial saving of items to a lookup table is simple. There are no other relationships defined, so we are doing a simple insert.

What happens when a user pulls up their UI again and attempts to save the same relationships with an additional relationship and one removed relationship? The easiest way to address this issue is to just toss away all the old relationships and then create the new relationships that we have in hand at that moment. This might be ok if we had no third column key, If we just had a clustered key with our two foreign keys, we could consider this. But do keep in mind that the "delete all" concept can thrash on your database a bit creating more traffic than is necessary.

Another way to manage this issue is to just remove the deleted relationships and continue to throw new relationships into the system. This creates redundant data (and possibly data corruption). This method also thrashes on the database with more traffic than is necessary.

The third and the best way to handle this is to determine what is to be removed and what is to be added before we hit the database. This can be performed regardless of the additional columns that we have. And this method doesn't cause any extra data or hits on the database.

```
//Fisharoo/DataAccess/Repositories/GroupToGroupTypeRepository.cs
public void SaveGroupTypesForGroup(List<long> SelectedGroupTypeIDs,
int GroupID)
        {
            using (FisharooDataContext dc = conn.GetContext())
            {
                //get a list of current selections
                List<long> currentTypes =
                    dc.GroupToGroupTypes.Where(gt => gt.GroupID ==
                    GroupID).Select(gt => gt.GroupTypeID).ToList();
                //make a list of items to delete
                List<long> itemsToDelete = currentTypes.Where(
                ct => !SelectedGroupTypeIDs.Contains(ct)).ToList();

                //make a list of items to insert
                List<long> itemsToInsert =
                    SelectedGroupTypeIDs.Where(
                    s => !currentTypes.Contains(s)).ToList();
                //delete grouptogrouptypes
```

```
                List<GroupToGroupType> GrouptoGroupType=
                dc.GroupToGroupTypes.Where(g => itemsToDelete.
                Contains(g.GroupTypeID)

                && g.GroupID == GroupID).ToList();
                foreach (GroupToGroupType gptogpt in GrptoGrupType)
                {
                    dc.GroupToGroupTypes.DeleteObject(gptogpt);
                }
                //create the actual objects to insert and insert
                foreach (long l in itemsToInsert)
                {
                    GroupToGroupType g = new GroupToGroupType() {
                    GroupID = GroupID, GroupTypeID = l };
                    dc.GroupToGroupTypes.AddObject(g);
                }
                dc.SaveChanges();
            }
        }
```

As you can see, we are pretty much only using standard LINQ statements to create a unique list of items for each purpose. We first get a list of the current relationships. We then make a list of the items to be deleted and a list of items to be created. Next, we actually perform the delete on the relationships that need to be removed. And then we create the objects that represent the relationships. We then perform the insert of those objects. There is some work here in the extent of code to be created. But keep in mind that this results in minimal database thrashing and good clean data!

GroupForumRepository

The `GroupForumRepository` is even less interesting as compared to the last repository we considered. This repository is also supporting a standard many-to-many lookup table.

None of the methods here are special as they all are similar to what we have seen before in the other repository examples.

GroupMemberRepository

This particular repository provides many supporting type database lookups that allow us to do bulk executions, simple tasks such as promoting and demoting members to and from admin status, and tasks such as determining if a user is a member or an administrator.

GetMemberAccountIDsByGroupID

This particular method is not complex by any means. But you will notice that it is creating a list of members from two data sources. It first looks at all the members defined by the `GroupMembers` table. It then takes into account that the owner of the Group is not in that list, so it also extracts the owner to add to this list.

```
//Fisharoo/DataAccess/Repositories/GroupMemberRepository.cs
public List<int> GetMemberAccountIDsByGroupID(Int32 GroupID)
{
    List<int> result = new List<int>();
    using(FisharooDataContext dc = conn.GetContext())
    {
        result = dc.GroupMembers.Where(gm => gm.IsApproved &&
                                  gm.GroupID == GroupID).
                                  Select(gm => gm.AccountID).ToList();
        result.Add(dc.Groups.Where(g => g.GroupID ==
               GroupID).Select(gm => gm.AccountID).FirstOrDefault());
    }
    return result;
}
```

DeleteGroupMembers

This is a method that is performing a bulk-style action. We are selecting a list of members based on the IDs that were passed into the method. And we are then passing that list of `GroupMembers` into the `DeleteAllOnSubmit` method allowing us to perform a batch delete. This will support our multi-select page on the member management pages later.

```
//Fisharoo/DataAccess/Repositories/GroupMemberRepository.cs
public void DeleteGroupMembers(List<int> MembersToDelete, int
                                GroupID)
{
    using(FisharooDataContext dc = conn.GetContext())
    {
        IEnumerable<GroupMember> members =
            dc.GroupMembers.Where(gm =>
                                MembersToDelete.Contains(gm.AccountID)
                                && gm.GroupID == GroupID);
        foreach(GroupMember grpmember in members) {
            dc.GroupMembers.DeleteObject(grpmember);
        dc.SaveChanges();
    }
}
```

GroupTypeRepository

The `GroupTypeRepository` has a handful of methods to perform the basic tasks. None of them is out of the ordinary and so we will not be discussing them here.

AccountRepository

This particular repository is the one that has grown over several chapters. In order to support Groups we had to add a couple of new methods to this class—`GetApprovedAccountsByGroupID` and `GetAccountsToApproveByGroupID`. These allow us to use our `GroupMembers` table to look up an actual Account from a membership point of view. We will get users who would like to be a part of our group, and the members who are already a part of the group.

GetApprovedAccountsByGroupID

This method is primarily of interest for the reason that it supports server-side paging, that is to say, it has the ability to show a subset of records within the larger selection. This is accomplished using some standard LINQ expressions—`Skip()` and `Take()`.

```
//Fisharoo/DataAccess/Repositories/AccountRepository.cs
public List<Account> GetApprovedAccountsByGroupID(int GroupID,
                             int PageNumber, int
                             NumberOfRecordsInPage)
{
    List<Account> result = null;
    using (FisharooDataContext dc = conn.GetContext())
    {
        IEnumerable<Account> accounts = (from a in dc.Accounts
                   join m in dc.GroupMembers on a.AccountID equals
                   m.AccountID
                   where m.GroupID == GroupID && m.IsApproved
                   orderby a.AccountID
                   select a).Skip((NumberOfRecordsInPage *
                   (PageNumber - 1))).Take(NumberOfRecordsInPage);
        result = accounts.ToList();
    }
    return result;
}
```

In this method, we are accepting the `GroupID` and `PageNumber`. This tells us the set and also the subset of the data that we are interested in. The LINQ to Entity query is very standard up to the point of call to the `Skip()` method. This call allows us to tell the query which record we want to start at in the set of data. Directly after that we call the `Take()` method, that tells the query how many records from the starting record we want to include in our returned set of data.

The easiest way to perform the skip logic is to take the number of records we want our page size to be (stored in a `config` file somewhere) and multiply it by the page number we are currently on (minus one as this is technically a zero-based way of doing things). The `Take()` method just wants to know how many records you are interested in to make up your page set of data.

GetAccountsToApproveByGroupID

This method isn't anything more than a simple query around `GroupMembers` and `Groups`.

```
//Fisharoo/DataAccess/Repositories/AccountRepository.cs
public List<Account> GetAccountsToApproveByGroupID(int GroupID)
{
    List<Account> result = null;
    using (FisharooDataContext dc = conn.GetContext())
    {
        IEnumerable<Account> accounts = (from a in dc.Accounts
                   join m in dc.GroupMembers on a.AccountID equals
                   m.AccountID
                   where m.GroupID == GroupID && !m.IsApproved
                   select a);
        result = accounts.ToList();
    }
    return result;
}
```

Implementing the services/application layer

Once all the repositories are built for single serving purposes we can begin to create the services layer. Again, this layer is responsible for assembling aggregates and performing complex actions with our entities. We will create and modify the following services:

- `GroupService`
- `AlertService`
- `Redirector`
- `WebContext`

GroupService

The `GroupService` is really just an abstraction layer from the `GroupRepository` for the most part. There are a couple of cases wherein we do something other than pass calls through to the repository layer. For the most part, it is there to be expanded later. Let's look at a few relevant methods of this class.

IsOwnerOrAdministrator

This method is taking two methods—`IsOwner` and `IsAdministrator`—aggregating their result into one result.

```
//Fisharoo/BusinessLogic/GroupService.cs
public bool IsOwnerOrAdministrator(Int32 AccountID, Int32 GroupID)
{
    bool result = false;
    if (IsOwner(AccountID, GroupID) || IsAdministrator(AccountID,
                                                        GroupID))
        result = true;
    return result;
}
```

SaveGroup

Other than the `SaveGroup` method, all other methods are pretty much pass-through methods to a repository method. The `SaveGroup` method on the other hand does some pretty heavy lifting for us. It takes care of creating all the other data items that surround a group. It is currently creating a `BoardForum` and the `GroupForum` data that links this group to the new forum as well as saving the Group as normal.

```
//Fisharoo/BusinessLogic/GroupService.cs
public int SaveGroup(Group group)
{
    int result = 0;
    if(group.GroupID > 0)
    {
        result = _groupRepository.SaveGroup(group);
    }
    else
    {
        result = _groupRepository.SaveGroup(group);
        BoardForum forum = new BoardForum();
        forum.CategoryID = 4; //group forums container
        forum.CreateDate = DateTime.Now;
        forum.LastPostByAccountID =
        _webContext.CurrentUser.AccountID;
```

```
            forum.LastPostByUsername = _webContext.CurrentUser.Username;
            forum.LastPostDate = DateTime.Now;
            forum.Name = group.Name;
            forum.PageName = group.PageName;
            forum.PostCount = 0;
            forum.Subject = group.Name;
            forum.ThreadCount = 0;
            forum.UpdateDate = DateTime.Now;
            int ForumID = _forumRepository.SaveForum(forum);
            //create relationship between the group and forum
            GroupForum gf = new GroupForum();
            gf.ForumID = ForumID;
            gf.GroupID = group.GroupID;
            gf.CreateDate = DateTime.Now;
            _groupForumRepository.SaveGroupForum(gf);
        }
        return result;
    }
```

AlertService

In case if you have not yet read the previous chapters, the `AlertService` is woven through all the other code in this site as it provides us with a way to let our users know that something has happened in our site. With Groups this is no different—with the exception that a user doesn't actually do much with our groups. They can join the groups and then make posts in our group-owned forum though! The difference here is that rather than sending an alert to all their friends about a post in the forum, we will send an alert to all the group owners.

Apart from the various alert methods that we added, the only one of interest to be discussed here is the `SendAlertToGroup()` method.

```
//Fisharoo/BusinessLogic/AlertService.cs
private void SendAlertToGroup(Alert alert, Group group)
{
    List<int> groupMembers =
                         _groupMemberRepository.
                         GetMemberAccountIDsByGroupID(group.GroupID);
    foreach (int id in groupMembers)
    {
        alert.AlertID = 0;
        alert.AccountID = id;
        SaveAlert(alert);
    }
}
```

This method takes in the newly-created alert. It then gets a list of `groupMembers` for the specified group. With these items in hand, it iterates through each `groupMember` and adds their `AccountID` to the Alert and then sends the Alert.

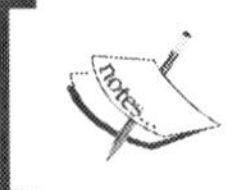

This could potentially be a performance bottleneck. A better way to possibly do this is to create all the alerts first and then create a new `SaveAlert()` method that takes in a list of Alerts to do a bulk insert.

Redirector

While the `Redirector` class is not that complex, it is very important as it abstracts our redirection logic out of the pages and puts it higher up into the business layer. This means that if things change in our page structure we have one place to go and make changes. There are of course times when we can't fit redirection into the `Redirector` class—just be sure that you don't put your redirection logic in a page out of sheer convenience! Look up the source code associated with this chapter to see the new methods added to this class.

WebContext

Similar to the `Redirector`, the `WebContext` class is not all that complex. Its purpose is simple and the way it conforms to its purpose is equally simple. This class is responsible for acting as a gateway to all requests to the `HttpContext` class. This means that any time we are making a call to query string items, post form items, or anything directly represented by the `HttpContext` class such as application variables; we should be hitting this class rather than going to the source.

There are two additions made to this class—we now have a `NewGroup` property and a `GroupID` property. You can look up the source code associated with this chapter to see these.

Implementing the presentation layer

With all the backend out of the way, let's get to building the front end. It is always difficult to decide where to begin when creating an application of this nature. Do you populate the database with some sample test data and build the display page first? Or do you start with the data creation pages first and then work on the display pages? This time we will work with the data creation pages first, and then work our way out to the display pages towards the end. With that in mind, let's get started.

ManageGroup

While we could have created two pages to manage our group data—one for new groups and the other to edit groups—we find it far easier to create one page and one UI that allows us to both create and edit groups. This particular page has a couple of interesting features in it that we are providing a WYSIWYG editor as well as an image upload feature. These two topics are the features that we will work with the most in this discussion.

Before we get started, it is important to know that the page knows its different states by the presence of two query string variables. The first variable is `newgroup=1`. This obviously tells the page that we intend to create a new group. The second variable is `GroupID={number}`, which allows us to populate the page with a specified group's data.

WYSIWYG

Our WYSIWYG editor of choice is Xinha (which we have covered before in the previous chapters). To use this editor, all we have to do is drop a textbox with the **TextMode** set to **MultiLine**. Then further down the page, we have to pass the full control ID into the Xinha engine with the following code:

```
//Fisharoo/Web/Groups/ManageGroup.aspx
<script type="text/javascript">
    xinha_editors[xinha_editors.length] = 'Content_txtDescription';
    xinha_editors[xinha_editors.length] = 'Content_txtBody';
</script>
```

This creates the full-featured WYSIWYG editor and you can configure more or less options globally depending on what you need.

Image upload

While we covered the topic of file uploads in the chapter that covers files, folders, image galleries, and the like we felt that we might want to recover some ground. In that chapter, we had the `FileUpload` logic stored in a helper page called `ReceiveFiles.aspx`. While this approach worked well when we had only one area of the site that required uploads, it no longer works when we have two areas of the site that require upload capabilities.

For that reason, we moved all the upload logic into an `UploadService`. It is pretty much 100 percent duplicated from that file (so we won't recover it here). Then in the `ReceiveFiles` page, we removed all the old code and replaced it with a single call to the `UploadService.UploadPhotos` method. Once this refactoring was completed, we were able to turn back to address the fact that we wanted the users to be able to upload a photo as their group's logo.

Here is the `SaveGroup` method from the `ManageGroupPresenter` (the rest of the code is standard plumbing code):

```
//Fisharoo/Web/Groups/Presenters/ManageGroupPresenter.cs
public void SaveGroup(Group group, HttpPostedFile file, List<long>
                      selectedGroupTypeIDs)
{
    if (group.Description.Length > 2000)
    {
        _view.ShowMessage("Your description is " +
                  group.Description.Length.ToString() +
                  " characters long and can only be 2000
                  characters!");
    }
    else
    {
        group.AccountID = _webContext.CurrentUser.AccountID;
        group.PageName = group.PageName.Replace(" ", "-");
        if (group.GroupID == 0 &&
         _groupRepository.CheckIfGroupPageNameExists(group.PageName))
        {
            _view.ShowMessage("The page name you specified is already
                             in use!");
        }
        else
        {
            if (file.ContentLength > 0)
            {
                List<Int64> fileIDs = _uploadService.UploadPhotos(1,
                                   _webContext.CurrentUser.AccountID,
                                    _webContext.Files, 1);
                //should only be one item uploaded!
                if (fileIDs.Count == 1)
                    group.FileID = fileIDs[0];
            }
            group.GroupID = _groupService.SaveGroup(group);
            _groupToGroupTypeRepository.SaveGroupTypesForGroup(
                           selectedGroupTypeIDs,group.GroupID);
            _redirector.GoToGroupsViewGroup(group.PageName);
        }
    }
}
```

As you can see in the preceding code, we are primarily performing some data validation and clean up tasks. If we have a new group we verify that the page name specified is unique to the system. If the page name is unique, then we are able to process the save request. Prior to processing the save, we check to see if a file is being uploaded. If it is, then we make a call to the `UploadService.UploadPhotos` method and pass in the upload file. From there, we perform standard save operations. The rest of this page is a standard MVP event and data plumbing.

Members

With a group successfully created, and with the ability to edit the group in place, we can turn our attention to managing membership. In the membership management page, we will be able to approve new membership requests. We can promote and demote existing members to the status of administrator (allowing them to perform various tasks down the road). And we can delete members. This UI will have a multi-select checkbox type interface but not with the standard `CheckBoxList` control. In addition to that we will support pagination functionality in a custom manner.

As we mentioned during the creation of our `AccountRepository.GetApprovedAccountsByGroupID()` method—where we pass in the `GroupID` and `PageNumber`—the `PageNumber` input specifies which subset of data we want to see in our display. You will notice in the preceding image that we have a **Back** link (which takes us back to the group page). Next to that if we were on any page other than the first one, we would see **Previous**. Additionally, if we had approved members in the UI, we would also have a **Next** link.

Data pagination

These next and previous concepts are handled in the `MembersPresenter` with the following two methods:

```
//Fisharoo/Web/Groups/Presenters/MembersPresenter.cs
public void Next()
{
    _redirector.GoToGroupsMembers(_webContext.GroupID,
                             (_webContext.PageNumber + 1));
}
public void Previous()
{
    _redirector.GoToGroupsMembers(_webContext.GroupID,
                             (_webContext.PageNumber - 1));
}
```

As you can see, with the pairing of the logic in the `AccountRepository`, we have a very simple pagination solution that can be performed with any set of data. Also while we haven't explicitly addressed it here, you should take care to not go past valid page numbers.

CheckBoxLists without the CheckBoxList control

The other easy thing to implement without being forced to use standard controls is the use of a `Repeater` and a `CheckBox` control to create a custom `CheckBoxList`, which is more preferred. This pairing is simply a `Repeater` control and a `CheckBox`. We can add any data that we need to capture for each selected checkbox to the `CheckBox` control as an attribute in the `Repeater`'s `OnItemDataBound` event.

```
//Fisharoo/Web/Groups/Members.aspx.cs
public void repMembersToApprove_ItemDataBound(object sender,
                                        RepeaterItemEventArgs e)
{
    if(e.Item.ItemType == ListItemType.AlternatingItem ||
                          e.Item.ItemType == ListItemType.Item)
    {
```

```
        ProfileDisplay p = e.Item.FindControl("Profile1") as
                           ProfileDisplay;
        CheckBox chkProfile = e.Item.FindControl("chkProfile") as
                              CheckBox;
        p.LoadDisplay(((Account)e.Item.DataItem));
            chkProfile.Attributes.Add("AccountID",
                    ((Account)e.Item.DataItem).AccountID.ToString());
    }
}
```

We then have a method in the code behind to extract the selected values for use later.

```
//Fisharoo/Web/Groups/Members.aspx.cs
private List<int> ExtractMemberIDs(Repeater repeater)
{
    List<int> result = new List<int>();
    foreach (RepeaterItem item in repeater.Items)
    {
        if(item.ItemType == ListItemType.AlternatingItem ||
                           item.ItemType == ListItemType.Item)
        {
            CheckBox chkProfile = item.FindControl("chkProfile") as
                                  CheckBox;
            if(chkProfile.Checked)
                result.Add(Convert.ToInt32(chkProfile.Attributes[
                                                  "AccountID"]));
        }
    }
    return result;
}
```

As you can see in the code, we are looking for the `AccountID` attribute that we added in the `OnItemDataBound` event. We do this by iterating through all the items in the `Repeater` and finding and casting our checkbox controls from each item. We can then work with the selected values no matter how many there are in the `Repeater`. One final point to note here is that as a membership is approved, an appropriate alert is sent to the user who had requested the membership. You can see the code of `ApproveMembers` method in `MembersPresenter.cs` for details. While not currently handled, a similar alert can easily be added if the request is denied.

Default

The homepage of our Groups section (see the first screenshot of this Chapter), the `default.aspx` page, is responsible for listing all the groups in the system when a user first enters this section of the site. This page makes a call to the `GroupService` to get all the latest groups. It then binds that collection of data to a `ListView` and outputs each group. Be aware that each of the group names has actual links to the custom group `PageName.aspx` (we will cover more on this in a moment). Nothing more to this page though.

See the code for specific examples of how this works.

URL routing

Before we dig too deep into data management, we find ourselves at a crossroads where we need to dig into our URL routing again. As we have a `PageName` field in our Groups we need to discuss how to handle Group `PageNames`. Once this is complete, we can move on to pulling up and viewing a group. This is handled by creating an additional routing entry in our route collection in `global.ascsx.cs` in the `RegisterRoutes` method.

```
//Fisharoo/Web/Global.ascx.cs
public static void RegisterRoutes(RouteCollection routeCollection)
{
    . . .
    routeCollection.MapPageRoute("GroupRoute",
            "groups/{groupname}.aspx", "~/Groups/ViewGroup.aspx");
}
```

Once we locate the appropriate keyword, we can load up an instance of our group by the specified page name. This part is handled in `ViewGroup.aspx` page.

ViewGroup

This page is responsible for showing the group details. The first thing to look at is the handling of URL routing. In the code behind, we extract the group page name from the route data collection and pass it to the presenter to load the specific page.

```
//Fisharoo/Web/Groups/ViewGroup.aspx.cs
. . .
string groupname = Page.RouteData.Values["groupname"] as string;
presenter.Init(this, IsPostBack, groupname);
```

In the presenter we load the specific group data using the `groupname` that we got from the route data collection and then do some more processing with regards to public/private viewing.

```
//Fisharoo/Web/Groups/ViewGroupPresenter.cs
public void LoadData(string groupname)
{
    Group group = _groupService.GetGroupByPageName(groupname);
    string url = "/files/photos/" + _uploadService.
    GetFullFilePathByFileID(group.FileID, File.Sizes.S);
    _view.LoadData(group, url);
    if(_webContext.CurrentUser != null)
        _view.ShowRequestMembership(true);
    else
        _view.ShowRequestMembership(false);

    //is this public or private data?
    if (group.IsPublic)
    {
        _view.ShowPrivate(true);
        _view.ShowPublic(true);
    }
    else if (ViewerIsMember(group.GroupID))
    {
        _view.ShowPrivate(true);
        _view.ShowPublic(true);
    }
    else
    {
        _view.ShowPrivate(false);
        _view.ShowPublic(true);
    }
}
```

In addition to displaying data, it will act as our jumping off point for viewing and managing other sections that are related to the group—such as the group-owned forum.

Private/Public

Determining whether a group is public or private is performed simply by checking a bit flag set in the database, determining who can actually see a private group is a bit more complex (refer to the presenter code above).

Recall that we had created a few help functions to determine if a user was the owner of the group, a member of the group, or an administrator of the group. In our `ViewGroupPresenter`, we make a call to our `ViewMembers` method to determine where the user stands.

```
//Fisharoo/Web/Groups/Presenters/ViewGroupPresenter.cs
public void ViewMembers()
{
    _redirector.GoToGroupsMembers(_webContext.GroupID);
}
```

This lets us know quickly and easily if we can display the private group. If not, then the user is shown the appropriate message stating that the group is private and they are prompted to request membership. When you request to become a member, an alert is sent to the group owner for this request.

```
//Fisharoo/Web/Groups/Presenters/ViewGroupPresenter.cs
public void RequestMembership(string groupID)
{
    . . .
  _alertService.AddGroupMembershipRequestAlert(gm.AccountID,
  gm.GroupID, _webContext.CurrentUser.Username);
}
```

Created:
7/7/2008
Last
Updated:
7/7/2008

This group is private! Request Membership

Lorem ipsum dolor sit amet, consectetuer adipiscing elit. Mauris eget lacus. Maecenas enim nisl, fringilla vel, fermentum vel, tempor vel, leo. Mauris orci arcu, tincidunt vitae, rutrum non, cursus id, magna. Nullam velit. Nulla felis elit, faucibus ut, viverra et, blandit et, dui. Sed enim. Nunc tincidunt. Mauris semper justo nec tellus. Fusce nec felis eleifend metus aliquam vestibulum. Maecenas lorem lacus, bibendum vitae, lacinia vel, vestibulum vel, dolor. In mi sem, porttitor eu, dapibus in, accumsan

If you are part of the group or the owner of the group, you would instead see the list of members below the group description.

MyGroups

The `MyGroups` page is a duplication of the homepage in that it streams a bunch of groups. The immediate difference is that all the groups on this page belong to the viewer of the page. In addition to the security check and changed data source, we also offer a couple of additional features. From this page, we can delete the selected group. We also have the ability to link to the `ManageGroup.aspx page`.

The security comes in the form that this page requires the viewing party to be logged in. From the logged-in user's `AccountID` (stored in session), we then load the page with a call to the `GroupService.GetGroupsOwnedByAccount()` method from within the `MyGroupsPresenter`.

```
//Fisharoo/Web/Groups/Presenters/MyGroupsPresenter.cs
public void LoadData()
{
    List<Group> list = _groupService.GetGroupsOwnedByAccount(_
                              webContext.CurrentUser.AccountID);
   _view.LoadData(Translator.GroupToPEGroup(list));
}
```

With each `ItemDataBound` event in the code behind, we pass in the `GroupID` to the attributes collection of our edit and delete buttons. We also add a bit of client-side JavaScript to confirm with the user that it is OK to actually perform the delete process on the selected group.

```
//Fisharoo/Web/Groups/MyGroups.aspx.cs
protected void lvGroups_ItemDataBound(object sender,
                                      ListViewItemEventArgs e)
{
    if (e.Item.ItemType == ListViewItemType.DataItem)
    {
        Image imgGroupImage = e.Item.FindControl("imgGroupImage") as
                              Image;
        Literal litImageID = e.Item.FindControl("litImageID") as
                             Literal;
        Literal litPageName = e.Item.FindControl("litPageName") as
                              Literal;
```

```
            LinkButton lbPageName = e.Item.FindControl("lbPageName") as
                                    LinkButton;
            ImageButton ibDelete = e.Item.FindControl("ibDelete") as
                                   ImageButton;
            Literal litGroupID = e.Item.FindControl("litGroupID") as
                                 Literal;
            ImageButton ibEdit = e.Item.FindControl("ibEdit") as
                                 ImageButton;
            ibDelete.Attributes.Add("GroupID", litGroupID.Text);
            ibEdit.Attributes.Add("GroupID", litGroupID.Text);
            ibDelete.Attributes.Add("onclick","return confirm('Are you
            sure you want to delete this group?');");
            lbPageName.Attributes.Add("PageName", litPageName.Text);
            imgGroupImage.ImageUrl = "/files/photos/" +
                                    _presenter.GetImageByID
                                    (Convert.ToInt64(litImageID.Text),
                                    File.Sizes.S);
        }
    }
```

Forum enhancements

We discussed earlier that we would have Group-owned-and-operated Forums. To pull this off, we had to add a new category to the board system specifically called **group-forums**. We then restricted that category from the board categories display (the forum homepage). This is handled in the `BoardCategoryRepository.GetAllCategories()` method. The forum homepage still looks like this:

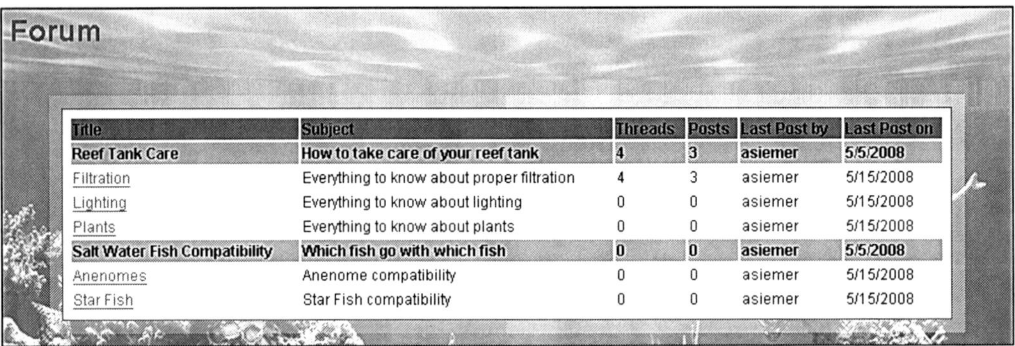

No group category exists here! Also note that there isn't a **sea-horses** present in the display whereas we can clearly link to the **sea-horses** forum from the **sea-horses** group. Recall that earlier we discussed when a group is created by the `GroupService`, we also create a new forum and attach it to the **group-forums** category (category 4). With this in place, when we load up the `ViewGroup` page, we can also load in the forum link for that group.

In addition to this, recall that we added a couple of methods to the `AlertService`. These methods allowed us to send alerts to all the members of the group rather than the friends of the poster. The only thing that we haven't covered up to this point to pull off this integration is how the posting forum page knows if it is a group-owned forum or not.

The only part of the forum system that was modified to create this addition is the `PostPresenter.Save()` method (covered in last chapter). At the very bottom of this method we added a bit of code to determine if we could load a group based on the `ForumID` or not.

> Recall that this logic is valid only if we specify that a group can own only one forum (and vice versa). We currently do that by only creating the link at the time the group is created. However, if you provide other tools for forum or group creation, you will need to keep in mind that some form of validation will need to be put in place, or this group/forum validation that we are currently discussing will need to be changed!

```
//Fisharoo/Web/Forums/Presenters/PostPresenter.cs
if (post.IsThread)
    thread = _postService.GetPostByID(post.PostID);
else
    thread = _postService.GetPostByID((long)post.ThreadID);

//CHAPTER 10. is this forum part of a group?
Group group = _groupService.GetGroupByForumID(forum.ForumID);

//add an alert to the filter
if (post.IsThread)
{
    //CHAPTER 10. is this a group forum?
    if (group != null)
        _alertService.AddNewBoardThreadAlert(category, forum,
        thread, group);
    else
        _alertService.AddNewBoardThreadAlert(category, forum, thread);
}
else
{
    //CHAPTER 10. is this a group forum?
    if (group != null)
        _alertService.AddNewBoardPostAlert(category, forum, post,
        thread, group);
```

```
        else
            _alertService.AddNewBoardPostAlert(category, forum, post,
            thread);
    }

    RouteValueDictionary values = new RouteValueDictionary {
            {"categoryname", category.Name}, {"forumname", forum.Name},
            {"postid", thread.PostID} };
    VirtualPathData vpd = RouteTable.Routes.GetVirtualPath(null,
                          "ThreadRoute", values);
                          _redirector.GoToForumsViewPost(vpd.VirtualPath);
```

With this code in place, our forum is not only aware that it is part of a group but is also able to send alerts to group members other than friends.

Summary

With this core framework in place you can see how groups can be used to bring many different systems together in a way that you start to create sub-communities. Obviously, this section has many other features which could be added to it. From the top of my mind I can think of integration in terms of the following features that might make some interesting additions to the group section:

- Messaging
    - You could create a "send to group" WYSIWYG section that sends messages to all the group members.
    - Additionally, you could integrate all the groups that a user is a member of into the messaging system so that the group name could be used as a contact name to blast messages directly from the mail section.
- Friends
    - Group members can be integrated easily as friends.
    - Not only can you specify public, private, and friends' areas in your user profiles but also have a filter such as `members of groups I am part of`.

You obviously don't have to think only about how you can bring groups out to your other community features. You could also bring some of your features into the group. Some examples of that are as follows:

- Blogs
    - Any blog posts that a member of the group creates could be flagged and shown on the group's homepage.
    - You could have a top N blog posts section on the group's homepage.
- Forum
    - Rather than force people to read into the forum, you could also post the latest threads on the homepage of the group.
    - You could have sticky threads (threads that never get pushed off the board—think memos or news) in the group forums that show up as bulletins on the group's homepage.
- Group filter
    - The group homepage could have group alerts posted on it in the same way a user profile has all the alerts posted on the filter.

Finally, the number of items that can be integrated into your group's homepage is limited to the number of features offered by your site.

11
User Interactivity

Giving our users the ability to comment, tag, and rate the content on our site provides them a level of interactivity that will make them want to come back again and again. There are mainly two reasons for these features to arouse the curiosity of users. First, it is human nature to want to provide their opinions about anything available to them. Once a group of users has offered its opinion on everything, you will find that a second group of users will rear their heads to look at and interact with the highest rated, most heavily commented and tagged content.

In this chapter, we will delve into what it takes to create a flexible system that will allow us to tag, rate, vote, and comment any object in our system (at the database level). We will apply tagging, rating, and commenting systems to our photo gallery section and vote, mark as answer, and medals to our forums section. Tagging and commenting will be somewhat straightforward in that they will simply take raw user input and tie it to the various content areas. The rating system on the other hand will use the ASP.NET AJAX library to provide multiple attributes in a modal window with the rating control, which when aggregated will provide us with an average score for that item.

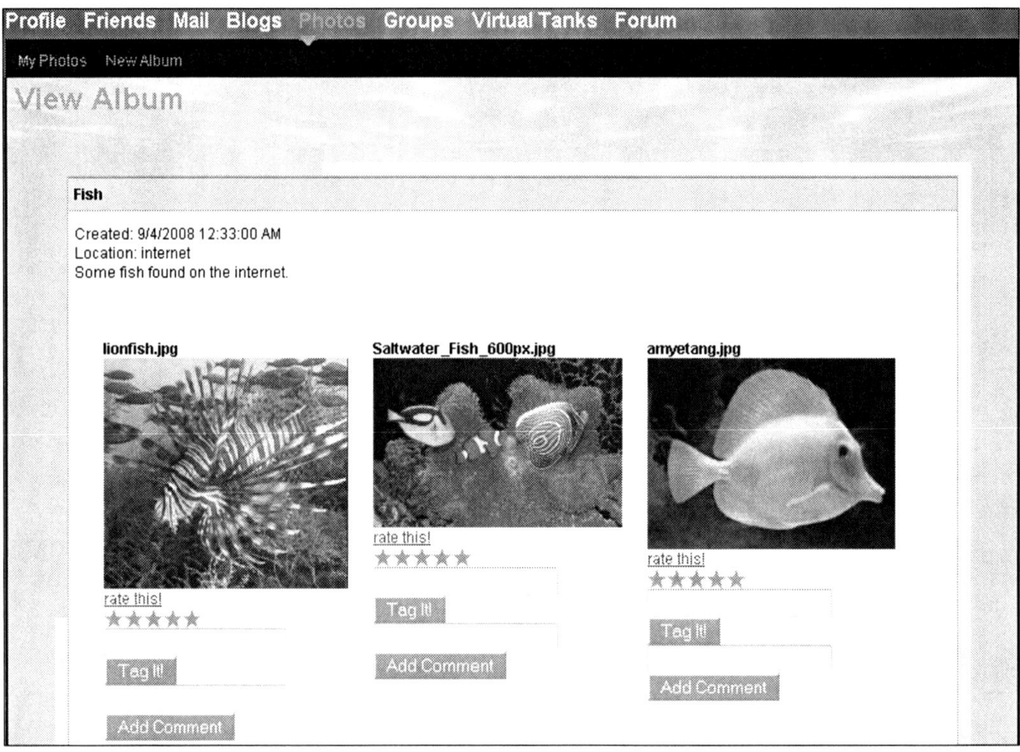

The voting control will also be AJAX-based and will allow forum users to vote a thread or a post as useful (+1 vote) or not useful (-1 vote). The mark as answer feature will allow the user who raised the initial query to accept a particular post as an answer to the query. Finally, voting and mark as answer together will help users to accumulate scores which will be reflected by medals that they can earn.

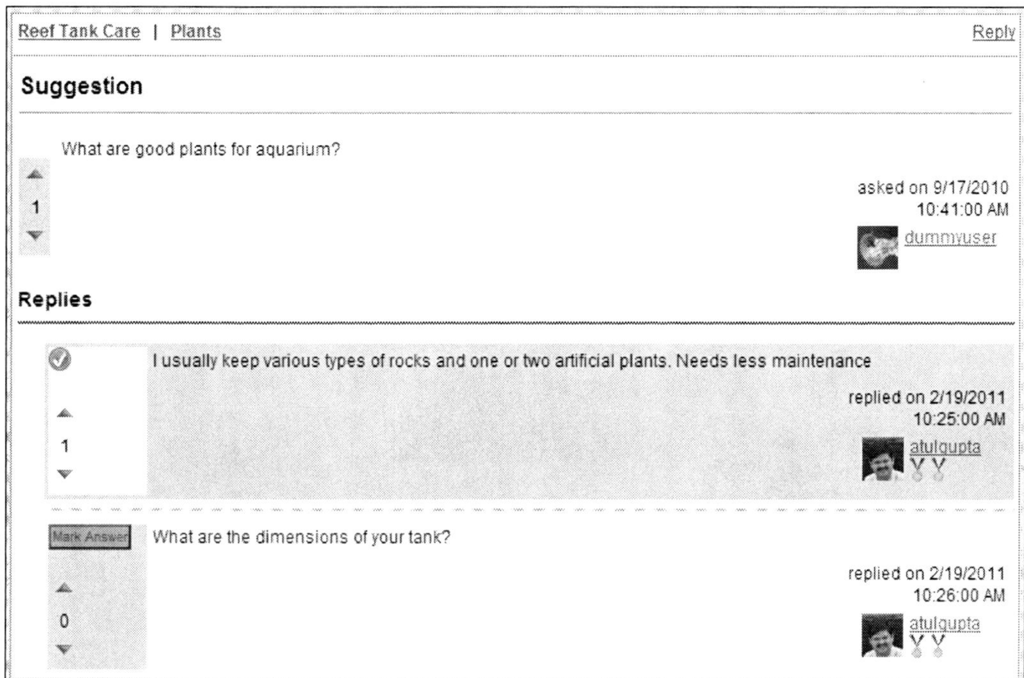

Problem

Let's take a look at the problems discussed in this chapter.

Ratings

The rating system included in the package of the ASP.NET AJAX controls works very well for a flat rating system. It has no issues with showing five stars horizontally or vertically, providing simple mouse over capabilities, capturing click events, and providing several properties to capture the selected input. What it doesn't do well is provide you with a way to capture multiple sub-ratings for a piece of content. That is what we will build here (refer to the first screenshot of this chapter)! Clicking on the **rate this** link will throw up a modal window.

In the modal window, the user will have several dynamically generated attributes to apply individual ratings to. All these ratings are then aggregated to provide the final rating for that item. Once we have received the rating for an item, we will thank the user for his/her input and then display the average rating as shown in the next screenshot:

Tagging

Tagging is a feature that allows us to attach keywords to any object (images in our case). Each keyword has a score attached to it that allows us to build a tag cloud with the largest tags shifted to the top showcasing the keywords that have the most use in the system. This particular control will be created in a flexible manner that allows us to capture new tags, display the tags that are attached to an object, display tags that are attached to a section, and those attached to the entire site.

We allow users to tag an image and then display the tags as sub cloud for that image.

Selecting the **large fish** tag will then take us to a page that lists not only other related images, but also any other content in the site with the same tag. In this case, selecting the **large fish** tag shows us three other resources with the same tag.

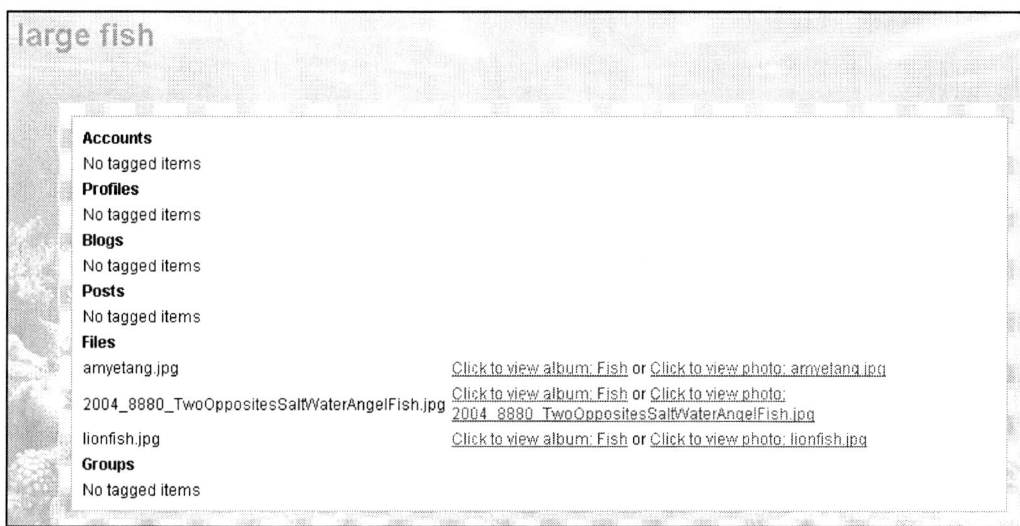

Also note that this page appears to be a resource in our site in the **Tags** directory. This we will handle via URL routing and this will help us feed the search engine spiders, which in turn should get more users to our site!

Finally, we can go out to the homepage to see a site-wide tag cloud. This tag cloud displays tags with a higher tag count, that is, the tags that are attached to more items, and having a larger font. This quickly identifies the most popular tags to the site's users.

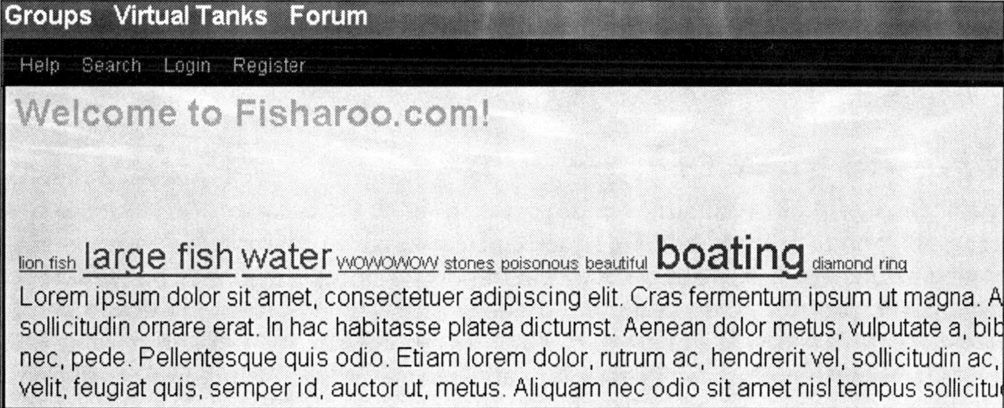

We will cover the algorithm used to determine the font size dynamically as well as some of the flexibilities that are baked into this control later in this chapter.

Commenting

Commenting allows our users to give more specific input about a resource. This can be integrated later into our search features to also help us get our content to our users. In addition to this, it allows our users to exchange comments about a resource, generating curiosity from other users.

Mark as answer

For any forum to be successful, it is important to have the basic infrastructure to post a question and to reply to existing posts. Once the basic infrastructure, which we created in Chapter 9, is available, the next important thing is to ensure resolution/responses to posted queries because ultimately that is what will drive the number of users to the forums. To ensure the forums are successful, they should provide the ability to accept a reply as an answer and at the same time allow other users to also vote on the question and its replies. These actions are internally linked to a scoring system. When a user attains a certain total score, they will be awarded a medal.

While each post that gets accepted as an answer will get some score, other posts also need to be valued to ensure users continue to show interest in posting replies. This is done by awarding scores to all replies, even if they aren't accepted as answers. The scores awarded in such cases are obviously lower than what one gets for posting an answer. We will go with a score of 10 for the accepted answer and 5 for all other posts.

Voting

Mark as answer, as discussed, is to be used by the user who raised the initial query. But how can we keep the community involved in the discussions? One way to address it is via voting. Users may find the questions and the replies useful for their own purposes and hence will like to give a positive vote. Similar users may not find the content relevant and can give a negative vote. A negative vote will cause the relevant user to lose on total score and will cause them to lose medals as well. This will act as deterrent for users to post irrelevant replies to threads.

Medals

Over a period the users build their credentials by accumulating scores. These credentials can be viewed as grades through medals. In Fisharoo, as the user attains certain total score, we assign him or her a medal. After attaining next level of score, we assign him or her additional medals and so on. The more medals the user has, the stronger the credentials the user carries on the social networking site. Similar to rating system, the medals will range from 1 to 5 with 1 being a beginner and 5 being the most reputed users on the site.

Design

Let's take a look at the design for this feature.

Ratings

With the ASP.NET AJAX Control Toolkit you are able to create horizontal or vertically positioned stars; stars that can be run from left-to-right, and right-to-left. You can even swap out the stars for any other image such as happy faces, if you really want to.

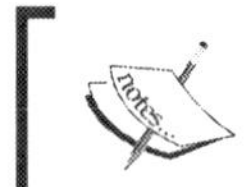

More information regarding the toolkit can be found here: `http://www.codeplex.com/AjaxControlToolkit` and `http://www.asp.net/ajax/ajaxcontroltoolkit/`.

The one thing that the control in the toolkit does not do, is allow you to show multiple attributes to be rated for an item. It also does not allow you to aggregate those ratings to be rolled up into one global rating. It is this more flexible control that we will discuss and build here.

Before we discuss rating attributes of an item, we need to discuss what an item is. In our community site, we may want to rate just about anything that is awfully vague and generally hard to work with. So we will say that our definition of "anything" is any table in the database (you will see more use of this object concept when we discuss comments and tags). In order to keep track of our objects, we will need to create a container which we can use as a hard reference.

For this, we will create a `SystemObjects` table. This will hold the name and `SystemObjectID` for each of the tables that we want to add ratings to. If we add more tables to our system that could benefit from ratings, we can easily extend our rating tool to work with the next object.

Now that we know what our objects are, we can discuss our attributes that will actually get individual ratings. For this, we will need the ability to have a flexible system that allows each unique object to have its own attribute definitions. We will create a `SystemObjectRatingOptions` table to manage these attributes. Here you will see the name of the attribute and its description. We will show the name in our display and add the description to a tooltip. In addition to this, we will create the relationship to our `SystemObjects` table. This will allow us to have custom attributes for something like images—as many as we like.

From there, we will need the ability to capture the actual end user feedback in the form of a rating. Each rating will apply to each attribute of a given `SystemObject` (or table). As individuals will be rating a unique item (an actual record) of the defined type of `SystemObject`, we will also need to track the record ID of the rated item in question. This will allow us to know that we are rating a specific record in the `Files` or `Photos` table so that we can easily query the data that we need.

With each rating we will also capture a score (1-5 in our demo). This will allow us to have an aggregate rating for each attribute. It will also allow us to have an aggregated rating for the actual rated item. We will simply average all scores collected for an item to provide us with a high-level, generic rating. With this system, we will also have the data that we would need for more sophisticated reports and displays as time permits.

Tags

Tagging allows the users of your community to provide keywords that categorize your content. This in turn helps other users to locate the appropriate content in your site. The more who apply a specific keyword to the content of your site, the larger that particular keyword will appear in the cloud.

This system will be built using the same `SystemObjects` concept. This will allow us to apply tags to any object defined in our system. In addition to the `SystemObjects` table, we will also have a `Tags` table. This will allow us to keep track of all of the unique tags that we collect over time. And this is where we will maintain our aggregated tag counts. While we could sum the count on the fly, it is easier and more efficient to build the sum as we collect new tags.

In addition to collecting new tags and maintaining the definition of our `SystemObjects`, we also need to maintain the relationship between our tags and the `SystemObjects`. We will do this with our `SystemObjectTags` table. This table will also keep track of who applied the tag and when.

With the tables defined, we should keep in mind that we want to build a flexible control. In our case, we will build a control that will not only collect tags for an object, but will also display the tags for a given item (a mini tag cloud if you will). We will also be able to keep track of all the tags for a parent (in case if we are tagging images, we can have a tag cloud for our image gallery). And finally, we will add functionality to our control that will allow us to build a high-level global tag cloud that could be used on your site's homepage. This cloud will display the most popular tags for all of the collected tags.

The final complexity is what completes the tag cloud. We will have the tables in place to hold the data appropriately. We will have the control to capture and display the data. But the real kicker to a tag cloud is how it is displayed. A **tag cloud** displays each tag (a keyword or words) with a size relative to its own ranking in the overall popularity of the cloud. This means that the more the tag is used in your cloud, the larger the tags will be in the cloud. On the other hand, a tag that is used less often will appear smaller in the cloud. We will fully discuss the algorithm behind this sorting when the time comes.

Comments

Compared to our fancy ratings and tagging controls, the commenting control is not very distinctive. Though it is not distinctive, it still fits this chapter where this is another method for your users to provide very specific content about your content. The comments will come in handy later when you integrate the gathered content into your site's search results. Also, our friendly search engines will love to eat up your new content-specific comments.

This system, like the other two, will be built around the `SystemObject` table. In addition to that table, we will have a `Comments` table. The `Comments` table will not only gather all the normal data but also the body of the comment. That's it!

Voting

To keep track of votes we have added not null integer column called as **VoteCount** in BoardPost table. To keep track of posts that are marked as answers, we also added the bit column **isAnswer** (not null) to the BoardPost table.

Medals

To keep track of the total Score for a particular account/user, we have added an integer column in Accounts table as **Score**. The score will be incremented based on the rules defined in the design section and accordingly Badges will be awarded.

Solution

Let's take a look at our solution.

Implementing the database

Let's take a look at what is needed in the database. The following screenshot shows the relevant tables:

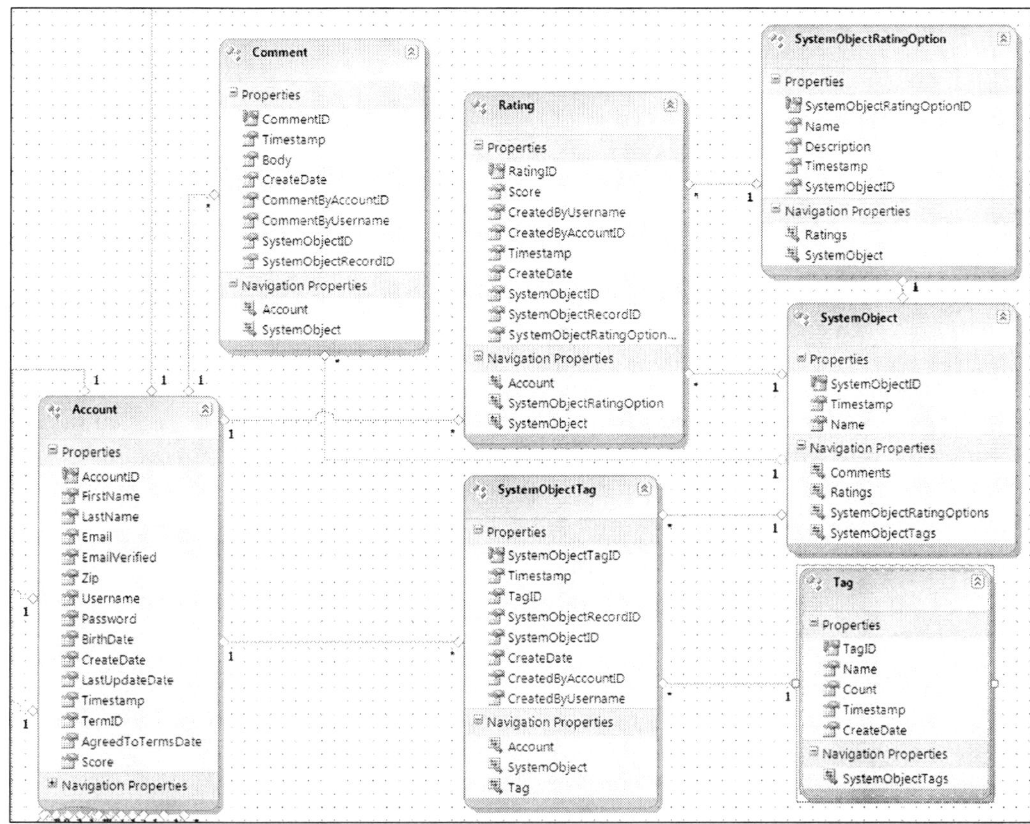

SystemObjects

The `SystemObjects` table is at the center of this chapter's list of features. Having said that, this table is the easiest part of this equation. It simply keeps track of all the tables in the system. Specifically, it keeps track of the table names and maintains an ID for each name.

Ratings

The `Ratings` table is responsible for holding all the end user ratings. As you can see each rating ties back to the `SystemObjects` table and also directly to the record within the specified table. In addition to that, we are also tracking the `Option` that was rated. The most important part of this table though is the **Score** field. The **Score** tracks the selected number of stars (in our case) that the end user has selected.

System object rating options

In addition to the ratings table we also have the `SystemObjectRatingOptions` table. This table tracks all the options that are available for each of our system objects.

Tags

The `Tags` table is responsible for holding all the textual tags that our users attach to the various objects in our system. Knowing that we intend to collect a number of the same tags for multiple objects in our system, it is important that we maintain a unique list of tags with counts rather than a single entry for every tag entered into the system and then having to sum up the tags to get a count. Performance-wise, maintaining the aggregate value as we collect tags will easily outperform determining the summed value each time we need the count.

System object tags

This then brings us to our `SystemObjectTags` table. It is responsible for maintaining details of which tag is connected to which record of a certain type of object. This table simply maintains various record IDs to keep track of the relationships.

Comments

This finally brings us to the `Comments` table. Of the five features, this is by far the easiest to implement as this table keeps track of everything for us directly. Each comment in this case is assumed to be unique and is therefore directly tied to an object and a record within that object. We also keep track of the user who left the comment (**CommentByAccountID**) and when (**CreateDate**) he/she did so. The current size of the comment can be up to 2,000 characters. However, if your community requires large comments, you can of course increase this number.

Votes and Mark as Answer

Votes are managed at individual thread/post level. We don't need a new table for this, but extend our `BoardPosts` table to add two new columns to it—**VoteCount** and **IsAnswer**. The change in vote count or setting of answer will result in the change of score for the relevant user.

Medals

The medals depend on the total score earned by a user. For this purpose we will extend the existing `Accounts` table and add a new column called **Score**. The `Medals` user control will display appropriate number of medals. We will look into that later when we discuss the presentation layer details.

Creating the relationships

Once all the tables are created, we can create all the relationships.

For this set of tables, we have relationships between the following tables:

- `Ratings` and `Accounts`
- `Ratings` and `SystemObjectRatingOptions`
- `Ratings` and `SystemObjects`
- `SystemRatingOptions` and `SystemObjects`
- `SystemObjectTags` and `Accounts`
- `SystemObjectTags` and `SystemObjects`
- `SystemObjectTags` and `Tags`
- `Comments` and `Accounts`
- `Comment` and `SystemObjects`

Setting up the data access layer

To set up the data access layer, we follow the steps as already done in earlier chapters. Open the `Fisharoo.edmx` file and add all the above mentioned tables.

Building repositories

With the addition of new tables will come the addition of new repositories so that we can get the data stored in those tables. We will be creating the following repositories to support our needs:

- `RatingRepository`
- `SystemObjectRatingOptionRepository`
- `TagRepository`
- `SystemObjectTagRepository`
- `CommentRepository`

Each of our repositories will generally have a method for select by ID, select all by parent ID, save, and delete. Once you have seen one repository you have pretty much seen them all. Review previous chapters, the appendices, or the included code, for example, of a standard repository. Here we will only discuss anything that varies from standard!

RatingRepository

Let's take a look at the `RatingRepository`.

HasRatedBefore()

The `HasRatedBefore()` method takes in a `SystemObjectID`, `SystemObjectRecordID`, and `AccountID` to perform a check against the account to determine if that account has already provided a rating for the specified object. If it has, then the `HasRatedBefore()` method returns `true`, otherwise `false`.

```
//Fisharoo/DataAccess/Repositories/RatingRepository.cs
public bool HasRatedBefore(int SystemObjectID, long
                           SystemObjectRecordID, int AccountID)
{
    bool result = false;
    using(FisharooDataContext dc = conn.GetContext())
    {
        if (dc.Ratings.Where(r => r.SystemObjectID == SystemObjectID
                                                                  &&
            r.SystemObjectRecordID == SystemObjectRecordID &&
            r.CreatedByAccountID == AccountID).Count() > 0)
            result = true;
    }
    return result;
}
```

GetCurrentRating()

The `GetCurrentRating()` method is responsible for determining the average rating across all the rated options for a specific object in the system.

```
//Fisharoo/DataAccess/Repositories/RatingRepository.cs
public int GetCurrentRating(int SystemObjectID, long
                            SystemObjectRecordID)
{
    double result;
    using(FisharooDataContext dc = conn.GetContext())
    {
        if (dc.Ratings.Where(r => r.SystemObjectID == SystemObjectID
                            && r.SystemObjectRecordID ==
                            SystemObjectRecordID).Count() > 0)
            result =
                dc.Ratings.Where(
                    r => r.SystemObjectID == SystemObjectID &&
                    r.SystemObjectRecordID == SystemObjectRecordID).
                    Select(r => r.Score).Average();
        else
            result = 0;
    }
    return Convert.ToInt32(result);
}
```

This method performs a check against the system to see if we have any ratings for the specified object. If we do, then we perform a query against our `Ratings` collection looking for our specified object. We are only interested in returning the average score for our object, so that we can locate our ratings and then call the `Select()` method. The `Select()` method fetches the **Score** field from all the objects. From there, we can call `Average()` to get our average across all the scores for all the ratings we have received. If there were no ratings, then we set the result to `0`.

SaveRatings()

We are used to building a repository with a single object save method. This is fairly straightforward. Here we are going to focus on building a method that can handle more than one rating at a time.

```
//Fisharoo/DataAccess/Repositories/RatingRepository.cs
public void SaveRatings(List<Rating> ratings)
{
    using (FisharooDataContext dc = conn.GetContext())
    {
```

```
                int varCreatedByAccountID = ratings[0].
                CreatedByAccountID;

                // get a list of items that have been rated before
                List<long> previouslyRatedSystemObjectRecordIDs =
                            (dc.Ratings.Where (r =>
                            r.CreatedByAccountID ==
                            varCreatedByAccountID)
                            .Select(r => r.SystemObjectRecordID)).
                            ToList();

                foreach (Rating rating in ratings)
                {
                    if (!previouslyRatedSystemObjectRecordIDs.
                    Contains(
                    rating.SystemObjectRecordID))
                    dc.Ratings.AddObject(rating);
                }
                dc.SaveChanges();
            }
        }
```

This method is not really that complex. First, it takes in a generic list of `Rating` objects. Once it has opened a connection and got the DataContext, we determine which ratings the user has previously rated (as we don't want more than one rating per user, per object!). We then iterate through all the passed in ratings. Once we have made sure that the user has not already rated the option in question, we add the rating object to the DataContext. With all the appropriate ratings attached, we save our changes.

SystemObjectRatingOptionRepository

This particular repository has only three methods, `GetSystemObjectRatingOptionsBySystemObjectID()` (now that is a mouth full!), `SaveSystemObjectRatingOption()`, and `DeleteSystemObjectRatingOption()`. These are all very standard methods that do just what they say. Looking at the code for this repository is a good example of a standard repository!

TagsRepository

This repository is used heavily in the building of our tag clouds. We have several methods to look at here.

GetTagByName()

The `GetTagByName()` method is responsible for looking for a tag by its name.

```
//Fisharoo/DataAccess/Repositories/TagsRepository.cs
public Tag GetTagByName(string Name)
{
    Tag result = null;
    using(FisharooDataContext dc = conn.GetContext())
    {
        result = dc.Tags.Where(t => t.Name == Name).FirstOrDefault();
    }
    return result;
}
```

The `GetTagByID()` method is the same as the `GetTagByName()` with the exception that it looks for an item by its ID.

GetTagsGlobal()

The `GetTagsGlobal()` method is responsible for getting tags at the site level. It looks at all the tags for all the defined objects and returns a specified number. It orders the tags by their count in descending order and then uses the `Take()` method to specify how many tags to return. This method is used to build the site-level tag cloud.

```
//Fisharoo/DataAccess/Repositories/TagsRepository.cs
public List<Tag> GetTagsGlobal(int TagsToTake)
{
    List<Tag> results = null;
    using(FisharooDataContext dc = conn.GetContext())
    {
        results = (from t in dc.Tags
                   select t).Distinct().OrderByDescending(t =>
                   t.Count) Take(TagsToTake).ToList();
    }
    return results;
}
```

GetTagsBySystemObject()

This method is similar to the `GetTagsGlobal()` method in that it gets all the tags for a cloud. This method is a little different in that it gets the tag only for a specified object type. It returns a specified number of tags by their count in descending order.

GetTagsBySystemObjectAndRecordID()

Finally, we come to the method that gets all the tags for a specified object down to the record level. This is for a specific item of a certain type of object. This method is used to display all the tags next to the item that was tagged.

```
//Fisharoo/DataAccess/Repositories/TagsRepository.cs
public List<Tag> GetTagsBySystemObjectAndRecordID(int SystemObjectID,
                                          long SystemObjectRecordID)
{
    List<Tag> results = null;
    using (FisharooDataContext dc = conn.GetContext())
    {
        results = (from t in dc.Tags
                   join sot in dc.SystemObjectTags on t.TagID equals
                   sot.TagID
                   where sot.SystemObjectID == SystemObjectID &&
                     sot.SystemObjectRecordID == SystemObjectRecordID
                   select t).Distinct().OrderBy(t =>
                   t.CreateDate).ToList();
    }
    return results;
}
```

SystemObjectTagRepository

There are three methods in this repository, `GetSystemObjectByTagID()`, `SaveSystemObjectTag()`, and `DeleteSystemObjectTag()`. We will discuss only the `GetSystemObjectByTagID()` method here.

GetSystemObjectByTagID()

This is a rather large method. It is used to get all the objects that a tag is related to. This method is used when we display the tag and its links by clicking on a tag link.

This method allows for only one tag to be loaded currently. But that restriction is only on the method input side. All the internals of this method will work with more than one tag though.

```
//Fisharoo/DataAccess/Repositories/SystemObjectTagRepository.cs
public List<SystemObjectTagWithObject> GetSystemObjectsByTagID(int
TagID)
{
    . . .
```

```
using (FisharooDataContext dc = conn.GetContext())
{
    tags =
        dc.SystemObjectTags.Where(sot => sot.TagID == TagID).
        OrderByDescending(sot => sot.CreateDate).ToList();

    SystemObjectTags = GetSystemObjectSpecificTags(1, tags);
    accounts = dc.Accounts.Where(
           a => SystemObjectTags.Contains(a.AccountID)).ToList();

    SystemObjectTags = GetSystemObjectSpecificTags(2, tags);
    profiles = dc.Profiles.Where(
           a => SystemObjectTags.Contains(a.AccountID)).ToList();

    SystemObjectTags = GetSystemObjectSpecificTags(3, tags);
    blogs = dc.Blogs.Where(
             b=> SystemObjectTags.Contains(b.BlogID)).ToList();

    SystemObjectTags = GetSystemObjectSpecificTags(4, tags);
    posts = dc.BoardPosts.Where(
             bp => SystemObjectTags.Contains(bp.PostID)).ToList();

    SystemObjectTags = GetSystemObjectSpecificTags(5, tags);
    files = dc.Files.Where(
                  f => SystemObjectTags.Contains(f.FileID)).
                  ToList();

    fileTypes = dc.FileTypes.ToList();
    for (int i = 0; i < files.Count(); i++)
    {
        files[i].Extension =
            fileTypes.Where(ft => ft.FileTypeID == files[i].
            FileTypeID).Select(ft => ft.Name).FirstOrDefault();
    }

    List<long> tempfiles = files.Select(f => f.DefaultFolderID).
    ToList();
    folders = dc.Folders.Where(folder => tempfiles.
    Contains(folder.FolderID)).ToList();

    SystemObjectTags = GetSystemObjectSpecificTags(6, tags);
    groups = dc.Groups.Where(
            g => SystemObjectTags.Contains(g.GroupID)).ToList();
}

foreach (SystemObjectTag tag in tags)
{
```

```
switch (tag.SystemObjectID)
{
    case 1:
        result.Add(new SystemObjectTagWithObject() {
        SystemObjectTag = tag, Account = accounts.Where(a
        => a.AccountID == tag.SystemObjectRecordID).
        FirstOrDefault() });
        break;

    case 2:
        result.Add(new SystemObjectTagWithObject() {
        SystemObjectTag = tag, Profile = profiles.Where(p
        => p.ProfileID == tag.SystemObjectRecordID).
        FirstOrDefault() });
        break;

    case 3:
        result.Add(new SystemObjectTagWithObject() {
        SystemObjectTag = tag, Blog = blogs.Where(b =>
        b.BlogID == tag.SystemObjectRecordID).FirstOrDefault()
        });
        break;

    case 4:
        result.Add(new SystemObjectTagWithObject() {
        SystemObjectTag = tag, BoardPost = posts.Where(p =>
        p.PostID == tag.SystemObjectRecordID).FirstOrDefault()
        });
        break;

    case 5:
        //need to get the file for use in getting the folder
        as well
        File file = files.Where(f => f.FileID == tag.
        SystemObjectRecordID).FirstOrDefault();
        result.Add(new SystemObjectTagWithObject()
        {
            SystemObjectTag = tag,
            File = file,
            Folder =
                folders.Where(f => f.FolderID == file.
                DefaultFolderID).FirstOrDefault()
        });
        break;

    case 6:
        result.Add(new SystemObjectTagWithObject() {
        SystemObjectTag = tag, Group = groups.Where(g
```

```
                    => g.GroupID == tag.SystemObjectRecordID).
                    FirstOrDefault() });
                    break;
            }
        }
        return result;
    }
```

Though this method appears to be big and complex, it's not really. Initially, we get a list of tags by the `TagID` that was passed in. We then get a list of all the objects that the tag is attached to. Currently, in addition to Accounts, Profiles, Blogs, Posts, Files, and Groups, we also get `FileTypes` and `Folders`.

Once we have all this information uploaded, we can iterate through each tag and load the `SystemObjectTagWithObjects` object, which we have created especially for this purpose. It carries the `Tag` and the objects that are related to it.

We then return a list of `SystemObjectTagWithObjects`, which we can then bind to a `Repeater` on the display side.

CommentRepository

This repository is pretty close to a standard repository. Other than the normal `get` and `delete` method, we also have a `GetCommentsBySystemObject()` method which gets a list of comments for the object they are attached to.

BoardPost Repository

We have discussed this repository earlier in Chapter 9. Hence here we will only discuss the aspects which have changed and are related to Voting and Badges.

We have added `ScoreInput` enum in `BoardPost.cs`. It provides various types for incrementing the score as replying to a post, voting the post useful, and marking as answer. The saving logic of `BoardPost` remains the same.

Implementing the services/application layer

Once all the repositories are built for single-serving purposes, we can begin to create the services layer. Again, this layer is responsible for assembling aggregates and performing complex actions with our entities. We will create and modify the following services:

- `TagService`
- `Configuration`

- `WebContext`
- `Extensions`
- `AccountService`

TagService

The `TagService` has a few things that are responsible for adding tags and calculating font sizes.

AddTag()

We have the `AddTag()` method that takes care of adding Tags to our database. You may ask why we can't just take care of that in our `TagRepository`. In this case, we are doing more than just shoving a new record into the system. Here we need to see if we already have the tag or not. If we don't, then we need to create a new tag. If we do have the tag already, then we need to increment the count for that tag and we can save the tag back into the system.

In addition to adding a tag into the system, we also need to create the relationship for that tag and the object it is related to. This is a straightforward job. We simply spin up a new `SystemObjectTag` with the appropriate `TagID`. Then we can toss that into the database.

```
//Fisharoo/BusinessLogic/TagService.cs
public void AddTag(string TagName, int SystemObjectID, long
                   SystemObjectRecordID)
{
    Tag tag = _tagsRepository.GetTagByName(TagName);
    if (tag == null)
    {
        tag = new Tag();
        tag.CreateDate = DateTime.Now;
        tag.Name = TagName;
        tag.Count = 1;
    }
    else
    {
        tag.Count += 1;
    }
    tag = _tagRepository.SaveTag(tag);
    SystemObjectTag sysObjTag = new SystemObjectTag();
    sysObjTag.CreateDate = DateTime.Now;
    sysObjTag.CreatedByAccountID = _webContext.CurrentUser.AccountID;
    sysObjTag.CreatedByUsername = _webContext.CurrentUser.Username;
```

```
        sysObjTag.SystemObjectID = SystemObjectID;
        sysObjTag.SystemObjectRecordID = SystemObjectRecordID;
        sysObjTag.TagID = tag.TagID;
        _systemObjectTagRepository.SaveSystemObjectTag(sysObjTag);
    }
```

CalculateFontSize()

The `CalculateFontSize()` method is responsible for taking a collection of `Tags` and calculating the font size for each one. There is a bit to this calculation in that some tags may have a very large count while other tags may only have been applied to a couple of items. If those were the numbers we used to calculate the font size, we may end up with a tag that is larger than the page or one that is so small that you can't read it. For this reason, we need to get the numbers to fit between something more reasonable. This is the calculation that we will discuss.

Before we look at the method in its entirety, let's discuss some of the variables that we will be working with:

- `MinimumRange`: This variable will hold the smallest count in our set of tags. This will form the lower bound of our collection. It is global to the calculation.
- `MaximumRange`: This variable will hold the largest count in our set of tags. This will form the upper bound of our collection. It is global to the calculation.
- `Delta`: This variable will hold the difference between our `MinimumRange` and our `MaximumRange`. It is global to the calculation.
- `Tag.InitialValue`: This will hold a copy of the `Count` for each tag.
- `Tag.MinimumOffset`: This is the `InitialValue- MinimumRange`.
- `Tag.Ranged`: This value is the `MinimumOffset` divided by the Delta.
- `Tag.PreCalculatedValue`: This is the `Ranged` value multiplied by the difference of the largest font size and the smallest font size subtracted by one (largest-smallest-1).
- `Tag.FinalCalculatedValue`: This is the `PreCalculatedValue` plus one.
- `Tag.FontSize`: This is the `FinalCalculatedValue` plus the smallest font size.

The result of all of these calculations is a set of tags that grow smoothly regardless of the difference between your smallest tag count and your largest tag count and regardless of the difference between your smallest and largest font size.

The next complexity to this method is how we want to sort the tags in our cloud. Shall we sort them from small to tall or from tall to small, or randomly? We will leave this up to a configuration value. If we want to sort the tags small to tall, we can use the `OrderBy()` method on the `Tags` collection. If we want to sort the tags tall to small, we can use the `OrderByDescending()` method. What do we do if we want to sort the tags randomly? We will add a new method to our `Extensions` class that will extend a Generic List of type Tag called `ShuffleList()`, which will handle shuffling the items in the collection. We will discuss that shortly.

```
//Fisharoo/BusinessLogic/TagService.cs
public List<Tag> CalculateFontSize(List<Tag> Tags)
{
    decimal MinimumRange;
    decimal MaximumRange;
    decimal Delta;
    //get the smallest count in this list
    MinimumRange = (Tags.OrderBy(t => t.Count).Take(1).Select(t =>
                              t.Count).FirstOrDefault()) * 100;
    //get the largest count in this list
    MaximumRange = (Tags.OrderByDescending(t =>
                t.Count).Take(1).Select(t => t.Count).
                FirstOrDefault()) * 100;
    //determine the difference between the minimum and the maximum
    Delta = MaximumRange - MinimumRange;
    if (Tags.Count > 1)
    {
        for (int i = 0; i < Tags.Count(); i++)
        {
            //set a working value
            Tags[i].InitialValue = Tags[i].Count*100;
            //calculate the minimum offset
            Tags[i].MinimumOffset = Tags[i].InitialValue -
                                    MinimumRange;
            //calculate the ranged value
            Tags[i].Ranged = Tags[i].MinimumOffset/Delta;
            //calculate the pre calculation
            Tags[i].PreCalculatedValue = Tags[i].Ranged*
                       ((_configuration.TagCloudLargestFontSize -
                       _configuration.AddToTagCloudFontSize) - 1);
            //calculate the final value
            Tags[i].FinalCalculatedValue = Tags[i].PreCalculatedValue
                                           + 1;
            //calculate the font size
            Tags[i].FontSize =
```

```
                Convert.ToInt32(Tags[i].FinalCalculatedValue +
                               _configuration.AddToTagCloudFontSize);
        }
    }
    //if a standard sort is not what you require, you can call
      Tags.Sort
    //  The Tags.Sort() method (in the Tag.cs partial class)
        can be
    //  modified to use different properties to sort by
    if (_sortOrder == CloudSortOrder.Ascending) //small to tall
    {
        Tags = Tags.OrderBy(t => t.FinalCalculatedValue).ToList();
    }
    else if (_sortOrder == CloudSortOrder.Descending) //tall to small
    {
        Tags = Tags.OrderByDescending(t =>
                                  t.FinalCalculatedValue).ToList();
    }
    else
    {
        Tags.ShuffleList(); //randomize!
    }
    return Tags;
}
```

Extensions

We will add one extension method to our `Extensions` class called `ShuffleList()`, which is responsible for shuffling the items in our list of Tags. We found this snippet on Experts-Exchange.com at `http://www.experts-exchange.com/Programming/Languages/C_Sharp/Q_22571864.html`

```
//Fisharoo/Common/Extensions.cs
public static List<Tag> ShuffleList(this List<Tag> listToShuffle)
{
    Random randomClass = new Random();
    for (int k = listToShuffle.Count-1; k > 1; --k)
    {
        int randIndx = randomClass.Next(k); //
        Tag temp = listToShuffle[k];
        listToShuffle[k] = listToShuffle[randIndx]; // move random
                                              num to end of list.
        listToShuffle[randIndx] = temp;
    }
    return listToShuffle;
}
```

AccountService

We discussed this Service earlier so we will discuss only the changes here.

SaveAccount ()

This method invokes the corresponding repository's save method to save the account along with the updated score in the database. It also handles the logic of incrementing the scores for the account based on the `ScoreInput` variable. This score will be used to display medals for the user.

If the post is a reply to an existing question, then the post owner's account score is incremented by one. If the reply is voted as useful then the post owner's score is incremented by five and if it is voted as not useful the score is decremented by five. When decrementing we make sure that we don't go below zero. If the reply is marked as an answer then the post owner's account score is incremented by ten.

```
public void SaveAccount(Account account, BoardPost.ScoreInput value)
        {
            if(account.AccountID > 0)
            {
                switch (value)
                {
                    case BoardPost.ScoreInput.ReplyPost:
                        account.Score += 1;
                        break;
                    case BoardPost.ScoreInput.VoteUseful:
                        account.Score += 5;
                        break;
                    case BoardPost.ScoreInput.VoteNotUseful:
                        if(account.Score >5)
                             account.Score -= 5;
                        else
                             account.Score = 0;
                        break;
                    case BoardPost.ScoreInput.MarkedAsAnswer:
                        account.Score = post.Account.Score + 10;
                        break;
                    default:
                        break;
                }
            }
            __accountRepository.SaveAccount(account);
        }
```

WebContext

There are a few changes to the `WebContext` class that we will discuss here.

SelectedRatings

The `SelectedRatings` property handles a `Dictionary<int, int>` collection that is stored in the `Session`. This collection is responsible for handling ratings that are collected for various options attached to an object. The first `int` is the `RatingOptionRecordID` and the second `int` is the `Rating` (score) that was applied to that `SystemObjectRatingOptionID`. This collection is built up prior to the user saving their rating options. What we mean to say is that every time a user adds a dictionary item to the `SelectedRatings` property, it adds the item to a collection stored in the Session rather than resetting the value all together. We will see how this plays out once we start to build our `Ratings` control.

If you are wondering about how this collection is handled—if it continues to grow—you should know that there is another method (coming up next) that handles the clearing of this collection.

```
//Fisharoo/Components/WebContext.cs
public Dictionary<int, int> SelectedRatings
{
    get
    {
        Dictionary<int, int> result = new Dictionary<int, int>();
        if(GetFromSession("SelectedRatings") != null)
        {
            result = GetFromSession("SelectedRatings") as
                     Dictionary<int, int>;
        }
        return result;
    }
    set
    {
        //make sure that we add to the existing rating store rather
        //than creating a new one
        Dictionary<int, int> result = new Dictionary<int, int>();
        if (GetFromSession("SelectedRatings") != null)
        {
            result = GetFromSession("SelectedRatings") as
                     Dictionary<int, int>;
            foreach (KeyValuePair<int, int> pair in value)
            {
                if (!result.ContainsKey(pair.Key))
```

```
                    result.Add(pair.Key, pair.Value);
                }
                SetInSession("SelectedRatings", result);
            }
            else
                SetInSession("SelectedRatings", value);

        }
    }
```

ClearSelectedRatings

This method simply clears out the `Dictionary<int, int>` collection that is stored in the session behind the `SelectedRatings`.

```
//Fisharoo/Components/WebContext.cs
public void ClearSelectedRatings()
{
    SetInSession("SelectedRatings", null);
}
```

Configuration

The `Configuration` class is responsible for reading the values in our `config` files. In this last round of coding features we have added the following properties:

- `TagCloudLargestFontSize`: This value sets the largest font size for display in the tag cloud.
- `TagCloudSmallestFontSize`: This value sets the smallest font size for display in the tag cloud.
- `CloudSortOrder`: This value sets the sort order of the tags in the cloud.
- `NumberOfTagsInCloud`: This value sets the number of tags to be displayed in the cloud.

Implementing the presentation layer

This chapter is all about creating the necessary user controls—`Comments`, `Ratings`, `Tags`, `Votes` and `MarkAnswer`. In addition to the `Tags` control, we also have a `Tags.aspx` page that is responsible for displaying all the linked items for a specified Tag.

Comments Page

Let's get started by looking at the comments page.

Comments.ascx

The comment control is responsible for taking in a user's comment for an object in the system. This control is relatively simple, if compared to the others that we will be creating. It has a text box and a button to take in the comment. It also has a PlaceHolder to contain all the comments that we collect over time.

```
//Fisharoo/Web/UserControls/Comments.ascx
<asp:UpdatePanel runat="server">
    <ContentTemplate>
        <asp:Panel runat="server" ID="pnlComment">
            <asp:TextBox ID="txtComment" runat="server"></asp:
                        TextBox><asp:Button Text="Add Comment"
                        ID="btnAddComment" runat="server"
                         OnClick="btnAddComment_Click" />
             <asp:PlaceHolder ID="phComments"
                            runat="server"></asp:PlaceHolder>
        </asp:Panel>
    </ContentTemplate>
</asp:UpdatePanel>
```

Comments.ascx.cs

First, note that we are initializing the control in the overridden OnInit() method. This allows us to get the control's output into the ViewState so that we can access everything down the road.

There are two properties for this class—SystemObjectID, and SystemObjectRecordID. They allow us to know what data to save and load.

When the page is initialized, we check the state of the current user to see if they are logged in or not. We do not allow unauthorized users to post comments. If the user is logged in, we show the comment text box and button. If they are not, we hide those controls.

Next, we load the page. To load the page, we load the comments from the presenter. Then we have the event handler for capturing the added comments. We also have a method to toggle the visibility of the panel that shows the comments. There is also a method for clearing the panel of comments.

The most complicated method in this whole class is the `LoadComments()` method. This method is responsible for taking in a collection of comments, iterating through them, and adding them to the panel for display. Let's look at this method in particular:

```
//Fisharoo/Web/UserControls/Comments.ascx.cs
public partial class Comments : System.Web.UI.UserControl, IComments
{
    . . .
    public void LoadComments(List<Comment> comments)
    {
        if(comments.Count > 0)
        {
            phComments.Controls.Add(new LiteralControl("<table
                                    width=\"100%\">"));
            foreach (Comment comment in comments)
            {
                phComments.Controls.Add(new LiteralControl("<tr><td>"
                          + comment.CommentByUsername + " (" +
                         comment.CreateDate.ToShortDateString() + "):
                       " + comment.Body + "</td></tr>"));
            }
            phComments.Controls.Add(new LiteralControl("</table>"));
        }
    }
}
```

CommentsPresenter.cs

The `CommentsPresenter` is responsible for handling all the logic behind this control. It determines whether or not to show the control based on whether or not the user who is viewing the control is logged in or not. It also handles loading the comments for the specified `SystemObject` and `SystemObjectRecordID`. Finally, there is a method for adding a comment.

```
//Fisharoo/Web/UserControls/Presenters/CommentsPresenter.cs
public class CommentsPresenter
{
    . . .

    public void LoadComments()
    {
        _view.LoadComments(_commentsService.GetCommentsBySystemObject(
                       _view.SystemObjectID, view.
                       SystemObjectRecordID));
    }
```

```
    public void AddComment(string comment)
    {
        Comment c = new Comment();
        c.Body = comment;
        c.CommentByAccountID = _webContext.CurrentUser.AccountID;
        c.CommentByUsername = _webContext.CurrentUser.Username;
        c.CreateDate = DateTime.Now;
        c.SystemObjectID = _view.SystemObjectID;
        c.SystemObjectRecordID = _view.SystemObjectRecordID;
        commentsService.SaveComment(c);
        view.ClearComments();
        LoadComments();
    }
}
```

Ratings Page

Now let's take a look at the ratings page.

Ratings.ascx

The `Ratings` control is responsible for displaying a modal pop up that contains the various options that can be rated. It then captures those ratings and saves them away to the database. In addition to handling the user interaction, it also displays the overall rating average for that particular object.

In order to use the rating control or the modal pop up, we need to register the `AjaxControlToolkit` (version 4.1.40412.2). Once this is added, we can hook up the modal pop up to our `pnlModalPopup`. This panel contains a repeater that will show all the ratings available for this object. Outside of the modal pop up, we also have a rating control that displays the average rating for the object.

```
//Fisharoo/Web/UserControls/Ratings.ascx
<asp:Panel ID="pnlRating" runat="server">
    <asp:UpdatePanel runat="server">
        <ContentTemplate>
            <asp:LinkButton ID="lbRateThis" runat="server" Text="Rate
            this!" OnClick="lbRateThis_Click"></asp:LinkButton>
            <asp:Label ID="lblThankYou" runat="server" Text="Your
            ratings have been saved! " Visible="false"></asp:Label><br
            />
            <cc1:Rating ID="Rating1" Enabled="false" ReadOnly="true"
                runat="server" MaxRating="5"
                EmptyStarCssClass="ratingStarEmpty"
                FilledStarCssClass="ratingStarFilled"
                StarCssClass="ratingStar"
```

```
                WaitingStarCssClass="ratingStarSaved"></cc1:Rating>

            <asp:Panel ID="pnlModalPopup" runat="server"
            BackColor="White"
                ScrollBars="Vertical" BorderStyle="Inset">
                <asp:Literal ID="litSelectedRatings" Visible="true"
                runat="server"></asp:Literal>
                <asp:Repeater ID="repRatingOptions" runat="server">
                    <ItemTemplate>
                        <table width="180px">
                            <tr align="left">
                                <td>
                                    <asp:Label ID="lblOptionName"
                                        ToolTip='<%#
((PESystemObjectRatingOption)Container.DataItem).Description %>'
                                        Text='<%#
((PESystemObjectRatingOption)Container.DataItem).Name %>'
                                        runat="server"></asp:Label>
                                </td>
                                <td style="width:100px">
                                    <cc1:Rating id="Rating1"
                                    runat="server"
                                       MaxRating="5"
                                       EmptyStarCssClass="ratingStarE
                                       mpty"
                                       FilledStarCssClass="ratingStar
                                       Filled"
                                       StarCssClass="ratingStar"
                                       WaitingStarCssClass="ratingSta
                                       rSaved"
                                       OnChanged="rating_Changed"
                                       Tag='<%#
((PESystemObjectRatingOption)Container.DataItem).
SystemObjectRatingOptionID %>'></cc1:Rating>
                                </td></tr>
                        </table>
                    </ItemTemplate>
                </asp:Repeater>
                <asp:Button CssClass="SiteButton" ID="btnSave"
                UseSubmitBehavior="false" OnClick="btnSave_Click"
                runat="server" Text="Save" />
                 <asp:Button CssClass="SiteButton" ID="btnCancel"
                runat="server" Text="Cancel" />
            </asp:Panel>
            <cc1:ModalPopupExtender ID="ModalPopupExtender1"
                runat="server" TargetControlID="lbRateThis"
```

```
                PopupControlID="pnlModalPopup"
                OkControlID="btnSave" CancelControlID="btnCancel" />
                </ContentTemplate>
        </asp:UpdatePanel>
    </asp:Panel>
```

There are two things that are important to notice in this UI. The first is the line that assigns the `SystemObjectRatingOptionID` to the Tag of property of the `Rating` control.

```
Tag='<%# ((PESystemObjectRatingOption)Container.DataItem).
         SystemObjectRatingOptionID %>'
```

When a `Rating` is selected, it fires an event that contains the `Rating` control and the selected value (the star that was selected). We are passing the `SystemObjectRatingOptionID` in the `Tag` property of the `Rating`.

The second important thing to notice is the property in our `btnSave` button. The `UseSubmitBehavior` property turns off the submit behavior of the `btnSave` button. If we don't disable this property, then the modal pop up will disappear when you click the button and you will not be able to capture the `btnSave_Click` event. When you do turn this behavior off, we are able to capture the event.

Ratings.ascx.cs

In this class, we have two properties—`SystemObjectID`, and `SystemObjectRecordID`. These allow us to load and capture the data for the appropriate object. Next, we initialize our presenter. In doing this, we load the current options, set the display, and set the current rating.

Next, we have the event handler that captures when a user selects a rating in our modal pop up. This is straight through to the presenter.

Then we have the `btnSave_Click` event handler. This method not only sends the event upstream to the presenter but also sets the visibility of the `pnlModalPopup` to `false`, thus effectively hiding the pop up. (If this is not done, the `ModalPopup` seems to break and display itself in the page rather than above the page.) We also hide the label that acts as the link to show the `ModalPopup` and the `Rating` control that shows the average rating for the control. Finally, we thank the user for his/her input!

We then get to the `lbRateThis_Click` method, which shows the modal popup panel `pnlModalPopup`.

Finally, we have a method that sets the `lbRateThis` (link to show modal popup) and the `pnlModalPopup` visibility. This method is interacted with directly from the presenter:

```
//Fisharoo/Web/UserControls/Ratings.ascx.cs
public partial class Ratings : System.Web.UI.UserControl, IRatings
{
    . . .
    public void LoadOptions(List<PESystemObjectRatingOption> Options)
    {
        repRatingOptions.DataSource = Options;
        repRatingOptions.DataBind();
    }
    . . .
    protected void btnSave_Click(object sender, EventArgs e)
    {
        _presenter.btnSave_Click(sender, e, SystemObjectID,
                         SystemObjectRecordID);
        pnlModalPopup.Visible = false;
        lbRateThis.Visible = false;
        Rating1.Visible = false;
        lblThankYou.Visible = true;
    }
    protected void lbRateThis_Click(object sender, EventArgs e)
    {
        pnlModalPopup.Visible = true;
    }
    public void CanSetRating(bool Visible)
    {
        lbRateThis.Visible = Visible;
        pnlModalPopup.Visible = Visible;
    }
}
```

RatingsPresenter.cs

In the `RatingsPresenter`, we have started off with the `Init()` method. This method loads all the options for our `Ratings` control. It then moves on to determine if the user is logged in or not. If they aren't, then we disable the ability to set a rating. If the user is logged in, we check to see if the user has provided a rating for this control before or not. If they have, then we also disable the ability to set a rating. Otherwise, we allow the user to provide the ratings. Finally, we set the current rating for this control.

Next, we have our LoadOptions() method, which populates the display with all the available options. It does this by getting the properties from the view for SystemObject and the SystemObjectRecordID, and passing them to the SystemObjectRatingOptionService.GetSystemObjectRatingOptionsBySystemObjectID() method.

Then comes the rating_Changed() method, which captures the event from the display. We create a new Dictionary<int, int> object and add the SystemObjectRatingOptionID and the selected rating to it. We then add this to the Session for that user via the WebContext.SelectedRatings property. (Recall that this adds the rating to a collection stored in the session.)

Finally, we get to the btnSave_Click() method, which captures the Save button click passed up from the code behind. In this method, we load up the Dictionary<int, int> collection of ratings stored in the session. We then create a new list of Generic List of Ratings. If we have the ratings in hand, we iterate through the list of KeyValuePairs. With each iteration, we spin up a new Rating and add it to the collection of Ratings. We then save all the ratings to the RatingRepository.SaveRatings() method. Then we clear the session using WebContext.ClearSelectedRatings().

```
//Fisharoo/Web/UserControls/Presenters/RatingsPresenter.cs
public class RatingsPresenter
{
    . . .

    public void Init(IRatings view, bool IsPostBack)
    {
        _view = view;
        LoadOptions(_view.SystemObjectID, _view.SystemObjectRecordID);
        if(_webContext.CurrentUser == null)
                                _view.CanSetRating(false);
        else if (_ratingService.HasRatedBefore(_view.SystemObjectID, _
        view.SystemObjectRecordID, _webContext.CurrentUser.AccountID))
        _view.CanSetRating(false);
        else
            _view.CanSetRating(true);

        _view.SetCurrentRating(_ratingService.GetCurrentRating(
                _view.SystemObjectID, _view.SystemObjectRecordID));
    }

    public void LoadOptions(int SystemObjectID, long
    SystemObjectRecordID)
    {
```

```
        List<SystemObjectRatingOption> list = _
        systemObjectRatingOptionsService.GetSystemObjectRatingOptionsB
        ySystemObjectID(SystemObjectID);
        _view.LoadOptions(Translator.SystemObjectRatingOptionTOPESyste
        mObjectRatingOption(list));
    }

    public void rating_Changed(object sender, RatingEventArgs args)
    {
        AjaxControlToolkit.Rating rating = sender as
        AjaxControlToolkit.Rating;

        Dictionary<int, int> newRating = new Dictionary<int, int>();
        newRating.Add(Convert.ToInt32(rating.Tag), Convert.
        ToInt32(args.Value));
        _webContext.SelectedRatings = newRating;
    }

    public void btnSave_Click(object sender, EventArgs e, int
    SystemObjectID, long SystemObjectRecordID)
    {
        Dictionary<int, int> selectedRatings = _webContext.
        SelectedRatings;
        List<Rating> ratings = new List<Rating>();
        if(selectedRatings != null)
        {
            foreach (KeyValuePair<int, int> pair
                                    in _webContext.SelectedRatings)
            {
                Rating rating = new Rating();
                rating.CreatedByAccountID =
                                 _webContext.CurrentUser.AccountID;
                rating.CreatedByUsername =
                                 _webContext.CurrentUser.Username;
                rating.CreateDate = DateTime.Now;
                rating.Score = pair.Value;
                rating.SystemObjectRatingOptionID = pair.Key;
                rating.SystemObjectID = SystemObjectID;
                rating.SystemObjectRecordID = SystemObjectRecordID;
                ratings.Add(rating);
            }
            _ratingService.SaveRatings(ratings);
        }
        _webContext.ClearSelectedRatings();
    }
}
```

Tags Page

Now let's take a look at the tags page.

Tags.ascx

From the client side, the tags control that we are creating appears to be very simple. This control has two panels—one to show the tags and the other to collect them.

```
//Fisharoo/Web/UserControls/Tags.ascx
<asp:UpdatePanel ID="UpdatePanel1" runat="server">
<ContentTemplate>
    <asp:Panel runat="server" ID="pnlTag" Visible="false">
        <asp:TextBox ID="txtTag" runat="server"></asp:TextBox>
        <asp:Button CssClass="SiteButton" ID="btnTag" runat="server"
                              Text="Tag It!" OnClick="btnTag_Click" />
    </asp:Panel>
    <asp:Panel runat="server" ID="pnlTagCloud" Visible="false">
        <asp:PlaceHolder ID="phTagCloud" runat="server" />
    </asp:Panel>
</ContentTemplate>
</asp:UpdatePanel>
```

Tags.ascx.cs

In this file we have defined both a class and an enum. The enum of `TagState` is defined to modify the various states of the tag control. We have the following entries defined:

- `ShowCloud`: This option shows only the cloud for the object that the control is configured for.
- `ShowTagBox`: This option shows the text box to collect tags. It does not show any cloud.
- `ShowCloudAndTagBox`: This option shows both the cloud and the text box.
- `ShowParentCloud`: This option shows the cloud for a parent. This option can be used to show all the tags for something like a photo album.
- `ShowGlobalCloud`: This option shows all the tags from the site's point of view.

The `Tags` class implements a `Display` property, which is of type `TagState` (our previously mentioned enum). In the `Page_Load()` method, we initialize our `TagsPresenter` and in doing so set the state of the control and load the tags that were already collected.

Next, we have some methods which the presenter uses to interact with the view—`ClearTagCloud()`, `ShowTagCloud()`, `ShowTagBox()`, and `AddTagsToTagCloud()`. These are all fairly self-explanatory! You do want to pay attention to the `AddTagsToTagCloud()` method though, because this is where we actually create the tags. Each tag is created as a `Hyperlink`. In building these tags, we set the size of the link by adding a style attribute to the control where we set the font-size property. Also note that we are linking to the `Tags/Tags.aspx` page via the `TagRoute` where we display all the objects that have that particular tag linked to it. To handle the `TagRoute` we also add appropriate route definition to `Global.asax.cs`. You can look at the code to see this.

Finally, we have a method that captures the click event of the `btnTag Button` `btnTag_Click`. This is a pass through to the presenter to save the new tag to the database. Once it has saved the tag, it clears the UI to capture another tag. We show only the most important method `AddTagsToTagCloud()` here.

```
//Fisharoo/Web/UserControls/Tags.ascx.cs
    public void AddTagsToTagCloud(Tag tag)
    {
        HyperLink hlTag = new HyperLink();
        hlTag.Text = tag.Name;
        //navigation URL will follow the URL routing pattern
        hlTag.NavigateUrl = Page.GetRouteUrl("TagRoute",
                        new { tagname = tag.Name.Replace(" ", "-") });

        hlTag.Attributes.Add("style", "font-size:" + tag.FontSize +
                            "px;");
        phTagCloud.Controls.Add(hlTag);
        phTagCloud.Controls.Add(new LiteralControl(" "));
    }
```

TagsPresenter.cs

When the `TagsPresenter` is initialized, the `DetermineClientState()` method is called. This method looks at the various states of the user and the `Display` property to determine how to build the `Tag` control. It interacts with the view to show or hide various aspects of the control, from the text box to the tag cloud.

After that we have a few methods for building the different types of tag clouds based on the `Display` property. We can build the global tag cloud, a parent tag cloud, or a single object tag cloud. This is done by calling into the various methods of the `TagService` and getting the appropriate tags. The methods then iterate through the returned collection of tags and add each tag to the view through its `AddTagsToTagCloud()` method.

Finally, we have the `btnTag_Click()` method, which handles the passed through click event and captures the `TagName` of a new tag entry. This `TagName` is passed to the `TagService.AddTag()` method with the `SystemObjectID` and `SystemObjectRecordID`. We then determine if we have a cloud as part of our `Display` options. If we do, then we clear the cloud and rebuild it so that the new tag can be shown.

```
//Fisharoo/Web/UserControls/Presenters/TagsPresenter.cs
    public void DetermineClientState()
    {
        if (_webContext.CurrentUser != null && _
                               view.Display == TagState.ShowCloud) {
            _view.ShowTagCloud(true);
             BuildTagCloud();
        }
        else if (_webContext.CurrentUser != null && _
                           view.Display == TagState.ShowCloudAndTagBox)
{
            _view.ShowTagBox(true);
            _view.ShowTagCloud(true);
             BuildTagCloud();
        }
        else if (_webContext.CurrentUser == null && _
                          view.Display == TagState.ShowCloudAndTagBox)
{
            _view.ShowTagBox(false);
            _view.ShowTagCloud(true);
             BuildTagCloud();
        }
        else if (_view.Display == TagState.ShowCloud) {
            _view.ShowTagBox(true);
        }
        else if (_view.Display == TagState.ShowParentCloud) {
            _view.ShowTagCloud(true);
            _view.ShowTagBox(false);
             BuildParentTagCloud();
        }
        else if (_view.Display == TagState.ShowGlobalCloud) {
            _view.ShowTagCloud(true);
            _view.ShowTagBox(false);
             BuildGlobalTagCloud();
        }
        else {
            _view.ShowTagBox(false);
            _view.ShowTagCloud(false);
        }
    }

    public void BuildGlobalTagCloud()
    {
```

```
        List<Tag> tags = _tagService.GetTagsGlobal(_
                                    configuration.NumberOfTagsInCloud);
        tags = _tagService.CalculateFontSize(tags);
        foreach (Tag tag in tags) {
            _view.AddTagsToTagCloud(tag);
        }
    }
    public void BuildParentTagCloud()
    {
        List<Tag> tags = _tagService.GetTagsBySystemObject(_
             view.SystemObjectID, _configuration.NumberOfTagsInCloud);
        tags = _tagService.CalculateFontSize(tags);
        foreach (Tag tag in tags) {
            _view.AddTagsToTagCloud(tag);
        }
    }

    public void BuildTagCloud()
    {
        List<Tag> tags = _tagService.
        GetTagsBySystemObjectAndRecordID(_
                      view.SystemObjectID, _view.
                      SystemObjectRecordID);
        tags = _tagService.CalculateFontSize(tags);
        foreach (Tag tag in tags){
            _view.AddTagsToTagCloud(tag);
        }
    }

    public void btnTag_Click(string TagName)
    {
        _tagService.AddTag(TagName, _view.SystemObjectID,
                                          _view.SystemObjectRecordID);
        if (_view.Display == TagState.ShowCloud || _
                            view.Display == TagState.
ShowCloudAndTagBox) {
            _view.ClearTagCloud();
            BuildTagCloud();
        }
    }
```

Votes page

Now let's take a look at the votes page.

Votes.ascx

The `Votes` control has `ImageButton` controls that display up and down arrows and a label that displays the current vote count.

```
//Fisharoo/Web/UserControls/Votes.ascx
<%@ Control Language="C#" AutoEventWireup="true" CodeBehind="Votes.
ascx.cs" Inherits="Fisharoo.Web.UserControls.Votes" %>
<asp:UpdatePanel ID="UpdatePanel1" runat="server">
    <ContentTemplate>
        <table>
            <tr><td><asp:ImageButton ID="imgUp" runat="server"
            ImageUrl="~/Images/up.png" ToolTip="This post is useful"
               onclick="imgUp_Click" /></td></tr>
            <tr><td align="center">
                    <asp:Literal ID="litVote" Text="0"
                    runat="server"/>
            </td></tr>
            <tr><td>
                    <asp:ImageButton ID="imgDown" runat="server"
                    ToolTip="This post not useful" ImageUrl="~/Images/
                    down.png" onclick="imgDown_Click" />
             </td></tr>
        </table>
    </ContentTemplate>
</asp:UpdatePanel>
```

Votes.ascx.cs

The `Votes` control stores two properties. One is the `Count` i.e. the current votes and the `PostID` which is the ID for the related post. This same control is used to display vote count for a thread and a post. The only difference is in the tooltip that is displayed if it a thread (i.e. is a question).

Finally it has two button click handlers used to increment and decrement the vote count and the same is passed to the presenter to store in the database. Let's look at only the relevant part of the code:

```
//Fisharoo/Web/UserControls/Votes.ascx.cs
protected void Page_Load(object sender, EventArgs e)
{
    presenter = new VotesPresenter();
    presenter.Init(this);
    if (IsQuestion)
    {
        imgUp.ToolTip = "This question is useful";
        imgDown.ToolTip = "This question is not useful";
```

```
        }
    }

    protected void imgUp_Click(object sender, ImageClickEventArgs e)
    {
        Count++;
        presenter.IncrementVote(PostID, Count);
        litVote.Text = Count.ToString();
    }

    protected void imgDown_Click(object sender, ImageClickEventArgs e)
    {
        Count--;
        presenter.DecrementVote(PostID, Count);
        litVote.Text = Count.ToString();
    }
```

VotesPresenter.cs

The presenter primarily manages the saving of the new vote count by using the `PostService.SavePost` method and updating the account's score via `AccountService`. The relevant method is shown below:

```
//Fisharoo/Web/UserControls/Presenters/VotesPresenter.cs
private void SetVoteCount(long PostID, int Count, BoardPost.ScoreInput
score)
{
     BoardPost post = _postService.GetPostByID(PostID);
     post.VoteCount = Count;
    _postService.SavePost(post);
    _accountService.SaveAccount(post.Account, score);
}
```

MarkAnswer page

Now let's look at the mark answer page.

MarkAnswer.ascx

This is probably the simplest user control we have. It has a button on the UI which handles the click event that is in turn used to mark the related post as answer. Once a post is answered, the UI will display an image that indicates that this post has been accepted as an answer. We will skip looking at the code here.

MarkAnswer.ascx.cs

In this file we have two properties to work with. The `PostID` property that indicates which post we are working with and the `IsAnswer` property that indicates if this post has been marked as answer or not. When the button is clicked we pass it to the presenter for further processing. The relevant code is as below:

```
//Fisharoo/Web/UserControls/MarkAnswer.ascx.cs
public void ToggleDisplay(bool value)
{
    btnAnswer.Visible = value ? false : true;
    imgAnswer.Visible = value ? true : false;
}

protected void btnAnswer_Click(object sender, EventArgs e)
{
    _presenter.MarkAsAnswer(PostID);
}
```

MarkAnswerPresenter.cs

The only relevant part is saving the post stating that it is accepted as the answer and incrementing the score for the account appropriately.

```
//Fisharoo/Web/UserControls/Presenters/MarkAnswerPresenter.cs
public void MarkAsAnswer(long PostID)
{
    BoardPost post = _postService.GetPostByID(PostID);
    post.IsAnswer = true;
    postService.SavePost(post);
    accountService.SaveAccount(post.Account,
                                BoardPost.ScoreInput.
                                MarkedAsAnswer);
}
```

Medals page

Finally let's look at the medals page, which uses the score for the account to show relevant medals on the UI. Since this control is used only for the display of medals, there are no updates linked to it and hence there is no presenter also associated with this control.

Medals.ascx

The UI has five images that are used to display the medals that the user has earned.

```
//Fisharoo/Web/UserControls/Medals.ascx
<%@ Control Language="C#" AutoEventWireup="true" CodeBehind="Medals.
ascx.cs"
Inherits="Fisharoo.Web.UserControls.Medals" %>
<!-- keeping one visible to help with UI layout. Actual visibility is
controlled from code behind-->
<asp:Image ID="medal1" runat="server" ImageUrl="~/Images/medal.png" />
<asp:Image Visible="false" ID="medal2" runat="server" ImageUrl="~/
Images/medal.png" />
<asp:Image Visible="false" ID="medal3" runat="server" ImageUrl="~/
Images/medal.png" />
<asp:Image Visible="false" ID="medal4" runat="server" ImageUrl="~/
Images/medal.png" />
<asp:Image Visible="false" ID="medal5" runat="server" ImageUrl="~/
Images/medal.png" />
```

Medals.ascx.cs

There is only one property of relevance here and that is the `Score`, which is used to decide how many medals to display on the UI.

```
//Fisharoo/Web/UserControls/Medals.ascx.cs
    public int Score
    {
        get {
            if (ViewState["MedalScore"] != null)
                return Convert.ToInt32(ViewState["MedalScore"]);
            else
                return 1; }
        set {
            ViewState["MedalScore"] = value;
            /* We have picked some range to display medals. These are
            easily customizable based on specific needs
                * 0 - 5 = no medal
                * 6 - 20 = 1 medal
                * 21 - 100 = 2 medals
                * 101 - 500 = 3 medals
                * 501 - 2000 = 4 medals
                * > 2001 = 5 medals
                */
            medal1.Visible = (value > 5) ? true : false;
            medal2.Visible = (value > 20) ? true : false;
            medal3.Visible = (value > 100) ? true : false;
            medal4.Visible = (value > 500) ? true : false;
            medal5.Visible = (value >2000) ? true : false;
        } }
```

Installing the new user controls

Now that we have our controls built and ready for use, let's plug them into our existing pages.

Photos UI

Let's start with `ViewAlbum.aspx` page for this purpose. This page displays uploaded photos, which is fairly good content to collect ratings, comments, and tags from our users.

To get started, we need to register our user controls to the page so that we have access to them. We do that by adding `Register` declarations to the top of the page.

```
<%@ Register Src="~/UserControls/Ratings.ascx" TagName="Ratings"
                  TagPrefix="Fisharoo" %>
<%@ Register Src="~/UserControls/Tags.ascx" TagName="Tags"
                 TagPrefix="Fisharoo" %>
<%@ Register Src="~/UserControls/Comments.ascx" TagName="Comments"
                  TagPrefix="Fisharoo" %>
```

Once they are registered we are free to plug them in anywhere we like. We have chosen to add them just beneath the display of each photo.

```
//Fisharoo/Web/Photos/ViewAlbum.aspx
<li>
    <asp:Label Style="font-weight: bold;" ID="lblFileName"
    Text='<%#((PEFile)Container.DataItem).FileName %>'
        runat="server" /><br />
    <asp:HyperLink ID="linkImage" NavigateUrl='<%#((PEFile)Container.
    DataItem).Year + ((PEFile)Container.DataItem).Month %>'
        runat="server"></asp:HyperLink>
    <br />
    <asp:Label ID="lblDescription" runat="server" Text='<%#((PEFile)
    Container.DataItem).Description %>' />
    <br />
    <Fisharoo:Ratings ID="Ratings1" runat="server" SystemObjectID="5"
    SystemObjectRecordID='<%#Convert.ToInt64(((PEFile)Container.
    DataItem).FileID) %>'></Fisharoo:Ratings>
    <br />
    <Fisharoo:Tags ID="Tags1" runat="server" SystemObjectID="5" Syste
    mObjectRecordID='<%#Convert.ToInt64(((PEFile)Container.DataItem).
    FileID) %>' Display="ShowCloudAndTagBox" ></Fisharoo:Tags>
    <br />
    <Fisharoo:Comments ID="Comments1" runat="server"
    SystemObjectID="5" SystemObjectRecordID='<%#Convert.
    ToInt64(((PEFile)Container.DataItem).FileID) %>'></
    Fisharoo:Comments>
```

```
        <asp:Literal Visible="false" ID="litFileID" Text='<%#((PEFile)
        Container.DataItem).FileID %>' runat="server"></asp:Literal>
        <asp:Literal Visible="false" ID="litImageName" runat="server"
        Text='<%#((PEFile)Container.DataItem).FileSystemName %>'></
        asp:Literal>
        <asp:Literal Visible="false" ID="litFileExtension" runat="server"
        Text='<%# ((PEFile)Container.DataItem).Extension %>'></
        asp:Literal><br />
    </li>
```

Once we have the controls physically plugged into the page, we would want to set their `SystemObjectID` to `5`, which is the `File` object (in our database).

We would also want to set the `SystemObjectRecordID` to the `FileID` of the current iteration. Then for the `Tags` control we would want to set the `Display` property `ShowCloudAndTagBox`, which will allow our users to see the already assigned tags and also add their own tags.

Forums UI

The other set of controls (`Votes, MarkAnswer` and `Medals`) will be useful in the forums pages like `ViewForum.aspx` and `ViewPost.aspx`. We will look at `ViewPost.aspx` here as all three controls are used in it. You can look at the associated code to see changes made for `ViewForum.aspx`, the code behind, and the presenter as well.

As done with photos UI, we first register the controls to the page:

```
<%@ Register Src="~/UserControls/Votes.ascx" TagName="Votes"
TagPrefix="Fisharoo" %>
<%@ Register Src="~/UserControls/Medals.ascx" TagName="Medals"
TagPrefix="Fisharoo" %>
<%@ Register Src="~/UserControls/MarkAnswer.ascx" TagName="MarkAnswer"
TagPrefix="Fisharoo" %>
```

Next we plug them in at the appropriate places. The `MarkAnswer` and `Votes` controls are added just before the body of the post and the `Medals` are added next to the user details. Note the appropriate property bindings for these controls below:

```
<ItemTemplate>
    <table style="background-color: #dddddd; vertical-align: top;
    text-align: left;width:100%">
        <tr><td rowspan="2" style="width:70px" >
                <div style="background-color:#ffffff">
                    <Fisharoo:MarkAnswer ID="MarkAnswer1"
IsAnswer='<%#((PEBoardPost)Container.DataItem).IsAnswer %>'
PostID='<%#((PEBoardPost)Container.DataItem).PostID %>'
Visible='<%#((PEBoardPost)Container.DataItem).DisplayMarkAnswer %>'
```

```
                              runat="server" /> <br />
                        <Fisharoo:Votes ID="votePost" IsQuestion="false"
PostID='<%#((PEBoardPost)Container.DataItem).PostID %>'
Count='<%#((PEBoardPost)Container.DataItem).VoteCount %>'
runat="server" />
                  </div></td>
              <td>
                  <asp:Label ID="lblDescription" runat="server"
                  Text='<%#((PEBoardPost)Container.DataItem).Post %>'></
                  asp:Label>
          </td></tr>
          <tr>
              <td align="right">
                  <table width="120px">
                      <tr> <td colspan="2">
                              replied on
                              <asp:Label ID="lblUpdateDate"
runat="server" Text='<%#((PEBoardPost)Container.DataItem).UpdateDate
%>'></asp:Label>
                      </td></tr>
                      <tr><td>
                              <asp:Image Width="30" Height="30"
ID="imgProfile" runat="server" ImageUrl='<%# "/images/profileavatar/
profileimage.aspx?AccountID=" + ((PEBoardPost)Container.DataItem).
AccountID %>' />
                          </td>
                          <td align="left" valign="top">
                              <asp:HyperLink ID="linkUsername"
                              NavigateUrl='<%# "/" + ((PEBoardPost)
                              Container.DataItem).Username %>'
                                  runat="server" Text='<%#((PEBoardPost)
                                  Container.DataItem).Username %>'></
                                  asp:HyperLink> <br />
                              <Fisharoo:Medals ID="medalPost"
                              Score='<%#((PEBoardPost)Container.
                              DataItem).Score %>' runat="server" />
                          </td> </tr>
                  </table>
              </td></tr>
    </table>
</ItemTemplate>
```

There are minor changes in the code behind where we set the property value of these newly added controls. In the presenter, we make changes to our load method. The `MarkAnswer` control will be displayed only if the user is logged in and is the same user as the one who had asked the initial question. Also along with querying the post details, we also need to make additional call to the `AccountService` to get appropriate scores for the user accounts so that the medals can be displayed.

```
//Fisharoo/Web/Forums/Presenters/ViewPostPresenter.cs
private void LoadData(string categoryname, string forumname, int
postID)
{
    List<BoardPost> list = _postService.GetPostsByThreadID(postID);
    BoardPost bp = _postService.GetPostByID(postID);

    bool displayMarkAnswer = IsUserLoggedIn() && (bp.AccountID ==
                   _webContext.CurrentUser.AccountID) ? true : false;
    int score = _accountService.GetAccountByID(bp.AccountID).Score;

    _view.LoadData(Translator.BoardPostToPEBoardPost(bp, score),
              Translator.BoardPostToPEBoardPost(list, _accountService,
                  displayMarkAnswer), categoryname, forumname, score);
}
```

ProfileDisplay UserControl

Finally we will also add the `Medals` control to the `ProfileDisplay` user control. The changes are similar to what we have done for the scenarios just discussed. We will register the `Medals` control in the `UserControl/ProfileDisplay.ascx` and add it at a relevant place. In the code behind we set the `Medals.Score` property to the `Account.Score`.

That's it! Your new user controls are officially ready for action.

Tags page

Now that our user controls are built and plugged into our site, we have one final thing to do. In our tag cloud, each Tag links to the tag name directly, which take the users to the `Tags.aspx` page so that we can see all the objects that share the same tag. The tags could eventually be used to perform search on the site as well. This page is fairly straightforward as most of the heavy lifting is done behind the scenes. Let's take a look.

Tags.aspx

The display side of this page simply has a handful of repeaters—one repeater for each type of object to which we allow the tags to be attached. When we load our UI, the presenter sends the view a list of `SystemObjectTagWithObjects` objects. We iterate through this collection and for each object, we bind the specific collection of objects to its corresponding `Repeater`. In the case of `Files`, which is what we have plugged our controls into; we would take the `Files` collection and bind it to the `repFiles Repeater`. As we add our new user controls to other sections of the site, we can hook up to new sections in this page.

```
//Fisharoo/Web/Tags/Tags.aspx
<asp:Repeater ID="repFiles" runat="server">
    <ItemTemplate>
      <tr><td>
      <%#((PESystemObjectTagWithObjects)Container.DataItem).FileName%>
      </td><td>
                <asp:HyperLink runat="server" Text='<%# "Click to
                                       view album: " +
                                       ((PESystemObjectTagWithObjects)
                                       Container.DataItem).FolderName
                                       %>' NavigateUrl='<%# "~/photos/
                                       ViewAlbum.aspx?AlbumID=" +
                                       ((PESystemObjectTagWithObjects)
                                       Container.DataItem).
                                       DefaultFolderID %>'></
                                       asp:HyperLink> or
          <asp:HyperLink runat="server" Text='<%# "Click to
                      view photo: " + ((PESystemObjectTagWithObjects)
                      Container.DataItem).FileName %>
                               ' NavigateUrl='<%# "~/files/photos/"
                               + ((PESystemObjectTagWithObjects)
                               Container.DataItem).URL %>'></
                               asp:HyperLink>
          </td></tr>
    </ItemTemplate>
</asp:Repeater>
```

Tags.aspx.cs

All that this file does on its own is hook up to its presenter by passing the route data that captures the tag name. When the presenter's `Init()` method is called, the presenter calls into the `LoadUI()` method of the view.

The LoadUI() method takes in a collection of PESystemObjectTagWithObjects. It then proceeds in setting the data source for each repeater with a subset of the collection of PESystemObjectTagWithObjects by specifying which SystemObjectID is to be used. Once all the lists are built, the repeater's Items.Count property is interrogated to see if we have any empty sections, and if we do, we add a "No tagged items" message.

The last method is the SetTitle() method, which allows the presenter to set the page title that is viewed as a header in our page as well as in the title bar of the browser (a property in the Master page).

```
//Fisharoo/Web/Tags/Tags.aspx.cs
public partial class Tags : System.Web.UI.Page, ITags
{
    private TagsPresenter _tagsPresenter;
    protected void Page_Load(object sender, EventArgs e)
    {
        _tagsPresenter = new TagsPresenter();
         string tagName = Page.RouteData.Values["tagname"] as string;
        _tagsPresenter.Init(this, IsPostBack, tagName);
    }
    public void LoadUI(List<SystemObjectTagWithObjects>
                       tagWithObjects)
    {
        repAccounts.DataSource = tagWithObjects.Where(t =>
                        t.SystemObjectTag.SystemObjectID == 1);
        repAccounts.DataBind();
        repProfiles.DataSource = tagWithObjects.Where(t =>
                        t.SystemObjectTag.SystemObjectID == 2);
        repProfiles.DataBind();
        repBlogs.DataSource = tagWithObjects.Where(t =>
                             t.SystemObjectTag.SystemObjectID == 3);
        repBlogs.DataBind();
        repPosts.DataSource = tagWithObjects.Where(t =>
                             t.SystemObjectTag.SystemObjectID == 4);
        repPosts.DataBind();
        repFiles.DataSource = tagWithObjects.Where(t =>
                             t.SystemObjectTag.SystemObjectID == 5);
        repFiles.DataBind();
        repGroups.DataSource = tagWithObjects.Where(t =>
                             t.SystemObjectTag.SystemObjectID == 6);
        repGroups.DataBind();
        if (repGroups.Items.Count == 0)
            repGroups.Controls.Add(new LiteralControl("<tr><td
                         colspan=\"2\">No tagged items</td></tr>"));
```

```
        if (repFiles.Items.Count == 0)
            repFiles.Controls.Add(new LiteralControl("<tr><td
                         colspan=\"2\">No tagged items</td></tr>"));
        if (repPosts.Items.Count == 0)
            repPosts.Controls.Add(new LiteralControl("<tr><td
                    colspan=\"2\">No tagged items</td></tr>"));
        if (repBlogs.Items.Count == 0)
            repBlogs.Controls.Add(new LiteralControl("<tr><td
                    colspan=\"2\">No tagged items</td></tr>"));
        if (repProfiles.Items.Count == 0)
            repProfiles.Controls.Add(new LiteralControl("<tr><td
                    colspan=\"2\">No tagged items</td></tr>"));
        if(repAccounts.Items.Count == 0)
            repAccounts.Controls.Add(new LiteralControl("<tr><td
                    colspan=\"2\">No tagged items</td></tr>"));
    }
    public void SetTitle(string TagName)
    {
        ((SiteMaster)Master).Title = TagName;
    }
}
```

TagsPresenter.cs

The presenter for this file has one method: `Init()`. The `Init()` method sets the title by passing the `Name` property of the `Tag` that is loaded from the `TagService` using the `TagName`. The presenter also calls the `LoadUI()` method of the view and sends it a collection of `PESystemObjectTagWithObjects`. This collection is retrieved from the `SystemObjectTagService.GetSystemObjectsByTagID()` method.

```
//Fisharoo/Web/Tags/Presenters/TagsPresenter.cs
public void Init(ITags view, bool IsPostBack, string tagName)
{
        view = view;
        Tag tag = _tagService.GetTagByName(tagName.Replace("-", " "));
       _view.SetTitle(tag.Name);
        List<SystemObjectTagWithObject> list =
                     _systemObjectTagService.GetSystemObjectsByTagID(
                                                 Convert.ToInt32(tag.
                                                 TagID));
       _view.LoadUI(
       Translator.SystemObjectTagWithObjectToPESystemObjectTagWithObj
       ect(list));
}
```

Summary

In this chapter, we have successfully created six controls to allow our users to express their opinions about various content areas of our site and also show their own participation level. We built a tagging control that allows us to take in tag keywords as well as display all the tags for various levels of our site from specific records all the way out to the entire site. We built a rating control that allows us to configure many options per system object for individual ratings, which are then averaged across all ratings and displayed as a general score. We created a commenting control so that our users could express very specific opinions regarding any of our content items. We created a mechanism to vote and mark as answer the replies to posts on the forum. Finally, we created a medals control that displays appropriate number of medals based on the score that the user has. While we have not done it, it is fairly straightforward to include the medals in the user's profile page as well. We have however added medals to the user's short profile display that is used as part of the friends display.

With these new user controls, we have created new avenues of interest for our users. We now have the ability to allow users to touch just about anything in our system. In addition to allowing users to provide input, we have also created another avenue of interest for our users who enjoy reading and seeing other users' inputs. We have come a long way in including our users in the community feel of our site.

12 Moderation

We are finally at a point where we have a community with pretty much every feature that represents a great community. To that point, a lot of the things that we allow our users to create are text-based or resource-based content items such as images, movies, and so on. This is wonderful! Now all we have to do is deploy our site, invite some users, and watch our community grow.

Not so fast! Allowing your user base to have complete freedom in filling your site with content is not a good idea. It means that you don't have any control over the destiny of your site. It also means that you will eventually have someone adding inappropriate material. You might even have a tech-savvy user attempting to steal some of your user's information for less than appropriate ventures. All these issues might eventually drive out all the good users leaving you only with bad users. Possibly, in the worst case, you might end up with legal issues on your hands due to the actions of your uncontrolled users.

We don't mean to scare you. We only mean to inform you that with a community driven by your user's content, you will need to take some responsibility and keep a tight grip on the reigns. This tight grip that we're talking about is what this chapter is all about.

In this chapter, we will discuss various forms of moderation. With user-generated content, we can take advantage of user-generated moderation. After all, why not give the offended a method to report what offended them? We will also discuss gagging users who are habitual offenders. And we will create a filter that will block bad words, and competitor's spams.

Problem

The core problem in this chapter is that we do not want to give willy-nilly control to our user base. We should maintain as much control over our site as possible with regards to what goes into it and what is displayed on it. Let's discuss the core features.

Community moderation

The user moderation takes place with a simple AJAXed `ImageButton` that allows them to flag inappropriate content inline along with the content.

The content that is flagged by the community will show up in the administration console under the **Moderation** section as shown in the following screenshot. Here you can approve or deny the content.

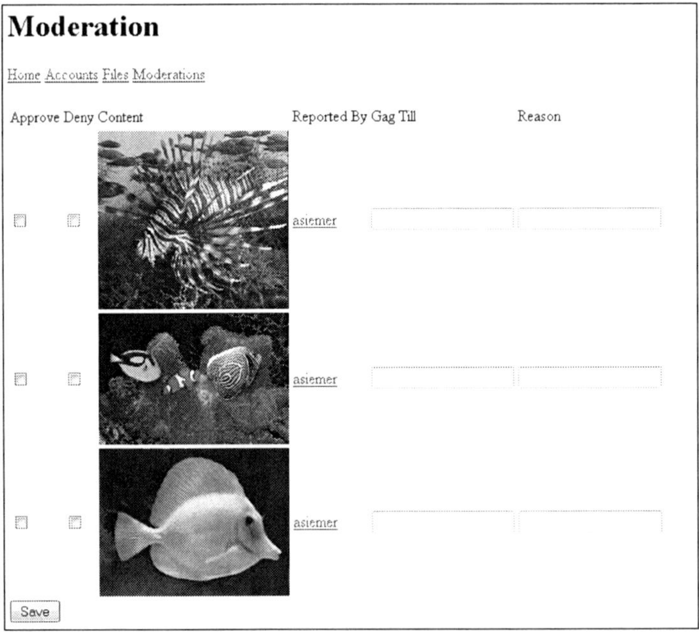

Gagging users

Once you have a list of moderated content, you will eventually start to notice some repeat offenders. For that reason, we need a way to slap the hands of those offenders. When viewing your flagged content, you will also see the owner of the content. If you find that you are seeing repeat offenders, you can apply a Gag to the user. A Gag will restrict the user from continuing to add content to the site as a form of punishment for bad behavior. Part of the Gag is to specify the reason and the date that the Gag order ends, as shown in the following screenshot. If you don't want to specify an end data, you can apply a 20 year ban!

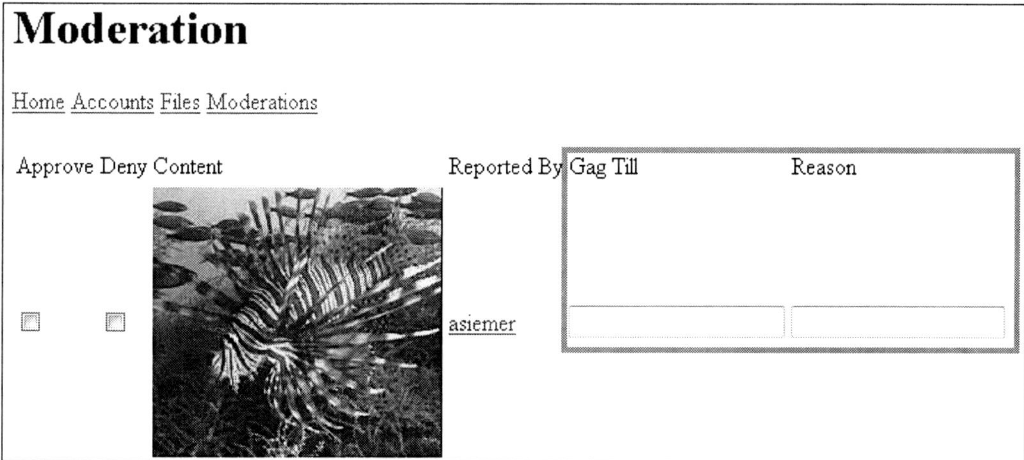

Dynamic filter

The dynamic filter will address a few issues. You can use it to effectively remove profanity from your site. You can also use it to intercept competitor postings or advertisements on your site. And most importantly, you can use it to restrict the types of scripting that you allow. This tool could block HTML, JavaScript, and just about anything else that you don't want on your site, which can aid you in dealing with cross-site scripting issues.

As an example, we are posting to the forum, and chose to use the offensive California term **dude**, as shown in the following screenshot:

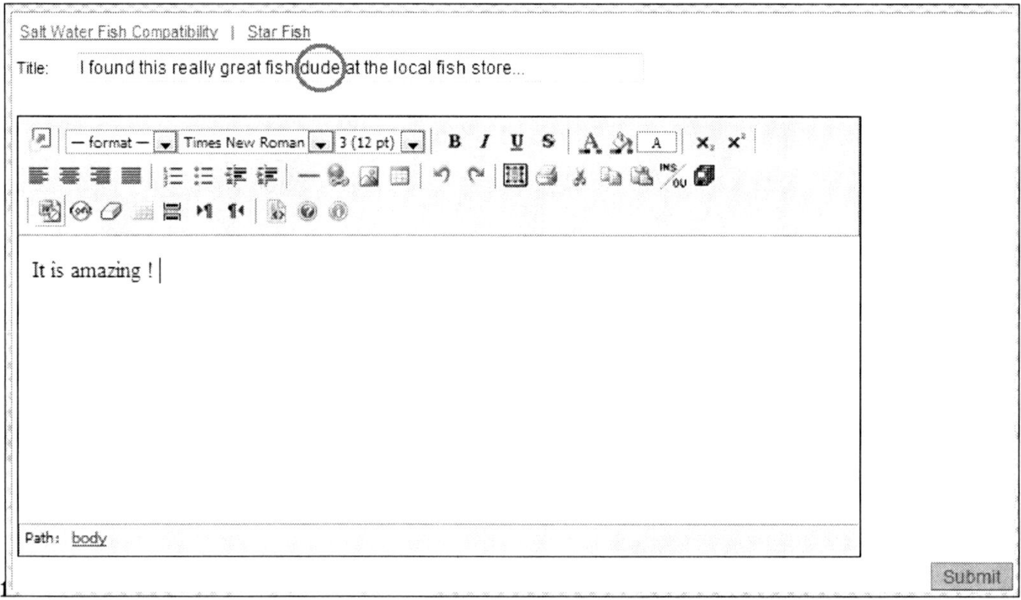

As shown in the following screenshot, we have added a filter entry to our `ContentFilter` list that disallows the word **dude** in the site and instead replaces it with **[filtered]**, as shown in following screenshot:

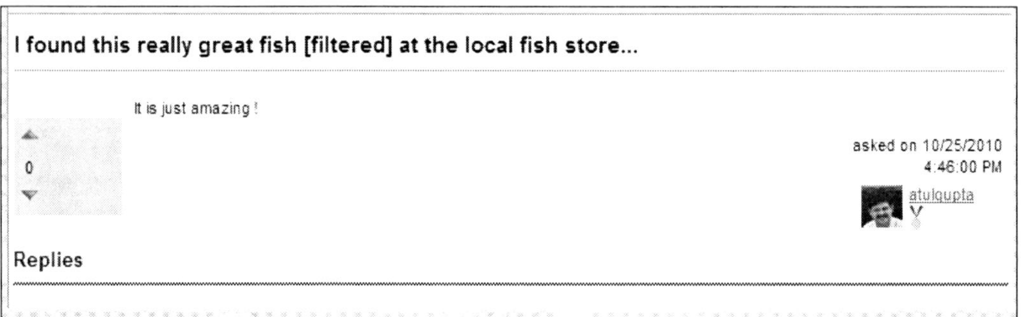

Design

Let's take a look at the design for this feature.

Moderation

For us to enable Moderation, we will take advantage of the same concepts that we used in Chapter 11. This feature will be implemented as another `UserControl` that we can plug in wherever we need it. As it will tie in to the **SystemObjects** table of objects, we are free to allow our users to moderate any database-oriented content—be it textual, image based, or just about anything else. As long as it has a record ID and a table associated to it, we can moderate it.

In addition to letting our users flag content for approval, we will need to create a page to manage what was flagged. We will implement a simple administration page that will show everything that is listed. For each listed item we can approve or deny the content. Approved content will no longer be visible on the site. This page will also house our gagging capabilities, which we will discuss later.

This structure is identical to our other users of the **SystemObjects** table. It has a **SystemObjectID** and a **SystemObjectRecordID**, which allow us to add a Moderation entry and see where it points to. When we build the administration page, you will see how we can use this data to get all the objects, regardless of the type, for administration viewing purposes. In addition to the **SystemObjects** table, we are also linking to the **Accounts** table with the **AccountID** of the account that published the questionable content and the **AccountID** of the user that took action on the questionable content. Tracking this second AccountID is useful as it helps us keep track of which user is raising flags. If we find that the content isn't questionable, we can actually track the user who raised the request to find out if this is a malicious user attempting to get other innocent users banned.

Gags

To gag a user—such as in a legal gag order—is to suppress them from being able to make comments publicly. We will extend this concept to say that we will not allow a user to publish content on our system if they have a gag order placed on them! As with flagging of questionable content, not having an automatic gagging, but having a moderator intervene will help to prevent instances where innocent users may otherwise be gagged.

The most important thing to note in the Gags table is the **GagUntilDate** field as shown in the preceding screenshot. The date in this field is the date that the user can interact with the community again.

Filtering

The filtering system will provide us with the ability to map out content that we don't want, and swap it with the content that we actually need. We will first address this simple mapping issue with the concept that someone has used foul language on our site. We will be able to add the word that we don't like to our content filter list and insert a better word in its place so that our content is less offensive. In the case of the "dude" scenario we swapped in "[Filtered]".

While our filter can and should be used in this simple way, it can also be used to destroy a client-side script. To possibly destroy a script, you can add these text strings to our filter list (two different entries) <script> and </script> along with an empty string as the replacement value. This will effectively replace all <script> and </script> entries with an empty string. This will leave the code/text between the remaining script tags. That would effectively break the script—we think.

In order to just use this concept of filtering, we would have to have an extensive database of possible entries to test for. Not only is this difficult, it would also be tremendously inefficient! Even if we had the greatest dictionary in the world, there is still a chance that we could miss something. And of course it would be fairly ugly as you would have all the code that we didn't catch displayed in the page. But at least they couldn't run the script at that point. It's a step in the right direction.

In order to address the issue of unaccounted for tags, and to bypass the need for a tag library, we will use UrlEncode() on the string to be filtered prior to filtering it. The first pass of UrlEncode() will convert the <script> and </script> tags into <script> and </script>. It will also convert all the other special characters in the entry and make them encoded as well. This effectively renders all the HTML, CSS, and JavaScript code useless!

Now that we have killed all the possible markup and script in the text, what about the stuff that we want to allow on my site? We can make exceptions in our filter list by adding encoded words to be translated back to acceptable terms. In the case of a bold tag <b> the encode function would make it look like <b&rt;. We can simply add the <b&rt; to our list of words to be filtered with a replacement value <b>. Now we can build back what we want to accept. An acceptance list is much easier to manage than a database of possibilities for the content to be filtered.

Solution

Now let's take a look at the solution.

Implementing the database

First let's take a look at what tables are needed. The following screenshot shows the relevant tables:

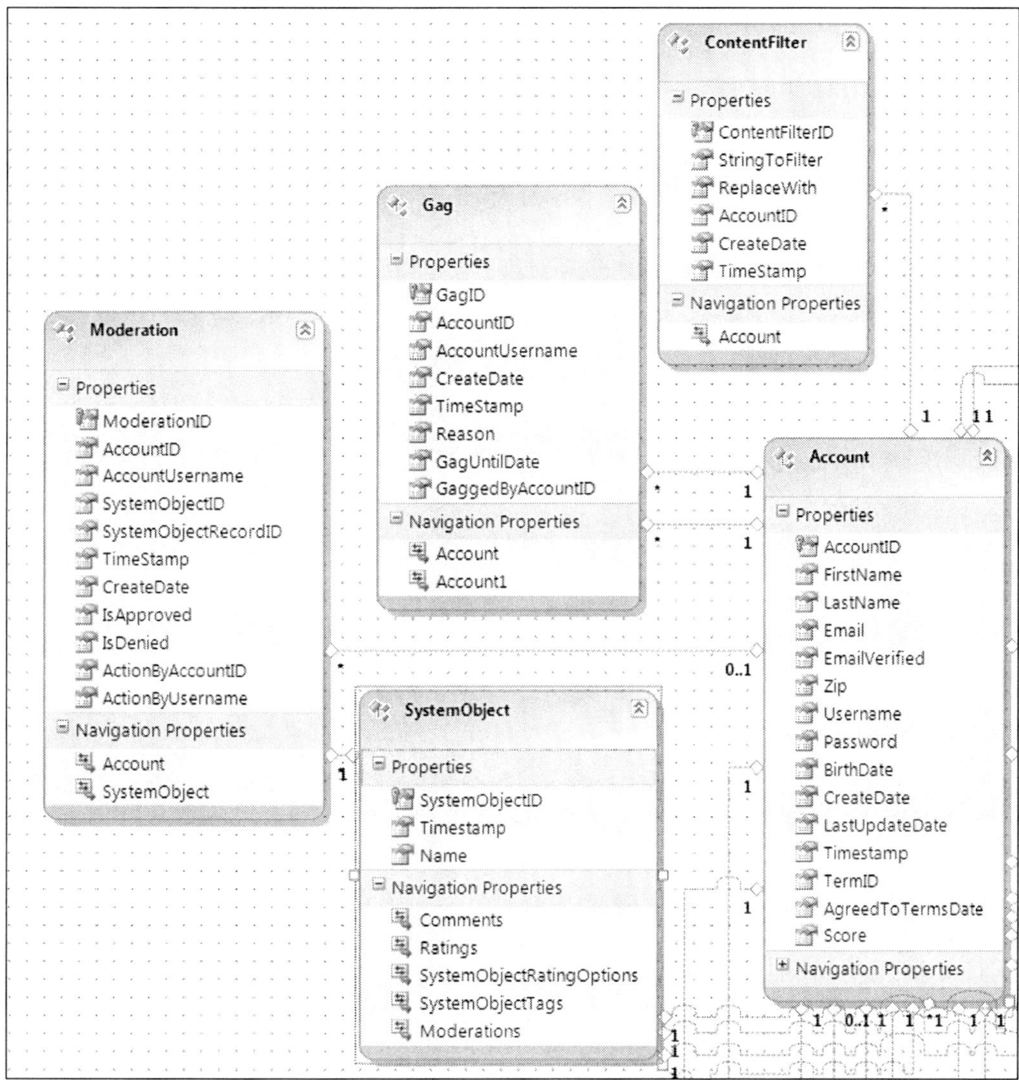

Moderations

The moderation table shown in the previous screenshot holds the **SystemObjectID** and **SystemObjectRecordID** as well as the Account that created the content in question. It also carries the Account that executed the resulting action as well as what that action is.

In addition to tables, we are going to need a way to quickly and easily obtain moderated files. We hate to say it, but we are going to dip into the actual SQL for this one. We will create a stored procedure that will take a `FolderID` and will return all the moderated files in that folder.

```
CREATE PROCEDURE [dbo].[pr_GetModeratedFiles]
@DefaultFolderID bigint
AS
BEGIN
    SELECT  f.* FROM Files f WHERE f.DefaultFolderID = @
    DefaultFolderID AND f.FileID
    NOT IN (SELECT f.FileID FROM Files f, Moderations m
            WHERE
            f.DefaultFolderID = @DefaultFolderID
            AND
            m.SystemObjectID = 5
            AND
            m.systemobjectrecordid = f.FileID
            AND
            m.IsApproved = 1
    )
END
```

We can then work with this information inside and outside of our queries quickly and easily.

Gags

The `Gags` table, as shown in the previous screenshot is responsible for determining if a user is on house arrest with regards to adding content to the community. It holds the gagged user's **AccountID**, their **AccountUsername**, when the gag was applied, why it was applied, who applied it, and when it is to be lifted.

ContentFilters

Though the content filter has a great deal of responsibility, it is a relatively simple system. All it keeps track of is which patterns to filter, what to replace each pattern with, who created each filter, and when. The strength of the system is more in the implementation than in the storage!

Creating the relationships

Once all the tables are created, we can create all the relationships.

For this set of tables we have relationships between the following tables:

- `Moderations` and `Accounts`
- `Moderations` and `SystemObjects`
- `Gags` and `Accounts`
- `ContentFilters` and `Accounts`

Setting up the data access layer

To set up the data access layer, we follow the steps as already done in earlier chapters. Open the `Fisharoo.edmx` file and add all the above mentioned tables we have discussed in this chapter.

Building repositories

With the addition of new tables will come the addition of new repositories so that we can get the data stored in those tables. We will create the following repositories to support our needs.

- `ModerationRepository`
- `GagRepository`
- `ContentFilterRepository`

Each of our repositories will generally have a method—for select by ID, select all by parent ID, save, and delete. Once you have seen one repository, you have pretty much seen them all. Review previous chapters, the appendices, or the included code for examples of a standard repository. However, we will discuss anything that varies from the standard.

ModerationRepository

For this repository, we have a standard save method that will take in one ModerationRepository at a time and deal with it appropriately. It essentially creates entries as our users flag content. This is great for *one-at-a-time* record creation for our community users.

GetModerationsGlobal()

Once we have our Moderation records created, we need to be able to see the issues so that we can accept some content and deny the others. To do this, we have a method that gets all the moderations from a global point of view GetModerationsGlobal().

```
//Fisharoo/DataAccess/Repositories/ModerationRepository.cs
public List<Moderation> GetModerationsGlobal()
{
    List<Moderation> result = new List<Moderation>();
    using(FisharooDataContext dc = conn.GetContext())
    {
        var groups = (from m in dc.Moderations
                      where m.IsDenied == null || m.IsApproved ==
                                          null
                      group m by m.SystemObjectRecordID
                      into g
                          select new { g, NumberOfReports = g.Count()
                                     }).OrderByDescending
                                     (g1 => g1.NumberOfReports);
        foreach (var v in groups)
        {
            result.Add(v.g.ToList()[0]);
        }
    }
    return result;
}
```

This method allows us to get all the moderations, grouped by the SystemObjectRecordID as many people could report the same bit of content. This reduced view is what we will see in our admin screens so that we can accept and reject content in a more streamlined fashion. There is no need to view every complaint!

Our admin screen will be built similar to a web-based email client so that you can interact with several moderation records at a time. It will gather a collection of moderation records and package them up into a collection of `ModerationResults`. Once we have a collection of those items, we can pass them to our bulk save method, `SaveModerationResults()`.

```
//Fisharoo/DataAccess/Repositories/ModerationRepository.cs
public void SaveModerationResults(List<ModerationResult> results, int
ActionByAccountID, string ActionByUsername)
{
    using (FisharooDataContext dc = conn.GetContext())
    {
        foreach (ModerationResult result in results)
        {
            List<Moderation> moderations = dc.Moderations.Where(
                    m => m.SystemObjectID == result.SystemObjectID &&
                    m.SystemObjectRecordID ==
                                result.SystemObjectRecordID).
                                ToList();

            for (int i = 0; i < moderations.Count(); i++)
            {
                if (result.IsApproved)
                {
                    moderations[i].IsApproved = true;
                    moderations[i].IsDenied = false;
                }
                else
                {
                    moderations[i].IsDenied = true;
                    moderations[i].IsApproved = false;
                }
                moderations[i].ActionByAccountID = ActionByAccountID;
                moderations[i].ActionByUsername = ActionByUsername;
            }

            if (moderations.Count() > 0)
                dc.SaveChanges();
        }
    }
}
```

This method is responsible for taking in a collection of `ModerationResults`, which is possibly a grouped result set of individual moderations. For this reason with each iteration over the `ModerationResults` collection, we must first attempt to get a list of applicable `Moderation` records. We then set all the values for each of these records and save them back into the database.

We now have everything we need to get complaints from our users as well as the ability to respond to the complaints. What we are still missing is the ability to actually remove the content from our site based on the complaints. We can deal with this issue in two ways. We can add a delete content functionality that physically removes the offending content from the server entirely, or we can simply hide flagged content so that the user can possibly fix it. We would be very upset if a site administrator removed a ten page blog post just because it had one accidental dirty offensive word! So we will stick with the concept that the content will simply be hidden from the site when it is flagged. This concept unfortunately doesn't have a magic bullet fix in C# or LINQ—at least not the right one! This is where that `GetModeratedFiles ()` SQL stored procedure comes in. We will need to add our `GetModeratedFiles ()` call to our existing repositories where appropriate. Here is the `FileRepository` with an example highlighted:

```
//Fisharoo/DataAccess/Repositories/FileRepository.cs
public List<File> GetFilesByFolderID(Int64 FolderID)
{
    List<File> result;
    using (FisharooDataContext dc = conn.GetContext())
    {
        result = dc.pr_GetModeratedFiles(FolderID).ToList();
        foreach (File file in result)
        {
            var fileType = dc.FileTypes.Where(ft =>
            ft.FileTypeID == file.FileTypeID).FirstOrDefault();
            file.Extension = fileType.Name;
        }
    }
    return result;
}
```

This addition will effectively block the output of all the files that are flagged in our moderation system.

GagRepository

There are two methods in this repository that we will discuss:

- `GetActiveGags()` will give us the ability to get a listing of all the Gags in the system so that we can manage who is gagged, who is about to be ungagged, and possibly a user who may need a Gag extension.
- `IsGagged()` will allow us to check to see if a user is currently gagged. It will allow us to restrict a gagged user from creating new content. We can also use it to make changes to the display such as hiding the new post button.

```
//Fisharoo/DataAccess/Repositories/Gagpository.cs
public List<Gag> GetActiveGags()
{
    List<Gag> result = new List<Gag>();
    using(FisharooDataContext dc = conn.GetContext())
    {
        result = dc.Gags.Where(g => g.GagUntilDate >
                 DateTime.Now).OrderBy(g => g.GagUntilDate).
                 ToList();
    }
    return result;
}
public bool IsGagged(Int32 AccountID)
{
    bool result = false;
    using(FisharooDataContext dc = conn.GetContext())
    {
        if(dc.Gags.Where(g=>g.AccountID == AccountID &&
                     g.GagUntilDate > DateTime.Now).
                     FirstOrDefault() != null)
        {
            result = true;
        }
    }
    return true;
}
```

ContentFilterRepository

The `ContentFilterRepository` currently has only one job. It returns a list of all the filters in the system.

Implementing the services/application layer

Once all the repositories are built for single-serving purposes, we can begin to create the service layer. Again this layer is responsible for assembling aggregates and performing complex actions with our entities. We will create and modify the following services:

- `ContentFilterService`
- `Extensions`

ContentFilterService

The `ContentFilterService` is responsible for applying our `ContentFilters`. This method consolidates the call into the `ContentFilterRepository`, the `HtmlEncode()` of the string, and the actual work of applying the filters to the string being filtered.

```
//Fisharoo/BusinessLogic/ContentFilterService.cs
public string Filter(string StringToFilter)
{
    List<ContentFilter> _contentFilters = _contentFilterRepository.
    GetContentFilters();
    StringBuilder sb = new StringBuilder(StringToFilter);
    //encode the final output for further security
    sb = new StringBuilder(HttpUtility.HtmlEncode(sb.ToString()));
    //replace all the dirty words and forbidden tags
    foreach (ContentFilter cf in _contentFilters)
    {
        sb.Replace(cf.StringToFilter, cf.ReplaceWith);
    }
    return sb.ToString();
}
```

Our initial entry into this method provides us with the string that we will be working with. Next, we get a list of `ContentFilters` to work with. In order to work with our string in a more efficient manner we are going to create a new `StringBuilder`. Our first pass of filtering our string will start with encoding our string using the `HttpUtility.HtmlEncode()` method. Once we have our base string to work with, we can begin iterating over our collection of `ContentFilters`. With each `ContentFilter`, we perform a `Replace()` where we swap out our `StringToFilter` for our `ReplaceWith` value. We then convert our `StringBuilder` back to a string prior to returning the result of our filtering process.

Implementing the presentation layer

The majority of our work in this chapter will be in the form of user controls and function calls. The changes that are made are more about how the content disappears rather than seeing new items.

Moderation

Now let's look at the feature of moderation.

The user control

Our moderation feature begins its life as a rather simple user control. This control is made up of an AJAX.NET `UpdatePanel`, one `Panel`, and one `ImageButton` for flagging our content. If the user is not logged in, we will hide the Panel. And once the user clicks the `ImageButton`, we will add the `Moderation` content to our table. Directly after the filter is captured, we will hide the button. From that point onwards when the users load their content they will no longer see the option to flag that content.

```
//Fisharoo/Web/UserControls/Moderations.ascx
<asp:UpdatePanel runat="server">
    <ContentTemplate>
        <asp:Panel ID="pnlFlagThis" runat="server" style="float:left;
                                      padding-left:5px;padding-
                                      right:5px;">
            <asp:ImageButton ToolTip="Flag this content!"
            ID="ibFlagThis"
                            runat="server" ImageUrl="~/Images/
                            redflag.png"
                                            OnClick="ibFlagThis_
                                            Click" />
        </asp:Panel>
    </ContentTemplate>
</asp:UpdatePanel>
```

Note that we have a few properties. These are the same as our Tagging, Rating, and Commenting controls. These properties allow us to track the item that we are allowing our users to flag. Once we have the UI loaded for this control, we initialize our presenter and make a call to initialize the control.

Nothing fancy in the code behind so let's look at the presenter. There we set all the properties for our control and determine if we should show the control or not.

```
//Fisharoo/Web/UserControls/Presenters/ModerationPresenter.cs
public class ModerationsPresenter
{
    . . .

    public void Init(IModerations view, bool IsPostBack)
    {
        _view = view;

        if (_webContext.CurrentUser == null)
            _view.ShowFlagThis = false;
        else if (_moderationRepository.HasFlaggedThisAlready(
              _webContext.CurrentUser.AccountID, _view.SystemObjectID,
              _view.SystemObjectRecordID))
            _view.ShowFlagThis = false;
        else
            _view.ShowFlagThis = true;
    }

    public void SaveModeration(int SystemObjectID, long
    SystemObjectRecordID)
    {
        if (_webContext.CurrentUser != null)
        {
            Moderation moderation = new Moderation();
            moderation.AccountID = _webContext.CurrentUser.AccountID;
            moderation.AccountUsername = _webContext.CurrentUser.
            Username;
            moderation.CreateDate = DateTime.Now;
            moderation.SystemObjectID = _view.SystemObjectID;
            moderation.SystemObjectRecordID = _view.
            SystemObjectRecordID;
            _moderationRepository.SaveModeration(moderation);
        }
        _view.ShowFlagThis = false;
    }
}
```

The `SaveModeration()` method is the button click event that is transferred from the code behind and into the presenter. From the presenter we create a new `Moderation` and save it to our database.

Once the user control is complete, we are able to plug it for all to use.

Remember that this is simply a link button that displays a small icon.

```
//Fisharoo/Web/Photos/ViewAlbum.aspx
<ItemTemplate>
    <li>
         <Fisharoo:Moderations ID="Moderations1" SystemObjectID="5"
                 SystemObjectRecordID='<%#Convert.ToInt64(
                              ((PEFile)Container.DataItem).FileID)
                              %>'
                               runat="server"></Fisharoo:Moderations>
        <asp:Label style="font-weight:bold;" ID="lblFileName"
                  Text='<%#((PEFile)Container.DataItem).FileName %>'
                  runat="server">
        </asp:Label>
```

Note that we are loading the properties directly in the page. This may or may not work depending on when you load the repeater. You may need to locate and load the control in the `OnItemDataBound` event handler.

```
//Fisharoo/Web/Photos/ViewAlbum.aspx.cs
protected void lvAlbum_ItemDataBound(object sender,
                                     ListViewItemEventArgs e)
{
UserControls.Tags Tags1 = e.Item.FindControl("Tags1") as
                           Fisharoo.Web.UserControls.Tags;
                           Tags1.SystemObjectRecordID = Convert.
                           ToInt64(litFileID.Text);
UserControls.Moderations Moderations1 =
    e.Item.FindControl("Moderations1") as Fisharoo.Web.
    UserControls.Moderations;
Moderations1.SystemObjectRecordID = Convert.ToInt64(litFileID.Text);
}
```

Once this is complete, the community will be off and running to moderate content!

Moderating flagged content

Now that we have a working flagging system, it is time to stand up a page where we can manage the newly collected data. To achieve this, we have added a new project to manage our administration area. This page has a repeater that shows some checkboxes to capture whether the item is to be approved or denied. There are also some Gagging tools here to capture the gagging of a user. We will discuss this in more detail later. Do also note that we have just provided a bare minimum page without much attention to creating a good looking user interface. This interface will show us the content that was flagged and, who posted the content, and provide us with the opportunity to take appropriate action.

With the UI created, we can take a quick look at the code behind. For the most part, the code in this page is a very normal loading and rendering of a `Repeater` control. The one place that may be a bit new to you though is in the `Save` button's `click` event. Here we will iterate through all the controls in the `Repeater` to extract the data that we need to work with.

```
//Fisharoo/AdminConsole/Moderations/Default.aspx.cs
protected void btnSubmit_Click(object sender, EventArgs e)
{
    List<ModerationResult> results = new List<ModerationResult>();
    foreach (RepeaterItem item in repModeration.Controls)
    {
        if(item.ItemType == ListItemType.AlternatingItem ||
           item.ItemType == ListItemType.Item)
        {
             CheckBox chkApprove = item.FindControl("chkApprove") as
             CheckBox;
             CheckBox chkDeny = item.FindControl("chkDeny") as
             CheckBox;
             Literal litSystemObjectID =
             item.FindControl("litSystemObjectID") as Literal;
             Literal litSystemObjectRecordID =
             item.FindControl("litSystemObjectRecordID") as Literal;
             TextBox txtGagDate = item.FindControl("txtGagDate") as
             TextBox;
             TextBox txtReason = item.FindControl("txtReason") as
             TextBox;
             Literal litAccountID = item.FindControl("litAccountID")
             as Literal;
             Literal litAccountUsername =
             item.FindControl("litAccountUsername") as Literal;
            if(chkDeny.Checked || chkApprove.Checked)
            {
                ModerationResult mr = new ModerationResult();
                mr.SystemObjectID =
                Convert.ToInt32(litSystemObjectID.Text);
                mr.SystemObjectRecordID =
                Convert.ToInt64(litSystemObjectRecordID.Text);
                if (chkApprove.Checked)
                {
                    mr.IsApproved = true;
                    results.Add(mr);
                }
                //deny wins
                if (chkDeny.Checked)
                {
```

```
                    mr.IsApproved = false;
                    results.Add(mr);
                }
            }
            if(!string.IsNullOrEmpty(txtGagDate.Text))
            {
             _presenter.GagUserUntil(Convert.ToInt32
                                    (litAccountID.Text),
                                    litAccountUsername.Text,
                                    DateTime.Parse(txtGagDate.Text),
                                    txtReason.Text);
            }
        }
    }
    if(results.Count() > 0)
        _presenter.SaveModerationResults(results);
}
```

There appears to be a lot going on here, but a fair amount of the code at the top of the method is dedicated to locating and loading the controls from the UI. Once we have the controls in hand, we can interrogate the state of each flagged item. When we find something with a checkbox selected for approving or denying, we add the item to our `List` of `ModerationResults` (recall that we created this earlier in the repository in the previous section).

Once we have worked our way through the data, we then send our list of alterations through to the `ModerationRepository` where it is saved in bulk.

Gagging

In the moderation pages UI you can notice that we have two text box controls. We have one text box for capturing the reason why we have decided to gag a user. And the other text box is for providing the date, which indicates when the gag would ultimately be revoked for a user.

In the `btnSubmit_Click()` method (discussed previously), you will also see some code that interrogates the state of those text boxes. If we find something in the Repeaters control collection, then we call into the `GagUserUntil()` method of our presenter and effectively gag the user. The presenter creates a `new Gag` object and persists it out to our database.

```
//Fisharoo/AdminConsole/Moderations/Presenters/DefaultPresenter.cs
public void GagUserUntil(int AccountID, string AccountUsername,
                         DateTime GagTillDate, string Reason)
{
```

```
        Gag gag = new Gag();
        gag.AccountID = AccountID;
        gag.CreateDate = DateTime.Now;
        gag.AccountUsername = AccountUsername;
        gag.GagUntilDate = GagTillDate;
        gag.Reason = Reason;
        gag.GaggedByAccountID = _webContext.CurrentUser.AccountID;
        _gagRepository.SaveGag(gag);
    }
```

Filtering

The filtering process is responsible for removing vulgar language, competitors' advertisements and bad mouthing, and XSS attacks.

We have added this feature to our `PEBoardPost` presentation entity to demonstrate it. A thread/post has two textual parts—the title and the main content. We modified `PEBoardPost` to return filtered data for the title and the content. The changes to the code are shown below:

```
//Fisharoo/Web/HelperClasses/PEBoardPost.cs
private string _name;
public string Name
{
    get { return _contentFilterService.Filter(_name); }
    set { _name = value; }
}

private string _post;
public string Post
{
    get { return _contentFilterService.Filter(_post); }
    set { _post = value; }
}
```

Done, finally! All the work for the implementation of this feature is in the backend—crucial for a feature of this nature. The easier it is to use, the more likely it will be used. Wherever possible we would actually be better off filtering the text in the presenter or even further up the chain. The closer this task is done to the actual data retrieval, the less likely it is to be forgotten! But as you can see, it is flexible enough to be used whenever and wherever you need it.

Summary

In this chapter we discussed how and why to implement some form of moderation. We looked at how our community provided content could be managed by the same community using a very simple flagging tool that is flexible enough to be added to any major entity on our site. We also looked at methods to deal with habitual rule breakers in the form of gagging them or suspending their content by adding privileges. Finally, we took a high-level look at how to implement a filtering system to filter out unwanted language/words from the site content.

13
Scaling

If you have made it this far then you must be the proud new owner of a community site that is ready to start accepting new community members. We know from experience that you did not go this far to start a community that will only ever have 100 users. You, like everyone else, would like very much to start building a social network that gets 100,000 or more active users. Ten thousand users is considered a success. One hundred thousand users and you might be able to sell your community to someone else.

To get that many users to your site will require several things. You will have to have a great new concept for your site. Something that really makes it stand out as different. It will require excellent marketing skills either by way of viral marketing or through a more traditional marketing campaign. It will also mean that your site will need to stand up under a heavy daily load of users continuously until you reach your goals. This last point is what this chapter is all about.

Problem

There are many aspects of a site with a large number of users that can bring the site to its knees. Some of this can be slowness of the features while others can be physically locking the system to a point that it is no longer responsive. In this chapter, we will address some of the possible issues that might come up with a community and ways to fix them.

We will discuss issues at the database level in the form of indexing and partitioning our data. We will dive into how we can address scalability by application tier-ing, application slowness by throwing more hardware at it, and then load balancing that hardware. We will also discuss how to cache data dips and complex object creation so that we don't have to perform the queries or object manipulation every time. Next, we will speed up our search by creating highly optimized, indexed data sets. And finally we will look at reducing the number of systems our website speaks to directly so that our user experience is not directly impacted by infrastructure.

Design

Let's assume for this chapter that you have so many concurrent users on your site that you are starting to notice that the site and your servers are no longer able to keep up. What can we do? There are many approaches to this problem. You can tier the code. You can address some performance in your code and stay on one server. You can even address some optimizations at the database level. Eventually you will have to do all these to withstand the large loads of a successful community.

Also note that while we cover this topic towards the end of this book, in real world implementations, performance and scalability are by no means things that can be pushed to the end. They need to be planned alongside the requirements, architecture, design, and build phase and regular performance testing has to happen to ensure that as new features are added, it doesn't adversely impact the performance.

Solution

There is no one silver bullet for addressing Scalability. Ensuring the application is scalable in long run needs addressing multiple aspects; we have explained some of the important ones in the coming sections.

Tiered architecture

When we started with architecture in Chapter 2, we planned our application into multiple layers such as Presentation, Business Logic, Data Access, Storage, etc. It is important to note the difference between layers and tiers. A layer is logical whereas a tier is the physical separation of the code base.

For scaling an application with an increasing number of users, the complete code base can be either deployed on a maximum of two tiers or it can be split across different tiers. Each solution approach, with its respective strengths and weaknesses is discussed in the following sections.

Scaling with two-tiered approach

We designed the Fisharoo solution so far in such a manner that we can have a maximum of two tiers-i.e. presentation, business logic, and data access related code all on one tier, called the application tier; and SQL server code on another tier, called the database tier (see the following screenshot).

As the scale increases the application tier can be scaled out by duplicating it on another machine. With the help of load balancer in place, the user request can be routed to anyone of the various machines hosting the application tier. While doing so, one option is that the load balancer be configured in such a manner that it sends requests from one user to the same machine. This is referred to as sticky sessions. The other option is to do stateless design and let load balancing happen on its own. The load balancer is discussed in the *Web farming* section. The database can be further clustered or replicated to provide better availability and performance.

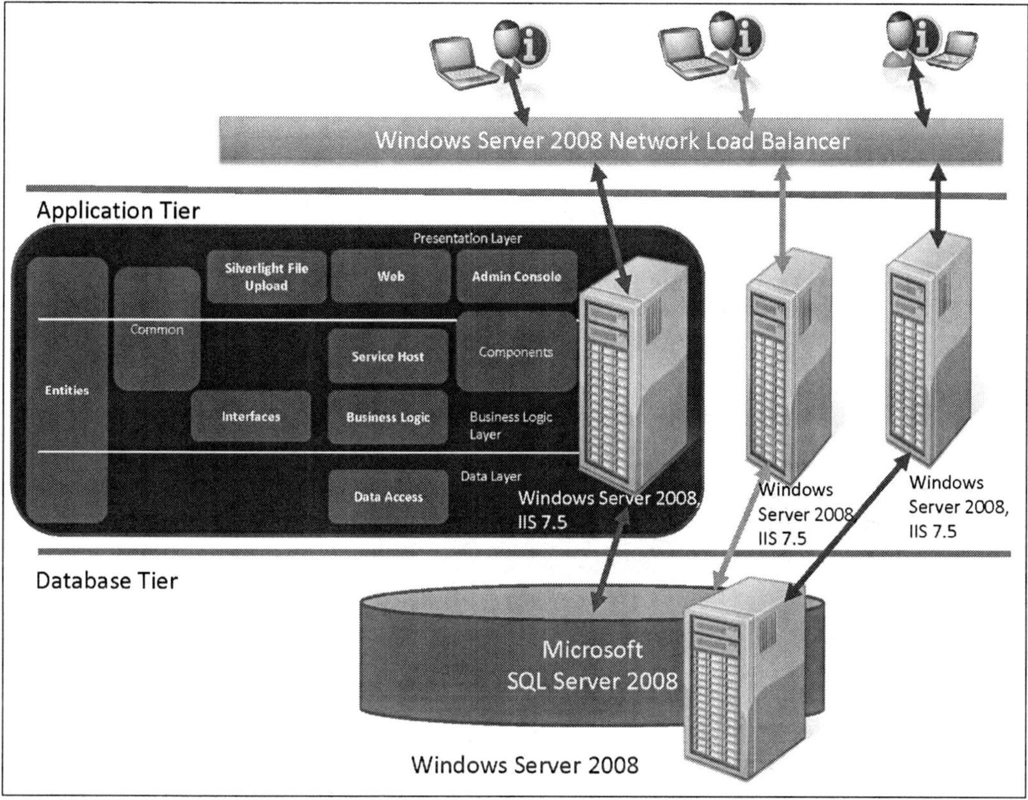

This approach has strengths in:

- Better performance as most calls are in-proc (within application tier) and there are less machine hops.
- Improved availability as the machine running with application tier can be taken offline for maintenance while others continue to serve the users.
- No upfront investment in infrastructure and as the user base grows, more machines can be added to support the increasing user base.

Scaling with multi-tiered approach

Another way of scaling is by deploying each layer on a separate physical machine called a Tier (see the following screenshot). The tiers would look like:

- Presentation Tier: Presentation Components (`Fisharoo.Web; Fisharoo.AdminConsole;Fisharoo.SilverlightFileUpload`)
- Application Tier: Business Logic (`Fisharoo.BusinessLogic; Fisharoo.Common;Fisharoo.Components;Fisharoo.WcfServiceHost; Fisharoo.Interfaces; Fisharoo.MailQueueProcessor; Enyim.Caching`) + DataAccess Logic (`Fisharoo.DataAccess`)
- Database Tier: Database

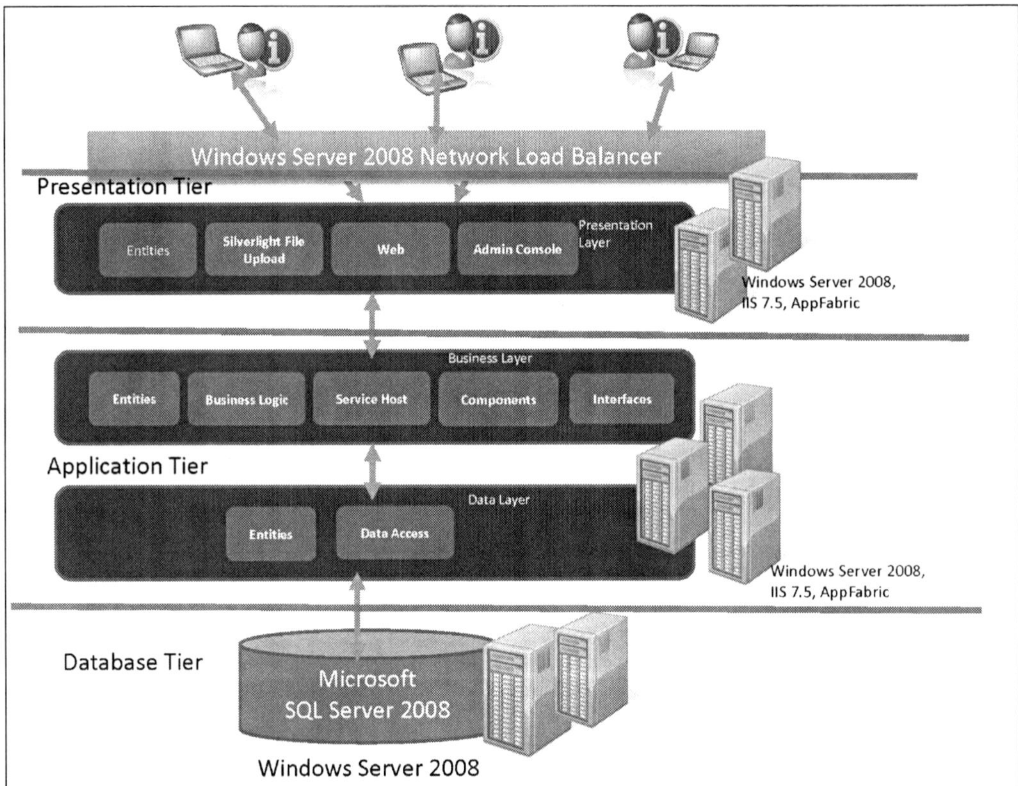

This approach has strengths in high scalability and availability but will give relatively less performance compared to the earlier approach.

However, it is not as simple as just moving the specific assemblies to different machines. The calls from presentation to business are now going to be outside of the machine boundary as the respective code would exist on different physical machines. To resolve this, one of the things we can do is to enable **Service Oriented Architecture (SOA)** for this application. SOA is very well known paradigm, and you can read it from `http://en.wikipedia.org/wiki/Service-oriented_architecture`.

In the following sections we will show how we can modify the current implementation to make it SOA enabled.

Presentation and application tier scaling

Before we dig further into scaling, let's do some architecture compliance validations.

Layered architecture validation

Architecture validation is an important aspect that we should be able to perform during various phases of the project. This helps in ensuring the architecture rules defined as part of the process are adhered to consistently throughout the development phases and are not violated unknowingly. Rules, such as presentation layer code should not directly call data access layer code, are essential, but difficult to locate unless code is reviewed thoroughly.

Visual Studio (VS) 2010's Architecture Validation feature provides this facility out of box. You need to first create an architecture diagram in the designer and then attach different projects in the solution to different layers in the diagram. VS can then validate calls across different projects as per the architecture diagram and point out violations.

Let's add a new project to our existing solution called as `ModelingProject` and add a new item using the **Layer Diagram** template. Drag three horizontal and one vertical layer on the canvas using the **View | Toolbox** menu. The horizontal layers from top to bottom are respectively named the Presentation Layer, Business Layer, and Data Access Layer. The vertical layer is called the Utility Layer.

Once these layers are created, drag `Web`, `AdminConsole`, and `SilverlightUpload` projects from solution explorer on to the presentation layer. Similarly corresponding projects are dragged in other layers as shown in the following screenshot. Once all the layers are mapped with projects, right-click the canvas and choose **Generate dependencies** which in turn displays relationships between various projects. The direction of arrow signifies calls from source to target layer.

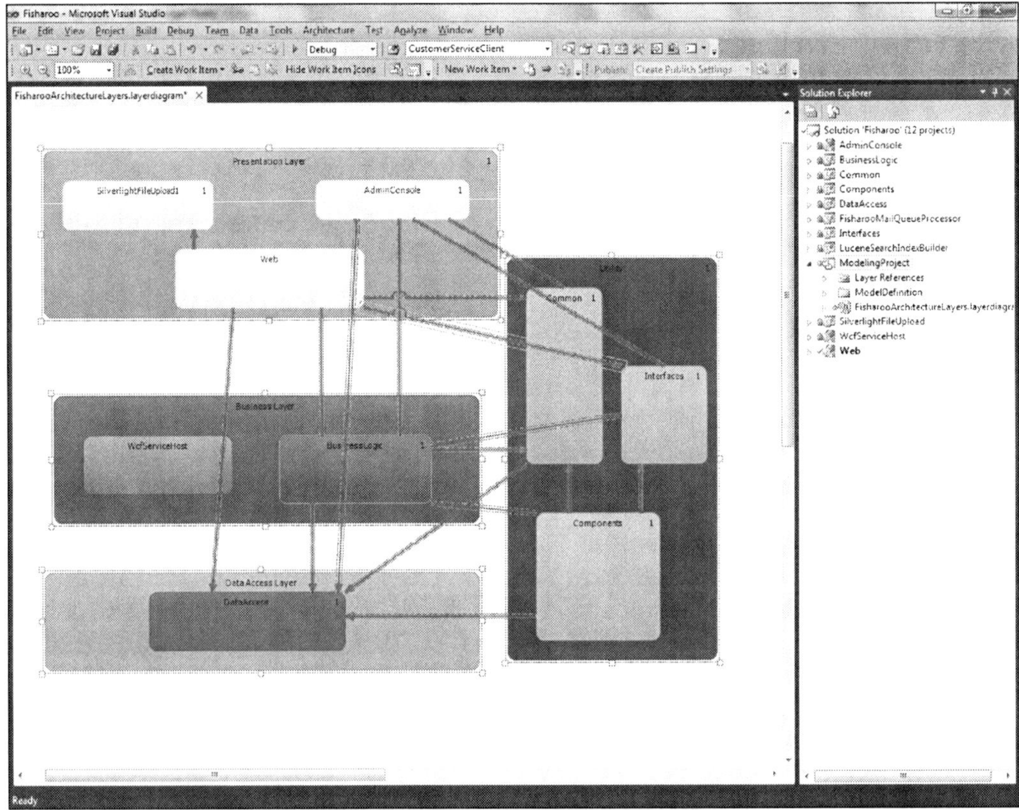

One can also right-click the canvas and choose the **Validate Architecture** option which will help in establishing that the architecture is valid. When we validated the Fisharoo architecture, it gave a few errors, as shown in the following screenshot:

Error List

49 Errors | 0 Warnings | 0 Messages

Description

1 AV0001 : Invalid Dependency : Fisharoo.AdminConsole.SiteMaster.CheckLogin(Method) --> Fisharoo.Da
Layers: Utility, Data Access Layer.DataAccess | Dependencies: Calls

2 AV0001 : Invalid Dependency : Fisharoo.AdminConsole.SiteMaster.CheckLogin(Method) --> Fisharoo.Da
Layers: Utility, Data Access Layer.DataAccess | Dependencies: References

3 AV0001 : Invalid Dependency : Fisharoo.AdminConsole.SiteMaster._userSession(Field) --> Fisharoo.Data
Layers: Utility, Data Access Layer.DataAccess | Dependencies: References

4 AV0001 : Invalid Dependency : Fisharoo.AdminConsole.Account.Accounts.Page_Load(Method) --> Fish
(Method)
Layers: Utility, Data Access Layer.DataAccess | Dependencies: Calls

5 AV0001 : Invalid Dependency : Fisharoo.AdminConsole.Account.Accounts.Page_Load(Method) --> Fish
Layers: Utility, Data Access Layer.DataAccess | Dependencies: References

6 AV0001 : Invalid Dependency : Fisharoo.AdminConsole.Account.Accounts._accountRepository(Field) --
Layers: Utility, Data Access Layer.DataAccess | Dependencies: References

7 AV0001 : Invalid Dependency : Fisharoo.AdminConsole.Moderations._default.LoadData(Method) --> Fis
Layers: Utility, Data Access Layer.DataAccess | Dependencies: References Generic Parameter

8 AV0001 : Invalid Dependency : Fisharoo.AdminConsole.Moderations._default.btnSubmit_Click(Method)
Fisharoo.DataAccess.Repositories.ModerationResult.IsApproved(Property)
Layers: Utility, Data Access Layer.DataAccess | Dependencies: Calls

9 AV0001 : Invalid Dependency : Fisharoo.AdminConsole.Moderations._default.btnSubmit_Click(Method)
Fisharoo.DataAccess.Repositories.ModerationResult.SystemObjectID(Property)
Layers: Utility, Data Access Layer.DataAccess | Dependencies: Calls

10 AV0001 : Invalid Dependency : Fisharoo.AdminConsole.Moderations._default.btnSubmit_Click(Method)

To trace back to the source code associated with the error, you can double click the error and it opens up the associated code as shown here. The errors we got are for use of interface and entities from data access layer directly in presentation layer (in `Web` project). You can fix all such errors or can plan to ignore it.

We will show you how we fix these as we move along. Converting the existing application into SOA could have been extremely difficult had we not followed layered, modular, and object based design. But since we adhered to these principles of design, we can convert existing solution into SOA based application with a few changes. Note that one of the key aspects of SOA is having business logic exposed as **services**. While we called all classes in our business logic project as services they aren't really the SOA services. Let's see how to translate one of the business functionalities into a service. Other business components can be translated in a similar manner. We will be using **Windows Communication Foundation (WCF) 4** for implementing our services.

Service enabling business logic

You need to follow the following steps to convert existing business logic to a WCF service:

1. We have built our Data Access Layer using Entity Framework's Entity object based approach which is the default option. For SOA design, we need to use self-tracking entities based solution. Right click `Fisharoo.edmx` designer and select **Add Code Generation Item** and then select **ADO.Net Self tracking Entity Generator** template and provide the name of the model. It will generate `Fisharoo.Model.Context.tt` and `FisharooModel.tt` as text transformation toolkit based files.

   The Entities in `DataAccess` project carry the data and move across tiers. We will create an independent class library project as `Entities` and move `Fisharoo.Model.tt` and its associated entity classes under it. We will also move our extended partial classes like `Account`, `Profile`, etc. to this new project inside a folder call **ExtendedEntities.** All our Entities are now under the `Fisharoo.Entities` namespace. This helps us remove the dependency of `Web` project on `DataAccess` project, which was one of the violations we got in architecture validation, as discussed earlier. We will need to now reference the `Entities` project in the `Web`, `BusinessLogic`, `Components`, and `Common` projects.
2. We will now convert `AccountService` class (`BusinessLogic` project) to a WCF service. SVC less activation is a new feature with WCF 4 which allows us to expose logic as service without necessarily having that logic written in file having SVC extension. This is the feature we will be using when converting our classes to WCF services.
3. Add reference of `System.ServiceModel` and `Fisharoo.Entities` assemblies in `BusinessLogic` project.
4. Go to `IAccountService.cs` and decorate Interface with `ServiceContract` attribute and decorate all public methods which need to be exposed outside the Service with `OperationContract` attribute. If there are any overloaded methods, use the `Name` attribute inside `OperationContract` as done in the `SaveAccount` method. We are showing relevant parts of the file below:

   ```
   //Fisharoo/BusinessLogic/Interfaces/IAccountService.cs
   [ServiceContract]
   public interface IAccountService
   {
       [OperationContract]
       bool UsernameInUse(string Username);
       [OperationContract]
       bool EmailInUse(string Email);
       . . .
   ```

```
        [OperationContract (Name = "SaveAccountWithScore")]
        void SaveAccount(Account account, BoardPost.ScoreInput value);
        . . .
    }
```

Entities like `Account` etc. generated in `Entities` project are already marked with the `DataContract` attribute hence there is no need to touch them.

5. To host the WCF service, we need to create a service host. Create `WCFServiceHost` project using **WCF Service Application** project template. Also add a reference to the `BusinessLogic` project.
6. Update the `WCFServiceHost` config file for relative Address:

```
<system.serviceModel>
    <serviceHostingEnvironment multipleSiteBindingsEnabled="true"
    aspNetCompatibilityEnabled="false">
      <serviceActivations>
        <add relativeAddress="AccountService.svc"
        service="Fisharoo.BusinessLogic.AccountService"/>
      </serviceActivations>
    </serviceHostingEnvironment>
    <behaviors>
      <serviceBehaviors>
        <behavior>
          <serviceMetadata httpGetEnabled="true"/>
          <serviceDebug includeExceptionDetailInFaults="true"/>
        </behavior>
      </serviceBehaviors>
    </behaviors>
  </system.serviceModel>
```

Note that this `.config` file does not mention endpoint and behavior information because it uses the default ones. This feature of WCF 4 helps reduce complexity in WCF configurations.

If you intend to provide endpoint, binding for each service, following is the way to do:

```
<system.serviceModel>
  <services>
    <service name="Fisharoo.BusinessLogic.AccountService.cs" behavio
    rConfiguration="AccountServiceBehavior">
    <endpoint name="AccountServiceEndpt" address=""
    binding="basicHttpBinding" contract="Fisharoo.BusinessLogic.
    Interfaces.IAccountService.cs"
                bindingConfiguration="AccountBinding"> </endpoint>
      </service>
```

```
    </services>
    <serviceHostingEnvironment multipleSiteBindingsEnabled="true" aspN
    etCompatibilityEnabled="true">
      <serviceActivations>
        <add relativeAddress="AccountService.svc" service="Fisharoo.
        BusinessLogic.AccountService"/>
      </serviceActivations>
    </serviceHostingEnvironment>
    <behaviors>
      <serviceBehaviors>
        <behavior name ="AccountServiceBehavior">
          <serviceMetadata  httpGetEnabled="true" />
          <serviceDebug includeExceptionDetailInFaults="true"/>
        </behavior>
      </serviceBehaviors>
    </behaviors>
    <bindings>
      <basicHttpBinding>
        <binding name ="AccountBinding" allowCookies= "true">
        </binding>
      </basicHttpBinding>
    </bindings>
  </system.serviceModel>
```

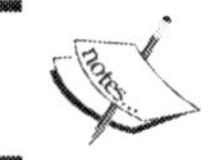

Ensure that the connection string for the `DataAcess` project is mentioned in `.config` of `WCFServiceHost` project.

```
<connectionStrings>
      <add name="FisharooDataContext"
       connectionString="metadata=res://*/Fisharoo.csdl|res://*/
       Fisharoo.ssdl|res://*/Fisharoo.msl;
                          provider=System.Data.SqlClient;
                          provider connection string=&quot;Data
                          Source=.\SQLEXPRESS;Initial
                          Catalog=Fisharoo;Integrated Security=True;Mu
                          ltipleActiveResultSets=True&quot;"
       providerName="System.Data.EntityClient" />
  </connectionStrings>
```

7. Ensure that the `DataAccess` assembly is explicitly loaded so that the connection to the Database happens successfully. The assembly is explicitly loaded in the `BusinessLogic` layer in `AccountService.cs` constructor as follows:

```
public AccountService()
{
    MEFManager.Compose(this);
    Assembly.Load("FisharooDataAccess");
}
```

This is a quick way of doing it. A more elegant way would be to specify the assembly name in the `.config` file and read it from there instead of hard coding it.

8. Now we are ready to consume the service in the client. For this we need to add service reference (`AccountProxy`) in `Web` Project for `Account` service.

   Eventually we would host services on IIS, but for now we need to add a proxy URL from the ASP.NET environment. If we leave this to the ASP.NET runtime, it will assign a new port every time it runs the service. However, we want a static port for the proxy to be generated. So we assign a static port to the service in its project properties. We have set the port to 63043.

   To generate Service proxy, right-click the **Web** project and add **Service Reference** and provide the URL of the service to `http://localhost:63043/AccountService.svc`

   Remember, in `.config` for the `WcfServiceHost`, we have provided the relative address for `AccountService`, the same has to be used in the above URL after **machinename:port**

   Provide the name for the service proxy as `AccountProxy` and click **Advanced** on the page and **Service Reference Settings** window will appear. Check the **Reuse types in all referenced assemblies** checkbox, as shown in following screenshot and then click **OK** and the proxy will be created under the Web project.

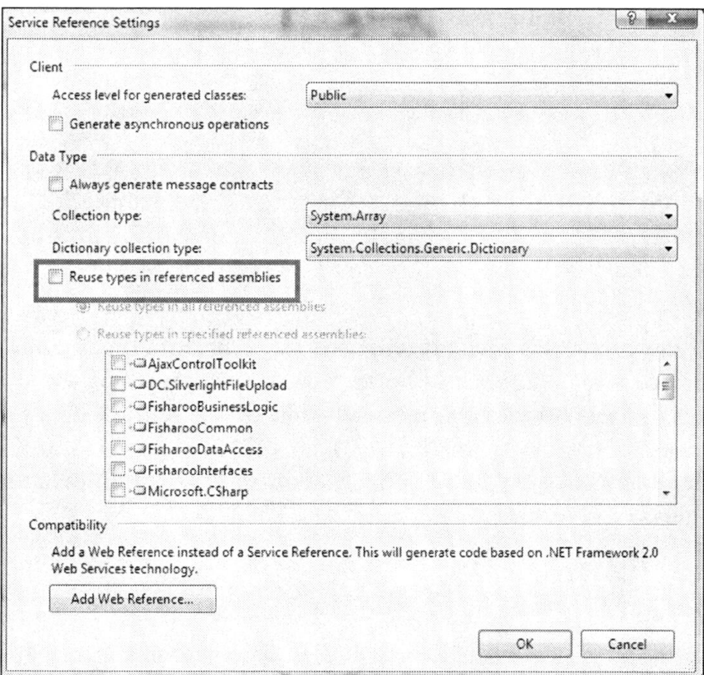

By using the option **Reuse types in referenced assemblies** the data contracts and operation contracts are available on the client side through referenced assemblies in the `Web` project.

Also note the update in `Web.config` in `Web` project, reflecting the Service related configuration settings.

Anytime, contract changes on service side that impacts the operation contract (interface) or data contract (entities) do update the service reference by right-clicking the proxy and selecting **Update Service Reference**. Failure to do so will result in a mismatch between the proxy and the service and can cause runtime exceptions.

9. With the proxy successfully added, let's now see how we can invoke the operations of services. To do this, create the instance of `AccountProxy` and invoke the required methods. Let's see the changes needed in the code for this:

```
//Fisharoo/Web/Accounts/Presenters/LoginPresenter.cs.
using Fisharoo.Web.AccountProxy; //proxy for Account WCF Service
public AccountProxy.AccountServiceClient _accountService;

Instantiate the proxy in the Init method
        public void Init(ILogin view)
        {
            . . .
            _accountService = new AccountServiceClient();
        }
```

You would note the key change in the above code is that the `AccountService` is no longer instantiated using MEF, but is based on the `AccountProxy` we added as service reference. The rest of the code remains the same.

With these changes done, lets shift our focus back to the `AccountService`. Our service uses `IWebContext` interface. This means that our service relies on `HttpContext` and `Session` objects. However, with SOA we are crossing the process boundary from ASP.NET into WCF Services (and the machine boundary as well) and the `HttpContext` and `Session` information won't be available on the service side.

We can address this design change in two ways. We can either design the service operations in a completely autonomous manner with all relevant in-out parameters OR we can pass the `HttpContext` and `Session` information to the WCF Service.

10. While the first one is a better approach, it is more intrusive and will need lot more changes in our code. For now we will go with the second option. For this we need to add an attribute to decorate our service:

```
[AspNetCompatibilityRequirements(RequirementsMode =
AspNetCompatibilityRequirementsMode.Required)]
public class AccountService : IAccountService
```

And in `WcfServiceHost` project's `web.config` file, mark `aspNetCompatibilityEnabled` as `true`.

```
<system.serviceModel>
    <serviceHostingEnvironment multipleSiteBindingsEnabled="true"
    aspNetCompatibilityEnabled="true">
      <serviceActivations>
        <add relativeAddress="AccountService.svc"
        service="Fisharoo.BusinessLogic.AccountService"/>
      </serviceActivations>
```

With this we are done with converting `AccountService` into a WCF Service and consuming it into `Web` client project.

Web Server and application server—Windows IIS 7.5 and AppFabric

It is important that we deploy the Presentation and Application tier onto the software's which can scale. We will use Windows **Internet Information Server (IIS)** 7.5 for deploying the presentation layer (`Web` project) and Windows Server AppFabric for deploying services, business, and data access logic.

Windows Server AppFabric is a Microsoft server for hosting and managing WCF and **Workflow Foundation (WF)** services and also provides distributed caching services. It gets installed on top of IIS 7 or above. Deployment of the `Web` and `WcfServiceHost` project in IIS can be done as follows.

Ensure you have IIS 7.5 installed (assuming you are running on Windows Server 2008 R2). Windows Server AppFabric is free and can be downloaded from the following site:

`http://www.microsoft.com/downloads/en/details.aspx?displaylang=en&FamilyID=467e5aa5-c25b-4c80-a6d2-9f8fb0f337d2`

You can refer to this link for information about the software's installation and configuration: `http://msdn.microsoft.com/en-us/library/ff637707.aspx`

Once installed launch IIS and deploy the `Web` project by:

- Right-clicking on **Default Web Site** and selecting **Add Application.**
- Providing the alias for application pool and ensuring that you selected a dedicated app pool running under .NET v 4.x.x.x (a dedicated App pool can be created under **Application Pools** node).

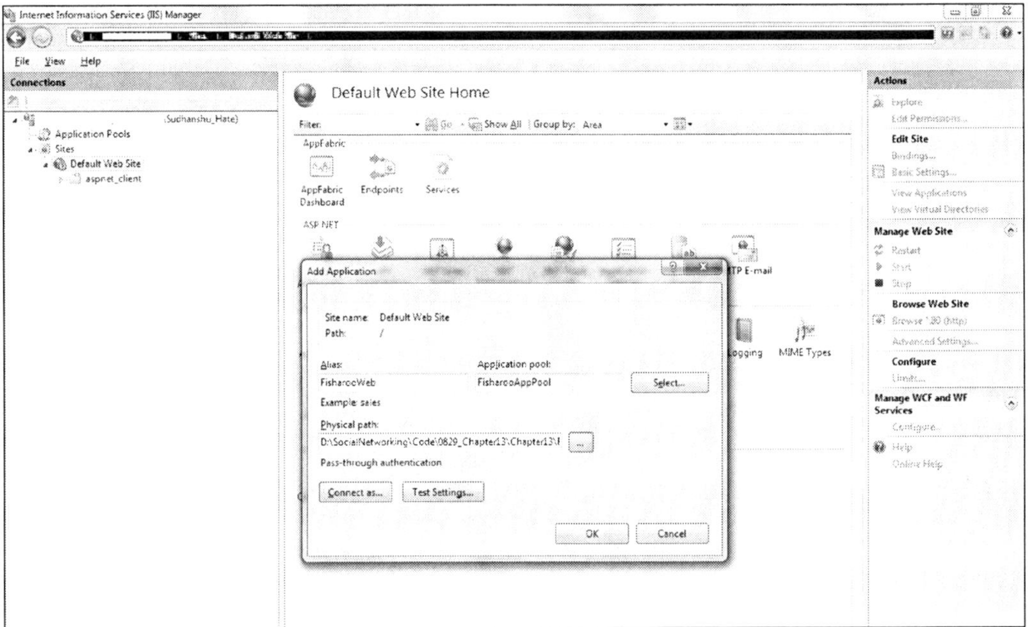

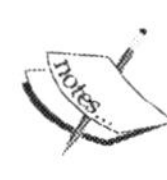

It is important that the application gets a dedicated application pool. This helps in ensuring the necessary application isolation level as each application pool runs in a dedicated w3wp process. If more than one application is run under the same application pool and w3wp crashes due to any issues in any one application, then the other applications running under the same w3wp will also crash.

With this, you will see the `Fisharoo Web` application is created under the default web site.

Now let's look at how to deploy the services. For this, first we need to package the services. For packaging select `WcfServiceHost` project, right click and provide package properties such as **create deployment package as a zip file**, the location where the package will be created, and the web application name.

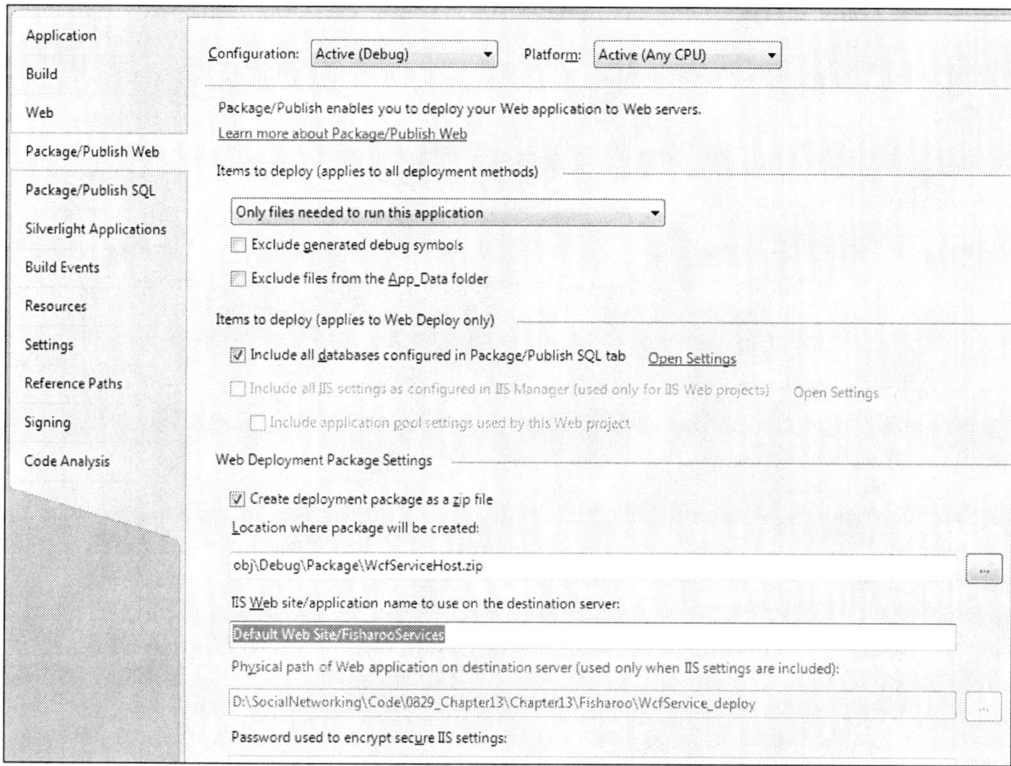

Once this is done, right click the project and select **build deployment package**. This will create a deployment package which we need to import on to IIS. Right click **Default web site | Deploy | Import** and provide the path from where to import.

This will get the Services installed. You can configure, manage, and monitor the WCF services from AppFabric's dashboard.

Web farming

Web farming (or load balancing) is the concept of spreading out your site's traffic over many servers. This addresses most of the performance problems whether in the application or on the server, by expanding your infrastructure and sharing the load across many servers. Generally, whoever is doing your load balancing will take a look at all the servers in your farm and route the user to the server with the lowest load. There are several ways to do this, and we will touch upon many of them lightly.

We are going to assume that we are interested in learning how to create a web farm in a windows environment.

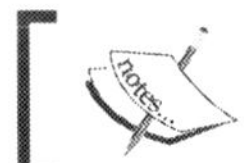

For those who need a Linux solution you might try **Ha Proxy** (`http://haproxy.1wt.eu/`) or something similar.

Specifically, we are going to talk about setting up a web farm using Windows using the **Network Load Balancing** (**NLB**). This allows you to host a handful of servers behind one virtual IP address on your network.

For this to work, each server in the farm needs to be configured identically so that any request that goes to any server will be handled in the same fashion. When a request comes to the virtual IP address, the packet will be routed to the least busy server. This configuration allows support of the concept of a reliable service. Meaning that if one server goes down, the farm will simply rebalance itself and route traffic to the servers that are still up.

To set this up, you need at least two machines running the Windows Server 2008. Each machine will need to have one fixed IP address. While the machine can run on one network card, two cards are preferred—one card having the fixed IP address and the other using the virtual IP address. The IP addresses must be on the same class C network.

Windows Server 2008 comes with limited preinstalled features. You will need to enable **Network Load Balancing** on it. For this go to **Server Manager** from **Administrative Tools** and in **Features** section select **Add Features** option.

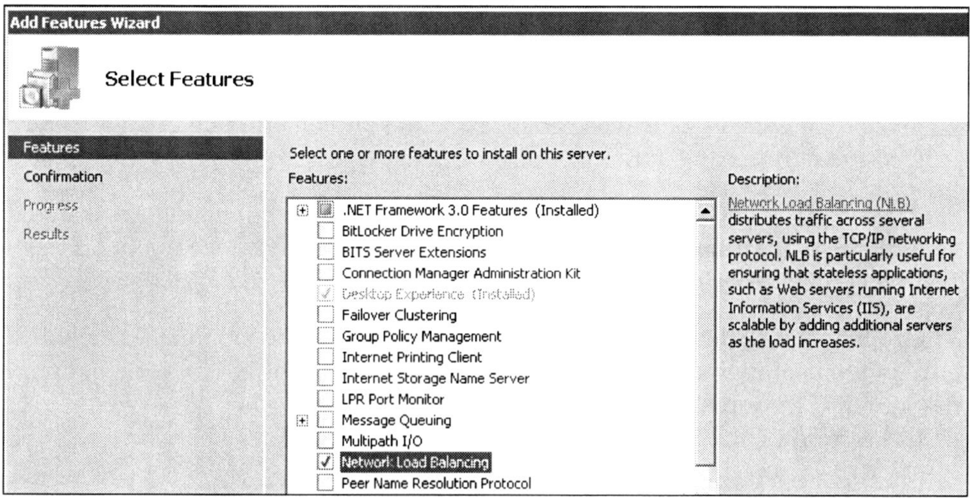

Once installed, open the **Network Load Balancing Manager** from **Administrative Tools**. Right-click on the **Network Load Balancing Clusters** and select **New Cluster** and continue to follow the wizard steps to configure load balancing.

For more detailed information about setting up a network load balanced web farm in Windows Server 2008, check out:

- `http://technet.microsoft.com/en-us/library/cc771300(WS.10).aspx`
- `http://www.techotopia.com/index.php/Building_a_Windows_Server_2008_Network_Load_Balancing_Cluster`
- `http://telnetport25.wordpress.com/2008/03/24/quick-tip-configuring-network-load-balancing-nlb-on-windows-2008-for-exchange-cas-servers/`

Caching

Typically, to cache is to take some data or objects from backend database and store them in memory for later use. When we need the data/object, we can simply retrieve it from the cache (memory). In terms of caching data from a database, we can take queried results and store them in memory. This means that when we need the information again, we don't have to perform a server-to-server connection, we don't have to wait for the query to be executed, and we don't have to wait for the results to be sent back to us. We can just pluck the data from RAM. Take this one step further up the chain and we can enjoy further optimizations. We can take the data from the database, parse that data, build a list of fully hydrated objects, and then store that list in the cache. This means that in addition to skipping the database stuff we can also skip creation and hydration of our objects.

Caching, like indexing, comes with some downfalls. If we put data into our cache and then modify/delete that data from the database, we may find that our site is using stale data. For example, if we try to create blog entries with an account that no longer exists, we will get a database error. So while implementing a caching layer we must be vigilant in making sure that our data is kept clean.

Another problem is if we have data in the cache that is stale but valid. We again end up showing data that is incorrect to the user. It is important that we maintain this side of the clean data equation too!

One more aspect is to decide how much data to cache? Cache too much data and you end up with out-of-memory problems as cached data is going to consume memory on the server. If the intent is to cache large data, you should plan for servers with large RAMs (multi GB to TB) which are commonly used in social networking sites.

Caching—AppFabric solution

Windows Server AppFabric caching services are useful for building highly scalable and available applications in distributed and non-distributed scenarios. Let's see how we can use this in our solution.

Client

In `Components` project, create an `AppFabricCache` class. This class will implement `ICache` interface and expose AppFabric Caching APIs. The current interface `ICache` (we had looked at this in Chapter 2) has limited methods than what AppFabric caching services can provide. However for now we will stick with these many only. If you intend to use more of the AppFabric APIs, you can add the corresponding method signatures in `ICache` interface and implement the same in `AppFabricCache.cs` class.

We need to add reference of the following AppFabric caching assembles to the `Components` project.

```
Microsoft.ApplicationServer.Caching.Client.dll
Microsoft.ApplicationServer.Caching.Core.dll
```

These assemblies contain the cache methods that will be used by the application. The assemblies can be found in `~:\Windows\System32\AppFabric` folder.

The `AppFabricCache` wrapper class with relevant methods is as shown below. We have implemented a few get and set methods. There are lot many APIs provided by AppFabric caching service which can be wrapped up, but for simplicity we are just focusing on two methods and in other methods we are just throwing exception. See the full code for this class in the code associated with this chapter.

```
//Fisharoo/Components/AppFabricCache.cs
using System.Web.Caching;
using System.ComponentModel.Composition;
using Microsoft.ApplicationServer.Caching;

namespace Fisharoo.Components
{
[Export(typeof(ICache))]
public class AppFabriCache : ICache
{
private static DataCache dataCache;
private static TimeSpan timeSpan = new TimeSpan(
    Settings.Default.DefaultCacheDuration_Days,
    Settings.Default.DefaultCacheDuration_Hours,
    Settings.Default.DefaultCacheDuration_Minutes, 0);

private static DataCacheFactory dataCacheFactory;
private static string namedCache = "FisharooCachedData";

static AppFabriCache()
{
    if (dataCacheFactory != null)
    {
        dataCacheFactory = new DataCacheFactory();
        dataCache = dataCacheFactory.GetCache("FisharooCachedData");
    }
}

public object Get(string cache_key)
{
    return dataCache.Get(cache_key);
}

public void Set(string cache_key, object cache_object)
{
    dataCache.Put(cache_key, cache_object);
}

. . .

}
}

static AppFabriCache()
{
    if (dataCacheFactory != null)
    {
        dataCacheFactory = new DataCacheFactory();
        dataCache = dataCacheFactory.GetCache("FisharooCachedData");
    }
}
```

The constructor creates a `DataCacheFactory` and further creates a named region in the name of `FisharooCachedData` where the cached data would be stored. This named region needs to be created only once and is hence done through the static constructor of the class.

Once the region is created, we have `Get` which retrieves data from the cache based on the key provided and `Set/Put` which overwrites data into cache based on the key provided.

With this class ready, the next step is to configure the cache client. Configuration can be done either in the application configuration file or programmatically.
For configuration, open the `App.config` file of `Components` project and add the following configuration to it:

```
<?xml version="1.0" encoding="utf-8" ?>
<configuration>
    <configSections>
      <section name="FisharooCachedData" type="Microsoft.
      ApplicationServer.Caching.DataCacheClientSection,
      Microsoft.ApplicationServer.Caching.Core, Version=1.0.0.0,
      Culture=neutral, PublicKeyToken=31bf3856ad364e35" />
    </configSections>
    <dataCacheClient>
      <clientNotification pollInterval="500" />
      <hosts>
        <host name="FisharooCacheServer1" cachePort="22233" />
        <host name="FisharooCacheServer2" cachePort="22233" />
      </hosts>
    </dataCacheClient>
</configuration>
```

We add a configuration section for caching and name it as `FisharooCachedData`. It adds the list of cache host and the host port. Change the name and port of the cache host according to the cache cluster you have created.

Now let's take a look at how we use it to cache the actual data. We will demonstrate using it in `BusinessLogic` project, in `FolderService` where we will cache Folders for specific `AccountID`.

```
//Fisharoo/BusinessLogic/FolderService.cs
namespace Fisharoo.BusinessLogic
{
//CHAPTER 7
[Export(typeof(IFolderService))]
public class FolderService : IFolderService
```

```
{
[Import]
private IFriendRepository _friendRepository;
[Import]
private IFolderRepository _folderRepository;
[Import] //CHAPTER 13 - For Caching
private ICache _cacheService;

public FolderService()
{
    MEFManager.Compose(this);
}

//CHAPTER 7
public void DeleteFolder(Folder folder)
{
    //CHAPTER 13 - first removing the folder from the cache
    if (_cacheService.Exists(folder.AccountID.ToString()))
    {
         _cacheService.Delete(folder.AccountID.ToString());
    }

    //actual physical delete
    _folderRepository.DeleteFolder(folder);
}

public List<Folder> GetFoldersByAccountID(int AccountID)
{
    //CHAPTER 13, Implemented a sample for Caching
    List<Folder> cachedFolders = _cacheService.Get(
                             AccountID.ToString()) as List<Folder>;
    if (cachedFolders != null)
    {
        return cachedFolders;
    }
    else
    {
        cachedFolders = _folderRepository.GetFoldersByAccountID(
        AccountID);
        _cacheService.Set(AccountID.ToString(), cachedFolders);
        return cachedFolders;
    }
}
}
```

First we use MEF to plug `ICache` in our class using the `Import` attribute.

In `GetFoldersByAccountID()` we check if the `Folders` exists in cache and if it exists it returns from the cache directly. If it doesn't exist in the cache, we call the appropriate method in `FolderRepository` and make it a point to store the returned value in the Cache.

In `DeleteFolder()` first we check if the `Folder` exists in the cache. If exists, we remove the folder from the cached object and then also delete it from backend using `FolderRespository.DeleteFolder()` method.

You should also consider the ways in which to invalidate the cache data in case if the data gets stale. This can be done using **Notification Services** feature with AppFabric.

Windows Server AppFabric provides failover solution for cache data which was not possible with State Server or SQL Server based OutProc caching solutions prior to AppFabric. It has lot more application in distributed caching and covers more varied kinds of caching needs. For more details on Windows Server AppFabric, check `http://msdn.microsoft.com/en-us/windowsserver/ee695849.aspx`.

Caching—MemCached solution

The page at `http://memcached.org/about` explains that:

> *memcached is a high-performance, distributed memory object caching system, generic in nature, but intended for use in speeding up dynamic web applications by alleviating database load.*

Simply put, the MemCached software allows you to create a farm within your web farm. This tool is used to create and manage a state farm. There aren't any limitations as to how many servers you can have in this farm. There aren't any hardware requirements for this tool either. This means that you can easily set up some very cheap Linux boxes with a load of RAM, and expand your state farm as your application(s) require.

Did you say Linux? This is what we used to say too. No worries though. MemCached has been ported to the Windows platform, and is now offered as MemCached for Windows (`http://code.google.com/p/memcached/wiki/PlatformWindows`). The same rules apply to this product from the hardware perspective. The only reason we brought up the Linux option is that every instance of Windows that you set up will cost you an initial outlay of cash for both a new box and the OS. On the other hand, the Linux boxes could be a farm of deactivated desktops and a free copy of your favorite Linux distro. This cache implementation can do for you exactly the same thing as the one done by AppFabric caching solution. You can point your session wrapper (or Context in our case) to your memcache implementation.

The server

Get the windows version of MemCached from the URL given in the *Caching* section. You can download the assemblies or the source code. If you downloaded the source code, you need to build the solution. With the assemblies in hand, you can unzip/put them into a directory on your local drive. Once you have the assemblies installed, you can run these simple directions:

1. Unzip the assemblies in your desired directory (eg. `c:\memcached`).
2. Install the service using the command:

   ```
   c:\memcached\memcached.exe -d install
   ```

3. Start the server from the Microsoft Management Console or by running the following command:

   ```
   c:\memcached\memcached.exe -d start
   ```

4. Use the server, by default listening to port 11211.

You can run several instances of this program on each server if you need to. Also, you can change the port that you run the server(s) on. You could run a different instance per application if you like.

That's it!

The client

Once you have the server installed and running you will need a client. There are the currently a few C# clients available:

- `https://sourceforge.net/projects/memcacheddotnet/`
- `http://code.google.com/p/beitmemcached/`
- `http://memcached.enyim.com`

There is also a host of other clients for other languages too.

`http://memcached.org/`

In our implementation, we will use the `Enyim Memcached client`. We have used this client on several projects and have not seen it having any issues. This client comes in the form of a solution that you can get from `codeplex.com`. It has a test client, the actual code, and so on. We take the `Enyim.Caching` project from within the solution and plug it into my current project solution.

With this in place you can then add a reference to `Enyim.Caching` from your project.

Using the client

With our new client in place we can then create a new cache wrapper that inherits from the same interface as our current cache wrapper.

We will call the new cache wrapper `MemcachedCache`. The big difference here is that we have a different `Pluggable` attribute of `MemCached`.

```
//Fisharoo/Components/MemecachedCache.cs
using System.ComponentModel.Composition;
using System.Web.Caching;
using Enyim.Caching;
using Enyim.Caching.Memcached;

namespace Fisharoo.Components
{
    [Export(typeof(ICache))]
    public class MemcachedCache : ICache
    {
        private MemcachedClient cache;

        public MemcachedCache()
        {
            cache = new MemcachedClient();

            List<string> keys = new List<string>();
            cache.Store(StoreMode.Add, "keys", keys);
        }
        public object Get(string cache_key)
        {
            return cache.Get(cache_key);
        }
............
    }
}
```

Caching in the Business logic layer

We can now wire our caching concepts into our existing Business logic layer. For example, we are going to add it to the `FolderService`. We will take the `GetFoldersByAccountID()` specifically.

```
//Fisharoo/BusinessLogic/FolderServic.cs
  public List<Folder> GetFoldersByAccountID(int AccountID)
        {
```

```
            //CHAPTER 13, Implemented a sample for Caching
List<Folder> cachedFolders = _cacheService.Get(AccountID.ToString())
as List<Folder>;
            if (cachedFolders != null)
            {
                return cachedFolders;
            }
            else
            {
   cachedFolders = _folderRepository.GetFoldersByAccountID(AccountID);
                _cacheService.Set(AccountID.ToString(),
                cachedFolders);
                return cachedFolders;
            }
        }
```

Caching doesn't just take care of database calls. It is also worth wrapping complex code that does long processing to return a result set that doesn't change with every call. Places to consider wrapping with cache might be the database, file system access, web service results, and so on.

While implementing a caching layer, be cautious to take into account what happens when new data is added and more importantly when the data is deleted. If the data that is added is not in the cache, it may or may not be important to update the cached item. However, leaving deleted data in the cache is pretty much never a good idea! For that reason, we want to add some code to our `delete` method that will remove a deleted folder from the cached entries.

```
//Fisharoo/BusinessLogic/FolderService.cs
  public void DeleteFolder(Folder folder)
        {
            //CHAPTER 13 - first removing the folder from the cache
            if (_cacheService.Exists(folder.AccountID.ToString()))
            {
                _cacheService.Delete(folder.AccountID.ToString());
            }
            //actual physical delete
            _folderRepository.DeleteFolder(folder);
        }
```

Now when a user deletes a folder we will remove it from the cache if it exists there. Then when a user goes to get a list of folders that used to contain a deleted folder, we will build the list again rather than finding it in the cache.

Configuration

We have demonstrated three caching solutions one uses `System.Web.Caching` (check `Cache.cs` in the code), another with AppFabric Caching, and last one using MemCached. For this we have built one interface `ICache` and built a specific implementation wrapper `Cache.cs`, `AppFabricCache.cs`, and `MemcachedCache.cs` for each of the solution respectively in `Components` project.

In the real world you will need only one solution; whereas we have shown three so that you can build an understanding with each one. When you want to actually run the project you should use just one caching solution and exclude the other two caching class implementations from `Components` project because failure to do so will have MEF raise an exception at runtime. This happens because for `ICache` interface exporting MEF will find three matching imports (with the three class implementations) and the composition container will not know which one to use.

However, MEF also provides a solution to such a problem by providing `ImportMany` attribute, which can match multiple `Import` interfaces to one `Export` interface. Alternatively, one can mention the priority of matching `Import` in [Metadata] attribute and the highest priority `Import` will get assigned. However, to keep things simple you can just exclude the other two class files here.

Where do I start?

The easiest way to know where to put caching is to analyze the performance of your site and find the slowest parts. There are at times sections of code that may benefit from a tweak to squeeze out better performance. But frequently, there are highly optimized sections of code that just can't run any faster. These are the areas that may benefit from a cache wrapper. To get major gains from your caching you don't necessarily need to stow your items away in the cache for days on end. You can see gains by caching something for only a few seconds. The key is how frequently your data changes, and how frequently that data is accessed by your users. If the data changes constantly and it is accessed constantly, huge gains can be made from seconds of caching. If the data doesn't change much you can put it into the cache and remove it only when your data changes.

Email

How can sending email make the site slow? If you think about the normal emailing process, you will find that the web server has to, at the very least, connect to an SMTP server. This connection can take time. If you need to send hundreds of emails, then you need to possibly make the same amount of connections to an SMTP server.

To reduce this slowness, we will build a system that allows us to stuff our emails into a queue and send the email later from another system. This will greatly improve our users' experience as they will not have to wait for the web server to make a connection to SMTP and send an email. We will instead stuff the email into our queue and assume that the email will be delivered from another system. The mails will have some delay before they are delivered, but for our community site requirement, we don't expect the users will need real time communication anyway.

To this point we have discussed speeding up the site from a hardware point of view, and a caching point of view. We are sure that it didn't take you too much convincing that all these are wise places to look for eking that last bit of performance out of your site. Now we are going to look at speeding up the site from an infrastructure point of view. Specifically, we are going to look at how to handle our email processing in such a way that we will reduce the number of network connections required to be made by the website directly.

> The concept of queuing up system-to-system communications is not a new one. This can be done with almost any communication that does not need real-time feedback. Any asynchronous communication is a prime candidate. And you don't necessarily need to employ a database as your queue. You can use MSMQ, the file system, or any other responsive local or semi-local resource. The concepts are mostly the same even though the technologies are vastly different.

Specifically, any time your website needs to connect to an external server—say FTP, HTTP or SMTP, —the site takes a major hit in trying to establish a connection, and once connected, to actually perform its work with the third-party resource. Any time we can come up with a way to remove this connection, our users will be much happier. From the users' point of view, they want to create a message, click a button, and get feedback on whether their message was sent. We can simulate that by allowing them to create a message, stuff it in a database, and then tell the user that the message was sent. The connection to a database for a transaction is much quicker than the connection to the SMTP server. So we will store our messages in the database and have another application process outbound email at a later time.

Creating services to send email

We currently have an `Email` class which handles the creation of email, the actual connectivity to the infrastructure, and finally the sending of the email. You will agree that this particular class is way overtasked. For this reason, we will move out the infrastructure and sending of an email to an `EmailService`.

This service will have one method—`Send()`—to begin with. This method will be responsible for taking in a `MailMessage`, connecting to the mail server with a `SmtpClient`, and finally sending the email.

```
//Fisharoo/BuinessLogic/EmailService.cs
public void Send(MailMessage Message)
{
    Message.Subject = _configuration.SiteName + " - " +
                      Message.Subject;
    SmtpClient smtp = new SmtpClient();
    smtp.Send(Message);
}
```

We will then go into the `Email` class and modify the implementation of the `Send()` method to invoke the `EmailService`:

```
//Fisharoo/Components/Email.cs
private void Send(MailMessage Message)
{
    _emailService.Send(mm);
}
```

Now that our infrastructure is separated out a bit, we can address the need for storing the email in some form of a queue rather than sending the email directly. To do this, we will start by first addressing our queue needs. We will use a queue in the database.

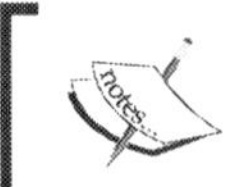

We could just as easily use an MSMQ or the file system with some XML files. Rather than adding something new to the project we figured we would build off our existing framework!

The database

We need to build three tables. Each table will have exactly the same structure, but a different purpose. We will have a receiving table that will take in new emails. This table can't be interrupted. We want to be able to receive new emails while also processing the existing emails. To do this we will need to have a working table where we will put all the emails that need to be processed. And finally, as we have a log of all the communications that we have sent, we will also have a history table. This table will hold all the emails that we have processed over time.

Our tables will hold serialized email. This means that we will actually have the email, as sent, in its entirety. This means that we could easily re-serialize a batch of emails to be resent if we ever needed to. The only thing that is different about each of these tables is their names!

In order to process email that is received, we may have to go outside of what LINQ was designed for. For this reason, we will create a couple of stored procedures to help us out. We will have two procedures—one to essentially put the data from receiving into the working table, and the other to put the working data into the history table. This is just the idea, not the actual implementation!

Here is how we create the first procedure:

```
create procedure [dbo].[pr_MailQueue_SwapReceivingAndWorking_
GetWorking]
as
begin tran
--rename working to temp
execute sp_rename
   @objname = 'MailQueue_Working',
   @newname = 'MailQueue_Temp'
--rename receiving to working
execute sp_rename
   @objname = 'MailQueue_Receiving',
   @newname = 'MailQueue_Working'
--rename temp to receiving
execute sp_rename
   @objname = 'MailQueue_Temp',
   @newname = 'MailQueue_Receiving'
select * from MailQueue_Working
commit tran
```

This procedure moves the data from one table to another in a manner that is more efficient than actually moving the data. We start by renaming the working table (an empty table at this point) to `MailQueue_Temp`. We then rename the receiving table (a full table) to `MailQueue_Working`. And finally, we rename the temp table to `MailQueue_Receiving` so that we can continue to collect new emails. With this complete, we then return all the records in the working table. If this process is not run frequently enough, you might find that there is more data in this table than you can process in a single chunk. For that reason, you either need to process it more often, or modify the selection to select pages of data. Our implementation will assume that you process your queue frequently enough so that the processor is never overloaded.

The next procedure, `pr_MailQueue_MoveWorkingToHistory`, cleans up after our email processor has completed its work.

```
create procedure [dbo].[pr_MailQueue_MoveWorkingToHistory]
as
begin tran
```

```
insert into MailQueue_History (SerializedMailMessage, CreateDate,
                               SendDate)
(select SerializedMailMessage, CreateDate, GetDate() from
                               MailQueue_Working)
truncate table MailQueue_Working
commit
```

This procedure inserts all the data from the working table into the history table. It then truncates the working table (which is why it was empty in the other procedure).

With the details worked out in the database, we can now drag these newly-created objects into our LINQ design surface so that we can work with them in our application.

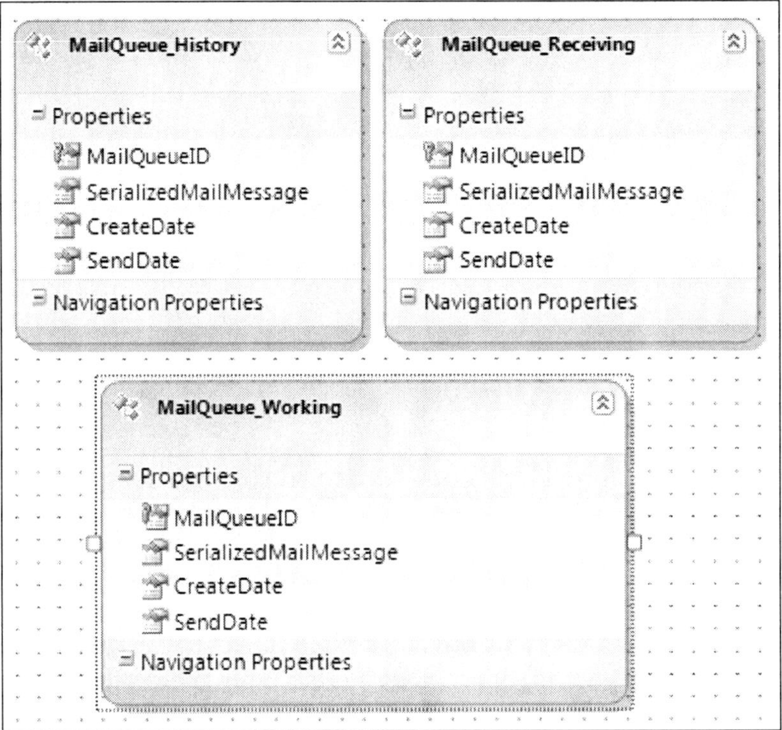

You should have the three new tables and the two new procedures similar to the ones shown in the previous screenshot. With these objects in place we can now create our new `EmailRepository`. This repository will have three methods—one to save a new email, the other to get all the email that needs to be processed, and the third one to copy the working table to the history table.

```
//Fisharoo/DataAccess/Repositories/EmailRepository.cs
public void Save(MailQueue_Receiving MailQueue)
```

```
{
    using (FisharooDataContext dc = conn.GetContext())
    {
        dc.MailQueue_Receivings.InsertOnSubmit(MailQueue);
        dc.SubmitChanges();
    }
}
public List<pr_MailQueue_SwapReceivingAndWorking_GetWorkingResult>
            GetMailQueueToProcess()
{
    List<pr_MailQueue_SwapReceivingAndWorking_GetWorkingResult>
          results = new List<pr_MailQueue_SwapReceivingAndWorking_
          GetWorkingResult>();
    using (FisharooDataContext dc = conn.GetContext())
    {
        results =
       dc.pr_MailQueue_SwapReceivingAndWorking_GetWorking().ToList();
    }
    return results;
}
public void MoveMailQueueWorkingToHistory()
{
    using (FisharooDataContext dc = conn.GetContext())
    {
        dc.pr_MailQueue_MoveWorkingToHistory();
    }
}
```

Services

With the repository and database out of the way, we need to create a new service. We already have an `EmailService` that directly sends email through an SMTP server. But what we need is a new service that can be swapped in place of the `EmailService`—the `DBMailService`. This service will need to conform to our `IEmailService` interface so that none of our application will need to know anything about how the email is sent.

Recall that our `EmailService` only had one method—`Send()`. We will have a `Send()` method that will deposit email into the new `EmailRepository`. But our `DBMailService` will also need a way for our email processor to process emails. So we need a second method of `ProcessEmails()`.

```
//Fisharoo/BusinessLogic/EmailService.cs
public void Send(MailMessage Message)
{
```

```
        Message.Subject = _configuration.SiteName + " - " +
                          Message.Subject;
        MailQueue_Receiving mq = new MailQueue_Receiving();
        mq.CreateDate = DateTime.Now;
        mq.SerializedMailMessage = Message.SerializeEncrypted();
        mq.SendDate = Convert.ToDateTime("1/1/2000");
        _emailRepository.Save(mq);
    }
    public void ProcessEmails()
    {
        //make sure we are only processing this in one thread!
        //otherwise we might lose emails
        lock (this)
        {
            try
            {
                List<pr_MailQueue_SwapReceivingAndWorking_
                GetWorkingResult> results =
                    new List<pr_MailQueue_SwapReceivingAndWorking_
                    GetWorkingResult>();
                results = _emailRepository.GetMailQueueToProcess();
                foreach (var result in results)
                {
                    MailMessage mm =
                             XMLService.Deserialize<MailMessage>
                             (result.SerializedMailMessage);
                    SmtpClient smtp = new SmtpClient();
                    smtp.Send(mm);
                }
                _emailRepository.MoveMailQueueWorkingToHistory();
            catch(Exception e)
            {
                Log.Fatal(this, e.Message);
                return;
            }
        }
    }
```

As you can see, the `Send()` method is fairly straightforward. We do need to serialize our `MailMessage` prior to sticking it into our queue, which we will go over shortly. Otherwise, it is just an `EmailRepository` call.

The `ProcessEmail()` method on the other hand is a bit more involved. First and most important is the fact that this method should only be run one at a time. We don't want the method to be accessed by anything, so we need to lock it. Next, we need to get a list of emails to process. We then iterate through each email. Note that as we iterate over the email message, we are de-serializing each message (we will cover this shortly). We then connect to our mail server and send our email.

> Rather than connecting to an IIS SMTP server or some other non-bulk sending application, you could connect to something like PMTA or other bulk email delivery system. These systems would make this process even faster as they take in the email similar to the database and process the mail after receiving it. IIS SMTP attempts to send it straightaway, which can cause a delay in any application trying to send emails.

As we added a new method to our `DBMailService`, we will also want to update our `IEmailService` interface and the `EmailService` class (so that we can get our `DBMailService` and `EmailService` through MEF in all the cases). To do this, add a new method to your `EmailService` for the `ProcessEmails()` method. This method will throw up an error as we don't plan to implement it.

```
public void ProcessEmails()
{
    throw (new Exception("ProcessEmails is not implemented by this
                         class!"));
}
```

Serializing email

To start this section we have to rant a bit! We are trying to send a `MailMessage` through a queue process. This means that we need to be able to serialize the `MailMessage`. We think many people would need similar functionality either to stuff it into the database, or into an MSMQ, or onto the file system. The `MailMessage` is not serializable though!

There are two approaches to this issue. We can tap into the serialization of the `MailMessage` and specify how each of the objects in the `MailMessage` is to be serialized. Or we can fake the serialization. Hacking into and overriding the serialization could be a chapter in itself. So we are going to fake it.

To fake this process, we created a class called `MyMailMessage` with a subclass `MailAddress`. This encompasses all the features that we need to be represented in our emails at this point. We are avoiding the headers, attachments, and so on. At this point, we only care about the sender, the receivers, subject, body, and a few other things.

```
//Fisharoo/BusinessLogic/MailMessageService.cs
[Serializable]
public class MyMailMessage
{
    public MailAddress[] Bcc { get; set; }
  …//refer to actual file for complete code
    public MailAddress Sender { get; set; }
    public string Subject { get; set; }
    [Serializable]
    public class MailAddress
    {
        public string Address { get; set; }
        public string DisplayName { get; set; }
    }
}
```

Note that it is marked as `Serializable`!

With this in place, we were then able to create a few methods that effectively shuffle data in and out of the `MailMessage` class into and out of our new `MyMailMessage` object.

```
//Fisharoo/BusinessLogic/MailMessageService.cs
private static MailAddressCollection ConvertMyMailAddressesToMailAddre
sses(List<MyMailMessage.MailAddress>
MyMailAddresses)
{
    MailAddressCollection mac = new MailAddressCollection();
    foreach(var a in MyMailAddresses)
    {
        mac.Add(ConvertMyMailAddressToMailAddress(a));
    }
    return mac;
}
private static MailAddress ConvertMyMailAddressToMailAddress(MyMailMes
sage.MailAddress
MyMailAddress)
{
    MailAddress ma = null;
```

```
        if(MyMailAddress != null && MyMailAddress.Address != null &&
                             MyMailAddress.DisplayName != null)
            ma = new MailAddress(MyMailAddress.Address,
                 MyMailAddress.DisplayName);
        return ma;
    }
```

And finally, we have the `Serialize()` and `Deserialize()` methods that operate on the `MailMessage` with the helper methods.

As a great side effect of this class, we were also able to create the `SerializeEncrypted()` and `DeserializeEncrypted()` methods that take the returned string from the `Serialize()` method and wash them with our `Cryptography.Encrypt()` and `Cryptography.Decrypt()` methods respectively.

Connecting the new DBMailQueueService

Now that we have this new service up and running and ready to be tested, we hook it into our existing system without changing much of our existing code using MEF approach.

The queue

Now we are actually able to collect email from our site to be deposited into our `MailQueue`. Since the implementation of this new feature is transparent to the site, all areas that send email will now deposit them into our queue.

> Keep in mind that you have the option of encrypting emails that are to be stored in the queue. This might be a good idea considering that you have emails that go out with users' passwords in them. Just something to think about!

Processing the queue

With a couple of emails in our queue, we can now focus on building a sample processor. We will build a quick console application to demonstrate this. Technically, you could take the console application and hook it up to your windows server as a scheduled task. But for production work, we suggest that you convert this console application to a Windows service, which is vastly more reliable (just not as easy to show demos of!).

To get started, we added a new console application project called `MailQueueProcessor`. We added an `app.config` file. The `app.config` file has a copy of all the properties that our `Configuration` class would expect to see, as well as an entry for the `system.net/mailSettings`, which points to our mail server.

```
<?xml version="1.0" encoding="utf-8" ?>
<configuration>
  <system.net>
    <mailSettings>
      <smtp>
        <network host="www.fisharoo.com" port="25"
             userName="admin@fisharoo.com" password="tm-es@as"/>
      </smtp>
    </mailSettings>
  </system.net>
  <appSettings>
    <add key="SiteName" value="Fisharoo"/>
    <add key="NumberOfRecordsInPage" value="20"/>
    <add key="NumberOfTagsInCloud" value="30"/>
    <!--
      CloudSortOrder - Possible options include the following:
        Random: randomly sorts the cloud each time
        Ascending: sorts the final value of the tag cloud from small
        to tall
        Descending: sorts the final value of the tag cloud from tall
        to small
    -->
    <add key="CloudSortOrder" value="Random"/>
    <add key="TagCloudSmallestFontSize" value="10"/>
    <add key="TagCloudLargestFontSize" value="30"/>
    <add key="RootURL" value="http://localhost:64810/"/>
    <add key="WebSiteURL" value="http://localhost:64810/"/>
    <add key="AdminSiteURL" value="http://localhost:64948/"/>
    <add key="DefaultCacheDuration_Days" value="0"/>
    <add key="DefaultCacheDuration_Hours" value="0"/>
    <add key="DefaultCacheDuration_Minutes" value="15"/>
    <add key="ToEmailAddress" value="website@fisharoo.com"/>
    <add key="FromEmailAddress" value="website@fisharoo.com"/>
  </appSettings>
</configuration>
```

Finally, we have the actual guts of the program:

```
using System.ComponentModel.Composition;
using Fisharoo.BusinessLogic.Interfaces;
using Fisharoo.Common;

namespace Fisharoo.MailQueueProcessor
{
public class Program
{
    [Import]
    private static IEmailService _emailService;

    static void Main(string[] args)
    {
        MEFManager.Compose(null);
       _emailService.ProcessEmails();
    }
}
}
```

As we did most of our work in the `DBMailService`, we have very little work left to do to actually process our email queue. We import an interface IEmailService, compose it, and call the `ProcessEmails()` method. We just wanted to show you that this could be done trivially. This means that the entire application that processes the email in our queue is just two lines of code!

Alerts

Alerts are notifications sent between users of the site. The question you may ask is how will this impact the performance of the site? As the community grows with more and more people and they become friends with each other, they become members of the groups, write blogs, access forums, etc. the amount of alert messages flowing in the system increases. This means rapid growth in data that needs to be stored and displayed to each user.

We will talk about database optimization below, where we address data file sizes. In case of alerts, while we need to handle the growth of the alert messages, we will also need to look at providing means to delete alerts that are no longer useful. This will help ensure to keep the data growth in check. We can further automatically purge data that is older than a certain date as needed. Another change we will do is restricting the alerts to be sent to only friends. There is no need to add an alert to self as the user already knows what activity he/she has done on the site.

We could also easily add another feature like subscription of alerts. In our current design, alerts are always fired to all the friends (and group members). We can provide option for users to select the kind of alerts they will like to receive, which can further reduce the load on the system. We have updated the `Default.aspx` in our Profiles folder to provide for a checkbox to the users. They can use it to select which alerts they want to delete. Additionally, we have modified `AlertService` to not fire alert for self and only for friends. You can check these updates in the code associated with this chapter.

Database tier scaling

Up to this point in the book, we have not spent too much time discussing the database level. We will try to maintain that theme here as well, this book being more about ASP.NET and C# than it is about SQL! That being said, there are some things that we can do at the database level that we just can't do elsewhere.

Flagged for delete

Flagging content to be deleted rather than actually deleting it is not only going to be faster from the user's perspective but also from the database's perspective. When you attempt to delete a record, the database must lock that table prior to performing the delete. Also, with each deletion an entry must be made to the transaction log. And when a record is finally deleted, the database maintains the log sequence number and doesn't necessarily de-allocate the data pages for the deleted information. The bottom line is that a delete statement is one of the most expensive commands that can be executed.

So, instead of deleting the record when the application says it needs an item deleted, we could set the `FlaggedForDelete` column to `true`. Then when our queries fetch data from this table, we could have a parameter in our `WHERE` clause checking that the data that we are selecting is not flagged for delete. We could then have an administrative process that runs however frequently best for the current load that selects all the active data out of our table into a temp table, drops the table with our flagged for delete data, and then renames our temp table to the original name. When the table is truncated, the data pages are re-allocated to the system for re-use.

Keep in mind that there is no "undo" feature for this method. If you need your data to be persisted to the transaction logs for auditing purposes, this may not be the best method for you. Also, if you have any foreign key references to the table that you are truncating, you must drop those references prior to performing the truncate command. When you are through with your process, you will then have to recreate your keys.

The FlaggedForDelete concept is not one we are going to spend too much time on. You simply need to add FlaggedForDelete columns to each of your tables with false as the default value. As we are using Entity framework, you would then need to update all the tables in your design surface. Then specify the default value of the FlaggedForDelete field as false in all your INSERT statements (you will need to set this value as objects come in to be inserted). With this in place, you would next need to update all your SELECT statements to check against the FlaggedForDelete field excluding items that are marked true. Don't forget that when you are running joined queries check the FlaggedForDelete field on the linked tables as well.

Indexing

Indexing is a way of optimizing your database in such a way that the data is organized for fast searches. Analyzing Query in Database Engine Tuning Advisor can help in creating indexes. Without an index, various functions such as WHERE, ORDER BY, GROUP BY, TOP, and DISTINCT will have to perform a full table scan, which will impact performance heavily. Without an index, when you are looking for a user's profile where ProfileID = 89734, SQL Server will have to look at every row to find the data that it is looking for. With an index in place, SQL Server will keep a list of ProfileIDs in a specific order so that locating the one we are interested in will be easy.

With an index in place, you will find that querying with a WHERE clause will be much faster. The downside to an index is that each time data is deleted from the index; the index must be rebuilt or recreated. The creation or rebuilding of an index can take time if the data set is large. This is a known downside and but it is generally accepted that having an index is better than not having one.

There are several types of indexes that can be created on a table—unique, clustered, non-clustered, and so on. A **unique** index is one where the key of the index is unique across the entire table. Think of an auto-generated int value as a unique index. A **clustered** index keeps the sort of the table's data the same as the sort of the index. This makes for a very fast index. There can be only one clustered index on a table, as the table can have only one physical sort order! And then there is the non-clustered index. This index type keeps the indexed keys sorted logically, but this does not impact the physical sort of the table's data. An index can be made up of a single column such as the primary key of the int type. Or, you can create a composite key which is made of up to sixteen columns.

By default, when you create a table, the ID field or the primary key is established as the clustered index. If we wanted to create a new clustered index for the `Accounts` table using the Username field, we would first have to drop all the references to this primary key before we could remove the clustered index. We will focus on creating a unique non-clustered index on the `Accounts` table out of the Username field as the current clustered index will be used more often than the one we are going to create (as we frequently query on `AccountID`). To create this index, follow the steps given next:

1. Go into the `Accounts` table details.
2. Select the `Indexes` folder.
3. Then right-click in the empty space and select **New Index...**.
4. Then specify the **Index name** as **nci_Accounts_Username** (nci = non-clustered index), select **Unique** as we know that the **Username** field should be unique in our system, and then add the **Username** field to the columns that we want to build an index for.
5. Then click **OK**, and we should have a **New Index** in place. If you have large amounts of data in the table that you created an index for, the index will be created right away. But SQL Server may need some time to generate the index.

The use of an index is transparent to us. It is sort of like a phone book for SQL Server. Hence when we specify that we want the data for a user with the username of "Sudhanshu", it knows how to find that data in a more efficient manner.

Partitioning

Partitioning is the concept of splitting up a table's data into multiple tables. This can be done both vertically and horizontally. Both types of partitioning can be useful. We will explain both types, but we will go into further detail regarding horizontal partitioning.

Vertical partitioning is about slicing the table vertically such that some columns in the table are made part of one and the remaining with another physical table. Such partitioning style is useful if the query patterns are such that they need only specific columns because it benefits from having set of columns as part of one table on one disk and another set on another disk. However, this partitioning style can backfire on performance, if the query patterns need columns from vertically split two tables as these two tables needs to be joined using a unique key column which joins two split tables.

Horizontal partitioning is where you would take a physical set of data—the whole row—and store it in an identical table (schema wise). Each set is generally a ranged set of data. So for an ordering system you might put one quarter worth of data in table A, another quarter in table B, and so on. Generally, you would want to work with dates or numbers or geographies as your range set. However, in our case, we would only know the users by their usernames and passwords. So we might keep an indexed table of Usernames and UserIDs. Once we have the User's ID, we could then go to a partitioned table of user data partitioned on UserID in the range of 1-100000, 100001-200000, and so on. Horizontal partitions speed up queries due to the fact that we are working with smaller sets of data. Also we can easily and quickly work with smaller sets of data in terms of adding to and deleting from those sets.

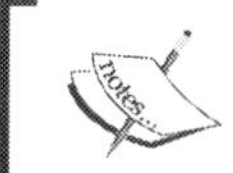

If you follow the Cloud Computing related trends, you would know what Microsoft's Azure Table storage essentially follows this horizontal partitioning pattern.

We will focus on how to build and utilize a partitioned table. Keep in mind that we only need to do this once the database has gotten to a point where it is starting to feel a bit sluggish (actually, you want to do this prior to feeling sluggish!). These are the general steps for creating the horizontal partition:

1. Create filegroups if you want to put the data on multiple physical disks. This is the best way to feel the most gain out of this particular performance hop up. This way when you are querying across the partition, the work is split up across multiple disks.
2. Create a partition function. This defines the range that we will be working with.
3. Create a partition scheme. This allows us to specify which partition sits on which filegroup.
4. With these steps out of the way, we can then start to create the partition tables.

FileGroups

To create a new filegroup, use this syntax:

```
Alter Database Fisharoo ADD FILEGROUP FG1
```

Once the filegroup is created, you can then add files to it.

```
ALTER DATABASE Fisharoo
ADD FILE
(
    NAME = FILE1,
    FILENAME = 'c:\Projects\Fisharoo\Trunk\DataBase\ FILE1.ndf',
    SIZE = 1MB,
    MAXSIZE = 10MB,
    FILEGROWTH = 1MB
)
TO FILEGROUP FG1;
```

You can add as many files to the file group as you think you will need. One file per disk per partition is the best thing you could do! You can always add to and modify this later.

Partition function

To create a partition function, use the following code:

```
CREATE PARTITION FUNCTION pfAccounts(int)
AS
RANGE LEFT FOR VALUES(10,000,20,000,30,000)
```

This partition function specifies that there will be three partitions. Each partition will hold 10,000 account records (you would probably want to define larger ranges). In the first partition, we will have accounts 1 through 10,000. The second partition will have 10,001 through 20,000. The third partition, that is, the final one will have accounts 20,001 through 30,000.

Partition scheme

To create a partition scheme use the following code (assuming that you made these file groups):

```
CREATE PARTITION SCHEME psAccounts
AS
PARTITION pfAccounts TO (FG1,FG2,FG3,[PRIMARY])
```

If you only have one file group defined then you can use this code:

```
CREATE PARTITION SCHEME psAccounts
AS
PARTITION pfAccounts ALL TO (FG1)
```

Partition tables

With these items in place we can then create the actual partition table.

```
CREATE TABLE Accounts
(
   AccountID INT,
   Username VARCHAR(20),
   ...
)
ON psAccounts(AccountID)
```

How does this affect our current system?

Unfortunately, this is not a behind-the-scenes fix all for your system like the indexes are. Querying a partitioned table requires a bit more syntax as you need to tell the SQL Server in which partition to look. This is not overly complex though. To get the account of a user with an `AccountID` of `25,000`, you would run this query:

```
SELECT *
FROM Accounts
WHERE $PARTITION.pfAccounts(AccountID)  =
      (SELECT $PARTITION.pfAccounts(25,000))
```

The key here is the `SELECT` statement in the `WHERE` clause.

```
SELECT $PARTITION.pfAccounts(25,000)
```

This line returns the partition number to search for based on the range value that we build our partition function around. In this case, it knows that you are interested in the third partition. So it returns a `3` as partition `3` holds the account with `AccountID 25,000`. Beyond this querying, data is unchanged.

Take a look at this resource for further information regarding partitioned tables:

`http://www.dotnetspider.com/resources/1082-Partitioning-Tables-SQL-SERVER.aspx`

For SQL Server 2008 R2, look at

`http://msdn.microsoft.com/en-us/library/ms188730.aspx`

Gotchas

Do take note that table partitioning, as described in the previous section, is available only in the Enterprise Edition (EE) of SQL Server.

Scaling is a wide subject area; we could go on and on. With constraint on the number of pages, we would like to close this discussion here and suggest that you take a look at this blog for some additional points:

`http://www.infosysblogs.com/microsoft/2009/10/considerations_for_developing.html`

Searching

Although a properly implemented set of indexes and a caching layer can really improve the performance of your site, it is not a fix all for everything. There is no reason to add search results to cache as each search could differ and produce different results. This would quickly fill our cache with bogus data. In addition to this shortcoming from cache, indexing doesn't fix everything up either. While an index can add some new legs to our search, it is not the best option for searching as people are generally interested in searching fields of text (not something we would want to index). And while we could implement FREETEXT search capabilities in SQL Server, there are better solutions out there.

In this section, we will discuss using Lucene.NET, which is a tool that allows you to index and search data efficiently. There are many big sites out there that currently use Lucene for their search capabilities, and we will show you how to do it. While we won't be able to create a Google search engine, we can create all the fast searching features that any community site might need.

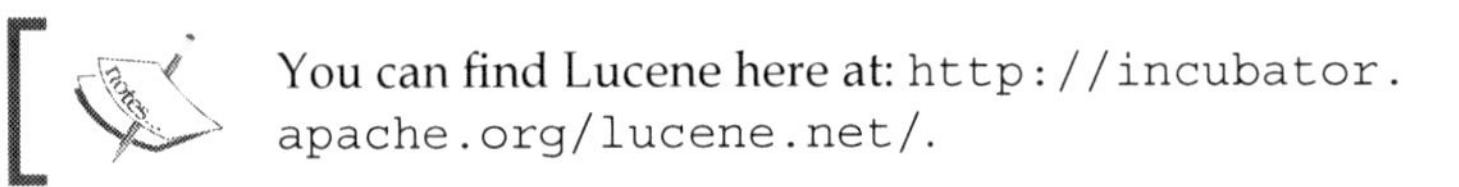

You can find Lucene here at: `http://incubator.apache.org/lucene.net/`.

We talked about database optimizations from the point of view of creating indexes, streamlining our deletion process, and partitioning our data. It is apparent that the deletion process won't help us here. Let's discuss why the other two don't really help us either.

You might think that adding indexes to a table will help optimize our search process. But if you think about it, we need to search within the data of a column. We will rarely have the full string that exactly matches the string that is found. In addition to that, we need to be able to support something more than wild card searches. We also want to support Boolean searches, multiphrase queries, and so on. For these reasons, indexing doesn't help us with searching.

Partitioning helps us deal with large amounts of data. It doesn't help us with searching that data though. Again, neither does this process help us make our search faster, nor does it allow us to support additional feature-rich forms of searching.

We have also discussed caching to help speed up our site. Unfortunately, caching search terms won't help us a whole lot either unless we cache the search terms for very long periods of time. For short term caching, we won't reap benefits here. And of course, there is the nagging issue that caching doesn't give us additional search capabilities.

This is where Lucene.NET comes in handy. The thing to know about Lucene.NET is that it works best in searching already indexed data. So this is where we will start creating indexes.

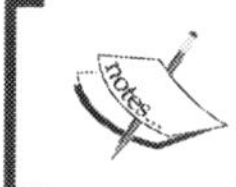

Disclaimer: Lucene and Lucene.NET are huge tool sets. There is no way that we can completely cover this tool in this chapter! Turn to Google if you have more questions after reading this!

Getting Lucene.NET

To get us started, we first need to download Lucene.NET. You can get that here: `http://incubator.apache.org/lucene.net/download/`.

All that you really need are the `Lucene dll` and `config` files. Toss those somewhere on your hard drive and add a reference to your `Fisharoo.BusinessLogic` project. With this completed we can start to build an index builder.

Building indexes

We will start building our index builder by first creating a `LuceneSearchService` class. This class will contain everything from our index builders to our index searcher. Let's add a method called `BuildIndexes()`. This method should be locked so that it can be called only once (as building indexes could take a while with a lot of data).

```
private object _indexBuildLocker = new object();

...
private void BuildIndexes()
{
    lock (_indexBuildLocker)
    {

    }
}
```

Note that we have an object declaration at the top of the class called _indexBuildLocker. We can then place a lock on this object any time we call into the BuildIndexes() method. If the object is locked when another call is made to this method, the call will be blocked until the lock is released.

With this method in place as the gateway to our other methods that will build our indexes, we can get started. Let's start by creating a BuildBlogIndex() method. This method will be responsible for building the index for our blog data. Refer code at //Fisharoo/BusinessLogic/LuceneSearchService.cs.

The first major step to build an index is to open an IndexWriter. This is done by passing in a Directory and a StandardAnalyzer. As we will have more than one index builder, we pulled out the Directory logic and put it into the getCacheDirectory() method to return the appropriate Directory.

```
private Directory getCacheDirectory(string SubFolder)
{
    if (!System.IO.Directory.Exists(_indexPath + "\\" + SubFolder))
    {
        System.IO.Directory.CreateDirectory(_indexPath + "\\" +
                                            SubFolder);
    }
    _directory = FSDirectory.GetDirectory(_indexPath + "\\" +
                                          SubFolder, false);
    return _directory;
}
```

The StandardAnalyzer is used to clean out the busy words from the index that is being created. This way, words such as 'the', 'and', 'is', and so on, will be removed.

It is important that if you clean the words going into your index, you also need to remove any busy words from your queries!

The next set of code allows us to work with smaller sets of data. We don't want to get a million records to work with as we build our index. Instead, we will work in smaller sets of data. So we are carefully watching to see if we have more records using the while (moreRecords) statement. Once we get the remaining records from our BlogRepository we will set the moreRecords variable to false.

As we get the records for building into our index, we need to iterate through each record to actually add to the index. A Lucene.NET index is made up of Documents. So with each new Blog record we want to create a new Document, as done in the foreach block in the code above.

Then for each Document we will add new fields. The thing to know about building an index is that you only need to put the data that is to be searched and the data that you need to link the search results back to the actual data, in your database. For this reason, we will track the SystemObjectID and the SystemObjectRecordID. This effectively lets us index just about anything in our system. Then we need to decide what we want to add to the Document to help us with our actual search. In this case we will have the DisplayText to show in our search results. We will also have a Content field to hold all the data that we want to search for each item. We will have a URL to get us to the item from within our search results. There will also be an Order field to contain any internal search orders. And finally, we will have an AccountID field so that we know whom the content belongs to (in case we need to display a profile next to the results). With the Document created, we then add it to the IndexWriter.

There is some code in here that we don't need to worry about such as the counter and firing events. This is more for UI stuff than for building indexes!

Once we have iterated through all the pages of data and finally all the records, we then need to call the Optimize() method of the IndexWriter. This will make the index more efficient to work with.

In case you didn't notice that we had a try statement started at the top of the class! The reason we bring this up is that you are working with the file system. Any time you are working with the file system, it is very important that you clean up after yourself (indexWriter.Close()) in the finally section. This is no exception.

Building the search

Once we have an index built, we can then create a search process. The searching of Lucene is relatively easy compared to determining what you want to be represented in the index. Again, we want our process to be locked as this is a file-based process. So it is important that we have a method as a gateway that can be called externally.

```
// Fisharoo/BusinessLogic/LuceneSearchService.cs
public List<SearchResult> Search(string InputText)
{
    List<SearchResult> results = new List<SearchResult>();
    if (string.IsNullOrEmpty(InputText))
        return null;
    lock (_searchLocker)
    {
        results = SearchIndexes(InputText.ToLower());
    }
    return results;
}
```

Once we have a method to initialize our search, we can safely start the search process. In our case, we will be searching the `Profiles` and `Blogs` indexes (we created an index for both). Note that in the beginning of the search we have an array of indexes to search. Then we iterate through that list to perform searches on each index in the collection.

We then open the appropriate index. Also note that we are initializing a `Hits` object, which will hold the results of our search. In this implementation, we have created three types of searches. One is a wild card search, which will allow our user to specify an `*` as the wild card to search with. We then check to see if we have multiple words in our search phrase, which to us will represent a `MultiPhraseQuery`. And finally, we have a simple `PhraseQuery`.

The wild card search will look for whatever you specify with anything else in place of the wild card. If we specify "Atul*" as our search phrase, it should easily pick up "Atul Gupta" or anything else that starts with Atul. Be careful with this type of search as you might return a slew of data no different from `Select all` from SQL.

A `MultiPhraseQuery` query allows you to search for the first word in the phrase query, then search for the second word within the search results of the first word, and so on. This can be used to whittle down the search results with a fair amount of accuracy. Finally, we have a simple `PhraseQuery`. This query takes in one word and searches the index for instances of that word.

With each search we are returned a collection of `Hits`. The `Hits` object holds all the documents that were found via your search. Each hit has a relevancy as well as the document so that you can use the record IDs of the found document and hence can get back to the data you have stored in your SQL table.

From there, we then iterate through each of our hits creating a new `SearchResult` (a custom structure that we made), which we can use to generically feed our UI. Please refer code at `// Fisharoo/BusinessLogic/LuceneSearchService.cs.`

We use this structure to populate a grid or a repeater in our search result UI.

We did not plug this directly into the site instead we created a simple webpage, `LuceneSreach.aspx`, for you to see how it works. There is a code to build the indexes from this page as well as to perform a search. The code is very simple and we didn't do any MVP implementation for this as we wanted to just highlight how to put this to quick use. You can look up the code associated with this chapter for details.

Summary

In this chapter, we discussed various areas of the application that might experience some growing pains over time. We addressed issues surrounding application layer validation, looked at application tiering from the Web, Application and Database Server perspectives, and also looked at the possible strategies in each tier that we can employ to ready that specific tier to handle future user growth (scale).

In Application tier, we looked at how we can Service enable existing application without significant changes in the existing code. We looked at a way to speed up data and object access on the site by implementing a Caching layer using Windows Server AppFabric or MemCached.NET. Next, we looked at how network communications, emails in particular, could be speeded up by adding asynchronicity between your website and the actual process used to send emails. Then we looked at how we can better manage the various alerts that are sent out between users, for the actions that the users take on the site.

In the Database tier, we looked at possible inefficiencies in the database by discussing a better way to delete data, partition, and index it. We moved on to making our search capabilities better and faster.

The key to this chapter is leveraging existing technology stack to extract maximum features that help support scale, then look at your site for possible pain points, and addressing them with approaches that may not necessarily be ASP.NET or C# related. Frequently, your code may be optimized to a greater level, but may still appear to be slow. Poke around a bit to determine for yourself all the aspects that are involved with a problem, and learn to address it outside the box if that is best.

Comparing ASP.NET MVP with ASP.NET MVC

Web application development on Microsoft Platforms has evolved from CGI-based development to classic ASP pages to ASP.NET Web Form development to the most recent ASP.NET MVC. ASP.NET was introduced in early 2000 and it brought a significant change in the way web application were built and with its plethora of server controls (new controls were added with each new release), provided a tremendous productivity boost to application development.

The ASP.NET Web Form development model looks at providing the Windows Form type application development environment to web developers. Windows Form development is itself highly influenced by the rapid application development environment that VB 6.0 (and earlier) offered.

ASP.NET Web Forms

ASP.NET Web Forms solved a significant number of issues with the earlier classic ASP way of building web applications. Some of these are:

- Less spaghetti code and cleaner separation of HTML and code across ASPX and code behind files
- The ability to use first class citizen languages of .NET like C# and VB.NET
- Compiled code which gives a boost to performance
- The availability of server controls that enabled great productivity boost and helped write complex applications quickly
- An eventing model that again made it easy to deal with user actions on the page

- ViewState and ASP.NET Engine helped handle retaining the data between post backs (this had its side effects as well)
- Easy programming model and anyone can become productive quickly

The other benefits, like a better threading model, garbage collection, etc. came along with the core .NET framework and very soon a lot of developers had jumped onto this technology.

While this model solved lot of issues, it did introduce some of it's own as well. Some of these are:

- There isn't much adherence to web programming standards, such as the MVC pattern
- Testing ASP.NET applications isn't easy
- While business logic can still be tested, testing the UI code is a big hassle
- The code itself didn't promote separation of concerns and while spaghetti code was avoided in the ASPX page, it was seen at the backend in the mixing of data access logic with UI code
- Building cross browser and accessible applications wasn't always easy due to limited control over generated HTML

However, all is not lost and some patterns did evolve to address some of these short comings.

Web presentation patterns

Microsoft **Patterns and Practices (PnP)** team came up with various patterns categorized as Web Presentation patterns. These are as discussed briefly below. To know more details on these, check this: `http://msdn.microsoft.com/en-us/library/ff650511.aspx`.

Page cache

Many times it happens that users accessing a web page get to view similar information on the page. The page itself is dynamically constructed, but possibly due to the nature of the query, the resultant view is similar. So similar to data caching that there is a way in which we can ASPX page caching itself by making use of the expiration policies. This behavior is what the Page Cache pattern supports.

Page controller

Across the various web pages, there will typically be functionality reuse like authentication, access to session variables, logging. Additional pages serving related use cases may have overlapping business functionality as well like searching, displaying data in paginated grid, etc. The page controller pattern talks about extracting such common logic to a common base class and use it to derive the specific web pages instead of deriving from the default `System.Web.Page` class.

Model view presenter

This is the pattern that we have used while building our social networking site and we have discussed this in Chapter 2. This pattern is similar to the MVC pattern and uses model and view, but instead of controller it uses a presenter class. The key difference is that the controller is invoked directly by the runtime based on the resource request from the user's browser, while presenter is actually invoked by the view itself. There is typically one presenter per view and it offloads the processing logic and logic to connect to the model and get the data to itself. This **separation of concern (SoC)** enables testing on the presenter without having to necessarily create the view.

The challenge is that there is still dependency on some objects of ASP.NET runtime like Session, Cache, etc. As they are managed by the runtime, when testing, it becomes difficult to recreate them and make available to the presenter.

Model view controller

What the PnP team then proposed in early days is no longer used today as now we have a full blown ASP.NET MVC 2 implementation as part of ASP.NET 4. We will look at this in detail in later section.

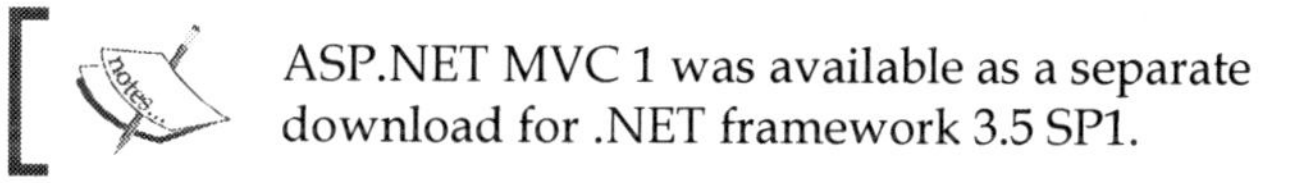

ASP.NET MVC 1 was available as a separate download for .NET framework 3.5 SP1.

Front controller

The page controller pattern does help bring common logic at one place, but it is still following the regular page cycle. The front controller is all about implementing a new HTTP Handler that intercepts the requests early on and suitably redirects them based on requested action.

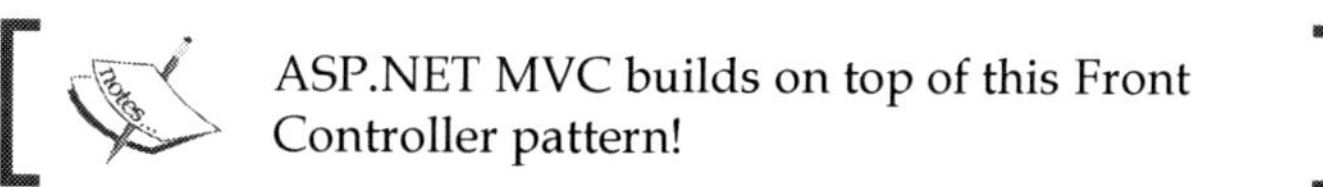

ASP.NET MVC builds on top of this Front Controller pattern!

Intercepting filter

The intercepting filter pattern extends the concept of Front Controller by actually using an HTTP Module so that it can intercept the requests before and also after they are processed by the ASP.NET runtime engine.

ASP.NET MVC

We looked at the various patterns and also briefly discussed the key issues that developers today are facing while building web applications using ASP.NET Web Forms techniques. It has been close to a decade and in a way we had to have some new model coming out soon. However let's clarify that ASP.NET MVC is not a replacement to the ASP.NET Web Form style of programming. It does address some of the key concerns and should really be treated as a new programming paradigm in the ASP.NET world. In short it means that when you start to build a new web application, you have to pick between ASP.NET Web Form and ASP.NET MVC.

But before we get into the choice, let's quickly highlight the key aspects of ASP. NET MVC. **Model-View-Controller (MVC)** is an architectural pattern and has been around for many years now. The pattern as such is fairly easy to understand. The **model** represents the data of the application as per the need of the application domain. Many times it will also support capturing updates to the data and storing it back to the appropriate storage. The **view** is how this data is visualized on the user interface. The **controller** is the one that handles requests for resources/data, reaches out to the right model and then passes it in suitable format to the view for the final display to the user. You can read more on MVC pattern here: `http://en.wikipedia.org/wiki/Model-view-controller`.

Microsoft has modified the way the incoming requests are processed and passed to the ASP.NET engine. The requests no longer are in the form of `.aspx` pages and instead are as more RESTful in nature and are action oriented. A handler intercepts these requests and passes them to the right action/method in the controller.

ASP.NET MVC enforces following the SoC principle to the core. Since controller is pure logic, it is easy to instantiate it from within a testing framework and test the functionality without having the need to get the entire ASP.NET runtime engine to load. While you can't still test how the final data has rendered, you can very well test the data that has to be rendered. This coupled with some manual UI validation can help in overall testing of the application. Unlike ASP.NET MVP, this pattern still relies on the full runtime engine, ASP.NET MVC was designed with testability in mind. It has abstract classes for intrinsic objects like `HttpContext`, `HttpRequest`, and `HttpResponse`, thus allowing easier testing.

The view in the ASP.NET is built by MVC using standard HTML (done by using HTML helper methods). There are no ASP.NET server controls available and hence the developers end up writing most of the HTML themselves, but in turn this provides them complete control over the HTML and thus handle the accessibility requirements in a much better way. While the support in Visual Studio at this time is limited in terms of HTML controls for ASP.NET MVC, you need not write everything on your own as you get the option to use different view engines. There are third party controls available today that can be used with ASP.NET. You can pick from NVelocity, Brail, NHaml, Spark, etc. view engines to build your views.

For more details on ASP.NET MVC you can refer to the MSDN library here: `http://msdn.microsoft.com/en-us/library/dd381412.aspx`.

Now let's address the final question on selecting between MVP (essentially using ASP.NET Web Forms approach) and MVC.

Choosing between MVP and MVC

Both MVP and MVC patterns are capable of generating enterprise class applications. While MVC is definitely a much better pattern, it is also true that as of today the productivity benefits that you get with the MVP approach is far superior. MVC pattern adds a significantly steep learning curve for the current web developers or even the new ones who are just starting.

Given the expectation of rich user interface for a social networking site, using MVC also additionally means lot more work towards creating custom controls for almost every display requirement. MVP allows us to work with the large number of ASP.NET server controls.

When starting on a new application you can argue more convincingly in favor of MVC. However in our case, since this is an update of the book and the associated source code is building on top of the previous edition, using MVC would have meant a significantly long cycle.

There are no migration wizards available today that help in easily taking some MVP based code and converting it to MVC. Had we selected MVC, it would have meant a rewrite of the presentation layer and would have impacted the release timelines of this book.

Summary

We have discussed the various web presentation patterns available when working with ASP.NET Web Form application development. We also looked at what ASP.NET MVC has to offer and compared between the MVP pattern that we used in previous edition of this book and MVC. After multiple debates we eventually concluded that it is best to retain the MVP pattern for the presentation layer. In future if time permits, we will definitely look at an MVC based front end for our Fisharoo website.

Index

Symbols

A

B

C

D

E

F

G

H

I

N

O

P

R

T

U

V

W

X

About Packt Publishing

Packt, pronounced 'packed', published its first book "*Mastering phpMyAdmin for Effective MySQL Management*" in April 2004 and subsequently continued to specialize in publishing highly focused books on specific technologies and solutions.

Our books and publications share the experiences of your fellow IT professionals in adapting and customizing today's systems, applications, and frameworks. Our solution based books give you the knowledge and power to customize the software and technologies you're using to get the job done. Packt books are more specific and less general than the IT books you have seen in the past. Our unique business model allows us to bring you more focused information, giving you more of what you need to know, and less of what you don't.

Packt is a modern, yet unique publishing company, which focuses on producing quality, cutting-edge books for communities of developers, administrators, and newbies alike. For more information, please visit our website: `www.packtpub.com`.

Writing for Packt

We welcome all inquiries from people who are interested in authoring. Book proposals should be sent to `author@packtpub.com`. If your book idea is still at an early stage and you would like to discuss it first before writing a formal book proposal, contact us; one of our commissioning editors will get in touch with you.

We're not just looking for published authors; if you have strong technical skills but no writing experience, our experienced editors can help you develop a writing career, or simply get some additional reward for your expertise.

CPSIA information can be obtained at www.ICGtesting.com
Printed in the USA
LVOW092059060412

276539LV00002B/4/P

9 781849 690829